AA

Essen...

<u>expl</u>...

BOSTON & NEW ENGLAND

Tim Locke
and
Sue Gordon

AA Publishing

Essential

Written by Tim Locke and Sue Gordon
Original photography by Molly Lynch
Edited, designed and produced by AA Publishing
Maps © The Automobile Association 1995

Distributed in the United Kingdom by AA Publishing, Norfolk House, Priestley Road, Basingstoke, Hampshire, RG24 4NY.

The contents of this publication are believed correct at the time of printing. Nevertheless, the publishers cannot be held responsible for any errors or omissions or for changes in the details given in this guide or for the consequences of any reliance on the information provided by the same. Assessments of attractions, hotels, restaurants and so forth are based upon the authors' own personal experiences and, therefore, descriptions given in this guide necessarily contain an element of subjective opinion which may not reflect the publishers' opinion or dictate a reader's own experiences on another occasion. We have tried to ensure accuracy in this guide, but things do change and we would be grateful if readers would advise us of any inaccuracies they may encounter.

Extract from 'Birches' on page 209 reproduced from *The Poetry of Robert Frost* edited by Edward Connery Lathem. Copyright 1944 by Robert Frost. Copyright 1916, © 1969 by Henry Holt and Company, Inc. Published by Henry Holt and Company, Inc, New York and Jonathan Cape, part of Random House UK Limited.

A CIP catalogue record for this book is available from the British Library.

ISBN 0 7495 0941 4

Published by AA Publishing (a trading name of Automobile Association Developments Limited, whose registered office is Norfolk House, Priestley Road, Basingstoke, Hampshire RG24 4NY. Registered number 1878835).

Colour separation by Fotographics
Printed by LEGO SpA, Italy

Cover picture: Autumn colours
Page 4: Mist over Mystic Seaport, Connecticut
Page 5 (top): York's Nubble Lighthouse, Maine
Page 5 (bottom): Longfellow Bridge and the city of Boston
Page 9: East Orange, in Vermont's Northeast Kingdom
Page 27: A 19th-century engraving showing the landing of the Pilgrim Fathers
Page 247: Trinity Church and the John Hancock Tower, Boston
Page 267: Mount Washington Hotel, New Hampshire

Tim Locke is the author of Fodor's *Exploring Britain*, and contributed to *Germany* and *Thailand* in the same series. He is also the author of several walking guides, including *The Good Walks Guide* published by the Consumers' Association.

  Sue Gordon is the author of the AA's *Explore Britain's Villages* and a contributor to the AA's *Weekend Walks* and the Marks & Spencer/AA guide *100 Country Walks in Britain*. She is also an experienced guidebooks editor.

The white clapboard Congregational Church (1806) at Peacham in Vermont's Northeast Kingdom

How to use this book

This book is divided into five main sections:

❏ Section 1:
New England Is
discusses aspects of life and living today, from films to the fall

❏ Section 2:
New England Was
places the region in its historical context and explores those past events whose influences are felt to this day

❏ Section 3: **A to Z Section**
is broken down into regional chapters, and covers places to visit, including walks and drives. Within this section fall the Focus-on articles, which consider a variety of topics in greater detail

❏ Section 4: **Travel Facts**
contains the strictly practical information vital for a successful trip

❏ Section 5:
Hotels and Restaurants
lists recommended establishments in New England, giving a brief résumé of what they offer

How to use the star rating
Most places described in this book have been given a separate rating:

▶▶▶ **Do not miss**

▶▶ **Highly recommended**

▶ **Worth seeing**

   Not essential viewing

Map references
To make the location of a particular place easier to find, every main entry in this book is given a map reference, such as 176B3. The first number (176) indicates the page on which the map can be found, the letter (B) and the second number (3) pinpoint the square in which the main entry is located. The maps on the inside front cover and inside back cover are referred to as IFC and IBC respectively.

Contents

Quick reference

This quick-reference guide high-lights the features of the book you will use most often: the maps; the introductory features; the Focus-on articles; the walks and the drives.

Quick reference

Top: Boothbay Harbor, Maine
Left: Waits River, Vermont
Right: weathervane, Vermont

My Boston

by Polly Logan

> And this is the city of Boston
> The land of the bean and the cod
> Where the Lowells talk only to Cabots
> And the Cabots talk only to God.

This ditty speaks volumes about my beloved Boston – city of clannish families, great food and the ocean. Boston also has the smallest landmass of any major American city and is great for exploring on foot.

I love to walk around Harvard University, founded by America's first families, or wander through the house of Paul Revere, one of the fathers of the American Revolution. I enjoy touring the old Yankee neighbourhoods of Louisburg Square and Beacon Hill, then browsing through the many antique shops on Charles Street. Finally, I like to wander through the beautiful Boston Public Gardens, where you can pedal swan boats past a replica of the Brooklyn Bridge and see statues based on the characters of the children's book, *Make Way for Ducklings*.

Boston's most famous political family is the Kennedys; visit the great Kennedy Library on the peninsula in Boston Harbor. The statue of Irish-American Mayor James Michael Curley stands watch over Faneuil Hall.

For culture seekers, Boston is endowed with some of the country's finest art museums and maintains a world-class symphony orchestra.

A warm welcome awaits you in Boston...come with walking shoes and I will be your tour guide.

Polly Logan
For four decades Polly Logan and her late husband, General Edward Logan, opened their estate to a myriad of charitable, environmental and political causes. As Massachusetts representative to the Republican National Committee for 12 years, Polly Logan is prominent in Boston and Washington, and was honoured by presidents and government leaders – in particular for her role as an advocate of women's rights.

8

My New England

by Dick Hamilton

Some say New England is what America was. To a degree I guess it is, as America's roots began here. Much of the region's history is displayed in wonderful museums, re-creations and preservations such as Sturbridge, Newport, Strawbery Banke and Mystic.

The soft, rolling hills of Vermont, the majestic peaks of New Hampshire's White Mountains and the classic rocky coast of Maine make New England a special place. The rural charm of the countryside and the open friendliness of our people, with generations of experience in hospitality, make this a most welcoming destination. Except for Boston, Providence and Hartford, New England is a region of small towns, white clapboard homes, quaint farms, covered bridges and white-steepled churches. And, best of all, New England has wonderfully distinct seasons, crowned with a fall that has the most spectacular foliage display in the world.

My New England never ends. Country fairs and concerts, lobster festivals and antique shows, auctions and maple sugaring, leaf-peeping and skiing are all played out on America's most charming stage.

New England is America.

Dick Hamilton
Dick Hamilton, a native New Englander from the White Mountains, has spent his life promoting the region to prospective visitors. President of the White Mountains Attractions Association and Ski New Hampshire, he serves on many tourism-related boards and commissions in the region, and was founder of New England USA. He is also a photographer, a historian and a collector of White Mountains memorabilia.

NEW ENGLAND IS

■ The states of Massachusetts, Connecticut, Rhode Island, New Hampshire, Vermont and Maine constitute New England. Although relatively small in area, this is the cultural and historic cradle of the nation. There are qualities that characterise the region as a whole, but there are also subtle differences within it.....■

The elements The clichés have their own element of truth: against a blue sky the wooden steeple of a church stands high over a village green fringed with neat, white clapboard houses. Back roads wind over covered bridges and through seemingly endless forests which in autumn burst into brilliant hues of russet, gold and crimson. Bright orange pumpkins lie stacked in mounds by wooden barns and on farm stands. Lighthouses look out over the ocean from shores of rock and sand. Fishing boats unload the daily catch, and lobster and clam chowder appear on virtually every menu.

New England is a region of firsts, in industrialisation and historical events. It has been the seed-bed of intellectual and political thought for three centuries. It has magnificent art collections in museums, colleges and universities. New England has produced – and continues to produce – many great names in music, art and literature. New England has little of the brashness associated with many other parts of the country, and has been described as 'America with the volume turned down'. Many of the region's inhabitants greatly value their lifestyle and

A white steeple framed by autumn foliage: quintessential New England at Sugar Hill, NH

are fiercely proud of their history and roots. The Yankee mentality – formed by a keen work ethic, frugality, shrewdness and a serious, conservative outlook – is deeply ingrained.

Early days The great ice masses that once covered this land have left their mark. Glaciers sculpted the mountains and valleys, and created a deeply indented coastline. The landscape was scoured, and the bedrock and boulder-strewn earth proved infertile for the first farmers. On this soil the first European settlers established themselves, primarily along the coast and the rivers. The Pilgrim Fathers arrived from England aboard the *Mayflower* in 1620. More than a century later, in 1775, the first shots

Point Judith Light, Rhode Island

of the American Revolution at Lexington and Concord signalled the end of British colonial rule.

As settlers moved westwards over the continent, New England's farmlands were abandoned, and the trees, once cleared by the farmers, re-established themselves. Today some 80 per cent of New England is forested, and much of Vermont, New Hampshire and inland Maine is also hilly or mountainous and sparsely settled.

Visiting the region Boston is by far the largest city, and one that every visitor to the region should see. The Freedom Trail wends an intricate route past the city's historic sites. This is a city of superb museums, excitingly contrasting neighbourhoods and striking architecture. Visitors without a car can find plenty of places within reach by public transport.

New England's thick tree cover can mean that sweeping panoramic views are hard to come by, at least from a car. For the most spectacular views, however, you can take high-level walks in the White Mountains or Acadia National Park, or explore the coast by boat. Outdoor pursuits in the hills and mountains of northern New England are well developed and include winter sports, watersports, hiking and fishing. The southern states of Massachusetts, Rhode Island and Connecticut are more densely populated and have more historic sights.

The long and complex seaboard has a lasting appeal, with the sandy beaches of Cape Cod, the islands and southern Maine among the most popular. There are many opportunities for cruises and sailing, and a number of museums commemorate New England's maritime heritage, including the vanished whaling industry. Today, whale-watching cruises are big business, and no visitor should miss the chance to join an exhilarating tour to the feeding grounds of the humpback whales.

New England's charms change with the seasons. Spring brings freshness and greenery. In summer, delicious Atlantic breezes make the coast a pleasant retreat from the heat, while autumn's foliage is deservedly famous. Winters are harsh but bring photogenic snowfalls and a Christmas-card look as sports enthusiasts put on their skis.

With so much of the area heavily forested, clapboard is universal

■ **Explore New England and you experience a range of building styles from early colonial through to post-modernism. White clapboard is an integral feature of New England's charm, and is a dominant theme outside the major cities; observe closely and you should be able to identify stylistic variations.....**■

Early colonial The early English colonists brought with them a tradition of building in wood and, as hardwoods were plentiful in New England, the timber-framed house became – and remains – universal. The frames were covered with cedar shingles or clapboards (which originally were painted in a variety of colours). Built with steep roofs, as they had been back home to help the rain run off, the earliest colonial houses had an overhanging upper storey, central chimney and small, irregular casement windows. The steeper the roof, the older the house. Quite commonly a lean-to was added at the back under one sloping roof, the outline giving rise to the term 'saltbox'. Few of the very earliest houses survive, but Paul Revere's House in Boston and the House of Seven Gables in Salem, MA, both date from the late-1600s.

❏ In colonial times tree trunks more than 2 feet thick were kept aside for timber for the British navy, and therefore no floorboards were allowed to exceed this limit. In some houses, however, these extra-wide boards were sneaked into the attic, out of sight. ❏

Georgian The classical Palladian style that was introduced to Britain from Italy reached eastern New England in the 18th century. The handsome houses in this style, many built by wealthy maritime traders, are recognisable by their strict symmetry. Still clapboarded, they typically have a hipped roof, a central door which is sometimes pilastered, and equally spaced sash windows; Portsmouth, New Hampshire, has a good collection (see pages 202–3). Many modern clapboard houses are still built in this style.

Federal After Independence, Charles Bulfinch (see panel, page 72) introduced the neo-classical Adamesque style, known as Federal, with public buildings such as the State House in Boston and, notably, his Beacon Hill development of genteel, red-brick homes for the élite (see page 64). The North Shore seaports also have some excellent Federal-style buildings, built by merchants and often constructed of brick. These buildings – public and domestic – stand proudly four-square, lightly detailed, with a shallow, sometimes balustraded, hipped roof, an imposing porch and a fan-shaped window over the door. Inside, rooms may be oval,

The Mission House (1739) at Stockbridge, MA

12

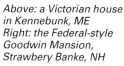

Above: a Victorian house in Kennebunk, ME
Right: the Federal-style Goodwin Mansion, Strawbery Banke, NH

circular or polygonal, with cornices and fireplaces decorated with garlands and urns of flowers. Salem, Massachusetts, and Providence, Rhode Island, have some of the finest examples of the Federal style. In Vermont, first settled in the late 1700s, this is the earliest major style.

Victorian After the mid-1820s the design of public, academic and domestic building becomes more diversified, reflecting European influences. Boston's Quincy Market is an example of the Greek Revival style, featuring the columns and pediments of ancient Greek temples. The Gothic Revival style is easily recognised by its steeply pitched gables, turrets and intricately carved bargeboards. The architect of Boston's Trinity Church gave his name to the uniquely American Richardson Romanesque style, notable for its heavy stonework with chunky columns and arches. Many Victorian styles are represented in Newport's fabulously over-the-top mansions. Boston's Back Bay, one of history's most splendid pieces of urban planning, also makes a wonderful sampler of Victorian architecture, with bow-fronted 'rowhouses' of various styles lining Parisian-style leafy boulevards (see pages 62–3).

A Cape Cod vignette: painted clapboard, screen door and wreath

Modern By far the most exciting contemporary architecture in New England is to be found in Boston and Cambridge: walk around Boston's financial district, and at every corner is another exhilarating vista. Try to see the view across Boston Harbour of the grey-glass tower blocks rising behind the red-brick buildings of the revamped waterfront. The leading architects are international: IM Pei, responsible for the city's 1970s rejuvenation scheme; the Bauhaus architect and Harvard professor, Walter Gropius; and Le Corbusier.

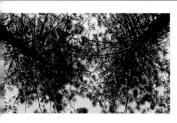

■ After the demise of its maritime trade and then its textile industry, the region is now one the country's main centres of technology. Tourism is of major importance, and while agriculture and fishing are of somewhat diminishing significance, the pulp and paper trade is a major growth area.....■

14

Farming meets tourism: orchards and cider mills welcome visitors

Insurance, industry, education and research Hartford, Connecticut, is the 'Insurance City'. The business started in the 19th century, in the heyday of New England's shipping trade, and today some of the largest US insurance companies have their headquarters here.

The academic institutions of New England make a significant contribution to the economy, partly by generating business locally, but chiefly through the research and development work on which the electronics and communications industries of the region depend. Connecticut is New England's most high-tech state, but the manufacture of electronic components and machinery is also the economic mainstay of Rhode Island, Massachusetts (particularly along Route 128) and the southern part of New Hampshire.

Tourism The wealthy of the Northeast recognised New England's potential as a summer playground at the end of the 19th century. Today, with the spawning of snow sports, the region attracts as many visitors in winter as in summer to its mountain and coastal areas. In addition to these natural assets (and not forgetting the glory of the region's autumn foliage), the tourist industry can draw on a particularly fine maritime heritage. Tourism is New England's second largest industry, after manufacturing.

❏ Pulp and paper mills at Rumford and Jay in Maine manufacture 1,500 tons of paper daily for books, magazines, catalogues and business stationery, with those at Bucksport and Madawaska following not far behind. ❏

The timber trade A visitor to the northern areas of New England cannot fail to be impressed by the extent of the tree cover – some 80 per cent in New Hampshire and Vermont, and 90 per cent in Maine. It should come as no surprise that these forests make a substantial impact on the region's economy, to the tune of some $6 billion a year, although in Maine, for instance, less than 3 per cent of the total forested area is actually harvested. Maine is the second

I Have Visited
COLD HOLLOW
CIDER MILL
-terbury Center
-mont 0567-

largest paper-producing state (after Wisconsin) in the US, making around 4 million tons of paper per annum. The building trade and furniture-makers also make significant use of what is a relatively new natural resource, for only a century ago most of the region's timber had been cleared for farmland. Today both environmentalists and the trade are anxious to ensure that this rapidly expanding industry is managed well.

Farming, fishing and quarrying
Vermont is traditionally associated with dairy farming and this is still an important part of the state economy, albeit a declining one. Vermont too specialises in turkeys (and Rhode Island is known for the breed of hen named Rhode Island Red). Immense quantities of potatoes are grown in northern

There are now about 2,400 dairy farms in Vermont, each with an average of 70 milking cows

Maine, the third largest crop in the country after Idaho and Washington. Other crops include tobacco in the Connecticut river valley, blueberries in Maine and cranberries near Plymouth, Massachusetts, and on Cape Cod and the nearby islands.

The fishing industry is now in decline. There is foreign competition in the Atlantic fishing grounds, and stocks of cod and haddock have been depleted, but fishing is still vital in ports such as Gloucester and Cape Ann in Massachusetts, and in the many lobstering ports along the coast of Maine.

New Hampshire, the 'Granite State', has many granite quarries. Vermont's Green Mountains are also quarried for granite (see Barre, page 226) and for marble at Proctor (see page 235).

Lobstering in Maine alone brings in over $70 million a year

15

■ **For anyone who considers shopping one of life's greatest pleasures, New England has to be paradise. It is particularly famed for its antiques and crafts, for the local produce sold at farm stands and in country stores, and for its factory outlets .....■**

For a taste of everything New England has to offer, shopaholics need to visit a factory outlet, an antique shop or fair, a crafts gallery or show, a village store, a farm shop, and some of the one-of-a-kind shops that proliferate throughout the region. Look at the amazing range of goods in a big hardware shop, such as the Portland Stove Company, and walk round a large department store like Jordan Marsh or Filene's. Then there is the shopping mall, a cultural experience in itself; try a really grand

❑ The serious factory outlet shopper should invest in a copy of the *Factory Outlet Guide to New England* by A Miser and A Pennypincher, available in bookshops and published by The Globe Pequot Press, Old Saybrook, CT. ❑

shopper – prices are not invariably cheaper than elsewhere). Well-known brand names to be found include LL Bean (the famous mail-order clothing company), Liz Claiborne, Calvin Klein, Benetton, Black & Decker, Van Heusen, Polo/Ralph Lauren – the list is endless. The outlet capitals of New England are Kittery and Freeport (also the home of LL Bean) in Maine (see also page 128), Fall River in southern Massachusetts and North Conway in New Hampshire (particularly popular because New

16

The outlet store (above, one of dozens in Freeport, ME) and the village store (right) offer two very different shopping experiences. Every visitor should try them both at least once

one such as Chestnut Hill in Boston. (For more on shopping in Boston, see pages 82–3.)

Factory outlets Love it or loathe it, outlet shopping is one of New England's big draws. All manner of merchandise – clothing, household goods and gifts – is offered at these manufacturers' and distributors' outlets, either at wholesale prices or at discounts varying from 25 to 80 per cent (but you do need to be a 'savvy'

Bargain-hunters in Boston's downtown area make for Filene's Basement, where goods are reduced according to how long they have been on display

Hampshire has no sales tax), but there are scores of smaller complexes in many other towns.

Antiques While some visitors come to New England simply for the outlets, others come purely for the antique-hunting. Cape Cod, the Berkshires, much of Vermont, and Newport, Rhode Island, have particular concentrations of antique shops, but it is hard to go anywhere without coming across an emporium of some sort, whether it trades in rusty farm tools or exquisite European furniture. The best bargains may be in flea markets and antique shows (listed

❑ New England's most famous country store is in Weston, Vermont, where artefacts from the past jostle for space with Vermont Common Crackers, penny candy and much more. For a mail-order catalogue, tel: 802/824 3184. ❑

❑ For a full list of crafts outlets, including shows, see official state guides and local listings. The League of New Hampshire Craftsmen (205 North Main Street, Concord, NH 03301), the Maine Crafts Association (PO Box 228, Deer Isle, ME 04627) and the Vermont Crafts Council (PO Box 938, Montpelier, VT 05601) publish touring guides to studios, shops, fairs and galleries. ❑

locally), but you need to know what you are about. The biggest show is held in May and September in Brimfield, Massachusetts.

Crafts Visitors to New England can buy examples of traditional and contemporary crafts at a broad range of prices in shops and galleries. At any time, in any area, they will also be able to find a craft fair within easy distance. The Annual Craftsmen's Fair, the oldest in the nation, is held in the second week of August at the base of Mount Sunapee in New Hampshire. Some fairs are restricted to 'juried' designers who have been judged to meet, or exceed, the highest of standards. These standards are reflected in the prices, but the quality really is outstanding. While excellent crafts can be found all over New England, it is in Vermont that the arts and crafts are particularly important. The Vermont State Craft Center at Frog Hollow has retail galleries in Burlington, Middlebury and Manchester, and there are dozens of other outlets throughout the state.

■ **In the northeast states of America the weather conditions and the variety of broad-leaved trees combine perfectly to produce a sensational display of autumn colour. During September and October virtually the whole of New England is given over to 'the fall'.....■**

The red maple brings the first hint of colour to the hillsides

Vast areas of New England are forested and where, over the years, loggers have felled the evergreen softwoods, hardwoods have grown in their place, creating a full palette of autumn colours. Like the richest of oriental carpets, the vivid reds of the red maple, sugar maple, sweetgum, blackgum, sassafras, red oak and scarlet oak interweave with the deep reddish-purples of the sumacs and dogwoods, the golden-yellows of the hickories, trembling aspen and birches, and the rich bronzes and browns of beech and the other oaks.

❏ From mid-September, call Fall Foliage Hotlines for a free calendar of events, a foliage guide (giving suggested leaf-peeping tours) and regularly updated reports. Connecticut: 203/566 5348. Maine: 207/287 5711. Massachusetts: 617/727 3201. New Hampshire: 603/271 2343. Rhode Island: 401/277 2601. Vermont: 802/828 3239. ❏

The cause of the colour When the Great Bear was hunted down in the heavens, so goes the Native American legend, his blood dripped on to the forests, turning some of the leaves red, while the fat that spattered out of the hunters' cooking pot turned others yellow. A more scientific explanation has to do with the food-making process that goes on in leaves. The cells in which this takes place contain pigments, notably chlorophyll, which makes leaves green. Leaves also contain carotenoids which give them a yellow colour, masked during spring and summer by the larger amount of green. When the days get shorter and the nights cooler, food-making slows down, the green goes as the chlorophyll breaks up, and yellows come to the fore. Similarly, when temperatures at night drop below 45°F, sugar made during the day is trapped, forming the pigment anthocyanin, responsible, for example, for the 'fire engine' red of the swamp or red maple.

No one can predict exactly when the leaf change will come, how long the season will be or how bright the colour. The most brilliant foliage occurs when warm, sunny days are

followed by cool nights. The season (about three weeks) starts in the northwest of New England around mid-September and progresses in a southeasterly direction.

Seeing the show Every state has its comprehensive list of fall foliage attractions for enthusiasts, known locally as 'leaf-peepers', with suggested car and cycle tours (see box). Roads such as the Kancamagus Highway in New Hampshire's White Mountains (see Drive on pages 206–7) and the Mohawk Trail in

> ❑ 'No pen can describe the turning of the leaves – the insurrection of the tree people against the waning year. A little maple began it, flaming blood-red of a sudden where he stood against the dark green of a pine-belt. Next morning there was an answering signal from the swamp where the sumacs grow. Three days later, the hill-sides as far as the eye could range were afire, and the roads paved, with crimson and gold.'
> – Rudyard Kipling, *Leaves from a Winter Notebook*, 1900. ❑

western Massachusetts can get extremely busy, and you may be better off on the back roads (see Drives on pages 98–9 and 240–1).

In Vermont you can combine leaf-peeping with craft shows, antiques fairs and apple festivals, taking in some covered bridges on the way. In Maine family outings can include visits to lighthouses and fishing villages, craft festivals and antiques fairs, farm stands and bean suppers. In New Hampshire, the Isle of Shoals Ferry runs cruises out of Portsmouth for a view from the sea, while the Lakes region offers a choice of cruises where the reflections of the trees in the water provide a double dose of colour. The Massachusetts fall foliage guide suggests hot-air balloon trips and areas that are particularly good for excursions by boat or canoe. In Connecticut, cruises go down the prettiest part of the Connecticut river.

The gold of sugar maple, most prominent around mid-October

■ **Lobster may be undisputed king but seafood does not end there. And while New England is the home of maple syrup, there are many more traditional treats for the sweet-toothed to enjoy. Orchard fruits and farm produce are of the very best.....■**

Traditionally, the New Englander's day starts with a pancake breakfast, the pancakes accompanied by lashings of maple syrup. Alternatively, it might be blueberry muffins, banana bread, French toast, Belgian waffles or an English muffin. Any of these may be served with eggs and ham or fruit. Only rarely does a hotel or restaurant limit itself to anything as plain as cereal or yoghurt, though the more health-conscious New Englanders may prefer this in their own homes. At weekends, brunch is traditional and, later in the day, depending on the season, there may be an outdoor cookout, an ice-cream social, a clam bake (see box) or a bean supper.

Baked beans, a favourite at church suppers, were invented by thrifty early colonists. Boston baked beans, however, may be less easy to find in a restaurant than Boston cream pie, which is actually a custard-filled sponge cake covered in chocolate. Desserts tend to be sweet and wicked. Indian pudding is a traditional recipe, a light, spicy dessert made with cornmeal and molasses. Pumpkin pie, also learned from the Native Americans, is traditional fare at Thanksgiving celebrations. A more recent New England speciality is Ben & Jerry's ice-cream (see page 234).

A blue lobster, a rare sight

❏ The clambake is a Rhode Island tradition, an outdoor event for at least 30 or 40 people. Traditionally, a deep hole is dug in wet sand, and clams, lobsters, potatoes, corn, sausages and chicken are steamed in it over hot rocks and covered with seaweed (or, nowadays, canvas). ❏

Seafood Imagine a lobster 5 feet long, as they were reported to be back in colonial times, and you can understand why the Pilgrim Fathers, setting eyes on *Homarus americanus* for the first time, thought it had been sent by the Devil. Seeing the Native Americans catching the beasts, however, and feeling pangs of hunger as they waited for their first crops to take root, the early colonists soon recognised the lobster as an important food source. Before long it was regarded as poor-man's fodder, a far cry from the gourmet food of today. Lobster appears on menus throughout New England, but the best place to try it is from the boiling cauldrons of one of the many lobster 'pounds' or 'shacks' along the coast roads of Maine.

A mainstay of the New Englander's diet is the chowders, notably clam, fish

Sweetcorn should be eaten as fresh as fresh as can be: peel back the end of each cob to check it is succulent

or corn. Menus rarely exclude one or other of these delicious, thick creamy soups. Other seafoods which may not be familiar to Europeans include scrod (a flaky, tender white fish) and the strangely named large clam, the quahog (pronounced 'ko-hog'), native to southeast New England.

Fruits in season The sweetcorn season (from mid-July to early September) is short, but to be relished. Ideally you should eat the corn within three hours of its being picked – a sweet, moist, tender treat. A favourite is the yellow and white variety called 'butter and sugar'. In September, just before the first frost, the orange pumpkins are harvested. Stacked against a traditional red barn,

they make a sight as colourful as the autumn foliage itself.

Fall also sees the start of the Pick Your Own apple season, while farm stands sell apple cider as well as ready-picked apples. Try Paula Reds, one of the earliest, and McIntosh, Cortland, Empire or Northern Spy.

Blueberries are a speciality of Maine, and turn up baked into anything from muffins and pancakes at breakfast to pie for dinner. Cranberries, traditionally eaten as a sauce with roast turkey, are exported all over the world from the bogs of the southeast corner of Massachusetts.

Above: Bean Suppers, often held in church halls, are a New England tradition. Visitors are welcome

■ **Education is a way of life in New England. With a concentration of highly regarded preparatory schools and well over 250 universities and colleges, it courses through the veins of social and cultural life. As a spin-off, New England leads the field in technological and medical research.....** ■

Lowell House, typical of Harvard's elegant Georgian buildings

❑ In October 1958 MIT student Oliver Smoot was carried prostrate by his classmates across what to MIT's chagrin is called Harvard Bridge. They marked off each head-to-toe length with paint and chalk. Thus the official length of the bridge is 364.4 Smoots plus one ear. The Smootmarks are regularly repainted – look out for them. ❑

compete in intercollegiate football and other sports, it is for their high academic and social standing that these élitist Ivy League colleges are so revered.

The origin of the name Ivy League is uncertain: traditional ivy-covered buildings? From 'IV', standing for Inter Varsity? Or perhaps because initially there were just four, in Roman figures IV, members?

❑ 'You can tell a Harvard man, but you can't tell him anything.' ❑

The Ivy League Four of New England's universities, Harvard, Yale, Brown and Dartmouth, together with four other eastern universities, Pennsylvania, Princeton, Columbia and Cornell, make up that prestigious group known as the Ivy League. In the 1870s the colleges used to meet for football matches and in those early years they were a major force in American football. In the 1920s, however, their prowess faded somewhat and, although they still

Harvard, the nation's oldest university, was founded in 1636 by the early colonists primarily as a training ground for Puritan clergymen. Many of Harvard's first graduates in fact went on to set up other educational institutions. By 1647, towns with 50 householders had to provide primary schooling and those with 100 or more to provide secondary schools. Today many of America's oldest and most highly regarded colleges and universities are in Massachusetts, notably the Massachusetts Institute of Technology (MIT), which was founded in 1861.

Yale, Harvard's traditional arch rival, is in New Haven, Connecticut. New England's second oldest university was founded in 1702 at Saybrook by Harvard graduates and renamed after its benefactor. It has a collegiate system modelled on that of Oxford and Cambridge universities in England, and its fine buildings recall their architecture (see pages 102–5).

Dartmouth College in Hanover, New Hampshire, the only Ivy League college in the northern part of New England, also has a beautiful campus. Founded in 1769 as a Native American charity school, Dartmouth by tradition waives tuition fees (so exorbitant as to eliminate most locals) for any resident of New Hampshire or Vermont with Native American ancestry. Consequently, the percentage of such undergraduates, although still tiny, is greater here than in other Ivy League universities. Brown University, in Providence, Rhode Island, was

Below and opposite, top: Yale's Gothic Revival architecture

❑ Fees at the Ivy League universities are currently in the region of $24,000 per year (tuition $18,000, board and lodging $6,000). Compare this with a state, or public, university where fees for a state resident range from around $1,500 to about $2,500. ❑

founded in 1764 as a Baptist college by one of the leaders in the China trade, John Brown.

The field of medicine If the state of Massachusetts is pre-eminent in education, it is also one of the world's major medical centres.and Boston has an illustrious tradition of leading the field in medical research. It was in Boston in 1846 that ether was first used as an anaesthetic during an operation, the first kidney transplant was performed there in 1954, and open heart surgery was first performed at the Boston's Children's Hospital in 1967.

■ One of the rich and diverse strands that make up the fabric of New England is its cultural life. Classical music, jazz and dance are a tradition not just in Boston's concert halls and churches but throughout the region in universities and colleges, at festivals and, not least, on the village-green bandstand.....■

Great composers One of America's first great modern composers was Charles Ives, who was born in Danbury, Connecticut, in 1874 and who graduated from Yale to become a successful insurance executive. In summer, outdoor concerts of classical music and jazz are held in Danbury at the Charles Ives Center for the Arts (see page 95). The third movement of Ives's *Three Places in New England*, 'The Housatonic at Stockbridge', was suggested by a misty Sunday morning walk with his wife along the riverbank.

The New England scenery has been inspirational to many works, including Edward MacDowell's *New England Idylls* (1902) and William Schuman's *New England Triptych*.

Seiji Ozawa conducts the Boston Symphony Orchestra at Symphony Hall

Another important New England composer (although the number of his works is small, because he destroyed his early compositions) was Karl Ruggles, a close friend of Charles Ives. Walter Piston, whose works include the orchestral suite *Three New England Sketches*, was born in Rockland, Maine, in 1894 and was an influential teacher at Harvard, one of his most distinguished pupils being Leonard Bernstein.

❏ For programme information and tickets for concerts in Boston see panel, page 79. For Tanglewood, see page 146. ❏

The highlights For more than a century, the Boston Symphony Orchestra's concerts in Symphony Hall have been a vital element in

24

Boston life during the winter months (see page 79). The orchestra's founding spirit was Henry Lee Higginson, who during the years he spent in Vienna as a music student had much enjoyed summertime garden concerts of light music and had a vision of giving Boston not only winter concerts of classical music but 'at other times, especially in the summer, concerts of a lighter kind of music'. So started, in July 1885, the

In 1929 outdoor concerts were introduced on the Esplanade along the Charles river in Boston. Every summer, thousands of young and old flock to the Hatch Shell with their rugs and picnic baskets for a summer evening's music in the open air.

One of Colonel Higginson's friends was Isabella Stewart Gardner, a patron of aspiring musicians, conductors and composers, as well as painters, sculptors, actors and writers. Her creation, Fenway Court, now the Isabella Stewart Gardner Museum, a fragrant oasis of beauty in Boston (see page 69), was a meeting-place for musicians and the venue for wide-ranging programmes of music, song and dance. Following in this tradition, the museum today puts on approximately 130 public concerts each year, including recitals by its own chamber orchestra.

Tanglewood, in western Massachusetts, is the Boston Symphony Orchestra's summer home, and the Tanglewood Music Festival is one of the cultural highlights of the Berkshires region, drawing hundreds of thousands of visitors annually to the open-

Summer music on the lawns of Tanglewood

'Popular Concerts', or 'Pops', that were to become a national tradition. The social élite flocked to Music Hall to sit at tables arranged between potted plants, partaking of refreshments and listening to 'light music of the best class'. Little changed in form or content, the concerts still remain a highlight of the year and the Boston Pops is the most recorded orchestra in the world.

sided Music Shed and the balmy lawns that surround it (see page 146). Jacob's Pillow Dance Festival, held near by at Becket from late June to August, offers 10 highly acclaimed weeks of dance programmes. Of the numerous regional festivals of music and dance, the recitals held in the opulent salons of some of Newport, Rhode Island's mansions have become a summer tradition. And all over the region the village bandstand provides many a delightful hour of informal entertainment.

■ **Hollywood, past and present, has not failed to tap the rich vein of New England's diversity. In the field of drama, theatre is as alive in small towns and villages as it is in the metropolis of Boston .....■**

Films Among the galaxy of films with New England associations is *On Golden Pond*, based on Ernest Thompson's 1978 play. Set on Great Pond, near Augusta, Maine, the film was actually shot at Squam Lake, New Hampshire. *The Whales of August* is another delightful film set in New England. *Mystic Pizza* (1988) was filmed in Connecticut, not in Mystic, but nearby Stonington, on a specially built pizzeria set. For the filming of Hitchcock's *The Trouble with Harry* in 1955, the village of Craftsbury Common, Vermont was painted white to make it a more 'ideal' New England village – and has remained so ever since.

Herman Melville's *Moby Dick*, with its settings on Nantucket, Henry James's *The Bostonians* and John Updike's *The Witches of Eastwick*, set in Wickford, Rhode Island, are but three New England novels to have been made into films.

Plays and players America's greatest playwright, Eugene O'Neill (see page 47), set his final

Madeleine Potter and Christopher Reeve in The Bostonians

masterpiece, *Long Day's Journey into Night* (1957) in his boyhood summer home, Monte Cristo Cottage in New London, Connecticut. Today, the Eugene O'Neill Theater Center, in Waterford, champions new work by American playwrights.

World-class performers are regularly brought in for pre-New York shows in small town theatres. In Vermont in particular many village communities enjoy theatre on an intimate scale in revitalised 19th-century theatres and opera houses. From 1938 to 1976 the Shubert Theater in New Haven, Connecticut, hosted the premières of many famous Broadway shows (see panel, page 103), and today the Goodspeed Opera House, a resplendent Victorian concoction on the banks of the Connecticut river at East Haddam, hosts musicals old and new. Festivals proliferate, offering strong local summertime theatre programmes. Those held in the Berkshires (see pages 143–7) make it a particularly popular area for theatre-lovers.

Veterans Katherine Hepburn and Henry Fonda in On Golden Pond

NEW ENGLAND WAS

■ **When the Pilgrim Fathers crossed the Atlantic in 1620 and founded the first permanent European colony in New England, they did so in the wake of many earlier explorers and merchant adventurers who had been probing a land that had been home to the Algonquin peoples since time immemorial.....■**

John Cabot, an Italian navigator and explorer based in London

It seems the ancestors of the Algonquin peoples of New England arrived in North America after the end of the last Ice Age, in a series of eastward migrations from Asia. By the time the first Europeans settled in the New World, Native Americans (the so-called American Indians) had been inhabiting these northeastern woodlands for well over 10,000 years.

European exploration To the Native American way of thinking, land – a

❏ In 1492 Native Americans in New England are estimated to have numbered about 100,000; by 1620 most were dead. ❏

source of food, like water – is not something that belongs to people; it is people who belong to the land. The 'People of the Dawnland', the Abenaki, once inhabited an area that extended from the Maine coast westwards to Lake Champlain, and from the St Lawrence south to the Merrimack river and northern Massachusetts. This was a forested land laced with lakes and waterways along which they travelled in their birchbark canoes to fish and hunt. These Abenaki would have been the first natives to meet with intruders, when in about AD1000, it is believed, Leif Ericsson arrived from Scandinavia with his dreaded Vikings. Over the following centuries a number of further forays were made across the Atlantic, many seeking the Northwest Passage round Canada. By the 1400s fishermen from Scandinavia, Portugal, Spain, France and Britain were coming regularly to enjoy rich pickings in the continent's then teeming offshore waters.

The excitement aroused by Christopher Columbus's voyages to the Caribbean between 1492 and 1504 tempted more and more Europeans. In 1497 King Henry VII of England authorised John Cabot to set sail from Bristol; exactly where he landed is uncertain, but Nova Scotia seems likely. Cabot staked an English claim to North America by hoisting the flag and returned home

with promising reports, but little else. In 1524 France sent the Florentine, Giovanni da Verrazano (who reported a frosty welcome from the Abenaki), then, in the 1530s and 1540s, Jacques Cartier, who explored the St Lawrence river. In 1568 David Ingram captured the imagination of all with tales of 'a magic city of Norumbega', glittering with 'pillars of crystal and silver'.

> ❏ The term 'New England' was coined by John Smith, English founder of the Jamestown colony in Virginia, when he wrote *A Description of New England* (1616). ❏

Attempts to settle The Spanish, British and French continued to look for potential sites for settlement and began to trade with the Native Americans for furs. By the turn of the 17th century, fisheries had been established and rival trading posts were in operation. Beaver hats were by now all the rage in Europe and fur trading was serious business. In 1605 the area was mapped by Frenchman Samuel de Champlain, who gave his name to the lake that is situated on Vermont's western boundary.

Attempts to establish settlements in the region, however, failed, and relationships between Europeans and Indians became increasingly prickly. George Popham

established a colony at Sagadahoc but it did not survive the harsh New England winter of 1607–8. A French Jesuit colony was set up on Mount Desert Island but in 1613 it was burnt down by the English.

Trading in disease The concept of hunting animals not for food and clothing but in order to sell their fur was an alien one to the Native Americans, but they were tempted by the Europeans' metal, which would improve their fish-hooks, snowshoes and canoe paddles, and welcomed their kettles and guns. However, traders also brought with them European viruses, to which the natives had no immunity, and which would in places wipe out practically the entire population. By the time the Pilgrims landed in 1620, the Indians were devastatingly weakened.

Pilgrims John Alden and Mary Chilton are the first ashore

■ **The successful establishment of the English colony at Plymouth in 1620 encouraged a flood of settlers. They came with the hopes and ideals of 17th-century England, but their vision of a new world was not easily realised.....■**

After a bad first winter, the Plymouth colony was soon settled and expanding, though closely dependent on contact with England and relying heavily on the advice of Native Americans for fishing, hunting and growing crops (see pages 180–1 for more on the Pilgrims). In 1630 another group of Puritans under the leadership of John Winthrop founded the Massachusetts Bay Colony on a spot they named Boston, after their home town in Lincolnshire, England. Quickly successful, it soon completely overshadowed Plymouth.

The meeting of Puritan and Native Americn was a meeting of two utterly different philosophies of life, yet at first, at least, they got on all right. Peace treaties made between the colonists and most of the neighbouring Native Americans held firm. Gradually, however, relations began to deteriorate. Not only had the Europeans brought diseases by which, catastrophically, the native people had been crippled, they had also introduced guns and alcohol which seriously disrupted their communities. Inter-tribal warfare broke out over trading, English missionaries tried to impose a foreign culture and, as colonists needed more land, the Native Americans were increasingly confronted by that totally alien, European desire to stake a claim on territory.

Wars of conquest By the mid-17th century the Puritans found themselves caught up in an unending round of skirmishes and shifting alliances between invader and native. In the Pequot War the settlers, aided by the Narragansett, annihilated the Pequots around the Connecticut river. In what is called King Philip's War (1675–6), however, the Puritans massacred the Narragansett, taking their land in Connecticut and Rhode Island. In the process hundreds of

Metacom or 'King Philip', sachem of the Wampanoags, who was finally driven to leading his people into vicious war in 1675

KING PHILIP

settlers were killed and many towns raided. During the French and Indian War (a part of Britain's Seven Years' War with France that basically was about beaver fur), which spluttered on from the late-17th century until the final flare-up that led to French defeat in 1763, the colonists were to fight countless battles alongside British troops against the French and their Native American allies.

A stand for freedom Even within their own communities, life was not all plain sailing for the settlers. Unlike the Plymouth colonists, the Massachusetts Bay Puritans were not Separatists who had broken with the Anglican Church. These were Puritans who were themselves dissenters in that they hoped to reform the Church, yet condemned any who showed signs of deviating from the (very) straight and narrow path of strict Puritanism. Men and women such as Thomas Hooker, William Coddington and Anne Hutchinson left to found new settlements. In 1636 a minister, Roger Williams, was banished for advocating freedom of religious thought. He went on to found Rhode Island, where church and state were always separate and religious freedom paramount.

John Winthrop: by 1670 his Boston colony had grown to 1,200

The Puritans were equally assertive in their public administration. Even when others joined them, power remained firmly in their hands and, with England absorbed in the Civil War, they were left to their own devices. When Charles II acceded to the throne in 1660, however, he found he did not like the extent to which the colony was running its own affairs. He therefore introduced the Navigation Acts, aimed at making New England merchants trade only with Britain, and ended the Puritans' monopoly of the vote. With suffrage, the merchants (who ignored the Acts) rapidly grew both wealthy and powerful. They no longer needed, or wanted, the close contact with England; soon they would want to be their own masters.

❏ When history is told by the victor, language is easily tainted by prejudice. Thus Native Americans had warriors, Europeans soldiers; Native American victories were massacres, European victories were battles; Native Americans had chiefs, Europeans generals and kings. ❏

■ **During the early 1700s New England was growing fat on its burgeoning international trade. Resentment mounted at the mother country's attempts to muscle in on this wealth, with events escalating in the 1760s to the inevitable shot famously 'heard round the world'.....■**

'No taxation without representation' Britain emerged supreme from the French and Indian War in 1763, but it also emerged practically bankrupt. King George III decided the wealthy American colonies should pay for their own defence and also help recoup financial losses.

A series of tax-levying acts followed, but were met with protests from a core of colonials who argued that no one should have to give financial support to a government in which he had no representation.

❏ While the Sons of Liberty were hailed as heroes, the Daughters of Liberty enforced boycotts of British goods by serving herbal teas, using maple syrup instead of sugar and wearing homespun cloth instead of imported silks. ❏

The Sugar Act of 1764 reinforced the 1733 Molasses Act which aimed to end trade with the West Indies (in fact it was so lax that smuggling, bribery and therefore the rum industry continued to prosper). The Stamp Act of 1765 taxed printed matter, but met with riots and was repealed the following year. The colonials also responded to the 1767 Townshend Acts, which taxed tea, glass, paint, paper and lead, by boycotting British goods. In 1770 all except the tax on tea were repealed, ironically on the same day as five colonials were killed in the so-called Boston Massacre. The colonials continued to smuggle tea in from Dutch traders.

The 'Boston Massacre', as portrayed by Paul Revere. The British resemble an execution squad firing on innocents at short range. Note the Custom House is labelled 'Butcher's Hall'

Disguised as Mohawks to escape detection, the Sons of Liberty tip East India Company tea into the harbour

The Boston Tea Party The Tea Act of December 1773 was seen as giving the British East India Company a monopoly on tea sales to the colonies. It so fuelled resentment at the British government's power to legislate and levy taxes, that when three East India ships docked in Boston loaded with 342 chests of tea, the 'Sons of Liberty', a group of patriots led by Samuel Adams, John Hancock, Joseph Warren and Paul Revere, agreed to take decisive action. Disguised as Mohawks, they boarded the ships and threw the tea into the water. Britain retorted in 1774 with the Intolerable, or Coercive, Acts. Boston Harbor was closed.

The opening shots The American colonies united in response to these further threats to their liberty, and at the First Continental Congress plans were laid for the organisation of an army (later to be led by George Washington). On 19 April 1775 the War of Independence, or Revolutionary War, began.

The British knew about a cache of arms in Concord (see pages 168–70) and sent troops to seize it. As they left Boston, Paul Revere (see page 55) made his famous ride to Lexington, on the road to Concord, to warn the Sons of Liberty there that the British were coming. There were minor scuffles in Lexington, but when the British reached Concord they met with organised resistance from the colonial Minutemen, and the 'shot heard round the world', as described by Emerson in his *Concord Hymn*, was fired.

In May, Ethan Allen and his Green Mountain Boys captured Fort Ticonderoga on Lake Champlain from the British. In June, around Boston, the British won the Battle of Bunker Hill in Charlestown, but only with heavy losses, and when George Washington fortified Dorchester Heights (with arms captured from Fort Tic) they decided to quit. The British left Boston in March 1776, never to return.

❑ The battle of Bunker Hill actually took place on what in 1775 was known as Breeds Hill; Bunker Hill was near by. In spite of the mix-up of names, the battle's name stuck and Breeds Hill was subsequently renamed Bunker Hill. ❑

The Battle of Bunker Hill, *one of a series of paintings by John Trumbull (1756–1843) recording events in the War of Independence*

■ The history of New England is inextricably bound up with the sea. Whether it be through fishing, whaling, trading or shipbuilding, it is the sea that has shaped the region's economy, its society and its traditions.....■

Fishing Even before the Europeans first established colonies on New England's shores, they were coming to fish the region's coastal waters, greedy for cod, haddock and pollack. For 200 years fishing was to be the mainstay of New England's trade with Europe. It declined during World War II, but there is still activity in harbours such as Gloucester, Provincetown, New Bedford and Boston, and in the lobstering ports of Maine.

34

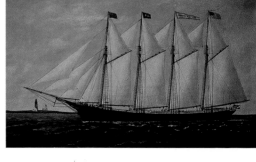

Marine art is a proud tradition

Whaling Today we look on whaling activities with revulsion, but in the

mid-19th century it was a brave, romantic enterprise – and also very prosperous. Right whales had long been caught by Native Americans and colonials in the in-shore waters, but

Ship's figurehead: the woodcarver's skill on show at Mystic Seaport, Connecticut

in 1712 Captain Christopher Hussey caught a sperm whale which, with its oil, spermaceti and ambergris, proved a much more valuable species. So began the Yankee enterprise that every year sent hundreds of whaling ships across the oceans of the world, to return with the oil that would light the lamps of America and Europe until the discovery of kerosene in the mid-1800s. Other exported whale products were spermaceti for candles, bones for corset stays and ambergris for perfume. Today, this legendary era is vividly recalled in whaling museums in New Bedford, Nantucket and Mystic.

Foreign trade If whaling brought wealth in the 18th century, so too did the infamous Triangle Trade involving slaves from Africa, molasses from the West Indies and rum from the colonies' distilleries, a trade that thrived on smuggling and bribery. After Independence in 1776, trade was opened up with China, and New

❑ Maine supplied the timber for the masts of 80 per cent of British Admiral Nelson's fleet. ❑

❏ In seaboard towns notice the 'widow's walk', a balustrade along the top of some of the sea captains' houses. From here wives would watch ships coming and going. ❏

England entered a golden age of commercial enterprise.

The capital of maritime New England during this 'Federalist Era', was not so much Boston as Salem, Massachusetts, and the elegant houses built here by the captains, ship-owners and merchants who amassed such vast fortunes are splendid monuments to their prowess. The Peabody Museum displays the trinkets they brought home, along with their cargoes of tea and silks. Boston's Back Bay and Beacon Hill neighbourhoods, Portsmouth (New Hampshire) and Newburyport (Massachusetts) also have their share of grand houses built on the China trade wealth.

Ship-building Seafaring activity supported a wide range of other businesses – rope-makers (a 1,000-ton vessel needed 12,000 feet of rope), sail-makers, caulkers, chandlers and, of course, ship-builders. Northern New England's plentiful forests supplied scores of shipyards, mostly along the Maine coast. The Merrimack river was also busy, and here was invented the little work-boat, the dory, which fishermen would stack in nests of five or six on their sea-going boats.

Boston Wharf in its heyday

A shipowners' advertisement for their 'first class clipper ship'

This was the era in which insurance agents first began to make a killing. With premiums based on the dimensions and type of wood used for the different parts of the ship, the wise ship-owner would follow their recommendations – hard (yellow) pine for the keel, Douglas fir for the deck planking, and so on. The Maine Maritime Museum in Bath (see page 118), is excellent for a study of boat-building.

The era of the clipper was brief, eclipsed by the steam-powered ship. New England's maritime trade began to decline, and rich merchants put their capital into manufacturing.

❏ Plaques on many houses in Marblehead, a delightful small town on the North Shore of Massachusetts, indicate the range of maritime trades. 'Built for Benjamin Pritchard, Tailor, 1753', reads one; others are 'Blacksmith', 'Housewright', 'Scribe', 'Shoreman', as well as 'Mariner' and 'Merchant'. ❏

■ **During the golden years of the China trade, it was the coastal areas of New England that generated the wealth. As maritime commerce declined and new industrial technology developed towards the end of the 18th century, the water-power of the inland river valleys became the basis for a new wave of prosperity.....■**

36

'Tuck' is the Algonquin word for 'river with waves', and Pawtucket is 'a divided river with waves' – ideal for powering mills. It was in Pawtucket, at the mouth of the Blackstone River Valley, which runs southeast from Worcester, Massachusetts, to Providence, Rhode Island, that the American Industrial Revolution was born. Craftsmen in metal, leather and wood, as well as handloom weavers and fullers, had worked in Massachusetts since the days of the early settlers, but in 1793 the first water-powered cotton mill in America, Slater Mill, opened in a clap-board building beside the river in Pawtucket.

Samuel Slater had worked in Richard Arkwright's revolutionary spinning mills in Britain. With financial backing from Rhode Island's prosper-ous shipping merchants, including one of the Brown brothers, he reproduced the machine designs he had learned there and made use of the local crafts-men's skills to harness water-power to drive the carders, spin-ning machines and looms that launched New England's textile industry and trans-formed daily life across the country. The mill and other buildings have been

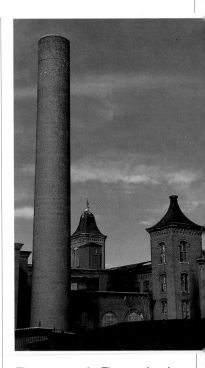

Thomson, on the Thames river in Connecticut, one of dozens of factory towns that sprang up during the 19th century to meet the growing demand for manufactured goods

❑ Some of New England's mill towns are being turned into Heritage Parks. Immaculately restored, they barely resemble the noisy, grimy towns of the 19th century, but they do offer an insight into a turning point in the region's history. ❑

❏ The exploitation of women and the use of child and slave labour in the factories were issues of great concern to 19th-century social activists such as feminist Margaret Fuller, anti-slavery campaigner William Lloyd Garrison (see panel, page 72) and the Concord circle of thinkers and writers (see pages 46–7). ❏

restored as part of the Slater Mill Historic Site in Pawtucket (see page 211).

Rise... Other merchants were quick to seize the opportunity for diversification. Alongside rivers such as the Blackstone and the Merrimack, the landscape of rolling farmland changed rapidly into a quite different scene of mills, warehouses and workers' housing, smoke stacks, dams, canals and, in time, railways. Millbury, for instance, a town positioned to benefit from both the Blackstone river and the Blackstone canal, had no less than six woollen mills in the 1830s. The most remarkable of these mill villages was Lowell, developed by the wealthy Boston merchant Francis Cabot Lowell on the Merrimack river northwest of Boston (see page 171). Lowell had seen the appalling conditions of some of the factory workers in Britain and planned decent company-owned housing, schools, places of worship and recreational facilities for his workers. Women as well as men were employed, daughters of New England farmers. Letters home describe good conditions, fair treatment and a lively social life. Lowell village became a showpiece. By 1850 it was producing 2 million yards of cloth a week and had one of the largest canal systems in the world.

...and fall As mills grew larger and more numerous, more labour was needed. Workers were attracted off the land and immigrants flooded in from Europe. Some of the earliest were the Irish who constructed the Blackstone Canal in 1828 to transport goods from Worcester to Providence, though 20 years later this was replaced by the railway. The mills (most of which had never operated on such caring principles as Lowell's) became overcrowded and, even in Lowell, families of Irish, Portuguese, Greeks and others were crammed into squalid tenements. Child labour was introduced and all workers were desperately exploited. Wages were cut, and protests, petitions and strikes ensued, culminating in a major strike in 1912.

Gradually industrialists were lured by cheaper, slave labour to the South, and by the 1920s 50 per cent of American cotton was being woven there. The Depression followed and most of New England's textile mills closed down. Industrial prosperity would only be regained with the development of the electronics industry in southern New England after World War II.

A look at the long-gone days of sweat and toil at Lowell Mill

■ **The 18th century saw a steady trickle of immigrants, but by the mid-1800s foreigners began to pour into New England in numbers significant enough to have a permanent effect on society, politics and the economy.....■**

Boston's Irish and Italians The Potato Famine in Ireland of 1845–50 resulted in a flood of families seeking better prospects. Thousands went no further than Boston; there, hungry and poor, they crowded into the North End district. Initially, the Roman Catholic Irish met with prejudice from Bostonians, whose blood was basically still Puritan, and their place remained at the lower end of social ladder. Gradually they improved their image and proved they could hold their own in public office alongside the blue-blooded Bostonian aristocrats (with the result that the Democrats began to break the Republican hold on power).

In 1884 Hugh O'Brien became the first of many Irish mayors of Boston. In 1905 came 'Honey-Fitz', as John F Fitzgerald (grandfather of John F Kennedy) was known, and then the colourful James Michael Curley. What Curley lacked in education he made up for in charm, and between 1920 and 1950 he was not only mayor four times, but also governor and congressman – even though he was jailed twice, once while in office. Boston Irish politicians have become legendary, and today they make up half the city council.

Master of blarney, 'Honey-Fitz', JFK's grandfather

The Irish of the North End were joined by Jews from eastern Europe in the 1870s, who were in turn followed in the 1890s by the Italians. To this day the area has remained an Italian quarter, a mish-mash of cafés, food shops and festivals that is good for people-watching.

❏ St Stephen's Church in Boston's North End has bent to the winds of the religious and ethnic changes in this area. In 1714 the New North Meeting House was founded on the site as a Congregationalist institution. In 1804 Charles Bulfinch designed the present building, and in 1813 it became a Unitarian church. In 1862, by which time the population of the North End was mostly Irish, the church, renamed St Stephen's, became Roman Catholic. ❏

Hugh O'Brien, first in a long line of Boston's Irish mayors

38

A cosmopolitan mix Many Irish immigrants found employment in the building of the railways. In Vermont, for instance, descendants of labourers on the Rutland and Central Vermont lines today make up the Irish population in towns such as Burlington and Rutland (their railway long since gone). Some of the Italian immigrants, from marble-producing areas of Italy, went to work in the marble quarries in Barre, Vermont, bringing skills with them in the same way as the Welshmen who went to the slate mines. The work-force for southern New England's textile and shoe factories was also largely formed by European immigrants. At the turn of this century, eastern Europeans formed a significant group in Providence, Rhode Island, and Connecticut's Naugatuck Valley.

Today, the influence of all these immigrants on their adopted hometown often goes beyond just ethnic food shops. Middletown, Connecticut, for instance, has recently had a number of Sicilian mayors. Many fishing fleets were manned by Portuguese from the Azores, and those that remain – at Stonington, Connecticut, and Gloucester, Massachusetts, for example – still

❑ The Sicilians of Middletown, Connecticut, have for several generations come from just one village in southeast Sicily called Melilli. ❑

hold the two-day Blessing of the Fleet. Festivities include a parade of ships and the blessing of wreaths which are thrown into the sea.

Immigrants also came into New England from other directions. After the Civil War French-Canadians came from Quebec, particularly to industrial cities of New Hampshire such as Manchester, but also to Connecticut and the mill villages of Rhode Island and Massachusetts. After World War II Jamaicans and West Indians came from the South and New York, chiefly to Boston and Massachusetts, Rhode Island and Connecticut. So too did Hispanics, many from Puerto Rico. In Hartford, Connecticut, 20 per cent of the population is Hispanic (public notices are printed in English and Spanish).

Top, opposite: the Blessing of the Fleet, Gloucester. Below: an Italian pizzeria in Boston's North End

■ **As cities sweltered under a cloud of mid-19th-century industrial grime, New England's unsullied coast and mountains, now easily reached by steamship or train, began to appeal to the wealthy of the Northeast as summer homes.....■**

40

Some of the hotels had their own railways: the Profile and Franconia Notch ran from Bethlehem, NH, to the Profile House

From the 1830s the painter Thomas Cole and other artists (see page 44) had visited the then little-known White Mountains region, soon to be joined by the notable writers of the day, such as Hawthorne, Emerson and Thoreau (see pages 46–7). These early 'tourists' did much to publicise areas like this and, once steamships and railways had arrived, the stage was set for the development of New England as a playground for the wealthy new industrialists. Spas proliferated, and the rich built summer 'cottages', particularly in Bar Harbor and Acadia on the Maine coast, on the islands of Martha's Vineyard and Nantucket and, notably, in Newport, Rhode Island (see pages 216–18). It is the 'grand hotel', however, that best evokes these days of early tourism.

The first resorts A pioneer of the summer vacation in America was Appledore House, which opened its doors in 1848 as a resort hotel on the Isles of Shoals, off Portsmouth, New Hampshire. Boston's socialites, including literary and artistic celebrities, flocked here in the new coastal steamers to spend idyllic summer months away from the stresses of urban life. Appledore's success spawned many more grand-style summer resorts on the coast and in the mountains, and by about 1880, with the benefit of a good railway network, the tradition of summer holidaying was firmly established. Each year, wealthy families from the eastern seaboard would arrive at the hotels on magnificent trains such as the White Mountain Express, bringing young and old, servants and governesses – and the lifestyle

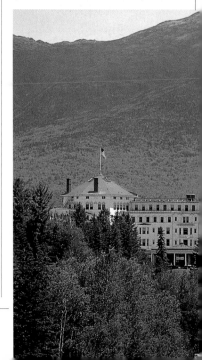

enjoyed by the top echelons of urbane society.

The grand hotel In the early 1900s there were 19 of these 'grand hotels' in the White Mountains alone. Many were self-sufficient, running their own farms, stables and ice-cooling barns. Some had post offices (envelopes franked by a grand hotel post office are nowadays collectors' items). Each had its resident orchestra, often made up of musicians who in the winter season played for the Boston Symphony Orchestra. Artists in residence were kept busy painting souvenirs of the landscape. Instruction was given in dancing (the tea dance being a favourite) and various sporting

❏ In the White Mountains, a daily newspaper, *Among the Clouds*, used to keep local hotel guests up to date with exactly who was staying where. ❏

facilities were offered, from croquet to boating, bathing and fishing. The more adventurous guests would go hiking or horse-riding into the mountains; some, however, would get no further than the hotel's veranda. The veranda was an important feature of the grand hotel, built wide and long (indeed, hotels were rated by its length), with cane rocking-chairs pushed well back so guests had room to promenade. Summer romances flourished, and it was important to see and be seen.

41

The cuisine of the grand hotel chef was legendary, and menus listed up to 70 items per meal. Guests would sit at the same table, with the same waiter, for the whole season. It was important, therefore, in order to see and be seen, not to be stuck in a corner, and for this reason the dining room in the Mount Washington Hotel was octagonal.

By the 1930s the automobile was bringing a different sort of person to the resorts, someone with less money and only a week or two to spare, looking for cheaper accommodation. It was the automobile that sounded the death knell of the grand hotel. Some were torn down, while others were gutted by fire and never rebuilt. Today, only a few remain, such as the Mount Washington in Bretton Woods and the Balsams in Dixville Notch, testaments to a gloriously romantic, sadly bygone era.

Above: wish you were here – an early postcard, of the Cannon Mountain Aerial Passenger Tramway
Left: the Mount Washington Hotel (1902) at Bretton Woods, NH, is one of the few grand hotels still operating today

■ **The political scene in Boston has always been an active one, and it is in New England that some of America's most influential politicians and diplomats, including five presidents, have cut their teeth.....■**

The Adams family The first member of the Adams family to come to prominence was Boston-born Samuel Adams (1722–1803). A complete failure as a businessman and tax collector, he emerged as a terrier-like political agitator, a patriot whose unscrupulous propaganda stirred up anti-British feeling in the run-up to Independence.

Sam Adams's second cousin, John Adams (1735–1826), was also a patriot. A more moderate man, he helped negotiate the Treaty of Versailles which ended the Revolution and was appointed the first US minister to Britain. On his return, he became George Washington's vice-president and a leading Federalist. When Washington retired in 1796, John Adams became America's second president, with his

Samuel Adams: an engraving of the portrait by Copley (1773)

President John Quincy Adams

wife Abigail, one of the intellectual women of the day, playing a strongly supportive role. Defeated by Thomas Jefferson in 1800, John Adams spent an active retirement in Quincy, Massachusetts (see page 182).

John Adams's eldest son, John Quincy Adams (1767–1848), had accompanied his father on various diplomatic missions and, after graduating from Harvard, pursued a distinguished career as a diplomat in Europe. Returning home, he became secretary of state and in 1824, when there was no clear majority in the presidential election, he found himself chosen in preference to Andrew Jackson. John Quincy's term of office was sullied by hostility from Jackson's supporters, and in the 1828 elections he was defeated. As a member of the House of Representatives, however, he put his energies into the anti-slavery campaign. During an impassioned speech on the subject he had a stroke and collapsed on the floor of the House, dying two days later.

'Keep cool with Coolidge' The life and death of Calvin Coolidge (1872–1933), America's 30th president, was not so colourful. Born in Plymouth Notch, Vermont (see page 233), Coolidge was a quiet and cautious man of few words who worked his way up the political ladder to become governor of Massachusetts. Elected Republican vice-president, he became president in 1923 when

The Kennedy era: Robert Rauschenburg's Retroactive *(1964)*

and by the time he announced his presidential candidacy in 1960 an aura of charisma surrounded the couple.

Kennedy was the youngest man, and the first Roman Catholic, ever elected president. At home his main concern was for social welfare, while in foreign affairs he won admiration for his handling of the Cuban missile crisis in 1962. Shortly afterwards he secured the Nuclear Test-Ban Treaty with Soviet leader Nikita Khrushchev and British Prime Minister Harold Macmillan. Seen by many as a symbol of hope, for America and the world, Kennedy was shot dead in Dallas on 22 November 1963.

George Bush President from 1989 to 1993, George Bush grew up in Greenwich, Connecticut, and graduated from Yale. He served under presidents Nixon and Ford before becoming loyal vice-president to Ronald Reagan. His presidency was marked by his involvement of American troops in the Gulf War. His holiday home is in Kennebunkport, Maine.

Warren Harding died unexpectedly. Coolidge's two terms of office were distinguished by such government inaction that when the writer Dorothy Parker was told he had died, she is reputed to have asked 'How can they tell?'.

The Kennedy style President John F Kennedy (1917–63) was the great-grandson of an Irish immigrant. JFK's father, Joseph P Kennedy (1888–1969), a Harvard graduate, married Rose Fitzgerald, the daughter of mayor 'Honey-Fitz' (see page 38). While Joseph made a successful career in politics and business – he was a millionaire at the age of 30 – Rose bore him nine children. Four would die a premature death: Kathleen, Joe, John and Robert.

John first ran as a Democrat for Congress in 1946. In 1953 the handsome young senator married the beautiful Jacqueline Lee Bouvier (in Newport, Rhode Island; see page 218),

George Bush, US president 1989–1993

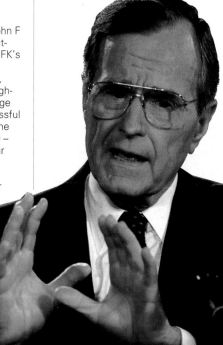

Colonial painting Colonial America produced three artists of note. John Singleton Copley (1738–1815) painted portraits of Boston's élite. His *Watson and the Shark*, in Boston's Museum of Fine Art, is a famous depiction of mankind's struggle with nature, but it is Benjamin West (1738–1820) who stands out as a historical painter during this period. Gilbert Stuart (1755–1828) was another eminent portrait painter (his George Washington appears on the dollar bill).

The White Mountain School Throughout the 19th century, New England artists continued to be influenced by Europe. Thomas Cole (1801–48) was a Romantic landscape painter and a founder of the Hudson River School. He frequently travelled about the Northeast making sketches, and in 1828 visited New Hampshire's White Mountains, instantly to be captivated by the scenery. Albert Bierstadt (1830–1902), another prominent member of the school, created grandiose views of the White Mountains and the Connecticut River Valley.

Top: from Boy in a Boatyard *by Winslow Homer (1836–1910)*

Coastal art colonies The Maine coast has been inspirational to many artists, notably Winslow Homer (1836–1910), who spent the latter part of his life at Prout's Neck. Here he painted a prodigious number of powerful seascapes. Look out too for the seascapes of Fitz Hugh Lane (1804–65). John Marin (1870–1953) was a more recent abstract landscape artist obsessive about the Maine coast. Edward Hopper (1882–1967), one of a group known as the Painters of the American Scene, also worked here, his static, silent figures set in humdrum surroundings. The area around Cushing, Maine, where Andrew Wyeth (born 1917) has his summer home, is the subject of many of his tempera and watercolour paintings. Another American Scene painter, Wyeth is best known for *Christina's World*, depicting a lonely figure in an open field.

Shipping in Down East Waters *by Fitz Hugh Lane (1804–65)*

Boston Common at Twilight *by Frederick Childe Hassam (1859–1935)*

Appledore, an idyllic summer artists' colony on the Isles of Shoals, was immortalised by the leading American Impressionist, F Childe Hassam (1859–1935). His *Boston Common at Twilight* is a favourite in Boston's Museum of Fine Art. Childe Hassam also worked in Old Lyme, at the mouth of the Connecticut river, where Florence Griswold opened her house (now a museum) to an influential colony which became known as the Old Lyme Impressionists.

Americans abroad No study of the art of 19th-century New England is complete without mention of two notable American artists whose work and influence straddled the Atlantic. These are James McNeill Whistler (1834–1903), who was born in Lowell, Massachusetts, and is perhaps best known for his paintings of London, and John Singer Sargent (1856–1925), born in Florence, Italy, who painted portraits of Boston's prominent men and women.

The 20th century The two New England artists who have won the most widespread popularity in recent times must be the illustrator Norman Rockwell (see page 150) and Anna 'Grandma' Moses (1860–1961), a primitive painter who created brightly coloured scenes of everyday New England life (see page 226).

Sculptors One of America's foremost sculptors, Augustus Saint-Gaudens (1848–1907), worked, after training in Europe, in Cornish, New Hampshire (see page 195). His work includes the 1897 Shaw Monument on Boston Common.

Chesterwood in Stockbridge, Massachusetts (see page 147), was the home of another notable sculptor, Daniel Chester French (1850–1931). Best known for his seated *Abraham Lincoln* in Washington DC, French first won acclaim with his *Minute Man* statue in Concord, Massachusetts.

■ **Writers in colonial times concentrated mostly on religious tracts and journals, but after the Revolution, American literature quickly established a new identity, and for two centuries New England has nurtured writers of prominence.....■**

❏ 'As the New England summer flamed into autumn, I piled cut spruce boughs all round the draughty cottage sill, and helped to put up a tiny roof-less verandah along one side of it for future needs.'
– From *Something of Myself* by Rudyard Kipling (1865–1936). ❏

The Concord circle Early in the 19th century there emerged a group of thinkers and writers, centred on Concord, Massachusetts (see pages 169–70), spiritual idealists known as the New England Transcendentalists. The leading figures were essayist and poet Ralph Waldo Emerson (1803–82), and Henry David Thoreau (1817–62), whose classic, *Walden* (1854), is a record of two solitary, transcendentalist years spent communing with nature in a log cabin in the woods around Walden Pond. Novelist Nathaniel Hawthorne (1804–64) also lived in Concord for a time, in the same house in which Louisa May Alcott

(1832–88) spent some of her teenage years, a period she was to draw on in *Little Women*.

The Berkshires Nathaniel Hawthorne also lived in Lenox, western Massachusetts, where he wrote *The Scarlet Letter* (1850) and *The House of the Seven Gables* (1851), inspired by the house of that name in his birthplace, Salem. In Lenox he became good friends with Herman Melville, who was living in nearby Arrowhead completing the whaling adventure story *Moby Dick* (1851) before fading into melancholia and virtual oblivion – it was not until the 1920s that his talent was recognised. In 1902 Edith Wharton, society hostess turned novelist, built The Mount, in Lenox, where she wrote her best-selling love stories (such as *Ethan Frome* and *The Age of Innocence*) in between entertaining her high-flying circle of friends, including Henry James.

❏ 'There are three kinds of lies: lies, damned lies, and statistics.'
– Mark Twain, *Autobiography* (1871). ❏

The Hartford colony In the Nook Farm area of Hartford, Connecticut (see page 96), Samuel Clemens, alias Mark Twain, and his wife built the exuberantly Victorian house where he wrote *The Adventures of Tom Sawyer* (1876) and his masterpiece of wit and insight, *The Adventures of Huckleberry Finn* (1884). Harriet Beecher Stowe was his neighbour, a minister's wife whose *Uncle Tom's*

Top: Tom Sawyer's band of robbers
Left: Mrs Keeley as Topsy, Uncle Tom's Cabin

[Mrs Keeley as Topsy. 'Is dreffol wicked.']
IN
"SLAVE LIFE, OR UNCLE TOM'S CABIN."

Cabin of 1852 was a touch-paper that lit popular anti-slavery feeling to the extent that it is counted by some as one of the causes of the American Civil War.

❏ Kipling and his American wife, Caroline, lived for a few years in Brattleboro, Vermont, and here he wrote some of his best-known works, including the Jungle Books. Their house, Naulakha, has been restored and is available for rent (tel: 0628 825925 in the UK for bookings, or toll-free 1-800/848 3747 for a brochure in the US). ❏

Poetry and drama Henry Wadsworth Longfellow, born in 1807 in Portland, Maine, wrote many of his narrative poems, including *The Song of Hiawatha* (1855), while teaching at Harvard. Longfellow was part of an aristocratic group of New England writers, closely linked with Harvard. Others were the poets Oliver Wendell Holmes and James Russell

Longfellow, one of a circle of writers associated with Harvard

Lowell. The sensitive recluse Emily Dickinson (1830–86) is also linked with Massachusetts (see page 176), while the poems of Robert Frost (1874–1963) are so steeped in the New England countryside he is often referred to as 'The Voice of New England' (see page 209).

The only American playwright to receive the Nobel Prize for Literature, Eugene O'Neill died in Boston in 1953. From a modest start with a one-act play performed in a wharf-side playhouse in the Cape Cod fishing village of Provincetown, O'Neill's troubled career – much of his material was drawn from the torments of his family life – was to bring him to a position of pre-eminence among 20th-century dramatists. He is commemorated at his boyhood summer home, Monte Cristo Cottage, in New London, Connecticut.

Louisa May Alcott

BOSTON

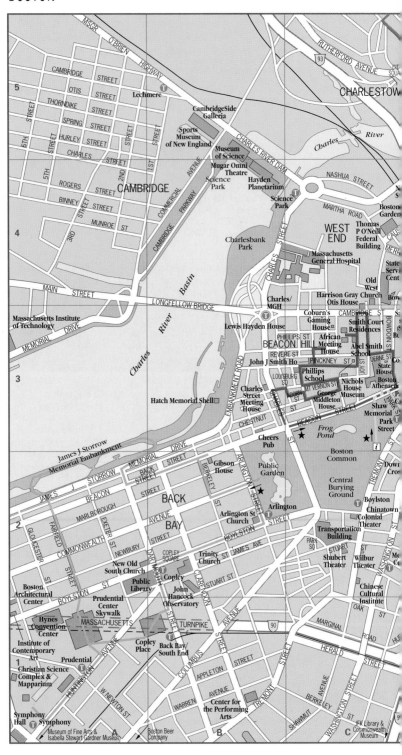

48

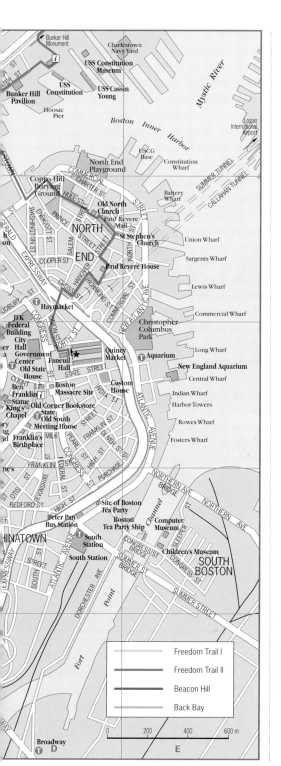

BOSTON

Boston A to Z Contents

50

Boston seen from the Charles river: Boston Common, the brownstone terraces of Back Bay and the State House dome backed by the tower blocks of the financial district

Boston The cradle of American history is a city of church spires, parks, statues and a remarkably thriving culture. To this, within the last 30 years, has been added an uncompromisingly American-looking high-rise skyline. To Americans and Europeans alike, the city's elements are partly familiar, partly refreshingly different. Boston also divides into strikingly contrasting neighbourhoods, from the trendy elegance of the Back Bay and the old-world charm of the North End to the striking modern skyline of the financial district and Waterfront.

Boston looks smart and pleased with life nowadays, with its elegant shops, gleaming office towers, refurbished wharves and historic buildings, lively eateries and bars. Although it is by far New England's largest city – with a population of around 575,000 – 'the Hub' (referring to its position in the universe) often presents a pleasant surprise to visitors who find it liveable and manageable.

Finding your feet Most Bostonians would tend to think of **Boston Common▶** and the neighbouring **Public Garden▶▶** as the true heart of the city. The Common is the oldest public park in the US, and is overlooked by the State House with its dazzling gold dome. A visitor information booth near by marks the start of the **Freedom Trail ▶▶▶** (see pages 58–61). To the east lies the main downtown district, with government buildings ranged around the huge piazza of **Government Center**. Here, too, is the renovated and ever-popular **Faneuil Hall Marketplace▶▶▶** (pronounced Fan'el), which comprises historic Faneuil Hall, Quincy Market and the adjacent North and South markets. Street performers entertain the shoppers and visitors, portrait artists sketch them and food stalls feed them: the atmosphere is conducive to lingering. The historic **North End▶▶**, the Italian quarter north of here, hosts lively street festivals on summer weekends, has excellent bakeries and restaurants, and has sites on the Freedom Trail.

Post Office Square is at the heart of the high-rise downtown Financial District. Near by rises Boston's first

Boston quirks
● Bostonians are seen in general terms by the rest of the nation as variously provincial, traditionalist and intellectual.
● Boston is a true peninsula; Boston Neck, which connects it to the mainland, was originally just 120 feet across. Since early times, much of the harbour has been filled in. Some 58 per cent of the city is built on landfill.
● The city's first squares were modelled on those laid out in 18th-century London.

51

'skyscraper', the Custom House, a slender Gothic-style clocktower that graces the downtown skyline. **The Waterfront** is no longer commercial, condominiums and offices having sprouted on the old wharves. It has some fine restaurants and the **New England Aquarium▶▶▶**. In 1994, work began to submerge the highway crossing the Waterfront in a tunnel and to landscape the area with a 73-acre park. South of the Financial District, **Chinatown▶** is a colourful neighbourhood with shops selling all manner of items and restaurants serving excellent food at bargain prices.

North and west of Boston Common are, respectively, the fashionable and delightful residential neighbourhoods of **Beacon Hill▶▶▶** and the **Back Bay▶▶▶**. South of **Copley Square▶▶** is the main hotel district, a convenient area in which to stay; eastward lies the Theatre District. The **South End** is a trendy up-and-coming area of bow-fronted Victorian townhouses, where Union Park is one of the most attractive streets. The district is full of excellent eateries, and is ethnically and socially mixed, with substantial numbers of blacks and Spanish-speakers as well as a sizeable gay community.

Southwest of the Back Bay, the Fenway occupies the area around Back Bay Fens, a lakeside park. It has the pick of the city's art museums – the huge **Museum of Fine Arts▶▶▶** and the intensely personal **Isabella Stewart Gardner Museum▶▶▶**. Fenway Park, the home of the Boston Red Sox, is one of the smallest and oldest baseball parks in the major leagues.

Cambridge▶▶, on the north side of the Charles river, is actually a separate city, although it is close enough to walk to from the Back Bay over the Harvard Bridge. Harvard University (the oldest university in the US), and the street activity and nightlife in and around Harvard Square are among Cambridge's prime attractions. Cambridge is also home to Massachusetts Institute of Technology (MIT) and boasts some of the finest restaurants in the Boston area.

Close-up on the bow-fronted houses of the South End

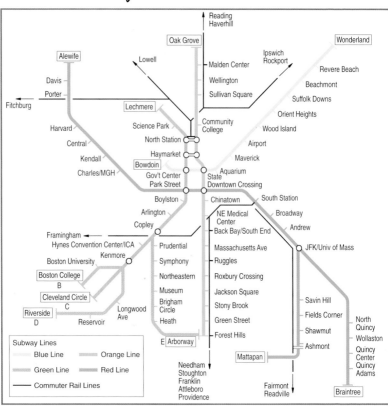

Subway Lines
— Blue Line
— Orange Line
— Green Line
— Red Line
— Commuter Rail Lines

'They say cows laid out Boston. Well, there are worse surveyors.'
– Ralph Waldo Emerson, *Worship*.

'Full of crooked little streets; but I tell you Boston has opened, and kept open, more turnpikes that lead straight to free thought and free speech and free deeds than any other city of living men or dead men.'
– Oliver Wendell Holmes, *The Professor at the Breakfast Table*.

Walking Everyone will tell you that Boston is a walking city. Distances downtown are small, and there is so much to look at. New visitors will often find that they have walked non-stop for days on end before noticing their tired feet.

During the day it is quite safe to wander around the central streets, although crossing them is another matter. Here, in what some people call the jay-walking capital of America, the tendency is to dodge the notoriously slow traffic lights and risk the traffic.

Beggars are becoming a more common sight in the centre, although nearly all go about their business in a totally unthreatening manner. Compared to many US cities Boston is safe for visitors, but some areas, such as the Common and the back streets of Chinatown, should be avoided at night.

Driving Don't drive in Boston unless you absolutely must. Anyone unacquainted with America's most bewildering one-way system will need good nerves to cope with the traffic, to navigate through the city's confusing maze of streets, to understand the priority systems where no lines are painted on the road surface, and to try to find one of those elusive parking spaces. The construction of three road tunnels may help to alleviate the traffic problem later in the 1990s. In the meantime, many visitors find it a handicap to have a car in Boston.

Public transport Fortunately, public transport in Boston is excellent, running from around 5am to 12:30am. The subway train network, known as the 'T', spreads across the city. You can buy tokens which you insert into a slot at the barrier; you do not get a receipt, and so travel without a ticket. Currently the cost is 85¢ for each journey on the 'T' (a little more for some journeys from the outer suburbs) irrespective of how many times you change lines.

A convenient visitor's pass provides from three to seven days' discounted 'T' travel. Passes are unlikely to save you money if you are only staying for a few days and making a couple of journeys each day; a better bet is to buy a stack of tokens first time round, thus saving time queueing at stations. Buses are slightly cheaper, but require a little more local knowledge.

From central Boston, journeys to Cambridge, the Museum of Fine Arts, the Isabella Stewart Gardner Museum and Logan Airport are best made by the 'T'. The colour-coded lines are reasonably straightforward even to a newcomer: just look for the colour and destination of the train.

Guided and self-guided tours Three companies run fleets of trolleys (quaint, wooden buses similar to old-style trams), with guided commentary, around the hotel area and the historic parts of the city, taking in most sights on the Freedom Trail. All of the routes on offer cover much the same ground. You can begin at any trolley stop. Tickets last a day, and you can get on and off where you like, then wait a few minutes for the next trolley. Additionally, Old Town Trolley Tours take in Cambridge. Doubledecker Tours make circuits by London-style doubledecker bus.

Boston By Foot (reservations not required) runs guided tours from May to October; for recorded information, tel: 617/367 3766.

A convenient and informative way of taking self-guided walks is provided by Cushing's Tours, where you hire a personal stereo and a cassette, and are given informative and entertaining tours. Look out for carts hiring the stereos on Boston Common by the start of the Freedom Trail and at other central destinations.

Boat cruises Boston Harbor Cruises runs trips from Long Wharf by the New England Aquarium. The short cruise to the Charlestown Navy Yard is the most direct and pleasant approach. Longer cruises pass by the airport, numerous container terminals and the world's largest sewage treatment plant. Views are far from scenic, but you glimpse the 17th- and 18th-century fortifications on Castle Island and there is an impressive panorama of the skyscrapers as the ship draws out into the bay.

Airport transfers See page 248.

Crowd-pullers
The top ten visitor attractions in Boston:
● Faneuil Hall Marketplace (page 59).
● Freedom Trail (pages 58–61).
● 'Cheers' Pub (page 84).
● Museum of Fine Arts (page 70).
● Museum of Science (page 71).
● New England Aquarium (page 72).
● USS *Constitution* (page 67).
● Swanboats and Public Garden (page 73).
● John Hancock Observatory (page 70).
● Filene's department store Bargain Basement (page 82).

53

Don't even think of driving in Boston. With a map in hand, finding your way around on foot is easy

For further information, contact the Greater Boston Convention and Visitors Bureau (see page 266).

January
Martin Luther King Day (18 January): commemoration of King's life and work.
Chinese New Year (January/February), Chinatown: fire-crackers, traditional music.

February
Black History Month, centred on Black Meeting House in Beacon Hill: plays, discussion, tours.
Festival of Food and Wine, World Trade Center: billed as New England's premier culinary event, with dining, wine-tasting and entertainment.

March
Spring Flower Show, Bayside Exposition Center: the third largest in the world.
St Patrick's Day Parade (mid-March): parade honouring Ireland's saint.

April
Boston Marathon (Patriot's Day), from Hopkinton to Boston: the oldest such race in America.
Patriot's Day Parade, City Hall to Paul Revere Mall.

Late April/Early May
Ducklings' Day Parade, Beacon Hill, Public Garden: make way for the mallard family and costumed relatives.

May
Boston Kite Festival, Franklin Park: attracts 15,000 participants.
Art Newbury Street: art, special exhibits, jazz and classical music.
Street Performers' Festival, Faneuil Hall Marketplace: weekend of continuous entertainments and parade.

June
Dairy Festival (first week): cows make an appearance on the Common (a colonial law mandates this); ice-cream, butter-making, milking.
Cambridge International Fair, University Park, Cambridge.
Boston Globe Jazz Festival, various locations.
Boston Annual Book Fair, Copley Square Park.

July
Boston Pops: free outdoor concerts at the Hatch Shell on the Esplanade.
Chowderfest, City Hall Plaza: sample a range of chowders produced by Boston restaurants and vote for the best.
Harborfest (week leading up to 4 July): celebration of Revolutionary War events in Boston Harbor, culminating in military parades, fireworks, concerts, and, once again from 1996, after its renovation, the entry into the harbour of the USS *Constitution*.

August
Boston Seaport Festival, Charlestown Navy Yard.
Caribbean Carnival, Franklin Park.
August Moon Festival, Chinatown.

September
Art Newbury Street (see May).
Boston Arts and Music Festival.

October
Columbus Day Parade.
Oktoberfest, Harvard Square, Cambridge.
Ringling Brothers Barnum and Bailey Circus, Boston Garden.
Head of the Charles Regatta: major rowing event (the world's largest), with 1,000 craft on the 3-mile river course.

November
Boston Globe Book Festival.
Holiday Happenings (19 November–24 December): holiday festivities, including Winter Wonderland and Sleigh Bell Parade.

December
Boston Tea Party Re-enactment, Tea Party Ship.
First Night Celebration: city-wide family celebration to ring in the New Year.

Part of the 4 July celebrations in downtown Boston

Paul Revere

■ 'Listen, my children, and you shall hear/Of the midnight ride of Paul Revere...' So begins Longfellow's *Paul Revere's Ride*, a ballad that was to turn a silversmith into America's favourite folk hero .....**■**

Until Longfellow's ballad was published in 1863, Paul Revere (1735–1818) was best known as a silversmith, though he dabbled in many things (see panel). An ardent patriot and an experienced express rider, he frequently carried messages for the Sons of Liberty (see page 33). On 16 April 1775, Revere rode out to Lexington to warn patriot leaders Sam Adams and John Hancock that British troops in Boston were making plans to march to Concord to seize a cache of rebel arms, and to capture Adams and Hancock in Lexington on the way. A plan was made for another message to be relayed as the soldiers actually left town.

In case he was unable to escape from Boston himself, Revere asked the sexton of Old North Church, Robert Newman, to signal to Charlestown, across the Charles river, by holding up one lantern in the church steeple if the troops left by land (across Boston Neck), two if by boat (across the river). On the night of 18 April, the signal was duly given, and Revere got out of Boston and headed for Lexington. He was joined there by William Dawes, and as they rode on they met Sam Prescott. All three were captured by the redcoats. Only Prescott escaped and reached Concord.

The legend Most newspaper reports of the night's events did not even mention Paul Revere by name. The *New York Gazette* reported him dead. A century on, however, thanks to Longfellow, Revere stepped into the annals of history. But Longfellow was a poet, not a historian, and so he could play around with the facts. He has Revere waiting for the signal in Charlestown; he has him making the heroic ride alone; and he certainly does not reveal that Revere never actually reached Concord, only Prescott. But then, 'Prescott' does not rhyme as easily as 'Revere'.

Left: Revere in middle age. Top: Revere as messenger

The man
Paul Revere was born in Boston on 21 December 1735. A silversmith like his Huguenot father, he became one of the country's finest artists in silver, gold and copper. A remarkable man of boundless energy and talent, he also turned his hand to engraving and printing, often for propaganda purposes (see panel below). He made spectacles, surgical instruments and false teeth. After the War of Independence Revere manufactured sheet copper, some being used on 'Old Ironsides' (USS *Constitution*) and on the State House dome. Revere died in 1818, aged 83, and is buried in the Old Granary burial ground.

The propagandist
In March 1770, a street brawl got out of hand when some youths started throwing snowballs at British troops. The soldiers panicked, opened fire and five men were killed. Paul Revere plagiarised an engraving of the incident by Henry Pelham (to Pelham's annoyance), fuelling resentment against the redcoats or 'lobsterbacks', as the British troops were derisively called. The term 'Boston Massacre' was coined by Sam Adams.

Bronze bell cast by Revere, a distinguished bellmaker

55

The pulse of Boston

■ **Boston could be forgiven for quietly basking in its venerable past and resting on its glorious cultural laurels. But life here is as much about computers as culture and, in this capital of academia, the pace is intellectually challenging. Boston has its share of blue blood, but it is above all a dynamic, youthful city.....■**

Brahmins and Boston

The physical development of Boston is closely linked to the Brahmins. In 1795 the society portrait painter John Singleton Copley sold land on Beacon Hill to a group of entrepreneurs. On it Bulfinch built the prestigious Beacon Hill estate into which Boston's blue-blooded élite moved, leaving their homes in the old North End *en bloc*. Beacon Hill was one of three major hills to be levelled off, the soil being used to fill in the swampy 'Back Bay' area along the Charles river. By about 1870 the Back Bay had been developed and many of the Brahmins then moved on to its more grandiose houses.

The thrusting, high-tech Boston

High-rise and high-tech For many years the Prudential Center was the only building in Boston higher than the State House dome. How different was the skyline then. In recent times, glassy skyscrapers and concrete office towers have risen rapidly one after the other to dwarf the elegant Victorian brownstone terraces of the Back Bay. The classic architectural image of Boston is the reflection of Henry Hobson Richardson's 1870s Romanesque-style Trinity Church in the glass windows of IM Pei's 1970s ultra-modern John Hancock Tower. And since IM Pei and his associates completed their commission to change the face of the blighted and downward-spiralling Boston of the 1950s and 1960s, a further proliferation of thrusting office towers has been occupied by financial and other leading institutions, and computer companies.

Boston today – together with Cambridge, across the river – is a high-tech place. Go to Harvard Square on a Friday or Saturday evening, and for every browser in the bookshops there are at least twice as many dads in the computer-ware shops showing their kids the latest educational software. It is not insignificant that Boston's Computer Museum (see page 68) is the first and only one in the world. Don't miss it – it's sensational.

In recent years, Boston and Cambridge may have become 'the Hub' (as Boston is known) of the computer industry, but this does not mean that their role as a leader in medicine has in any way diminished. The place is a hotbed of research – not for nothing has the Ether Dome, the Massachusetts General Hospital's operating theatre, where ether was first used as an anaesthetic, been completely submerged by modern buildings (it is open to visitors, if they can find their way through to it). As for education, it sometimes feels as if virtually everyone in town is somehow connected to the 67 colleges and universities on either side of the Charles river. The start of the academic year brings chaos; the streets seem to be full of walking mattresses, as 500,000 students move into their new accommodation. It is a city full of bright and lively people.

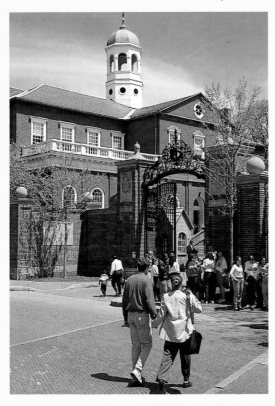

The proliferation of academic institutions on either side of the Charles river means a huge student population: left, Harvard Square, Cambridge

57

Boston Brahmins In the midst of all this ferment, a small but deeply significant element of Boston society calmly carries on with life just the way it has always done. These are the members of Boston's top families, the 'Proper Bostonians', the 'Boston Brahmins', as the city's Establishment was termed by Oliver Wendell Holmes in the 19th century. They trace their ancestry back to the 18th-century merchants and many claim to be related to early Puritan settlers (not, as is popularly misconceived, to the *Mayflower* Pilgrims, who landed not in Boston but in Plymouth and were definitely not so upper crust).

Certainly all are characterised by Puritan qualities of frugality and self-restraint, and a sense of superiority. Breeding, rather than money, has always been paramount. Indeed, the intermarrying of Boston's top families is surely matched only by that of European royals. A Brahmin is born with a name such as Adams, Cabot, Lowell, Bowditch, Appleton or Lodge, he is educated at Harvard (where else is there, after all?), he lives in the Back Bay and has a summer home in Maine.

In the 18th and 19th centuries it was the Brahmins who held all the power, and to a degree their blue blood continues to course through the city's veins today. Many of the financiers and businessmen in those downtown office towers are Brahmins; but perhaps it is families like the Kennedys (of Irish ancestry) and the intellectual élite who are the new generation of Brahmins?

Bar Harbor Brahmins
Bar Harbor, in Maine, is where the proper Bostonian traditionally has his summer cottage. There is one page in the Bar Harbor telephone book on which every name, with just one or two exceptions, is that of a Boston Brahmin family.

Lowell Brahmins
The story goes that there was some debate about whether or not a particular member of the Lowell family could be counted a true Brahmin, as he had not been born in Boston. 'Of course he is a Brahmin', pronounced his grand-mother, 'he was conceived in the Ritz'.

Walk The Freedom Trail: Part I

See map on pages 48–9.

Follow the red or brick line along the city pavements for colonial America's most historic walk. The route is the focus of Boston National Historical Park and passes many buildings associated with the Revolutionary War. Excellent free guided walks start every half-hour from the park visitor centre at 15 State Street opposite State subway station (in the Old State House).

Boston Common►, at the start of the walk, is a 44-acre, undulating grass expanse, formerly used as a pasture and parade ground. Follow the Freedom Trail across the Common up to the imposing State House with its gilded dome. Continue down Park Street to **Park Street Church** (1809), where William Lloyd Garrison made his first anti-slavery address in 1829 and where the song *America* was first sung in 1831. Adjacent is the **Granary Burying Ground,** containing graves from

King's Chapel graveyard, where John Winthrop lies

Revolutionary days, including those of John Hancock, Samuel Adams, Paul Revere and the five who perished in the Boston Massacre.

At the corner of Tremont and School streets, look inside **King's Chapel►** (1754), the first Anglican church in Boston, and later the first Unitarian Church. It has especially well-preserved furnishings, including white box-pews and a pulpit with sounding-board. A finely carved gravestone in the churchyard by the entrance is that of Joseph Tapping (1678), depicting Father Time extinguishing the candle of Life.

The **Old Corner Book Store** (1712; now called Globe Corner Bookstore), at the corner of School and Washington streets, was a literary meeting-house where the works of Longfellow, Stowe, Hawthorne and Emerson were first published. Today the store is largely devoted to books and maps on New England. Opposite is the **Old South Meeting House►** (1729), a former Puritan house of worship, and at one time the largest public meeting-hall in the city. Here heated meetings took place as the British sought to impose their taxes on the colony. On 16 December 1773 Samuel Adams addressed some 7,000 citizens just before the Boston Tea Party (see page 33) and pronounced the immortal words 'Gentlemen, this meeting can do nothing more to save the country.' Threatened with demolition in the 1870s, the building was the first in Boston to be preserved solely for its historic importance. Today the building contains an exhibition focusing on the events leading to the Tea Party.

Further north along Washington Street, the **Old State House►** (1713) has changed much over the years but externally is now restored to its original appearance, with the (renewed) British lion and unicorn flanking the gable above the balcony from where the Declaration of Independence was read to the public on 18 July 1776. Today the interior is a museum devoted to historical

One-time meeting place for writers and thinkers

THE GLOBE CORNER BOOKSTORE

Books & Maps for the Travell...

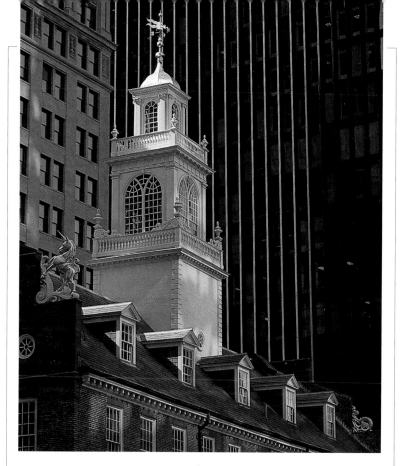

The Old State House, seen dwarfed by the new Boston

exhibitions about Boston, showing events preceding and following the Boston Massacre, and displays on the city's neighbourhoods.

A neat circle of stones embedded in a road island beside the Old State House marks the site of the Boston Massacre (see page 32).

Nearby **Faneuil Hall**▶▶ was donated to Boston in 1742 by Peter Faneuil, the 'bachelor of Boston', who died a few months after the building's completion of 'an excess of good living'. The building contains the meeting-hall known as the 'Cradle of Liberty' (open; free) where, over the years, revolutionary protests, women's suffrage, slavery and every war except the 1990 Gulf War (the building was closed for renovation) have been discussed. The top floor contains regimental memorabilia of the Ancient and Honorable Artillery Company (open free of charge). Behind Faneuil Hall is **Faneuil Hall Marketplace**▶▶▶, a lively scene with shops, restaurants and buskers centred on Quincy Market and North and South markets.

A typically colourful scene in Faneuil Hall Marketplace

Walk The Freedom Trail: Part II

See map on pages 48–9.

The second part of the trail leads from Faneuil Hall Marketplace, through the old Italian quarter of North End and past historic Charlestown Navy Yard to Bunker Hill. Many visitors prefer to end the walk at Old North Church in the North End and to take a ferry (from Long Wharf by the New England Aquarium), trolley or bus to Charlestown.

From Faneuil Hall Marketplace follow the trail along Union Street past the **Union Oyster House** (opened 1826), Boston's oldest restaurant, and the **Ebenezer Hancock House** (1767), home of John Hancock's brother, the deputy paymaster-general of the Continental Army. Near by, the Haymarket is a great place for bargain fruit and vegetables on Friday and Saturday. As you cross the street at the lights, notice the brass sculpture *Asaroton* (Greek for 'unswept floor'), by Mags Harries, representing fruit, vegetables and discarded rubbish embedded into the road surface.

North End►► is one of Boston's oldest neighbourhoods. Once a notorious slum, it has been home to wave after wave of immigrants. After the original 17th-century Puritan settlers came Irish refugees fleeing from the 1840s potato famine, then Jews from eastern Europe. Today the North End is the Italian quarter, known as 'Little Italy'. Lately the area has been gentrified.

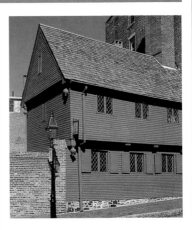

Paul Revere House, originally one of a terrace

Something of a freak survival from the old town, **Paul Revere House**► (*c* 1680), at North Square, was home to patriot Paul Revere (see page 55) and is Boston's oldest building. After Revere's time, the building functioned as a cigar factory, grocery, tenement and bank. Restored to its original appearance, the building now operates as a small museum, with some Revere family pieces.

Photogenic **Paul Revere Mall** features the famous equestrian statue of Paul Revere against the magnificent steeple of **Old North Church**►►► (1723), where Robert Newman, the sexton, lit two lanterns on 18 April 1775 to warn the citizens across the river of British plans to cross by sea rather than by land via Boston Neck (see page 55). The church is a magnificent colonial survival, with a gallery, box pews and brass chandeliers.

Copps Hill Burying Ground (1660) was used by the British as a vantage point for cannon while making preparations for the Battle of Bunker Hill. It is Boston's second oldest cemetery and has some fascinating early epitaphs. The headstone of Daniel

The North End, once a slum, is now a smart and lively district

BOSTON'S HISTORIC NORTH END

WELCOME

NORTH END BUSINESS ALLIANCE

Malcom (to the left if entering from Hull Street) records 'Here lies buried in a stone grave 10 feet deep. A friend to the Publick, an enemy to oppression', thus buried safe from British bullets. Though not an 'official' Trail site, **North End Garage Park**, on the left side of Hull Street, is of interest as the site of the famous Brink's robbery in 1950, which netted a record $2.5million; the FBI subsequently spent close on $29 million investigating it.

Across the road bridge is **Charlestown**, founded in 1629 and named after Charles I. It was razed by the British, and no house predates 1775. Charlestown was not incorporated into Boston until 1873. The trail passes **Bunker Hill Pavilion**▶ on the right (see page 66), on the way to **Charlestown Navy Yard**▶▶▶ (see pages 66–7), today home of the warship the **USS *Constitution***▶▶▶ and the World War II destroyer **USS *Cassin Young*▶**, as well as the **USS *Constitution* Museum**▶▶ and the Commandant's House.

Residential streets surround the **Bunker Hill Monument**▶▶, a tall obelisk that commemorates the first major Revolutionary War battle, fought on 17 June 1775. A 294-step climb is rewarded by an excellent view of the city. Musket firing takes place daily in summer and there is an exhibition inside the lodge.

'Old North', famous for the part it played in Paul Revere's ride

The Public Garden

Walk **Back Bay**

See map on pages 48–9.

This tour wends its way through the elegant Victorian brownstone district of the Back Bay, where almost every doorway deserves attention, and past the two great high-level viewing platforms of Boston – the Prudential and Hancock towers.

Begin at the west side of the **Public Garden**►► (see page 73) and cross the walkway along the centre of **Commonwealth Avenue**►►, often rated as one of America's finest streets. This forms the central axis of the Back Bay, an area subject to an ambitious landfill project in the late-19th century when Parisian-style avenues were laid out on a grand scale and with an eye for symmetry.

Turn right into Berkeley Street. At 137 Beacon Street, to the right, **Gibson House**► (*open*: 1 May to 1 November, Wednesday to Sunday; tours at 1, 2 and 3pm) is a wonderfully preserved example of the Back Bay brownstone, in pristine Victorian condition. Continuing west on Beacon Street, turn right at Dartmouth Street to take the footbridge over the highway to **Charlesbank Park**, a riverside strip popular with cyclists, sunbathers and joggers. The Hatch Shell, venue of outdoor concerts in summer, is to the right, while across the Charles river, the Massachusetts Institute of Technology (MIT) is prominent in Cambridge.

Return by another footbridge over the highway into Fairfield Street. Continue to Newbury Street, an inviting detour with its restaurants, sidewalk cafés and upmarket boutiques and galleries, and the **Newbury Street Mural** featuring historical and artistic figures. From Fairfield Street cross Boylston Street and the take the external steps opposite and slightly to the right that lead into the side of the Prudential Center. Walk through the building, and take an elevator to the 50th floor if desired for a panoramic view from the **Prudential Center Skywalk**►►► (see page 72).

Exit the building on Huntington Avenue and turn right. Pass the entrance of the **Bible Exhibit** (*open*:

Back Bay statue of local maritime writer, Samuel Eliot Morison (1887–1976)

Wednesday to Sunday; free), which has an electronic map charting travels across the Holy Land and telephones telling the listener of assorted miracle healings. The impressively large **Christian Science World Headquarters** is marked by a slender skyscraper, a huge oblong pool and the **Christian Science Church**▶ (1906), modelled on St Peter's in Rome and containing the largest pipe organ in the western hemisphere. Adjacent to the church (to its right) in a room in the publishing wing of the organisation, the **Mapparium**▶▶ (*open*: 9–4:30, Tuesday to Friday; free), is a stained-glass representation of the globe, created in 1932–5 to indicate the worldwide outlook of the Christian

The Christian Science World Headquarters

Science movement. Looking from within the sphere (with the map appearing in concave form) you can see the whole globe on a curved surface in one visual sweep. It is quite a sight, and the bizarre echo, with voices bouncing all around, makes this one of Boston's more offbeat experiences.

Return to the Prudential Center, take the escalator up the right-hand side of the courtyard in front of the Prudential Tower, go through the swing doors and turn right to cross Huntington Avenue by the covered walkway. This leads into Copley Place, an indoor shopping centre with exclusive department stores, shops and restaurants. Walk straight through, past the indoor waterfall to the escalators that lead to the street corner by the modern horse sculptures. Cross into **Copley Square**▶▶. On its west side is the supremely dignified Renaissance Revival **Boston Public Library** (1894), the first public lending library in the world, while on the north side is the **New Old South Church** (1875). This is usually locked, but its flamboyant exterior, inspired by the North Italian Gothic style, can be admired.

Physically the square is dominated by the huge skyscraper slab of the John **Hancock Tower and Observatory**▶▶▶, with its superb viewpoint 60 storeys up (see page 70). Its glass reflects the magnificent nearby **Trinity Church**▶▶▶ (1877), the French neo-Romanesque masterpiece of HH Richardson, with its sumptuously ornate interior which includes work by John LaFarge, William Morris and Edward Burne-Jones.

JOHN HANCOCK OBSERVATORY

The best place to see Boston

63

Walk Beacon Hill

See map on pages 48–9.

This walk explores Beacon Hill's tight network of narrow residential streets ranged on a sloping site. The neighbourhood is a fascinating early 19th-century mixture of patrician and artisan homes. Intricate iron balconies, crisply proportioned brick façades and carefully preserved front doors are much in evidence. Portrait artist John Singleton Copley sold land here to the Mount Vernon Proprietors, who included the great architect, Charles Bulfinch, and the lawyer and orator, Harrison Gray Otis. Here and there you can see some of the original purple window glass

Harrison Gray Otis House, built in post-Revolutionary 'Federal' style. A plain façade hides a supremely elegant interior

imported from Hamburg in the 1820s which discoloured because of the presence of manganese oxide in the material. Another Beacon Hill quirk is that the gas lamps stay on all day.

Start from the northeast corner of the **Public Garden**▶▶ (page 73) at the crossing of Charles Street and Beacon Street. Walk along Beacon Street eastwards. Number 45, built in 1805, was the last of three houses on 'the Hill' built for Harrison Gray Otis by Charles Bulfinch. At number 33 lived George Parkman, the Harvard undergraduate who in 1849 ended up

in several pieces in the laboratory of a Harvard professor of medicine; the sensational trial was the major scandal of Beacon Hill.

Opposite the **State House**▶▶ (see page 73), the **Robert Gould Shaw and 54th Regiment Memorial** acknowledges the role played by the first black regiment in the Civil War. Shaw, himself white, lived at 44 Beacon Street and led his regiment from here.

Turn left into Bowdoin Street. The column by the State House marks the site of the beacon which was erected here to warn the Puritans of Indians and foreign invasion and which gave the hill its name. The district was later to become a rough-and-ready jumble of disreputable bars and brothels, popularly known as 'Mount Whoredom'.

Turn left into Derne Street. From Hancock Street on the right, you can walk down to Cambridge Street and the first **Harrison Gray Otis House**▶ (see page 68). If not visiting the house, continue instead along Derne Street and turn right into Joy Street, off which is Smith Court. The **African Meeting House** here is the oldest black church building still standing in the US and the birthplace of the anti-slavery movement, where William Lloyd Garrison and 12 others founded the New England Anti-Slavery Society. Smith Court residences were typical homes of Beacon Hill's free black community who worked as servants in the 19th century. The meeting-house and **Museum of Afro-American History** are the starting point of the Black Heritage Trail.

Return along Joy Street and turn right into Pinckney Street, which was originally built to house service workers. Author Louisa May Alcott's family lived at **number 20**. **Number 24** (the 'house of Odd Windows') was converted by a relative of Ralph Waldo Emerson from a stable into a townhouse, while number 54 was the home of Nathaniel Hawthorne while working at Boston's custom house.

Detour right into Anderson Street and right again into **Revere Street,** and look for a tiny entrance on the left between numbers 25 and 29. The house with columns at the end is a false façade, with a sheer drop behind.

Retrace your steps via Anderson Street to **Louisburg Square,** laid out in 1834–44 by Bulfinch. Louisa May Alcott spent her last two years here at number 10. America's oldest home-owners' association maintains the square itself.

Mount Vernon Street▶▶, on the south side of the square, is one of Boston's finest architectural gems: Henry James called it 'the only respectable street in America'. Bulfinch's second Harrison Gray Otis

The more modest houses of lanes such as Acorn Street were built as servants' quarters

house (1800) is at number 85, while the **Nichols House Museum**▶ at number 55 (*open:* 12–5, Tuesday to Saturday), provides another opportunity to see a Bulfinch interior.

Follow Walnut Street into Chestnut Street, where abolitionist poet Julia Ward Howe resided at **number 13** in 1862 and penned *The Battle Hymn of the Republic.* Turn right into Willow Street and left into **Acorn Street**▶, picturesquely cobbled and perhaps the city's most famous, although certainly not its grandest, residential street. Finish by exploring the shops and restaurants of **Charles Street.**

Boston Beer's award-winning brew

We wish, finally, that the last object to the sight of him who leaves his native shore, and the first to gladden his who revisits it, may be something which shall remind him of the liberty and the glory of his country.
– Daniel Webster, address on laying the cornerstone of the Bunker Hill Monument, 17 June 1825.

Bostonian terms
The Black Maria was named after Maria Lee, who owned a disreputable hotel patronised by drunks and criminals. Police made frequent calls and took the offenders into the station by a 'paddy wagon', later renamed a 'Black Maria' to avoid disparaging the Irish population.
  The term 'gerrymandering' originated with Governor Elbridge Gerry, vice-president under James Madison, who re-apportioned electoral boundaries for his own advantage.

► **Boston Beer Company Brewery Tours**   *48A1*
Bismark Street
  Subway: Stony Brook (Orange Line).
  This renowned family-run brewery is the home of the award-winning Samuel Adams Boston lager. Guided tours give an overview of the brewing process. (*Open*: tours at 2pm Thursday, 12–2:30 Saturday, every half-hour.)

► **Boston Garden Tours and History Center**   *48C4*
Causeway Street
  Subway: North Station (Green and Orange Lines).
  Professional basketball is played at this stadium by the Celtics, and ice hockey by the Bruins. When games are not in progress, the stadium is open daily for tours behind the scenes. You can see the locker rooms, the teams' memorabilia and a video of sports highlights.

Boston Tea Party Ship and Museum   *49E2*
Congress Street Bridge
Bus: Courtesy shuttle bus from Quincy Market, at corner of State and Congress streets, in summer.
The ship moored here is a faithful replica of the brig *Beaver II*, one of the ships boarded in the Boston Tea Party protest (see page 33). You can view the ship for free from the road bridge. For your admission fee you can put on quasi-Indian feather headgear and dunk a tea chest in the river, sample a cup of cold tea and visit the small museum. It is very much an audience-participation venture: you are summoned to attend a 'town meeting' such as happened (more or less) at the old South Meeting House in 1773. Some children will enjoy it. A re-enactment of the Tea Party takes place here in December. (*Open*: daily, except 1 December to 1 March.)

► **Bunker Hill Pavilion**   *49D5*
Water Street, Charlestown
For public transport, see Charlestown Navy Yard.
The theatre (*open*: April to November) presents a 30-minute multimedia show, *Whites of their Eyes*, which plunges you into the Battle of Bunker Hill, seen through the narrative of 22 costumed mannequins 'acting' the parts. It is a spectacle and history lesson rolled into one.

►►► **Charlestown Navy Yard**   *49D5*
Subway: North Station (Green Line), then a 10–15 minute walk.
Charlestown Navy Yard (*open*: daily; free) served the United States Navy from 1800 until 1974. Some 30 acres of the yard now form part of Boston National Historical Park. It has very much the atmosphere of a shipyard, and visitors may enter only a few buildings. Tours are at 11am during weekends and also at 2pm on summer weekdays. The Visitor Center gives out informative leaflets.

BOSTON BEER COMPANY–CHARLESTOWN NAVY YARD

Restored to its full-masted glory, the frigate **USS Constitution**▶▶, the most famous of all historic American warships, was built near by in 1797 and served in three wars. In the War of 1812, British cannonballs bounced off the vessel, earning her the nickname of 'Old Ironsides', as she captured two sloops-of-war and sank two frigates. *Constitution* traditionally takes part in the annual Harborfest celebration and enters Boston Harbor on 4 July to fire a national salute, a role resumed in 1996 after dry-dock restoration. Throughout the rest of the year, cannon firing takes place daily at sunset, when the flag is lowered.

Maritime history is brought to life in the **USS Constitution Museum**▶▶, adjacent, for which there is an entrance fee. The museum displays ship models, documents and paintings, as well as some hands-on exhibits where you can try the ship's wheel or raise the sail. The **USS Cassin Young**▶ is a World War II destroyer that was hit by kamikaze raids at Okinawa.

The **Commandant's House** (*open*: 1–4pm, March to October) is a Federal-style building that was once the home of the commanding officers of the Navy Yard from 1805 to 1976; the interior has been preserved as it was when last occupied. The **Boston Marine Society** (*open*: 10–3) is situated next to the prominent octagonal Muster House of 1852 and has three rooms filled with nauticalia, including model ships and paintings of maritime scenes.

The Navy Yard is located along sight-seeing trolley routes. You can also get there by buses 92 and 93 from Haymarket station, or by water shuttle from Long Wharf, Boston, or ships operated by Boston Harbor Cruises (tel: 617/227 4320) and Bay State Cruise Company (tel: 617/723 7800).

Changing times
More than 160 ships were built in Charlestown Navy Yard. Over the years numerous buildings have been added, including boiler-maker shops, a marine railway, New England's first granite dry dock and America's last surviving ropewalk. The yard expanded in the Civil War, and in World War II employed nearly 50,000 people. From the 1960s it specialised in the modernisation and overhaul of old vessels.

Below: USS Cassin Young *in the Navy Yard, Charlestown. The Navy Yard is also permanent home to USS* Constitution, *the doughty revolutionary warship saved from the breaker's yard by Oliver Wendell Holmes' poem, 'Old Ironside'*

The Milk Bottle out-side the Children's Museum (a museum best visited on a weekday outside school vacations, for obvious reasons!)

▶▶ Children's Museum 49E2
300 Congress Street
Subway: South Station (Red Line)
Adults will wish they were kids again when they see this interac-tive museum, one of the oldest, largest and best of its kind any-where. Join a treasure hunt through Boston; learn about your body; visit a Japanese home or Tokyo subway station; try a work-out or a do-it-yourself medical check-up. (*Open*: 10–5pm, plus Friday 5–9pm, when the entrance fee is reduced; closed Monday outside school vacations.)

▶▶ Christian Science Center and Mapparium 48A1
See page 63.

▶ Commonwealth Museum 48C1
See page 69.

▶▶ Computer Museum 49E2
300 Congress Street
Subway: South Station (Red Line).
The world's first computer museum makes an excellent half-day visit for buffs and novices alike. On show are a gigantic walk-through mock-up of a computer, displays of robots and computers through the ages (including some very antique-looking specimens), and a range of inform-ative hands-on exhibits explaining various computer applications. (*Open*: daily July, August; at other times closed Monday, except school holidays. Entry half-price after 3pm.)

▶▶▶ Faneuil Hall Marketplace 49D3
See page 59.

▶ Harrison Gray Otis House 48C4
141 Cambridge Street
Subway: Bowdoin (Blue Line) or Charles Street (Red Line).
Dating from 1796, this was the first of the three houses built on Beacon Hill for Harrison Gray and Sally Foster Otis and the only one open to the public (*open*: Tuesday to Saturday; last tour 4pm). It is a fine example of the Federal style, and houses the headquarters of the Society for the Preservation of New England Antiquities (SPNEA), which maintains 23 historic house museums in New England. The Society has painstakingly researched and restored the original wall-coverings and the house con-tains period furnishings. The house can be visited on a walk around Beacon Hill (see pages 64–5).

Institute of Contemporary Art 48A1
955 Boylston Street
Subway: Hynes Convention Center/ICA or Prudential (Green Line).
Housed in the old stables of a Romanesque-style police and fire station, the ICA is a venue for changing art exhibi-

---

Computer dinosaurs
Some of the most fascinat-ing exhibits in the Computer Museum are the machines of the past.
● In 1970 the first robot capable of reasoning about its actions was created: one drawback – it took half an hour to make a move-ment.
● A 1930s vision of the 1960s saw the future as an age when safe driving dis-tance would be measured by radio control.
● On show is UNIVAC I, the first computer bought by a business in the US.

The founder of Christian Science Movement
The First Church of Christ, Scientist was founded in Boston in 1879 by Mary Baker Eddy. Born in 1821 into a strict Calvinist family in Bow, New Hampshire, Mary became convinced of the power of prayer in healing after making a sud-den recovery from a seri-ous fall. She began to teach spiritual healing and in 1875 published her prin-cipal work, *Science and Health*. In 1908, aged 87, she founded the daily newspaper, the *Christian Science Monitor*.
Published internationally by the Christian Science Publishing Society, it is rel-atively independent of the Church and is highly regarded.

tions. (*Open*: 12–9 Wednesday to Thursday, 12–5 Friday to Sunday; free Friday 5–8pm.)

►►► Isabella Stewart Gardner Museum   48A1
280 The Fenway
Subway: Museum (Green Line).
This magnificent museum (*open*: Tuesday to Sunday) is the creation of Isabella Stewart Gardner, the heiress of a wealthy New York family. The exterior of the building gives little hint of what lies within – a Venetian-style *palazzo* crammed with priceless art treasures and ranged around an exquisite flower-decked courtyard with fountains and statues. The rooms vary in styles, including Gothic, Veronese, early Italian and Dutch, with art treasures including ancient Egyptian artefacts, Renaissance paintings and French Impressionists.

The museum hosts weekend concerts between September and May (tel: 617/734 1359).

►   John F Kennedy Library and Museum   48C1
220 Morrissey Boulevard, Columbia Point
Subway: JFK/UMass (Red Line) for free shuttle bus every 20 minutes, 9am–5pm.
This striking library, designed by IM Pei and scenically sited on the waterfront in the southern suburbs, is the nation's memorial to JFK.

The adjacent **Commonwealth Museum** covers everything to do with the Commonwealth of Massachusetts. Changing and permanent exhibits feature Native Americans, immigrants, towns and cities, the political system, natural history and labour history. (*Open*: JFK Library and Museum, daily; free. Commonwealth Museum, 9–5 Monday to Friday, 9–3 Saturday; free.)

A strong character
Isabella Stewart Gardner was the talk of the Back Bay. She wore diamonds in her hair and raised a few eyebrows by posing for her artist friend John Singer Sargent. Once she hired a boxer to perform at a ladies' tea party. She slept late in early-rise Boston. After her son died at the age of two, she suffered depression and took a trip to Europe. She returned to Boston a new woman; her Back Bay home became a fashionable salon, where she held glittering galas and balls, and she devoted much of her time to collecting art.

69

The splendid courtyard of the Isabella Stewart Gardner Museum, with its fountains, statues and flowers

Night-time view of the John Hancock Tower, itself an excellent observation point

Local fine arts
New England is well represented at the Museum of Fine Arts in the sections devoted to furniture, which features a late-17th-century press cupboard from Wethersfield, Connecticut, with pillars painted black to resemble ebony, and two fine Newport chests of the mid-18th century. Many of the museum's 19th-century pictures have a New England theme, such as Frederick Childe Hassam's *Boston Common at Twilight* and Winslow Homer's *Look-out – 'all's well'*.

►►► **John Hancock Tower and Observatory**   48B2

200 Clarendon Street (Copley Square)
Subway: Copley (Green Line) or Back Bay (Orange Line). Boston's tallest building (built 1968–76), is a striking 60-storey slab of reflective glass designed by IM Pei and neatly reflecting adjacent Trinity Church. It suffered numerous teething problems just after completion when window panes repeatedly fell out and landed on the street below. On the top floor the Hancock Observatory offers, like the nearby Prudential Tower, superb panoramic views over Boston and the bay, to the highlands of Massachusetts, Vermont and New Hampshire (*open*: daily, last admission 10pm). There is little to choose from between the Hancock and the Prudential, although the Hancock has a marginally better view of the downtown area. It also scores over the Prudential with its model of Boston 1775, with a narration giving a general survey of the city's history. Unfortunately the building's glass is annoyingly reflective and you can see out of three sides only.

►►► **Museum of Fine Arts**   48A1

465 Huntington Avenue
Subway: Museum (Green Line) or Ruggles (Orange Line). New England's largest art gallery, often referred to as the MFA, is also one of the nation's finest. Among the **American art** is an unequalled collection of John Singleton Copley portraits of John Hancock, Samuel Adams and Paul Revere, in addition to his famous work *Watson and the Shark*.

European art is well represented: Canaletto's *Bacino di San Marco* (*c* 1735–40) shows characteristic mastery of perspective and light. JMW Turner's *Slave Ship* (1840) is striking for its use of colour, which makes the primary impact before grim details emerge. A wide selection of French masters features works by Manet (*Execution of the Emperor Maximilian*), Monet, Degas, Gauguin and Renoir. A highlight of the collection of European medieval religious art is an Austrian gold-crowned Madonna of the mid-15th century, carved from a single piece of poplar. The **Forsyth Wickes Collection** is made up of items from an affluent New Yorker's house, with 18th-century French furniture and decorative art.

The **Oriental collection** is of worldwide importance, with the largest collection of Japanese swords and prints outside Tokyo. Some 60,000 woodblock prints are shown on rotation. **Ancient art** features among the Greek collection the Bartlett *Aphrodite*, a representation of Greek beauty, often reproduced on covers of antiques magazines. Other treasures include Roman frescos from a house in Pompeii, Egyptian statues of King Mycerinus and Queen Kha-merer-nebty II, and a remarkably complete Egyptian tomb cover of 2100BC. (*Open*: 10–4:45 Tuesday to Sunday, 10–9:45 Wednesday; free 4–10pm Wednesday; Sunday concerts at 3pm.)

▶▶▶ **Museum of Science**   48B5

Charles River Dam

Subway: Science Park (Green Line). One of the great science museums of the world, this has more than anyone could hope to see in a single day. With the emphasis very much on interactive science and plenty of an introductory nature, it is an almost unfailing hit with the children who come here in throngs. At the **Theater of Electricity** you can watch high-voltage lightning sparks produced by the world's largest Van de Graaff generator. The **Observatory** delves into the unseen, including microscopic life and ultrasonic sounds, while **Earthworks** re-creates the process of gems growing beneath the Earth's surface. **Frontiers of Biotechnology** has interactive computers providing an introduction to genetics.

Two further attractions in the museum require separate admission; booking is strongly advised (tel: 617/723 2500). The **Charles Hayden Planetarium** gives tours of the New England skies and voyages through far-distant space as well as laser shows. The **Mugar Omni Theatre** has a wrap-around domed screen, 76 feet in diameter and as tall as a four-storey building. State-of-the-art projection and 84 speakers make it a far cry from the movie houses of the past. (*Open*: daily 9–5; Friday 9–9; school vacations 9–7. Closed Monday from January to April, except holidays and school vacations. Exhibit halls free on Wednesday 1–5pm September to April, except holidays and school vacations.)

Museum tours
Free tours of the Museum of Fine Arts provide an introduction to the collections. These take place on Wednesday at 6:15pm, Tuesday to Friday 1:30pm, and Saturday 11am and 1:30pm. Other themed tours depart between 10:30 and 2:30, Tuesday to Friday.

71

Pausing for reflection at the Museum of Science

Charles river cruises
An optional extra to a visit to the Museum of Science is to take a 50-minute narrated cruise on the Charles river. Departures are from the museum itself and from CambridgeSide Galleria Mall in Cambridge. For information contact the Charles Riverboat Company (tel: 617/621 3001).

▶▶▶ **New England Aquarium** 49E3
Central Wharf
Subway: Aquarium (Blue Line).
A spectacular place to end a day in Boston, the Aquarium stays open later than most sites. Time your visit to include the sea-lion show on **Discovery**, the museum's ship-turned-theatre. A spiral ramp gives views of marine life inside a huge cylindrical water tank (the world's largest), with fish of every size from sharks downwards swimming around a replica coral reef. More than 2,000 species are on show. Other features include luminous fish, fish noises, rare turtles, venomous frogs and an electric eel.

Perhaps Boston's most sobering exhibit is a display on the pollution of Boston Harbor, with a constantly changing counter announcing the alarming volume of sewage pouring into the waters each second. (*Open*: 9–6 daily, 9–8 Wednesday and Thursday, 9–7 weekends and holidays, 1 July to Labor Day; the rest of year the same hours except 9–5 Monday to Wednesday and Friday.)

▶ **Old South Meeting House** 49D3
See page 58, and panel opposite.

▶ **Old State House** 49D3
See pages 58–9.

▶ **Paul Revere House** 49D4
See page 60.

▶▶▶ **Prudential Center Skywalk** 48A1
Prudential Tower Building, Huntington Avenue
Subway: Prudential (Green Line, E train).
Although scarcely Boston's best-loved building, the prominent Prudential Tower offers a superb view of the city from its Skywalk (50th) floor, 700 feet above the streets (*open*: daily until 10pm). On a really clear day, the panorama stretches to the Berkshire Hills and to high points in New Hampshire and Vermont. Despite its lesser stature and popularity than the nearby John Hancock Tower, the

A hands-on (or in) experience at the New England Aquarium

Prudential has better glass for viewing, offers all-round panoramas and points out the sights. Both buildings are on the Back Bay walk (see pages 62–3).

The famous and perennially popular swan boats in Boston Garden

▶▶ Public Garden 48B2

Subway: Arlington (Green Line).
Well-fed squirrels and pigeons populate this charming park, graced with statues and some 350 varieties of trees. Since 1877 pedal-powered swan boats have conveyed visitors across the pond, past weeping willows and beneath a scaled-down replica of the Brooklyn Bridge. Look for the bronze statuettes of a duck and eight ducklings, modelled on the heroes of Robert McCloskey's children's story, *Make Way for Ducklings*.

▶▶ State House 48C3

Beacon Street
Subway: Park Street (Red and Green Lines).
Prominently sited at the top of the Common, the State House is the seat of government for the Commonwealth of Massachusetts. Road distances are traditionally measured from the gold-leaf dome.

The State House was originally designed by Charles Bulfinch. Subsequently extended, the building has a rich marble interior. The entrance is through the **Doric Hall**. It leads to the **Nurses Hall**, hung with a trio of paintings by Robert Reid (*Paul Revere's Ride, James Otis Arguing Against the Writs of Assistance* and *The Boston Tea Party*), and into the circular Hall of Flags and main staircase. The **House of Representatives** contains the Sacred Cod, a wooden fish carving that is the symbol of Massachusetts. The **Senate Chamber** and **Governor's Office** are part of the original building by Bulfinch.

The Great Hall, added to the State House in 1990, contains the controversial '$100,000 clock'. This was installed because of a law requiring 1 per cent of expenses in erecting such a building to be allocated towards purchasing works of art. (*Open:* 10–4, Monday to Friday; free guided tour.)

▶▶ USS *Constitution* Museum 48C3

See page 67.

Meeting-houses and churches
Old South Meeting House, with its Wren-inspired brick façade dating to 1729, replaced an earlier wooden meeting-house, built by Puritan settlers. These early colonists built their churches in the plain, square, meeting-house style, with a wooden spire or cupola and, inside, wooden panelling, box pews and galleries supported on wooden columns. Reflecting the unity of Church and State, the meeting-house often also served as town hall. It was not until the 19th century that new churches were built in such European-inspired styles as Gothic or Romanesque Revival.

Japanese print at the Arthur M Sackler Museum

Cambridge

Cambridge lies just across the Charles river from Boston, a short walk over the bridge from the Back Bay. Yet it is a separate city – a commercial centre as well as a famous seat of learning centred on Harvard University and the Massachusetts Institute of Technology (MIT). At night, Harvard Square comes alive with buskers and bustle. It is the busy atmosphere and the shopping, dining and nightlife facilities rather than the physical appearance of Cambridge that attract visitors.

Cambridge was founded in 1630 as Newtowne and became the capital of the Bay Colony, being chosen for its protected site away from the exposed Boston peninsula. Harvard University was founded in 1636, and two years later Newtowne was renamed Cambridge after the English seat of learning. Following the battles of Concord and Lexington in 1775, provincial militias grouped on Cambridge Common to form the new Continental Army under the command of George Washington. Today Harvard University is one of the pre-eminent Ivy League establishments in the country (see pages 22–3).

▶▶ **Harvard University Museums** *74C2/3*

The **Fogg Art Museum**▶▶ and the **Busch-Reisinger Museum**▶▶, at 32 Quincy Street, are two museums in one (*open*: 10–5, Tuesday to Sunday; free on Saturday mornings 10–12). Their noted collection of European and American art features big names such as Homer, Whistler and Sargent among the 19th-century Americans, and Lichtenstein, Warhol and Pollock among the 20th-century

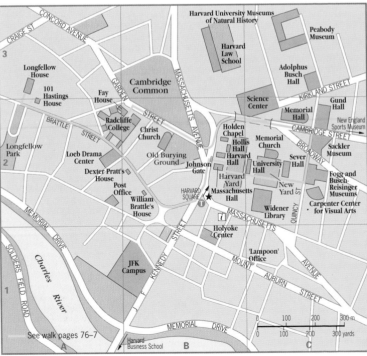

artists; Monet; the Paris School (Chagall, Picasso, Braque); the Pre-Raphaelites (Rossetti, Holman Hunt, Ford Madox Brown), and the German Expressionists.

The **Arthur M Sackler Museum**▶, at 485 Broadway Street, is housed in an innovative, if controversial, candy-striped building by James Stirling known as 'Stirling's Zebra'. It contains beautiful and rare items from Asia and the ancient world, including Greek Attic vessels, carvings of deities, Japanese woodblock prints and the world's finest collection of Chinese jade.

Entrances to the Harvard University **Museums of Natural History**▶ are at 24 Oxford Street and 11 Divinity Avenue (*open*: 9–4:30 daily; 1–4:30 Sunday). Admission covers the four museums in this rambling building. Much of it is the preserve of the specialist researcher, but the public mostly comes to see the unique collection of glass flowers in the Botanical Museum, more than 700 items in all, representing giant cross-sections, roots, rotting pears and insects (see panel). A 30-minute tape tour guides you to the highlights. The other museums are devoted to zoology (not for stuffed-animal phobics), including fossils, dinosaurs and the world's largest collection of spiders; archaeology and ethnology, and geology, with an attractive stone and gem collection featuring a cabinet of rocks from New England states.

Longfellow House 74A3

Henry Longfellow was 30 years old when he first saw this 1759 yellow clapboard mansion at 105 Brattle Street (*open*: daily; last tour 4pm), and felt like a 'prince in a villa' just to lodge here. Here he completed his translation of Dante, and penned *The Song of Hiawatha*, *Paul Revere's Ride* and *Evangeline*. His book collection reflects his passion for knowledge, and here he entertained Dickens, Emerson, Hawthorne, Twain and Wilde. Longfellow died here after living in the house for 45 years. Earlier, George Washington had his headquarters here during the siege of Boston.

▶ Sports Museum of New England 48B5

This popular museum (*open*: 10–9:30 daily; 12–6 Sunday) lies within the CambridgeSide Galleria at 100 CambridgeSide Place, accessible by free shuttle from Kendall Square station on the subway's Green Line. You can enjoy video highlights of Red Sox and Celtics games in mini-theatre mock-ups of Fenway Park and Boston Garden at this lively museum showing memorabilia and heroes of all the region's sports. There is a cross-section of a candlepin bowling alley (a sport unique to New England). Sporty kids will love it for the hands-on activities, where you can put your face into a baseball catcher's mask and feel what it's like to have Roger Clemens pitching at you as the ball hits your mitt. Time yourself having a go at the Boston Marathon in a wheelchair, or test yourself rowing on the Charles river.

Harvard's glass flowers
George Lincoln Goodall, the first director of Harvard's Botanical Museum, wanted three-dimensional plant models for teaching purposes. He travelled to Dresden in 1886 to visit Leopold and Rudolf Blashka, father and son, who were specialists in supplying museums with glass sea creatures. In this way he established a year-round laboratory for scientific study. The final models were created by Rudolf to illustrate plant diseases.

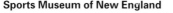

Longfellow House, home to the poet from 1837 to 1882

MIT
The Massachusetts Institute of Technology, founded in 1861, enrols 9,500 students. It is mainly of interest to visitors for its modern architecture and sculpture. Seek out the Chapel and the Kresge Auditorium (both by Eero Saarinen), and the Dreyfus and Wiesner buildings by IM Pei. Campus tours from 77 Massachusetts Avenue start at 10am and 2pm, Monday to Friday.

Harvard, the country's oldest, and richest, college

Walk Harvard and Cambridge highlights

See map on page 74.

This is a tour of Harvard University and historic Cambridge, encompassing the Common and the former home of the poet Henry Wadsworth Longfellow.

From Harvard Square Red Line subway station, walk north on Massachusetts Avenue to Johnson Gate, which gives access to **Harvard Yard**, the hub of the university. The first quadrangle, **Old Yard**, contains dormitories for freshmen and the oldest campus buildings; it was here that Washington gathered his troops against the British. To the left as you enter is **Harvard Hall**, a 1764 reconstruction of the original building endowed by John Harvard and destroyed by fire. Adjacent is **Hollis Hall** (1762), whose students included Emerson and Thoreau. Dents in the steps in front of the hall were

Leafy Harvard Yard

reputedly caused by the student practice of placing cannonballs in fireplaces to radiate heat, and throwing them out in spring! On the right is **Massachusetts Hall** (1718), the oldest building of all, which numbers John and Samuel Adams among its luminaries.

In the centre of Old Yard the **John Harvard Statue** (1885), known as the 'Statue of Three Lies', is not quite what it seems. A student, not Harvard, was the model, and the inscription 'John Harvard, Founder, 1638' errs on two counts: Harvard was the benefactor, not the founder, and the university was founded in 1636.

Beyond **University Hall** (1816), designed by Charles Bulfinch, is **New Yard**, a quadrangle formed by Memorial Church (1931), Sever Hall (1880) and the **Harry Elkins Widener Library** (1913). The latter is the largest university library in the world and was endowed by the mother of Harry Widener, an avid collector of antiquarian books who perished aboard the *Titanic*. True to his mother's wishes, the building has been unaltered, and for a time all applicants were required to undertake a swimming test (Harry could not swim). **Memorial Church** is dedicated to Harvard men who died in the two World Wars.

Leave the Yard and enter Quincy Street, opposite the concrete and glass **Carpenter Center for Visual Arts** (1963), the only building in the US designed by Le Corbusier, and one that has been likened by critics to

Above: there's always entertainment in Harvard Square, whether it's eating out, listening to buskers – or watching a game of chess

'two rhinos wrestling'. Continue past the Fogg Art Museum, turning left on to Cambridge Street to the cathedral-like **Memorial Hall** (1874), built to honour all the Harvard men killed in the Civil War.

Continue west across Massachusetts Avenue to Garden Street, where the **Old Burying Ground** ('God's Acre') contains the graves of the first eight Harvard presidents, as well as early settlers and Revolutionary soldiers. After its staunchly Tory Anglican congregation fled before the Revolution, **Christ Church** (1761), Cambridge's oldest existing church, was used as a patriot barracks and its organ pipes were pilfered for use as bullets. The **Common,** opposite, formerly functioned as the focus for Cambridge's religious, social and political life. Three captured British cannons stand on the grass close to where Washington took command of the 9,000 men who had gathered to form the Continental Army. Washington's Elm (not the original tree) marks the spot.

Cross the yard of **Radcliffe College,** which was founded as the Society for the Collegiate Instruction of Women in 1879, when Fay House (1807) was acquired. The college was incorporated into Harvard in 1894. Leaving Radcliffe, turn right along Brattle Street, known in the 18th century as Tory Row because of the British patriotism of its residents, as far as the **Longfellow House** (1759), described on page 75. Returning along Brattle Street, do not miss number 54, the home of Dexter Pratt, who was immortalised by Longfellow in *The Village Blacksmith* ('a mighty man is he, with large and sinewy hands'); the 'spreading chestnut tree' is no longer there.

Accommodation

78

City freebies
- Charlestown Navy Yard and the USS *Constitution*.
- Concerts at the Hatch Shell.
- Faneuil Hall Marketplace street entertainers and Faneuil Hall itself.
- JF Kennedy Library and Museum.
- Commonwealth Museum.
- Massachusetts State House.
- Ranger-led walking tour along the Freedom Trail.
- The Public Garden.
- Some major museums are free at certain times: Museum of Fine Arts (Wednesday 4–10pm), Museum of Science (Wednesday 1–5pm); New England Aquarium (Thursday from 3pm out of season), Harvard University museums (Saturday morning).

The upmarket Lenox Hotel on Boylston Street

Hotels Boston has world-class hotels right in the heart of the city. The principal hotel area begins at the Theatre District, just south of Boston Common, and extends westwards past the Prudential Tower towards Massachusetts Avenue. Most hotels are within easy walking distance of Copley Square and the start of the Freedom Trail at Boston Common. Other convenient hotels are found in the downtown and waterfront areas, and in Cambridge.

Boston is more expensive to stay in than is rural New England. At certain periods, especially during major conventions, it can be difficult to find a room, and rates are at a premium. Weekends are less busy than weekdays, and accordingly rates tend to be lower. Since the converse applies in summer resorts such as the North Shore, Cape Cod and the islands, you can make substantial savings by visiting Boston at the weekend and making for the coast during the week. As elsewhere in the US, hotel rates do not usually include breakfast, and state and local room tax are added to the room charge.

Bed and breakfast If hotels are too expensive, bed-and-breakfast (B&B) accommodation is a money-saving option. Several agencies organise hosted B&B accommodation, where you stay in someone's home. The most charming and convenient locations include the Back Bay, Beacon Hill and the North End. The Bed & Breakfast Agency of Boston (see page 268) is the largest of these operations.

You may be able to find less expensive places by opting to stay further out from the city centre. The subway and rail systems take you to most further-flung locations, such as the suburb of Brookline, southwest of central Boston, which has numerous inexpensive bed and breakfasts. For those on a tight budget, the Boston International AYH Hostel (for address and telephone number see page 268) near the Prudential Center has dormitory accommodation; non-members can join on the spot.

A visitor centre will help with finding accommodation

The BSO

■ **Boston has a reputation as the most musical city in the United States, a reputation that rests almost entirely on its being the home of one of the finest ensembles in the world: the Boston Symphony Orchestra.....■**

In October 1881 the BSO, or Boston Symphony Orchestra, gave its inaugral concert, bringing to reality the dreams of the philanthropist and amateur musician Henry Lee Higginson of founding a permanent orchestra in his home town of Boston. For the first 20 years or so concerts were given in the Old Boston Music Hall, initially under the directorship of Georg Henschel and then under a series of German and French conductors.

In 1900 the orchestra moved into Symphony Hall, which to this day remains one of the world's most acoustically perfect venues. Symphony Hall also became the venue for the orchestra's hugely successful 'Promenade concerts,' which had begun in 1885, fulfilling Higginson's ambition to provide a 'lighter kind of music' in addition to more serious programmes. Later called 'Popular Concerts' and then 'Pops', these have remained a favourite springtime tradition under the auspices of the Boston Pops Orchestra.

The Koussevitzky era In 1924 the Russian-born Serge Koussevitzky, a man of extraordinary talent and dynamic personality, took over as musical director of the BSO. During his 25-years' illustrious leadership, the orchestra began regular radio broadcasts. Arthur Fiedler initiated the free Boston Pops Esplanade concerts that are still given in summer beside the Charles river, while from 1937 onwards the BSO took up a summer residency at Tanglewood, in the Berkshires (see panel, page 146).

'The aristocrat of orchestras' Charles Munch followed Koussevitzky in 1949, introducing American audiences to quantities of French music. In the 1960s, promoted under Erich Leinsdorf as 'the aristocrat of orchestras', the BSO made numerous recordings and tours all over the world.

With Seiji Ozawa as musical director since 1973, Higginson's 'great and permanent orchestra' has consolidated its worldwide reputation, commissioning new works from composers such as Hans Werner Henze and John Cage, and presenting soloists of the highest calibre, such as Yo-Yo Ma, Pinchas Zukerman and Itzhak Perlman.

Above and left: John Williams conducts the Boston Pops

Concert information
The BSO season at Symphony Hall runs from the beginning of October to the end of April. Contact the Subscription Office, Symphony Hall, Boston MA 02115 (tel: 617/266 7575; fax: 617/638 9436). For the Tanglewood Music Festival, contact Symphony Hall, as above, or Tanglewood Ticket Office, Lenox MA 01240 (tel: 413/637 1940). For the Pops (April–June) tel: 617/266 1492 or 617/266 2378.

79

Opening night
When Isabella Stewart Gardner opened her Venetian-style palace (see page 69) on New Year's Night 1903, her guests were entertained in the concert hall by 50 members of the Boston Symphony Orchestra. Afterwards, the doors of the hall were opened and guests had their first view of the ravishing courtyard, filled with flowering plants and lit by lanterns.

Food and drink

'And this is the city of Boston,
The land of the bean and the cod,
Where the Lowells talk only to Cabots,
And the Cabots talk only to God.'
– James Collins Bossidy, toast at Holy Cross Alumni dinner, 1910.

'I've never seen a Lowell walk,
Nor heard a Cabot speak with God,
But I enjoy good Boston talk
And Boston beans and Boston cod.'
– RCH Bruce Lockhart, *In Praise of Boston*.

As the birthplace of the humble baked bean, Boston is nicknamed 'Beantown'. However, more sophisticated fare – such as Maine lobsters, quahogs (large clams), chowders and scrod (white fish) – is much easier to come by.

Faneuil Hall Marketplace is one of the best places to eat cheaply. Food stalls in Quincy Market offer take-aways in various forms – filled bagels, Greek and Chinese dishes, seafood, speciality milkshakes and swordfish kebabs – but the market starts to close down after 9:30pm.

Options for leisurely meals include restaurants in Beacon Hill's Charles Street, and in Newbury Street. Chinatown has some excellent eating-places: some of the best offer bargain prices and with functional décor to match! The North End can boast some of the highest-quality Italian food in the Northeast, and although Bostonians as a rule tend to eat early, it is often possible to stop by in the early hours for a cappuccino or bowl of pasta. Bargain-priced food stands are set up in the streets on Friday and Saturday, when you can take your fill of pasta, battered calamari and mussels. Some restaurants offer 'Early Bird' specials for senior citizens.

Cambridge has so much happening in the streets in the evening that to dine out there is part of the Boston experience. A branch of Au Bon Pain, an excellent city-wide sandwich bar chain, occupies one side of Harvard Square. Popular with chess-players, this is a pleasant point from which to watch Cambridge life going by. Cambridge is particularly strong on ethnic eateries, with Portuguese fare along Cambridge and Hampshire streets and a good choice of Korean, Creole and Indian restaurants.

Boston has some excellent beers: the Boston Brewery's Samuel Adams Lager is probably the best known. Some pub-restaurants produce their own brew: the Commonwealth Brewing Company, Cambridge Brewery and the Boston Beer Works.

Eating al fresco near Faneuil Hall

■ **Boston means different things to different people. To some it means simply the Red Sox. Add the Celtics and the Bruins and you begin to form a picture of a rich sporting tradition.....■**

The Red Sox The ups and downs of Boston's baseball team are inextricably entwined in the fabric of Boston life. Strong men go misty-eyed at the mention of such legendary names as Babe Ruth, Jimmie Foxx, Carl Yastrzemski, Jim Lonborg, Ted Williams (the last major leaguer to bat over 400 for a season), Dick 'The Monster' Radatz or Roger 'The Rocket' Clemens (both of whom regularly pitched at over 90mph). Revered too are the team's greatest benefactors, Tom Yawkey and his wife Jean, who owned and were deeply devoted to the Red Sox from 1933 to 1976.

The skill of the Fenway Park pros is phenomenal, but so too is the enthusiasm of the college and the local ballpark teams. To attend one of these games, along with the mayor, the cheer leaders and the fire engines, is every bit as thrilling.

The Celtics and the Bruins Basketball was born at the YMCA in Springfield, Massachusetts, in December 1891. The invention of a physical education teacher, Dr James Naismith, to keep his students out of mischief in the winter months, it is the only major sport founded in the US. Naismith originally used two half-bushel peach baskets as targets, hence the name of the game. Basketball caught on fast in schools and colleges across America, and a century later is played in 170 countries.

Boston is home to the Boston Celtics, who won 11 of 13 titles between 1956/7 and 1968/9, making them one of the most successful teams in the National Basketball Association. You will probably come across a local game – or, if you look into almost any Boston backyard, find a group of young Celtics fans in the team's green and white colours emulating a Larry Bird jump shot. The Celtics share Boston Garden (see page 66) with the Bruins, Boston's illustrious ice hockey team.

Ticket information
● The Boston Red Sox, Fenway Park, 4 Yawkey Way (tel: 617/267 1700, fax: 617/236 6640). The season runs from April to early October.
● The Boston Celtics and Bruins, Boston Garden, 150 Causeway Street – by North Station (tel: 617/227 3206). Celtics' season runs from October to May, Bruins' from October to April.
● New England Patriots Football Club, Foxboro Stadium, Route 1, Foxboro (tel: 508/543 8200). The National League is in action from August to early January.

81

*Above: basketball player Robert Parish
Left: Fenway Park*

And more...
Other great events in the Boston sporting calendar include the Boston Marathon in May; the Head of the Charles Regatta, in October; and the US Pro Tennis Championship in mid-July. Alternatively, visit the Sports Museum of New England (see page 75).

Above left: the Friday and Saturday Haymarket – lively, lusty and colourful Above right: altogether quieter, a bookstore near Tremont Street

Boston inventions
- Alexander Graham Bell invented the telephone in Sudbury Street, and the first telephone exchange followed in 1877.
- Charles Goodyear developed the vulcanisation of automobile tyres, in 1844.
- King Gillette invented the safety razor-blade in 1901.
- Other Boston innovations include the baseball catcher's mask, the polaroid film, the iron lung and the heart pacemaker.

The Back Bay and Beacon Hill If a competition was held to find New England's most chic shopping street, **Newbury Street** would be among the front runners. Running parallel to Commonwealth Avenue from the Public Garden through the fashionable district of Back Bay, the street has high-class designer shops, galleries, and boutiques; accordingly it makes for particularly enjoyable window-shopping. Near by in Beacon Hill, **Charles Street** is known for antiques. At the Boylston and Arlington street crossing is the Heritage on the Garden complex, offering jewellery, designer fashions, crystal and porcelain.

The revamped **Prudential Center** has Saks Fifth Avenue, Lord & Taylor and other high-class shops, while across Huntington Avenue fountains and piped classical music set an elegant (and expensive) tone in **Copley Place** indoor mall. Shops include Traveldays, with an excellent range of travel books and maps, including a New England section. Eastwards at 338 Boylston Street, the world's largest teddy bear marks the entrance to **FAO Schwarz**, the city's main toy store, a branch of the celebrated New York emporium. Close by at 330 Boylston Street, **Shreve, Crump and Low** sells fine-quality jewellery, china, glass and silver.

Downtown Crossing area There are over 300 retail stores around Summer and Washington streets, including the giant department stores of Jordan Marsh and Filene's; **Filene's Basement** is renowned for its bargain-price clothes and other lines. **Barnes and Noble** (395 Washington Street and 607 Boylston Street) is the city's largest discount bookseller. At the corner of School and Washington streets, on the Freedom Trail, **Globe Corner Bookstore** has a selection of New England books and maps.

Other Boston highlights Chinatown is great for browsing, with markets, restaurants, gift shops and supermarkets, as well as Vietnamese, Thai and Cambodian stores. Take your pick of jewellery, fabrics, joss-sticks, exotic foods and ginseng chewing-gum.

Another enjoyable place for window-gazing is **Pavo Real**, near Faneuil Hall, which stocks ceramics and clothes, many in outrageous styles. Elsewhere in the Marketplace are a number of kiosks and boutiques. By total contrast, the Haymarket is a no-frills fruit and vegetables market (Fridays and Saturdays only). Italian shops in the **North End** include some outstanding food stores and bakeries around Hanover and Salem streets.

Good **museum shops** are found at the Children's Museum, Computer Museum, Museum of Fine Arts (also at Copley Place), the Sports Museum of New England and the Museum of Science.

Cambridge Harvard Square has a concentration of bookshops offering new and second-hand volumes. **WordsWorth** and **Barillari Books** both offer discount prices: WordsWorth has a wider range while Barillari is generally slightly cheaper. Bookshops open all evening and Sundays, and you are welcome to browse for hours. There are also numerous music shops and boutiques. The **Harvard Coop Society** (known simply as the Coop) on the Square is the major department store, serving the town since 1882, and has books and music sections. There are further bookshops inside the MIT Coop at Kendall Square. From the square you can take the free shuttle service to the **CambridgeSide Galleria**, which comprises over 100 shops and restaurants, including Sears (a large general store); the New England Sports Museum is in the same complex. At Porter Exchange, north of Harvard Square, you can find specialist stores, and hair and skincare salons. Kendall, Harvard and Porter squares are stops on the subway's Red Line.

83

Suburban shopping An outstanding range of equipment and clothing for winter sports and hiking is found at **Eastern Mountain Sports** at 1041 Commonwealth Avenue, Boston.

Five miles west of the city centre on Route 9, the Mall at **Chestnut Hill** is a feast for the eyes, with over 100 stores, including Bloomingdales and Filene's. Concerts take place here at weekends. The Mall can be reached by Green Line (D train for Riverside) to Chestnut Hill station.

Further out of town, and accessible by commuter train, Cape Ann, Marblehead, Ipswich, **Essex** and **Newburyport** each have art galleries and antique shops.

Quincy Market, next to Faneuil Hall, dates back to the 1820s. Today, it is always an entertaining and lively place to be

Nightlife

Boston dining perspectives
Both the Prudential Tower and John Hancock Tower have stunning high-level views of the city by night. But the 52nd-floor Top of the Hub restaurant in the Prudential and the Bay Tower Room on the 33rd floor at 60 State Street allow diners to enjoy superb views at their leisure. Dinner cruises on the *Spirit of Boston* from Rowes Wharf get a low-level but equally fascinating perspective on Boston. *Odyssey* also offers dinner cruises.

There is a lot going on in Boston at night, although it is not an all-night city in the way New York is. The liveliest areas popular with visitors are Faneuil Hall Marketplace, Copley Square, Kenmore Square (near Boston University) and Harvard Square (in Cambridge, by Harvard University).

Listings and tickets Events listings for the week appear in the *Boston Globe* on Thursdays, the *Boston Herald* on Fridays, and the *Boston Phoenix* on Saturdays. For advance bookings and half-price tickets on the day of performance contact Ticketmaster (tel: 617/931 2000) or visit the Bostix ticket booth in Faneuil Hall Marketplace (tel: 617/723 5181).

Theatre The Theatre District, just south of Boston Common, has mainstream and avant-garde offerings, from anarchic student shows to lavish professional hit dramas and musicals.

Bars and clubs Piano bars, pubs, dance clubs, comedy clubs and dance venues proliferate around Faneuil Hall Marketplace. These tend to be mainly the haunt of visitors. The Bull & Finch pub, famed for its appearance in the TV series *Cheers*, is at 84 Beacon Street. Other pubs close by are The Sevens and the Beacon Hill Pub. Popular places with business people include the clubs in The Alley, and Esme, a nightclub in the Marais restaurant.

Boylston Street has outdoor bars, such as the Cactus Club, which attract the younger set. Small Planet is a funky bar for the environmentally conscious, with clouds painted on the ceiling. Number 29 Newbury Street is both outdoor and indoor, with late-1920s to 1940s décor and music. Ryles in Cambridge is a popular meeting-place, while Cantab on Massachusetts Avenue plays 1970s music. Rachel's on Long Wharf (296 State Street) is a nightly disco in the Boston Marriott Hotel, while The Paradise, an intimate club that

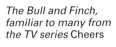

The Bull and Finch, familiar to many from the TV series Cheers

Jazz in the Charles Hotel's Regatta Bar

attracts big names, at 967 Commonwealth Avenue is excellent for live rock, blues and folk (booking essential; tel: 617/931 2000).

Columbus Avenue has plenty of neighbourhood bars, while gay venues abound in Kenmore Square and in the South End. The Kenmore Square area is also busy with college students and has numerous dance clubs, billiard halls, bowling and golf sports halls, and concert venues. Among them are Avalon, Jillian's Billiard Club, Venus De Milo, Bill's Bar and Lounge, and Boston Billiards. The Dick Doherty Comedy Club at Museum Wharf, and the Comedy Connection at Faneuil Hall are leading venues of their kind.

The jazz scene Some hotels have jazz and blues bars, including Diamond Jim's Piano Bar in the Lenox Hotel and the Regatta Bar in the Charles Hotel. The House of Blues and Black Goose on Beacon Street, and the Turner Fisheries Lounge by Copley Square are other jazz scenes. An excellent 'down-and-dirty' jazz venue is Wally's on Massachusetts Avenue; it is the only truly mixed venue of its kind, drawing all ages and colours. For jazz events, telephone the Boston Jazz Line on 617/787 9700.

Classical music venues The Boston Pops Orchestra performs light classics and popular favourites at Symphony Hall from May through July. The concert hall floor is cleared of conventional seating and has chairs and tables. The chatter and bustle tends to go on during the concert, to the annoyance of some, but to others it is part of the atmosphere. In early July there is a series of free Boston Pops outdoor concerts at the Hatch Shell on the Esplanade (tel: 617/266 1492). The Boston Symphony Orchestra performs at Symphony Hall from the beginning of October to the end of April (tel: 617/266 7575).

Boston Lyric Opera, New England's leading opera company, stages productions at 114 State Street (tel: 617/248 8811).

Ballet performances are given at the Wang Center for the Performing Arts (tel: 617/482 9393), at 270 Tremont Street, and by Boston Ballet, at 19 Clarendon Street.

Boston: firsts in US
- First fire law, banning wooden chimneys (1632).
- Law against smoking (1633).
- Public park (Boston Common, 1634).
- Public school (Boston Latin School, 1636).
- US post office (1639).
- Chocolate factory (1765).
- Lighthouse (1716).
- Electric fire alarm (1851).
- Burglar alarm (1858).
- Football game (Boston Common, 1862).
- Computer (Differential Analyzer at MIT, 1928).

CONNECTICUT

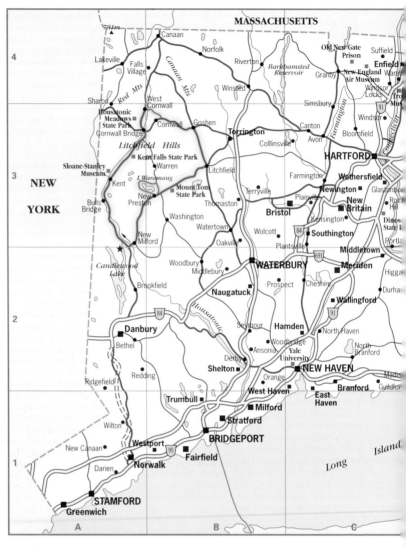

MASSACHUSETTS

NEW YORK

4

3

2

1

A   B   C

781m

Canaan

Norfolk

Lakeville

Falls Village

Riverton

Barkhamsted Reservoir

Old New-Gate Prison

Suffield

Enfield

Ware

Sharon

West Cornwall

Winsted

Granby

New England Air Museum

Windsor Locks

Tro Mus

Simsbury

Housatonic Meadows State Park

Cornwall Bridge

Cornwall

Goshen

Torrington

Collinsville

Canton

Avon

Bloomfield

Windsor

Litchfield Hills

Kent Falls State Park

Warren

Litchfield

HARTFORD

Farmington

Wethersfield

Newington

Glastonb

Sloane-Stanley Museum

Kent

L. Waramaug

New Preston

Terryville

Plainville

New Britain

Roc Hill

Bulls Bridge

Mount Tom State Park

Washington

Thomaston

Bristol

Kensington

Southington

Dinos State I

Portla

Candlewood Lake

New Milford

Watertown

Oakville

Wolcott

Plantsville

Middletown

Woodbury

Middlebury

WATERBURY

Meriden

Higga

Brookfield

Prospect

Cheshire

Wallingford

Durha

Naugatuck

Seymour

Hamden

North Haven

Danbury

Bethel

Woodbridge

Ansonia

Yale University

North Branford

Ridgefield

Redding

Derby

Orange

NEW HAVEN

Madis

Guildfor

Shelton

West Haven

Branford

Trumbull

Milford

East Haven

Wilton

Stratford

New Canaan

Westport

BRIDGEPORT

Fairfield

Long

Island

Darien

Norwalk

STAMFORD

Greenwich

Red Mts

Canaan Mts

Farmington

Connecticut

Housatonic

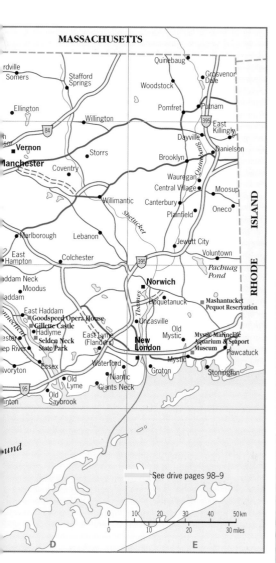

CONNECTICUT

Connecticut Named after New England's longest river, Connecticut extends some 90 miles west–east and 55 miles north–south. The state's rolling terrain is bisected by the Connecticut river, which flows south along a fertile valley into Long Island Sound. The shoreline has sandy beaches and quiet coastal towns, as well as more urbanised parts close to New York City. The coastal hinterland is a gentle plain, which rises further inland into forested uplands near the New York and Massachusetts borders. Connecticut is America's third smallest state (after Rhode Island and Delaware) and is densely populated. Yet the state has genuinely rural tracts that belie its proximity to the Big Apple. In all, two-thirds of Connecticut is rural, and most of that is forested.

Roseland Cottage in the quiet village of Woodstock

CONNECTICUT

A balloonist's view over Long Island Sound

'Here's to the town of New Haven,
The home of the Truth and the Light,
Where God talks to Jones in the very same tones
That he uses with Hadley and Dwight.'
– FS Jones, *On the Democracy of Yale*.

'Connecticut in her blue-laws, laying it down as a principle, that the laws of God should be the law of the land.'
– Thomas Jefferson, letter to John Adams, 24 January 1814.

The historic heritage The Connecticut river brought in the first Puritan settlers in the 1630s after Boston and Massachusetts had become too religiously intolerant for their tastes. Hartford, Windsor and Wethersfield were the original trio of towns they established, hence the three clusters of grapes on the state's coat of arms. These settlements merged to become the Hartford Colony, later named the Connecticut Colony. The Fundamental Orders of Connecticut, adopted in 1638, are widely held to have been the world's first written constitution of a democratic government – hence the state's official nickname, the Constitution State, on every vehicle licence-plate. Connecticut has also been named the 'Nutmeg State' – its inhabitants being 'Nutmeggers' (see panel) – and, during the Revolutionary War, the 'Arsenal of the Nation'. The state retains plenty of mementoes of those times.

Yankee ingenuity also made Connecticut the 'Gadget State'. This was the birthplace of the cylinder lock, the pay telephone, the steel fish-hook, the stone-crusher and the submarine torpedo. Samuel Colt's firearms company manufactured the famous .45 revolver and other guns in Hartford, while pioneer clock-makers Seth Thomas and Eli Terry had Thomaston and Terryville named after them. Eli Whitney devised interchangeable parts which effectively made him the father of mass-production. Charles Goodyear manufactured improved vehicle tyres and the first American copper coins were minted here. Even today, despite a decline in industrial activity, the state leans heavily towards manufacturing, including the output of ball-bearings, jet engines, nuclear submarines, sewing machines, cutlery and hardware. Since 1945 the more affluent inhabitants have left the larger towns for the picket fences of the suburbs and villages, and a significant ethnic blue-collar population has appeared in the towns themselves.

The state's oldest-established towns are found along the 253-mile shoreline and along the principal waterways, notably the Connecticut river. Early colonial days saw Yankee traders flourishing in ship-building, seafaring and commercial ventures at Mystic, Stonington, New London and elsewhere. The insurance industry that began in conjunction with this maritime activity gathered momentum. Today, insurance is still the state capital's *raison d'être*.

Visitor attractions For the visitor, Connecticut's maritime heritage is an obvious attraction, and is admirably presented in the great museums of Mystic and Norwalk. But other industrial ports bordering Long Island Sound in the state's southwestern territory have only patches of interest; one such oasis is Yale University, an architectural treasure-house in New Haven. In the Hartford area, the former homes of Mark Twain, Noah Webster and Harriet Beecher Stowe can be visited. Off-beat whimsicality can be found at Gillette Castle, in the Connecticut River Valley, while the Lockwood-Mathews Mansion in Norwalk, the most sumptuous house of its day, foreshadows the opulent 'cottages' at Newport in Rhode Island. Fine art collections are found at Hartford, Yale University and New Britain.

Elsewhere in the state, pristine white clapboard villages such as Litchfield, Wethersfield, Ridgefield and Farmington await discovery, grouped around their characteristic village greens, each stubbornly refusing to concede to urbanisation. By the Massachusetts border is the state's highest terrain and most scenic drive, along the fast-flowing Housatonic river in the Litchfield Hills, an area well endowed with arty crafts shops and galleries. The Connecticut and Housatonic rivers are both noted for fishing, the latter especially for trout, as well as for the more adventurous pursuits of tubing, canoeing and kayaking.

Several major venues exist for spectator sport. Hartford Whalers, a major-league hockey team, play in the state's capital city. The Basque sport of jai alai can be seen inexpensively at Milford (the biggest such venue in New England), Bridgeport and Hartford. Motor racing takes place at Lime Rock, and the Volvo International Tennis Tournament is held at New Haven. The Canon Greater Hartford Open is an annual golf event, and the state has over 70 public golf courses.

Connecticut superlatives
● The *Hartford Courant* is the oldest established newspaper in the US (1764).
● The Connecticut river is New England's longest.
● The Rocky Hill–Glastonbury ferry has been operating since 1655, the longest continuous service in the nation.

89

Below: at Coventry, in the northeastern corner of the state, the Nathan Hale Homestead was built by the patriot's family in 1776, the year he was executed

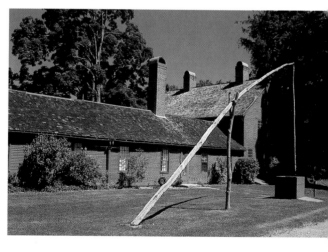

Events

For further information contact the state tourist office (see page 266) or chambers of commerce.

January–March
Warm Up to Winter, Farmington Valley area: a series of special events in which history and good food are combined at museums and period homes; weekend packages are offered from area hotels and country inns.

May
Dogwood Festival, Fairfield.
Lobster Fest, Mystic: lobster served al fresco, on the waterfront.

June
A Taste of Hartford: food, comedy, music and more.
Farmington Antiques Weekend.
Festival of Arts, Stamford.
Yale–Harvard Regatta, New London.
Canon Greater Hartford Open, Cromwell: attracting top names in golf.

June–July
Barnum Festival, Bridgeport: parade and festival to honour erstwhile mayor and circus-showman PT Barnum.

July
Antique and Classic Boat Rendezvous, Mystic Seaport.
Historic Homes Tour, Litchfield: houses open their doors to the public.
Riverfest, Hartford/East Hartford: 4 July river festival.
Sail Festival, New London: races, cruises, tall ships, concerts, fireworks.

August
Great Connecticut Traditional Jazz Festival, Moodus.
Outdoor Art Festival, Mystic: the streets close to traffic as the artists take over.
Quinnehtukqut Rendezvous and Native American Festival, Haddam Meadows State Park, by the Connecticut river: Native Americans from all over come to celebrate their past and customs.
Volvo International Tennis Festival, New Haven: major men's professional tournament at Yale University.

September
Woodstock Fair, South Woodstock: agricultural show, animals, crafts.
Fall Antiques Show, New Haven (also held in April).
Oyster Festival, Norwalk: tall ships, arts, crafts, oysters.

September–October
Mum Festival, Bristol: parade, arts, crafts, drama.

November
Thanksgiving Day Road Race, Manchester: a 4.77-mile race with thousands of runners.

December
Christmas season, Mystic Seaport: Lantern Light Tours give a one-hour 'interactive play' in a re-evocation of the 19th century; Yuletide Tours in the daytime.

Mystic Seaport, venue for a variety of events and activities

Early clock-making

Connecticut's clock-making industry, now all but defunct, originated in the late-18th century. In 1792 Eli Terry began making his name and money by mass-producing wooden cogs at his water-powered mill in Connecticut, by standardising gears and by introducing interchangeable parts. Brass gears were introduced after 1800. Further innovations included the bronze looking-glass clock and the banjo clock.

Furtive fishing

Another Bristol innovation was Everett Horton's collapsible fishing rod, which he conjured up for purely self-motivated reasons: fishing was banned on the Sabbath and his wife disapproved of his favourite pastime. The new rod could be hidden conveniently in transit.

▶ **Bristol and Area**   86C3

From the late-18th century until 1929 the neighbouring towns of Bristol, Thomaston, Terryville, Winsted and Waterbury played important roles as the centre of America's clock industry. Aptly, Bristol is home today of the **American Clock and Watch Museum**▶▶ in an elegant post-Revolutionary mansion at 100 Maple Street off Route 72 (*open*: March to November). The collection is eclectic, charting the history of American horology. In all, the museum has 1,600 watches and 1,800 clocks. Look out for the re-created 1825 clock-maker's shop, and an 1860 novelty clock from New York featuring a lion's eyes going up and down in time to the tick.

Also in Bristol, at 95 Riverside Avenue (Route 72), the **New England Carousel Museum**▶ has over 300 antique carved horses and carousel chariots. You can watch restoration in progress.

On Route 6, opposite the church at **Terryville**, the **Lock Museum**▶ occupies a site close to the former Eagle Lock mills, which opened in 1854, some 20 years after the lock industry began in Connecticut. The display features around 20,000 items from a 1580s Spanish Armada chest to a 1920s lock-demonstrating machine used at trade shows. Eagle locks are now collectors' items.

East of Bristol, **Farmington**▶, has numerous Federal-style houses and has become a select satellite of Hartford. In the village, the **Stanley-Whitman House** has been painstakingly restored to its 1720 colonial appearance and contains period furnishings. The house has diamond-pane leaded windows and an overhanging upper storey. The nearby **Hill-Stead Museum**▶, a turn-of-the-century colonial revival home, exemplifies good taste. It belonged to industrialist Alfred Pope. The family adorned the interior with French Impressionist paintings, first purchasing Manet's *View of the Maritime Alps* and later adding two of Monet's Haystack paintings.

Left: a carving in the Carousel Museum
Below: architecture from Bristol's 19th-century heyday

► Connecticut River Valley
87D2

After its 410-mile journey along the New Hampshire-Vermont border and through Massachusetts, the Connecticut river finally crosses Connecticut itself before flowing into Long Island Sound. The Connecticut scenery along New England's longest river is mild rather than spectacular, but a scattering of good sights, mostly in the county of Middlesex (at the southern end of the river's course), makes it worth taking in. Antique shops, art shows, country fairs, concerts and festivals are thick on the ground along the entire valley.

South of Hartford At the mouth of the river is **Old Saybrook**, the earliest settlement in the valley, which is home to the **Connecticut River Museum**, pleasantly sited by the river. Though not extensive, the museum's displays illustrate ship-building and maritime life in the context of the Connecticut River Valley. On show is a replica of the *American Turtle*, the first submarine, a claustrophobic-looking one-man vessel invented to sink British ships in the Revolution.

Genealogy at Middletown
Middletown was settled in 1650 and prospered in the late 18th century, as ship-building and trade with the West Indies made it the richest community in the colony. The town attracts genealogists on the trail of British and European ancestors, many of whom settled here. The Godfrey Library is the chief source of information and has records for the whole US before the 1850s.

Gillette Castle, home of an eccentric actor

At Essex, the **Valley Railroad▶▶**, one of only two steam railways in New England (the other is at North Conway, NH) operates 1½-hour round trips to Chester and Haddam. Period carriages make it a nostalgic treat: original 1920s furnishings include padded armchairs in Pullman class and cane seats as standard. An optional extra is to stop off at Deep River for a connecting boat trip upriver to East Haddam. The **Ivoryton Playhouse** provides entertainment at nearby **Ivoryton**, where there is a **Fife and Drum Museum**, open on summer weekends.

Gillette Castle▶▶, high above the river, south of East Haddam, is a fantasy re-creation of Rhenish medievalism, or something approaching that style. It was built in 1914–19 for actor William Gillette, who was famous for his Sherlock Holmes performances, but, despite public prominence, was something of a recluse. A system of mirrors was placed so that he could watch from his bedroom for unwelcome visitors and decide whether to be indisposed, and his dinner table was almost comically small. His passion for railways led to the creation of a 3-mile railway (no longer existing, although one carriage is preserved) in the grounds. The castle's idiosyncrasies reveal themselves inside, its 24 rooms displaying wooden light switches, Javanese matting, walls made of field stones, light fittings made with pieces of bottle glass, and bizarre lock systems.

Horse and carriage rides are provided daily in summer at the castle, and at weekends during most of the rest of the year. A scenic approach to the castle is on the **Chester–Hadlyme ferry** (April to September). There has been a ferry here since 1769, making it one of the oldest such continuous services in the US. It is feasible to leave the car on the far side, cross the river as a foot passenger and walk up a path to the castle.

Selden Neck State Park, devoid of facilities and accessible only by boat, is an ideal tonic for escapists who like to rough it. Canoe hire is available from below Gillette Castle.

At Middlefield, **Lyman Orchards** has been a family farm since 1741; its Apple Barrel Farm Store stocks a wide range of local produce.

Cultural life in **Chester▶**, a village graced with an unblemished main street, revolves around the delightful

Passengers on the Valley Railroad's early 20th-century steam train enjoy views of the Connecticut river and valley

New England's longest river
Named by Algonquin people as the Quinnetukut ('the long river whose waters are driven by wind and tide'), the 397-mile-long Connecticut river flows from its source near the New Hampshire-Canada border through four states and is tidal from Hartford.

First charted by Dutchman Adriaen Block in 1614, the valley was by the 19th century an important cigar-tobacco-growing area, but as in much of New England, the forest has taken over Essex, which once had six shipyards, and other communities grew as river settlements. Ship-building, however, never recovered from a flood in 1936 and a hurricane two years later.

Cruises

Deep River Navigation (tel: 203/526 4954) offers river trips from Old Saybrook, Middletown and Hartford. Camelot Cruises (tel: 203/345 8591) runs a sailing murder mystery cruise (tel: 203/345 4507) and New England Steamboat Lines (tel: 203/345 4507) makes trips to Greenport, Sag Harbor and Long Island. Paddle-steamer excursions are organised by Connecticut River Cruises (tel: 203/345 8373). *Sea Mist II* (tel: 203/488 8905), at Stony Creek, makes 45-minute trips around some of the 365 Thimble Islands; Money Island is where the pirate Captain Kidd reputedly used to draw in his boat.

Prisoners at New-Gate

A copper mine was worked at East Granby from 1707. When it became unprofitable, prison labour was used and the prison built in 1773. This became the first state prison in the US in 1776, and British loyalists were jailed here during the Revolution. The opportunities this presented, with shafts providing convenient exits and the availability of gunpowder, proved irresistible, and a mass escape by British prisoners of war and Tories occurred in 1781. The prison was abandoned in 1827.

Goodspeed Opera House (tours available; tel: 203/873 8668), with musicals usually running for six or seven weeks, and audience participation on Wednesdays. You can arrive for a performance by boat, picnic on the lawn and have drinks at the interval on a balcony overlooking the river. A tiny one-room schoolhouse at **East Haddam** was where patriot Nathan Hale taught in 1773–4 and is open on weekend afternoons for a nominal fee. Its bell was made in Spain in AD815 and is still in working order.

Historic Johnsonville is an old mill village, but without its mill since a fire destroyed it. The old houses that survived were renovated, while others were transported from elsewhere. Tours (Wednesdays at 10:30am) take in an old (non-functioning) store from Peru, Massachusetts, a chapel, an 1840s house, and an old meeting-house with a display of toys and clocks.

At Higganum, the **Sundial Herb Garden** is a compact but prettily contrived knot garden and topiary in 17th-century style, with miniature vistas opening up through its 'outdoor rooms'. It was created over a period of 20 years by an Irish and German couple who put on speciality teas (with English-style scones and clotted cream) and stocked a shop with a worldwide selection of herbs and spices.

Dinosaur State Park, on Route 91 at Rocky Hill (closed Monday), has in its exhibition hall some 500 dinosaur footprints in what was a shallow stagnant lake 185 million years ago. Life-size models, a diorama and a commentary flesh out the details, and there is a discovery room for children. If you bring your own plaster of Paris you can make casts of actual dinosaur prints. The impressions were uncovered in 1966 during building works.

For Hartford, see pages 95–7.

North of Hartford On Route 140 at **Windsor**, the **Trolley Museum** dates from 1940 and claims to be New England's oldest. Volunteers run 'trolleys' (or trams) along a 1½-mile section of the former Hartford–Springfield Street Railway and have rescued old trolleys from other

Cruising on the Connecticut river near East Haddam

places: one was found in a scout camp being used as a laundromat. On Route 75 near Bradley Airport, the **New England Air Museum▶** exhibits over 70 military and civil aeroplanes, from early biplanes to experimental fighters and modern home-built machines.

Old New-Gate Prison (*open:* Wednesday to Sunday, May to October), off Route 20 in East Granby, retains its castle-like walls (see panel opposite). The overgrown sandstone ruins have atmosphere, and children will enjoy exploring the mine.

Danbury 86A2

Danbury has two attractions for music-lovers. The **Ives House▶** (*open:* daily 2–5, April to December) was built in 1790 and acquired by the great-grandfather of composer Charles Ives (see pages 24–5) in 1829. The house has been moved three times and is now at number 5 Mountainville Avenue. It is furnished in the Victorian style appropriate to the time of the composer's birth in 1874, and family memorabilia, photographs, scores and Ives' death mask are exhibited. The piano is thought to be the one Ives first played and studied on as a child.

At the Westside campus of the Western Connecticut State University, the **Charles Ives Center for the Arts** holds outdoor summer concerts of jazz and classical music, providing a great excuse to picnic on the lawn (for details, tel: 203/797 4490).

Danbury's mixed ethnic population has given it a wealth of inexpensive Cuban, Thai, Hungarian and Portuguese eateries.

▶▶ Hartford 86C3

America's insurance industry capital stands on the Connecticut river. Downtown is dominated by high-rise office buildings (many belonging to insurance companies), the second tallest of which is the 527-foot **Travelers Tower▶▶**, offering a 37-mile view (free on weekdays from 10:30am to 3pm; there are 72 steps to climb). Virtually next door, at 600 Main Street, the Gothic Revival **Wadsworth Atheneum▶▶▶** (*closed:* Monday; free Saturday morning and Thursday) was in 1841 the first public art museum in the US (see panel). The original castle has been extended to form an architectural blend of five interconnecting buildings.

Wadsworth Atheneum highlights
A choice set of French Impressionist paintings includes Monet's *Beach at Trouville*, Matisse's *Woman with a Plumed Hat* and Van Gogh's *Self Portrait*. There are also important works by Thomas Cole and Frederic Church of the Hudson River School, as well as Caravaggio's *Ecstasy of St Francis* and Holman Hunt's *The Lady of Shalott*. Picasso, Dali, Warhol and Rauschenberg are also represented. Other rooms are devoted to applied arts: European porcelain, 17th- and 18th-century carved chests from Connecticut and Massachusetts, costumes, textiles and furniture.

95

Above left: a 'starburst' quilt in the Wadsworth Atheneum textile collection
Below left: local schoolmaster and patriot, Nathan Hale

CONNECTICUT

Insurance
Hartford's insurance industry began in the 18th century to cover ship-owners against loss of vessels. After the decline of shipping in the area, fire insurance grew in importance in the 19th century. Today about 40 companies, including Etna, Travelers and CIGNA, are based here.

Hartford's State Capitol: its exuberant design reflects Victorian pride

Bushnell Park, the nation's first landscaped public space, cuts a green swathe across the centre of the city and counts exotic rarities among its fine trees as well as a preserved carousel dating from 1914; a 1925 Wurlitzer organ provides the music. A grandiose brownstone structure known as the **Soldiers and Sailors Memorial Arch** (1886) honours citizens who served in the Civil War; its terracotta frieze depicts war scenes. In the park rises the gold-domed **State Capitol▶**, built in 1878 to the design of Richard Upjohn and adorned externally with bas-reliefs of historic scenes. Its lavishly ornate legislative chambers, Hall of Flags and gaudy silver and gold marble hall are grand gestures of civic pride. There are free tours from 9:15 to 1:15 every hour, and at 2:15 in July and August; (Saturdays only from April to October), or you can just walk in and look round yourself. Since 1988 the Capitol has been connected by walkway to the new Legislative Office, an impressive addition in polished granite.

At 800 Main Street is the **Old State House▶**, designed by Charles Bulfinch, which served as the state capitol from 1796 to 1878 and then the city hall up to 1915. Today it contains exhibitions of early Connecticut and Native American life, and a visitor information centre. Entrance is free. State memorabilia, including the 1662 royal charter and the Fundamental Orders of 1638, and a collection of Colt firearms are displayed at the **Museum of Connecticut History** at 231 Capitol Avenue (*closed*: Sunday; free).

West of downtown, at 351 Farmington Avenue, is the red-brick Gothic **Mark Twain House▶▶** (reached by bus E from the central transit station in Hartford). Samuel Clemens, alias Mark Twain (see pages 46–7), stipulated that his 19-room house should be unique. His personality still pervades what a local newspaper in 1874 described as 'the oddest house in Connecticut if not in the whole of America'. Here he wrote *Huckleberry Finn*, *Tom Sawyer* and five other major works up to 1891. Many of the original family pieces survive, including the items ranged on a mantelpiece, about which he used to tell stories to entertain his children. Each of these items had to feature in his story, and he had to start over again if he missed anything out.

Immediately adjacent is the **Harriet Beecher Stowe House►**, the home of the author of *Uncle Tom's Cabin* (see pages 46–7) from 1873 to her death in 1896, though most items here are not original. Harriet Beecher moved here while the Twain house was being built; at that time the neighbourhood was known as Nook Farm and comprised a small literary colony. Combined entry tickets for the two houses are available. (*Open*: daily, but closed Monday in winter.)

At 950 Trout Brook Drive, **West Hartford**, is the **Science Museum of Connecticut**, which has animal and planetarium shows and hands-on exhibits. At 227 South Main Street is the **Noah Webster House►**, the birthplace of the author of *An American Dictionary of the English Language* and *The American Speller* and has absorbing Webster memorabilia. (*Open*: daily in summer, except Wednesday; other seasons, afternoons only.)

On the north side of the city, at 200 Bloomfield Avenue at the University of Hartford, the **Museum of American Political Life►** (*open*: 11–4, Tuesday to Saturday) charts political campaigns, women's rights and prohibition movements from the time of George Washington.

Off I–91 at exit 26, the town of **Wethersfield►►**, settled in 1634, is one of the earliest settlements in the state. Its charming historic district, the state's largest, includes early 18th-century sea-captains' homes set along Broad Street, a huge, long green with houses set back. The **Webb-Deane-Stevens Museum►**, on Main Street (*open*: daily except Monday, May to October), comprises three restored houses. At the Webb House General George Washington and the Comte de Rochambeau planned the final campaign in the Revolution, leading to the British defeat at Yorktown in 1781. More period charm and a fascinating early kitchen are found in the **Buttolph-Williams House** of 1692, on Broad Street (also closed Monday). The **Keeney Memorial Cultural Center** has information and changing exhibitions on local history. Main Street ends at **Cove Park**, where one 17th-century warehouse survives from the days when Wethersfield was a port on the Connecticut river before it changed course.

Mark Twain's house, in the Nook Farm district of Hartford

The Charter Oak
A royal charter of 1662 gave a measure of independence to the Hartford colony; but in 1687 the new royal governor insisted it should be returned. At the meeting held to discuss the matter, the candles were suddenly extinguished and the charter vanished. It remained hidden (reputedly) in an oak tree for two years until the governor returned to England. In the 19th century Hartford's famous Charter Oak, as it had come to be known, was felled. Numerous items are said to be made from it, including the chair of the lieutenant-governor in the State Capitol.

Drive The Litchfield Hills

Early autumn in the Litchfield Hills

See map on pages 86–7.

A 64-mile tour of the highlands of Connecticut, taking in the best of the Housatonic Valley and the picture-postcard town of Litchfield. The autumn colours are superb .

Start from **New Milford**, with its attractive green, and where the Atelier Studio Gallery features work by over 100 artists. Take Route 7 north past **Bulls Bridge**, which boasts one of only two covered bridges in the state still open to motor traffic (off Route 7 to the left). The scenery becomes increasingly unspoilt and rugged along the **Housatonic Valley▶▶**, although foliage restricts views. The valley is known for trout-fishing and canoeing.

At **Kent** there are more antiques and crafts shops, and the **Sloane-**

Stanley Museum▶ (*open*: Wednesday to Sunday, May to October) exhibits bygone country tools collected by the late Eric Sloane. He considered these objects as 'symbols of American heritage, worthy of at least the same recognition as the popular current sculpture made from American junk'. He himself was a landscape painter and his studio has been re-created. Remains of an iron furnace in the grounds recall a vanished local industry. **Kent Falls State Park** is a roadside picnic stop-off, with pools for swimming where water tumbles down a 200-foot flight of natural steps. **Housatonic Meadow State Park** has picnic benches with a riverside setting and is popular with anglers. Just north, a sign on the west side of the road marks the start of the Pine Knob Loop Trail, leading up to a summit with a fine view. At **West Cornwall**, cross the covered bridge over the Housatonic river on the right.

Take Route 128 east to **Goshen** then Route 63 to **Litchfield▶▶**, the first National Historic District declared in the state and widely regarded as one of the finest towns in New England. In its heyday it was an industrial centre, with grist- and sawmills, iron forges, tanneries, fulling mills, carriage- and clock-makers and hatters' shops. During the Revolution it became a depot for military stores on roads linking Connecticut with the Hudson River Valley. The obvious legacy of the past is the wealth of Federal-style architecture along North, West, South and East streets, which radiate from the town's

A good place for an overnight stop is in this inn at Torrington

prominent and much-photographed Congregational Church (1829) on the spacious green.

In the middle of town, the **Litchfield Historical Society▶** maintains an archive library and a museum. By a genealogical fluke the Society inherited the world's largest collection of pictures by Ralph Earl, the foremost portrait painter in the US in the 18th century. The collection contains examples of Litchfield County furniture from the days when the area was a major craft-producing centre. Close by, the **Tapping Reeve House**

of 1774 (*open:* daily except Monday, May to October) belonged to Judge Tapping Reeve, who built America's first law college in 1784 in the grounds. A small exhibition commemorates its history and graduates.

Route 202 west passes the entrance to **Mount Tom State Park▶**, where a 1-mile trail leads to a tower at the 1,325-foot summit and a pleasant local view. At the junction with Route 45, divert northwest a short distance to take in **Lake Waramaug▶**, idyllically set beneath hills, and offering boating, swimming, picnics and camping; the far end of the lake has a tiny beach. Close by the lake, **Hopkins Vineyard** provides free tours and tastings.

Route 202 takes you back to New Milford. An optional detour is via Route 47 to the **Institute for American Indian Studies▶** at Washington. It has Algonquin arts and artefacts from up to 10,000 years ago. Highlights include a longhouse, a 17th-century Native American village and a simulated archaeological site.

Litchfield, an example of the perfect New England town

The New England village

■ **If there is one image that first-time visitors to New England bring with them, it is of white clapboard houses grouped round a village green, overlooked by the tall, white spire of a wooden church and set in rolling countryside against a backdrop of flaming, autumnal trees .....■**

A changing face

The New England village did not always present the face that is so cherished today. What is now a neat, attractive green, with its bandstand and war memorial, was once an unsightly, scrubby piece of common land. The clapboard house was not always archetypal white; until idealisation set in during the 19th century, houses were painted in a range of colours: reds, russets and blues. Even that icon, the tall, white church spire, has not always been there – many were added in the 19th century.

Farm buildings

While houses within the village itself are nowadays most often white, old wooden farm buildings are traditionally a deep red in colour. Particularly in the colder areas of New Hampshire and Maine, farm buildings are connected, so that the farmer can go from barn to shed to kitchen to house protected from the weather. (This also means, however, as many have learned to their cost, that fire too can move swiftly from barn to shed to house.)

The truth is that the New England village lives up to every expectation, serene as any calendar picture. The ingredients are always much the same. Facing on to a green is the white timber church, most often Unitarian or Congregationalist. Then there is the country store, a treasure chest that every visitor must delve into, selling anything from freshly made doughnuts and gourmet local products to cans of kerosene and farmers' rubber boots.

Larger villages often have a number of other, individually owned and equally enticing shops, selling clothes, gifts, books or crafts. Then there will be the town hall, seat of local government. And filling in the gaps around the green, and lining the roads leading to it are the timber-built houses that typify New England, usually painted white but occasionally traditional dusky shades. Some may fly the Union flag, many have a seasonal wreath of dried flowers on the door. One or two of these houses may be 'inns', private homes that offer accommodation and meals. Often dating back to colonial days and furnished with antiques, inns are a delightful way to enjoy the charm and hospitality of a New England village. Every village also has its burial ground, a plot of land set apart from the church or meeting-house.

The village way of life Because the houses are of timber, the local fire brigade is often a focus of social life, organising parades and, along with the churches, events such as barbecues and ice-cream socials. The green is a setting for regular flea markets and, during the Christmas season, for the tree which, like others, is decorated with white lights. Some villages boast a theatre.

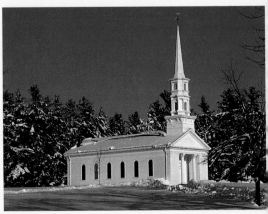

Village scenes: (top) autumn in Cohasset , MA, and (right) winter in Sudbury, MA

Masted sailing vessels moored on the Mystic river

▶▶▶ Mystic 87E2

Mystic Seaport▶▶▶ perhaps leads the field among New England's maritime museums. Built by the Mystic river, where numerous boat- and shipyards flourished before decline set in during the 1880s, the outdoor museum recreates life in a late 19th-century coastal community. Working craftspeople play the part; 22 period buildings make up the village, including a life-saving station, shipsmith's shop, meeting-house, bank, oyster house, school and chapel. Among the larger ships which you can board are the *Charles W Morgan* (1841), the last surviving American wooden whaler, and the *Joseph Conrad* (1882).

Mystic Marinelife Aquarium▶▶▶, with 6,000 living specimens, is a serious rival to the aquarium at Boston. There are blue lobsters, underwater views of penguins, whales and more. Gadgetry includes electronic quizzes and buttons to press which reverse the water flow in a tank. Whale, dolphin and sea-lion demonstrations take place hourly, and there are seal-, eagle- and whale-watching cruises in season (tel: 203/536 4200). Ocean samples are studied in Project Oceanology at Groton (see page 107).

Olde Mistick Village is an attractive speciality shopping area, replicated to look like the original colonial village. Both Mystic and neighbouring **Stonington** have a number of fine 19th-century homes recalling the maritime heyday. The **Denison Homestead**, on Pequot Sepos Road, Mystic, has been restored in the styles of five eras, ranging from colonial times to the early part of the 20th century. (*Open*: –5pm, Wednesday to Monday, 15 May to 15 October.)

On Route 2, on the Mashantucket Pequot Indian reservation, **Foxwoods Casino** is a growing success story (see page 125), drawing huge numbers of visitors. Like it or loathe it, the place is so bathed in commercialism as to be an experience despite itself. Other attractions include a Native American museum, a museum-experience' of American mankind and a turbo theatre (with a 360-degree screen).

Mystic cruises
River cruises on the last coal-fired passenger steamer to sail in the US, the SS *Sabino*, start from Mystic Seaport. The museum also runs trips on single-masted cat-boats. For reservations, tel: 203/572 5351.

The movie of the pizza
Mystic Pizza, a high-school kids' hang-out in the centre of town, became a legend when the movie *Mystic Pizza* put the town on the map. The eatery is plain for all to see, but filming actually took place in a lobster warehouse in nearby Stonington.

Life in a 19th-century seaport re-enacted at Mystic Seaport

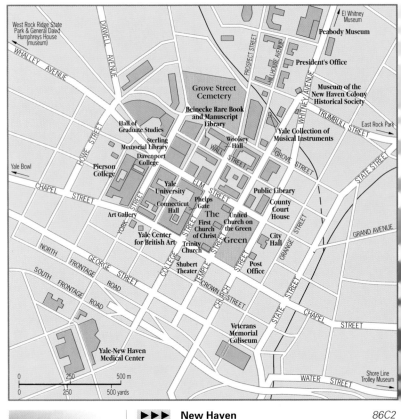

West Rock Ridge State Park & General David Humphreys House (museum)

WHALLEY AVENUE

DIXWELL AVENUE

PROSPECT STREET

LILAC AVENUE

El Whitney Museum

Peabody Museum

President's Office

Grove Street Cemetery

Beinecke Rare Book and Manuscript Library

Museum of the New Haven Colony Historical Society

WHITNEY AVENUE

TRUMBULL STREET

East Rock Park

Hall of Graduate Studies

Sterling Memorial Library

Woolsey Hall

Yale Collection of Musical Instruments

STATE STREET

Yale Bowl

HOWE STREET

Davenport College

WALL STREET

GROVE STREET

Pierson College

CHAPEL STREET

YORK STREET

ELM STREET

Yale University

Connecticut Hall

Phelps Gate

The

First Church of Christ

United Church on the Green

Public Library

County Court House

GRAND AVENUE

Art Gallery

Yale Center for British Art

Trinity Church

Green

City Hall

ORANGE STREET

STATE STREET

NORTH FRONTAGE

GEORGE STREET

Shubert Theater

TEMPLE STREET

Post Office

SOUTH FRONTAGE ROAD

CROWN STREET

CHURCH STREET

CHAPEL STREET

Veterans Memorial Coliseum

Yale-New Haven Medical Center

WATER STREET

Shore Line Trolley Museum

0   250   500 m
0   250   500 yards

Historic hamburgers
Not many fast-food establishments get on to the National Register of Historic Places. However, family-run Louis' Hamburgers in Crown Street, New Haven, made it by dint of being the birthplace of the American hamburger in 1900. Louis' retains its original grilling equipment. This is puritanical cuisine: toast, burger, lettuce and tomato only – strictly no ketchup or mustard. The turn-of-the-century fittings and Tiffany lamps are a far cry from McDonald's too.

▶▶▶ **New Haven**   86C2

Although it would take courage to rate the relative academic standards of Yale University at New Haven and Harvard University at Cambridge, Yale by far outstrips Harvard for visual interest for the day visitor. Eye-catching imitations of the medieval universities of Oxford and Cambridge in England are Yale's architectural hallmark. However, Yale and New Haven have little of the student–town interaction found between Harvard and Cambridge.

Founded in 1638 by the Puritans as an independent colony, New Haven is today a major cargo port, with a profusion of galleries, upmarket shops and good restaurants along Chapel Street.

Museums Natural history displays make up the bulk of the **Peabody Museum▶▶**. Most popular is the dinosaur collection, including the first discovered specimens of *Brontosaurus* and *Stegosaurus*. The *Deinonychus*, or 'Terrible Claw', inspired the vicious Raptor in the movie *Jurassic Park*. In the Hall of Mammals, an 11,000-year-old ground sloth (found in a tar pit in New Mexico) is remarkable for still having part of its skin and hair attached. Elsewhere, the museum displays Egyptian and Polynesian artefacts, geology exhibits, natural history dioramas and birds, and has a discovery room for children.

At 1080 Chapel Street, the **Yale Center for British Art▶▶** (*closed*: Monday; free) has a magnificent

collection of works by Turner, Hogarth, Constable, Reynolds and others, and puts on special exhibitions, talks and films (for details, tel: 203/432 2800). Less well known is the **Yale Collection of Musical Instruments▶**, at 15 Hillhouse Avenue, where 800 instruments include antique keyboards and entertaining oddities such as a 19th-century Italian-made Russian horn with a representation of a snake's head whose tongue vibrates when it is played. (*Open*: 1–4pm, Tuesday, Wednesday and Thursday; *closed*: July and August.)

The **Yale University Art Gallery▶▶** at 1,111 Chapel Street (*closed*: Monday; free), founded in 1832, has especially fine sections devoted to European paintings, a reconstructed Mithraic shrine, and a representative collection of American paintings and decorative arts.

The university Tours of **Yale University▶▶▶** from Phelps Gate on the Green are provided free by students at 10:30am and 2pm on weekdays; 1:30pm at weekends.

The university was founded at Branford in 1701, moved to Old Saybrook the same year and then to New Haven in 1716. Yale is the only collegiate university in the US, with students attached to the 12 colleges that belong to the university; the system is modelled on Oxford and Cambridge universities in England. Some 300 students live in each college, plus 100 freshmen on Old Campus.

In the present century, the architect James Gamble Rogers gave Yale an 'Oxbridge' look with his Georgian and Gothic-style buildings. To age the buildings, tiles were buried under different soils so that they would discolour and their edges become chipped. Acid was poured on the stonework, and glass was deliberately broken and releaded. Niches were left empty, as at Oxford and Cambridge, where so many statues have been stolen or otherwise destroyed through the ages.

The Green dates from colonial days when Puritan settlers laid out the town in neat squares, including this grazing ground. On one side, Phelps Gate leads into the **Old Campus**, where **Connecticut Hall**, built in the 1750s, is the oldest university building. The patriot Nathan Hale, industrialist Eli Whitney and lexicographer Noah Webster were students here. Hale's statue was made in 1914 by a sculptor who had no idea of his subject's true appearance, so a handsome Yale student was used as a model. The Theodore Dwight Woolsey statue is the only true likeness in the courtyard; his right foot is polished by students who rub it for good luck in their exams.

Above left and below: Yale University is an architectural show-piece, with buildings by leading 20th-century architects rubbing shoulders with Gothic Revival and Georgian creations

Where the shows began
From 1938 to 1976 New Haven's Shubert Theatre was the favourite venue to première new productions before transferring to Broadway. Début shows and plays have included *Oklahoma!*, *My Fair Lady*, *Blithe Spirit*, *The Sound of Music*, *A Streetcar Named Desire*, *Long Day's Journey into Night* and *Annie Get Your Gun*. WC Fields, the Marx Brothers, Sarah Bernhardt and Marlon Brando have all graced its stage. The theatre reopened in 1983 and gives performances between October and May.

CONNECTICUT

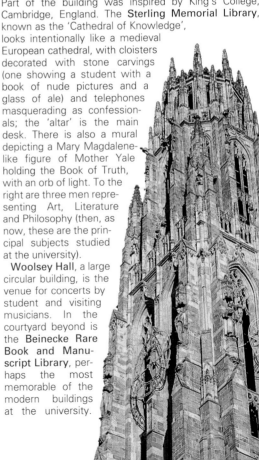

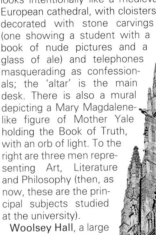

Above: home of the Yale Repertory Company
Right: Harkness Tower, a High Street landmark

Beyond the Old Campus, the neo-Gothic **Harkness Tower** (1920), the country's tallest free-standing tower when built (221 feet), was modelled on Boston Stump in Lincolnshire, England. Around its clock are sculptures of the eight great men of Yale: Nathan Hale, Eli Yale, Jonathan Edwards, Samuel FB Morse, Noah Webster, Eli Whitney, James Fenimore Cooper and John C Calhoun. **Wrexham Tower** was modelled on St Giles Church, Wrexham, Wales (where Eli Yale is buried), while **Pierson College**'s tower is based upon the design of Philadelphia's Independence Hall. **Davenport**, ex-President Bush's college, displays the ubiquitous Gothic treatment on the street frontage but its courtyard is in a very different Georgian style.

The art deco **Hall of Graduate Studies** (1932) resembles a miniature New York skyscraper with its chequered motif and flat relief. President and Hillary Clinton attended the **Law School**, opposite, whose stonework displays carvings of cops and robbers. Part of the building was inspired by King's College, Cambridge, England. The **Sterling Memorial Library**, known as the 'Cathedral of Knowledge', looks intentionally like a medieval European cathedral, with cloisters decorated with stone carvings (one showing a student with a book of nude pictures and a glass of ale) and telephones masquerading as confessionals; the 'altar' is the main desk. There is also a mural depicting a Mary Magdalene-like figure of Mother Yale holding the Book of Truth, with an orb of light. To the right are three men representing Art, Literature and Philosophy (then, as now, these are the principal subjects studied at the university).

Woolsey Hall, a large circular building, is the venue for concerts by student and visiting musicians. In the courtyard beyond is the **Beinecke Rare Book and Manuscript Library**, perhaps the most memorable of the modern buildings at the university.

Sporting spectaculars
Football in autumn at the Yale Bowl has been a major feature of New Haven life since 1913. Once every two years Yale and Harvard, the two old Ivy League rivals, battle it out in 'The Game'. Tennis superstars compete each August at the Volvo International Tennis Tournament. At Milford, jai alai, a Basque sport similar to squash, takes place daily (except Tuesday) from June to December. Although it is watched mainly for gambling, it is exciting and the entrance fee is nominal.

The library's ingenuity is revealed inside: the outer shell of Vermont marble shields a skyscraper-like stack of priceless books and manuscripts from the sun's ultra-violet rays, while halon gas is used to protect the contents from fire. The library is best seen on a sunny day when the translucence of the marble is apparent. There is no admittance to the stacks themselves, but a complete Gutenberg Bible of 1455, one of only 22 known, is displayed in the public area. Outside, you look down into the **Sculpture Garden**, a compact landscape of geometrical shapes formed in white marble by Isamu Noguchi (the library desk has a leaflet outlining the artist's ideas).

A windowless building close by is home to secret university societies, such as President Bush's Skull and Bones Society. Note how the **President's Office** is purposefully smaller than the other buildings: administration is seen as less important than academic life. In **Berkeley College**, Cross Campus Lawn is reputed to be the birthplace of the game of frisbee, first played here by students using pie dishes.

Take a trolley ride at the Shore Line Trolley Museum, East Haven

Out of town At Ansonia is **General David Humphreys House**, home of the aide to General Washington and the first US ambassador, (*open*: Monday to Friday; free). It is a museum with a difference, presented as a hands-on, late-18th-century experience, in which visitors dress up, spin, cook, and make bread and chowder in the manner of the period.

The **Eli Whitney Museum** at 915 Whitney Avenue (*open*: Wednesday to Sunday) Hamden, pays tribute to the inventor of mass-production and charts 200 years of industrial development in the New Haven area. Over 100 restored trolleys can be found at the **Shore Line Trolley Museum** at 17 River Street, East Haven, from where you can take a 3-mile trolley ride.

Northwest on Route 69 is **Shepherd's Farm**, a dairy farm whose Jersey herd provides the raw material for a celebrated ice-cream made on the premises. Further on, a sign on the left leads to the **Whitlock Book Barn** (*closed*: Monday), which has countless used and anti-quarian tomes, maps and prints crammed into two old turkey-brooder houses.

New Haven's stronghold
On 5 July 1779, 3,000 British and German Hessian troops were sighted in Long Island Sound. They succeeded in capturing the important port town of New Haven, but only after astonishing resistance from just 19 patriots ensconced at Black Rock Fort on the east side of the harbour. This fortification was rebuilt as Fort Nathan Hale and served in the War of 1812. It has since been restored and is open from Memorial Day weekend to Labor Day free of charge.

CONNECTICUT

A dramatic training centre
The Eugene O'Neill Theater Center at Waterford has been the training ground for hundreds of American actors; Meryl Streep and Al Pacino have been among them. Here, during the Playwright's Conference in July (drama) and August (musicals), you can watch new works in various stages of production. Performances are inexpensive, and the producer may substantially vary the presentation from one day to the next. You can listen in on rehearsals for free. (*Open*: daily except Sundays; at other times of the year, you can see students rehearse and perform.)

The US Coast Guard cutter Eagle, *a square-rigger used by the Coast Guard Academy as a training ship*

▶ **New London** 87E2

The seafaring town of New London has a mixture of gracious houses with lawns sloping to the water's edge and a brick-built port area. The latter has numerous survivals from its whaling days, which are also commemorated in the Maritime Museum inside the **Custom House**. The door timbers of this building were taken from the USS *Constitution*, the historic fighting ship of the War of 1812 (see page 67).

Captains of industry lived in Greek Revival mansions in Whale Oil Row (1832), which, together with the imposing railway station, echo former prosperity. Starr Street (1835) is strikingly uniform, its houses recently revamped. The **Joshua Hempsted House** (1678) and **Nathaniel Hempsted House** (1759) are typical of their period and are open to the public. Other notable survivals are the Burial Ground (1653), the New London County Courthouse (1784) and Union Station (1888). Incongruous beneath the huge I-95 viaduct, **Ye Olde Towne Mill** (free) originally dates from 1650 and retains its water-wheel and some historic documents.

On the harbour, a statue of the young Eugene O'Neill pays a belated tribute to the playwright, who was once held in popular esteem as no more than a drunken reprobate. His father bought **Monte Cristo Cottage**▶, close by the water, in 1880 and the summers spent here made a great impression on Eugene. The house (open to the public) was the setting of his autobiographical drama *Long Day's Journey into Night*.

The **US Coast Guard Academy, situated opposite Connecticut College,** trains aspiring coastguards from the age of 18. Below the visitors' centre in the grounds, the famous tall ship *Eagle*, where sea skills are taught, can be boarded free of charge on Sunday afternoons. Ironically for a vessel which has become a symbol of the US, it was built by the Germans in 1936, captured and brought back after World War II.

Ocean Beach Park, Waterford, a few miles south of New London

Across the Thames river is the naval base of **Groton**, no great beauty in itself but offering a free tour of the USS *Nautilus*▶ (*closed*: Tuesday), the world's first nuclear submarine, and film shows about life on board. At Niantic, the **South Eastern Connecticut Children's Museum** has plenty to keep youngsters occupied. At Waterford, mini golf, a 1-mile boardwalk and a water-slide are found at **Ocean Beach Park**.

Rocky Neck State Park, 3 miles west of Niantic, has a crescent beach, and is good for swimming, fishing and scuba diving. There are also picknicking and camping facilities.

▶▶▶ Norwalk   86A1

This oystering town is home to the **Maritime Museum▶▶▶**, one of New England's most ambitious to date. Housed in an old brick foundry, the museum features everything about the human and natural life of Long Island Sound, where even tropical fish can live because of the presence of the Gulf Stream. Its aquarium leads visitors through the inshore world of salt-marsh habitats and out to sea, with curved glass tanks and video selections explaining aspects of the ocean. Sharks and striped bass feature in the largest tank. Other displays include oyster boats, Long Island boats, diving equipment and boat-building. Hands-on activities make the atmosphere distinctly lively, with opportunities to design your own boat and to work out how sail and wind interact. Children can try out water flows and more in the 'Wet Lab'. Check ahead for details of lectures, events, cruises and demonstrations (tel: 203/852 0700); bookings are recommended for the IMAX movie theatre, with its screen as tall as a six-storey building.

Close by, at 295 West Avenue, the astonishing **Lockwood-Mathews Mansion▶▶** was the ostentatious 1860s precursor to the mansions of Newport (see pages 216–18) with its cavernous frescoed rooms, inlaid doors and magnificent staircase. Its semi-restored state (see panel) gives it an atmosphere of faded grandeur verging on the theatrical. Upper rooms give a good idea of the mansion's former glory and contain a wide-ranging collection of 19th-century music-boxes.

▶▶▶ Yale University   86C2

See New Haven, pages 102–5.

Stew Leonard's
Stew Leonard's in Norwalk is the world's largest dairy store, a food-lover's Disneyland with its animated displays of monkeys jumping between bananas and mock-ups of chickens laying eggs.

Sea adventure cruises
Project Oceanology, based at Mystic Aquarium (tel: 1-800/243 0416) operates 2½-hour trips from Groton to Ledge Light in summer. Participants set lobster pots, examine fish life and mud samples, and learn about marine pollution. Sunbeam Express (tel: 203/443 7259), runs whale-watching and deep-sea fishing excursions from Waterford. At South Norwalk, Island Girl cruises depart for Sheffield Island Lighthouse (tel: 203/334 9166), which guarded Norwalk Harbor from 1868; its ten rooms are open to the public.

Rebirth of a mansion
The Lockwood-Mathews Mansion was built for LeGrand Lockwood, who lost his fortune in a Wall Street crash in 1869. The house was sold to the Mathews family, then taken over by the city in 1938. The contents were sold, the floors covered with linoleum and the rooms used to store voting machines. Narrowly avoiding a threat of demolition in 1959, the mansion has been reunited with some of its former contents. Restoration began in 1966 but will take many years to complete.

MAINE

Mount Desert Island, near Somesville, has been popular with artists and summer visitors since the mid-19th century

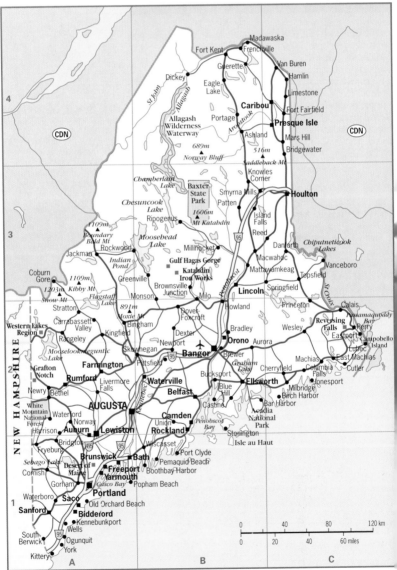

Madawaska
Fort Kent
Frenchville
Guerette
Dickey
Van Buren
Eagle Lake
Hamlin
Limestone
Caribou
Fort Fairfield
Portage
Presque Isle
Ashland
Mars Hill
St John
Allagash
Allagash Wilderness Waterway
689m
Norway Bluff
516m
Bridgewater
(CDN)
(CDN)
Aroostook
Saddleback Mt
Knowles Corner
Chamberlain Lake
Baxter State Park
Smyrna Mills
Houlton
Chesuncook Lake
Patten
1606m
Island Falls
1109m
Ripogenus
Mt Katahdin
Reed
Boundary Bald Mt
Moosehead Lake
Millinocket
95
Danforth
Chiputneticook Lakes
Jackman
Rockwood
Gulf Hagas Gorge
Macwahoc
Vanceboro
Indian Pond
Katahdin Iron Works
Mattawamkeag
Topsfield
Coburn Gore
1109m
Greenville
Brownsville Junction
Milo
Lincoln
Springfield
1203m Kibby Mt
Monson
Penobscot
Princeton
Calais
Snow Mt
Flagstaff Lake
891m
Dover-Foxcroft
Howland
St Croix
Passamaquoddy Bay
Stratton
Moxie Mt
Bingham
Bradley
Wesley
Reversing Falls
Perry
Carrabassett Valley
Kingfield
Newport
Dexter
Orono
Aurora
Eastport
Campobello Island
Western Lakes Region
Rangeley
Skowhegan
Bangor
Brewer
Machias
Lubec
Mooselookmeguntic Lake
Farmington
Pittsfield
95
Graham Lake
Cherryfield
Columbia Falls
East Machias
Cutler
Grafton Notch
Rumford
Livermore Falls
Waterville
Bucksport
Ellsworth
Jonesport
Newry
Bethel
Belfast
Blue Hill
Milbridge
Birch Harbor
White Mountain National Forest
Waterford
Norway
AUGUSTA
Castine
Bar Harbor
Acadia National Park
Harrison
Auburn
Lewiston
Camden
Union
Penobscot Bay
Stonington
Bridgton
Rockland
Isle au Haut
Fryeburg
Sebago Lake
Brunswick
Bath
Wiscasset
Port Clyde
Cornish
Desert of Maine
Freeport
Boothbay Harbor
Pemaquid Beach
Gorham
Yarmouth
Popham Beach
Casco Bay
Waterboro
Portland
Saco
Sanford
Old Orchard Beach
Biddeford
Kennebunkport
South Berwick
Wells
Ogunquit
Kittery
York

NEW HAMPSHIRE

| 0 | | 40 | | 80 | | 120 km |
| 0 | 20 | | 40 | | 60 miles | |

Maine The summer vacationland of Maine is slightly larger than all the other New England states put together and has the lowest population density. Even with a massive influx of summer visitors to the coast there are still places where you can find remoteness. Easily the most crowded part is from Camden to the New Hampshire border; even here there are areas of quiet charm if you are prepared to seek them out, but development along and around Route 1 is dense and often disappointingly drab. Further up the coast, **Acadia National Park** is the undisputed jewel in the crown and the coast's only appreciable hilly area. Beyond that, the crowds thin out substantially. Even then, the intricate coast is elusive: drivers won't see much of it, and access on foot is limited.

Although **Augusta** is the state capital, **Portland** is certainly the cultural epicentre, and the only place that feels like a substantial city. Freeport and Kittery are factory-outlet shopping towns.

Trees and more trees With forests covering 17 million acres, Maine is nicknamed the Pine Tree State. About 90 per cent of the land is forested, and Maine has for long lived off its appreciable timber supplies. The state is also referred to as Downeast, as the prevailing wind pushes sailing boats eastwards 'down' the coast. The term 'Downeaster' refers to any Maine-built ship.

Many Maine villages are now gentrified, but pockets of Downeast atmosphere remain at numerous fishing villages and coastal settlements. Distances between towns increase as you head north or east,and the towns get smaller and roads emptier. Inland, paper companies own vast tracts of Maine's forests; many of the roads are private. Today paper-making accounts for nearly 35 per cent of the state's total value of manufactured products.

On the few public roads, you will encounter huge and somewhat terrifying lumber trucks every few minutes or so, which have right of way (and should be given a very wide berth).

Rocky shores and dark coniferous trees typify the coast of Acadia National Park

Early days The state was settled by European explorers from early times. In the early 1600s, French and English settlers established themselves on the St Croix and Kennebec rivers respectively. Charles I then gave the territory to Sir Ferdinando Gorges and made him Lord of New England in 1635. The Massachusetts Colony purchased Maine, which remained part of Massachusetts until becoming an independent state in 1820.

From colonial times up until the latter part of the 19th century, Maine supported a flourishing ship-building industry. America's first sawmill was built in 1634 at South Berwick and by 1840 this number had increased to 1,400. Maine has produced more wooden sailing ships than any other state in the Union.

Sebago Lake offers boating, swimming and fishing

Maine salt-of-the earth

Lumber facts
● From the 1630s to 1850s sawmills made use of the 'sash saw', an up-down moving frame. A later invention was the circular-saw blade.
● Winter is the best season for felling, when the sap is down.
● In former times logs were placed on ice-covered lakes or rolled down to streams or rivers to be carried toward the sea each spring. As sawn logs could not be floated, sawmills were located close to shipping ports.

Blueberry bounties
Blueberries are harvested by a special rake, boxed on three sides. Cherryfield, the 'blueberry capital of the world', and Machias are the main processing centres.

Native Americans used to dry the berries for winter rations, and used them as healing potions.

Maine traits Inhabitants of Maine have a reputation for being frank and down-to-earth. They keep their cool and don't always smile at strangers (an off-putting attitude to some).

Maine is among the nation's poorest states. While that may seem hard to believe as you scan the antique and crafts shops in the smart resorts of Penobscot Bay, Kennebunkport, Ogunquit and elsewhere, the remoter areas see younger people drifting out of the state and there are high unemployment rates (particularly in the Native American reservations). Much employment is seasonal. Tourism is the biggest earner – hence the slogan 'Vacationland' on car licence-plates. Crowds flock to the coast in summer and, in the fall, foliage and winter sports draw visitors inland.

Maine at work Agricultural labourers spend August and September working on the wild blueberry harvest. Maine produces 90 per cent of the nation's output of this fruit, which grows mostly in Washington County in the state's eastern corner. Potatoes are the largest crop in the state, with over 20 million hundredweight harvested each year. From late October to early November, the Christmas wreath industry is at full swing. Maine has just the right type of balsam fir brush for this purpose, and the finished product graces the doors of many American homes.

Because of the harsh winters, the fishing and packing industries operate at maximum capacity when the weather allows it. Some three-quarters of the nation's lobsters come from Maine. Lobster is a ubiquitous menu item; even McDonald's restaurants offer lobster sandwiches in their Maine branches in summer. Meanwhile, Rockland, Prospect Harbor and Lubec are major centres for sardine canning.

Events

For further information contact the state tourist office (see page 266) or chambers of commerce.

January
Sugarloaf USA/Carrabassett:
Children's Festival Week: fireworks, torchlight parade, pool parties and more.

February
Western Mountain Winter Wonderland Week, Bethel: balloon and sleigh rides, dog sledding.
Annual National Toboggan Championship, Camden: races, chowder challenge, numerous events.

March
Ice-fishing Tournament, Rockwood, Moosehead Lake.
New England Sled Dog Races, Rangeley.
Log Drivers Bean Hole Bean Cookout, Island Falls: torchlight parade, bonfire and other events.

April
Fishermen's Festival, Boothbay Harbor.
Kenduskeag Stream Canoe Races, Bangor: whitewater open-canoe races.
Maine Maple Sunday, statewide: sugar houses demonstrate the production of 'liquid gold' maple syrup.

May
Moosemania, Rockwood: month-long moose-related activities and events.

June
Rodeo and Country Weekend, Farmington.
Windjammer Days, Boothbay Harbor: schooner races.

July
Bar Harbor Music Festival: classical and popular music (summer series; ends August).
Camden Garden House Tour: houses and gardens open to the public.
Clam Festival, Yarmouth: the biggest festival in Maine, with carnival, seafood, crafts, fireworks, children's parade, and other events.
Great Schooner Race, Rockland.

August
Blueberry Festival, Machias: harvest celebration.

Indian Day Celebration, Perry: Pasmaquoddy crafts, dancing, meals, traditional games.
Retired Skippers' Race, Castine.
Maine Lobster Festival, Rockland: a feast of Maine's most succulent crustacean in its busiest fishing port.

September
Blue Hill Fair, Blue Hill: on Labor Day weekend.
Tour d'Acadia: bike race from Bar Harbor.
Bluegrass Festival, Brunswick.

October
Living History Days, Leonard Mills, Bradley: water-wheel and sawmill demonstrations, horse and buggy rides, antique costumes.
Harvestfest, York: colonial celebration.
Fryeburg Fair: Maine's largest agricultural fair.

November
Lighting of Nubble Lighthouse, Long Sands Beach, York.
Christmas United Maine Craftsman Show, Brewer.

December
Christmas Prelude, Kennebunkport: Christmas events.

A maple sugaring demonstration at the big agricultural fair held annually in Fryeburg

MAINE

Acadia trips
Horse-and-carriage tours
can be taken from
Wildwood Riding Stables
from Memorial Day to
October (tel: 207/276 3622).
Sailing trips on *Blackjack*
run four times daily from
Northeast Harbor (tel:
207/288 3056), while two-
person glider rides leave
from Bar Harbor Airport on
Route 31 (tel: 207/667
SOAR). For mountain tours:
Jolly Roger's Trolley (tel:
207/288 3327), Oli's Trolley
(tel: 207/288 9899), and bus
tours run by the national
park. Cycling on the traffic-
free carriage roads and on
the Loop Road is possible;
for rentals, Acadia Bike &
Canoe, 48 Cottage Street,
Bar Harbor (tel: 207/288
9605).

▶▶▶   **Acadia National Park**   *108B2*

This scenic national park is dominated by the 1,530-foot
granite form of **Cadillac Mountain**▶▶▶, the highest
point on the US Atlantic coast. While no one can expect
solitude in high summer, Acadia is undeniably one of the
best places for hiking on the entire New England
seaboard. It gives outstanding opportunities for observing
wildlife, both flora (boreal northern and temperate southern species) and fauna.

In 1919 Acadia became the first national park east of the
Mississippi. Mount Desert Island (the major part of the
national park, connected to the mainland by bridge) was
endowed a 57-mile system of scenic carriage roads by
John D Rockefeller, Jr. He considered Mount Desert
Island 'one of the great views of the world' and donated
more than 10,000 acres to the national park. Meanwhile,
Bar Harbor became the summer society rival of Newport,
Rhode Island, as the Astors, Rockefellers, Vanderbilts,
Fords and others ensconced themselves here for the
season. In 1947, a fire destroyed more than 60 of the
millionaires' 'summer cottages'. Today everything is very
much visitor-oriented.

Visiting Acadia In July and August, **Bar Harbor** (outside
the park boundary) becomes one of the busiest points on
the Maine coast. It is the most practical place for accom-

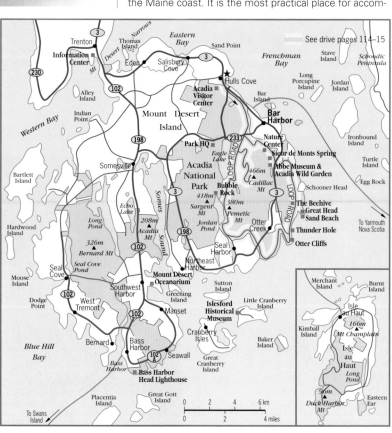

modation, eating and shopping, as well as a starting point for whale-watching cruises, bicycle hire, kayaking tours and sailing trips. Ferries sail from here for Nova Scotia. In the town are the Natural History Museum, the Oceanarium, the Wendell Tiley Museum of Bird Carving and the Bar Harbor Historical Museum.

Route 3 makes a drab entrance to Acadia, a virtually unbroken strip of motels, malls and amusement parks, but things soon get better. Most visitors concentrate on the east side of Mount Desert Island by following the **Park Loop Road**►►► (see pages 114–15).

The west side is much quieter and less dramatic, but tempting as an escape from the crowds, though many of the summits are wooded and viewless. Bass Harbor, Bernard, Southwest Harbor and Northeast Harbor are typical Maine fishing villages, and not particularly touristy. **Echo Lake** is good for swimming by virtue of being warmer than the waters on the coast. **Northeast Harbor** is a starting point for cruises into the Sound and out to the Cranberry Isles. From the village the **Sargent Drive** (cars and bicycles only) skirts the east side of **Somes Sound**►►, the East Coast's only fjord, carved by glaciers then flooded by the sea. An undemanding 2½-mile walk from Route 102 up Acadia Mountain on the sound's western side offers an outstanding view. **Bass Harbor Head Lighthouse** (1858) ranks among Maine's most photogenic lighthouses and can be reached by car.

Route 186 leads to **Birch Harbor** where you can follow the one-way coastal loop road to **Schoodic Point**►, which gives views of Mount Cadillac.

Acadia's furthest-flung outpost, **Isle au Haut**►, lies in Penobscot Bay and is reached by ferry from Stonington (no cars taken; tel: 207/367 5193). Quiet trails wind through the island's spruce forests and along its rugged shores; there is a small campsite. Ranger-led excursions are offered to **Great Cranberry Island**. **Little Cranberry Island** has a free museum covering maritime and local history. Ranger-led walks, often with a natural history content, are given free of charge in the park. Trailheads are mostly well-marked from the road.

With temperate and sub-Arctic species, such as this wild iris, Acadia is a rich hunting ground for naturalists

Information sources
Thompson Island Information Center can help with accommodation and campsites, while the national park Visitor Center provides information and hiking maps.

For information and reservations, contact Acadia National Park, Bar Harbor, ME 04609 (tel: 207/288 3338); for camping reservations, tel: 1-800/365 2267. Between June and October the park publishes *Acadia Beaver Log*, a free newspaper listing ranger-led tours, cruises and walks.

113

Bar Harbor

There are numerous viewpoints along the coastal roads

Drive **Acadia's Park Loop Road**

See map on page 112.

This scenic (mostly one-way) 27-mile road skirts Cadillac Mountain and provides a series of views that encapsulate the stunning beauty of Acadia. Although the loop can easily be driven in two hours or so, it merits a full day so that some of its trails can be experienced to the full. It may also be undertaken as a bicycle tour (there are several bike-rental shops in Bar Harbor), although some

ACADIA NATIONAL PARK

UNITED STATES DEPARTMENT OF THE INTERIOR
NATIONAL PARK SERVICE

Some of Mount Desert's early summer residents (in 1913) presented the US government with lands which in 1919 were declared a national park

may find the traffic at peak times mars enjoyment. Parking is rarely a problem as you can stop anywhere on the right-hand side of the two-track road along its one-way section. Week-long or seasonal passes must be bought on entering the park; entrance is free for US citizens over 62 or registered as having disabilities.

The **Hulls Cove Visitor Center▶** marks the start of the Loop Road and has a diorama of the park and a film show about Acadia's natural history.

The **Acadia Wild Garden▶**, created by the Bar Harbor Garden Club in co-operation with the national park, demonstrates the range of wild flowers and vegetation that can be found in contrasting sites such as beach, bog, mountain heath and mixed woodlands. Immediately adjacent are the Nature Center, the **Sieur de Monts Spring** and the **Abbe Museum▶** of Indian artefacts, which tells the story of the local Native American inhabitants before the Frenchman Samuel de Champlain discovered Mount Desert Island in 1604.

One of the toughest walks, definitely not for vertigo-sufferers, is the **Precipice Trail▶**, which ascends lofty crags by means of rungs and ladders. In recent years, peregrine falcons have been nesting here and consequently the trail has been closed in the summer months. **Sand Beach▶**, the only sandy beach in the park, has great beauty but the water stays decidedly cool on even the hottest August day. If you turn right out of

Silver birch trees growing behind the sandy shore of Sand Beach

Sand Beach car park along the road, the trailhead for the **Beehive Trail▶** is almost immediately on the left. The short but strenuous path makes a spectacular ascent. There is an easier (less interesting) route which may be taken as a safe descent. Go right at the first path junction, and from the summit go forward, following signs for the Loop Road.

Exquisite views can be enjoyed from the **Ocean Trail▶** (3.6 miles there and back), one of the most scenic easy walks in the national park. It runs closely parallel to the road, along the cliffs between Sand Beach and Otter Point. **Thunder Hole**, beside the road, needs bad weather to look its best, when the waves are tossed into the rock niche and the spray slants across its entrance. Otherwise it is little more than a minor chink in the coastline with pleasant rocks on which to sit.

The **Gorham Mountain Trail▶** offers further spectacular high-level views which are similar to those on the Beehive Trail (you can make a longer walk along the ridge to take in the Beehive), but the trail itself is less demanding. Just below the trail is Cadillac Cliff, an overhanging rock with a small cave.

Where the one-way traffic ends, you can detour south past **Seal Harbor**, a sandy beach, to **Northeast Harbor**, from where you can take a cruise (see panel on page 112). Alternatively, continue north to **Jordan Pond▶**, which has nature trails through the woods and along the lakeside. A longer scenic trail encircles the entire lake. The half-mile trail to South Bubble Summit, a 768-foot protuberance with a fine panorama, passes **Bubble Rock▶**, a classic glacial 'erratic' (deposited boulder), balanced on its side.

The summit road to **Mount Cadillac▶▶▶** needs careful timing for the best of the light and the view, both of which can change in quality for better or worse within minutes. When conditions are right you can see as far as Mount Katahdin (5,267 feet), Maine's highest point, located inland in distant Baxter State Park. Hikers who want the satisfaction of reaching a similar viewpoint without the crowds should follow the Dorr Mountain Trail, a short distance east of Sieur de Monts Spring.

115

■ **So prolific was the lobster in the days of the early colonists that they would catch it with hooks or spears in shallow waters and feed it to chickens and prisoners. Today lobstering is one of New England's proudest traditions and the king of seafood is dispatched to top restaurants across the world .....■**

Lobstering lore

Each harbour has its own close-knit society, one that guards its trade fiercely. Fishing territories are strictly defined, by tradition, and each fisherman's buoys are painted in his own colours. Trespass and you may find, as one Portland fisherman did in 1993, a bomb in your trap. The scalloper who drags his nets and scoops along the ocean floor and falls foul of a lobster pot or two won't find a warm reception either.

For a closer look

Several ports operate trips on lobstering boats in summer months, including Bar Harbor, Boothbay Harbor and Ogunquit in Maine, and Gloucester in Massachusetts. Remember to take warm clothes.

Lobster pounds are the best place to enjoy the day's catch – straight from the sea

The tradition The American lobster, *Homarus americanus*, lives along the Atlantic coast between Labrador and North Carolina, being particularly plentiful off the coast of New England. Trapping on a commercial basis began in southern New England by 1800. By the mid-1800s the hoop net had been introduced, which meant lobster could be caught without damage, and Maine, by now heading the trade, was transporting live lobsters in sailing 'smacks' to New York and Boston, where they were boiled and sold on the streets. The Maine fishery also supplied no fewer than 23 canning factories with smaller, less saleable lobster. Canning ceased at the turn of the present century, but lobstering is still a vital part of the coastal economy, not only attracting tourists but also providing work for local industry producing the boats and the slatted trap that, with modifications, has been used for decades.

The catch Harbours bobbing with boats and wharves stacked high with traps and buoys reveal little of the tough life the 'trapper' leads. In all weathers he heads out to his line of buoys (pronounced 'boo-ies') at daybreak and winches up the strings of pots. Many trappers have up to 50 traps per string and 1,000 traps in all. Each lobster is measured to ensure it is of legal size; 'keepers' are typically 10 inches long overall, 1–1½ pounds in weight and about five years old. The bait (dead fish) is renewed, the lobster pots are returned to the ocean floor, and then the catch is turned in to the dealer. It's no easy way to make a living.

► **Augusta** *108A2*

Maine's state capital is not a place that routinely attracts visitors, but it has a handful of good sights justifying a brief detour. The town lies on the Kennebec river at the site of an early Pilgrim colony. Along the river extends the green swath of 34-acre Capitol Park. Above stands the prominent **State House►**, dating from 1832 but extended twice since Charles Bulfinch designed it. The façade is original, although the dome replaced a cupola in the early 1900s. The building is open in normal office hours (*closed*: weekends). Wall panels provide a self-guided tour to its function and history.

Next door, the **Maine State Museum►** presents attractive displays covering various aspects of the state's industry and life from the Ice Age to the present. Lumbering and ice-harvesting, two of the city's former mainstays, feature in the 'Made in Maine' displays, together with exhibits of the state's ship-building, sardine-canning and farming industries.

Fort Western►, the oldest wooden fort in the US (1754), occupies the site of a Pilgrim trading post established near the river in the 1620s. The need for the fort arose from the colonists' nervousness of the French and Indians. It was never besieged and it became a trading post during its 12-year history as a fort. Its design was that of a typical New England fort, with a 100-foot-long main house. William Harvard, the commander, made the fort his home from 1766 to 1810, which is why it has survived; today it is presented as a house rather than a barracks. Reconstructions of the stockade blockhouses, with replica cannons and guns, date from 1921. Cannon firing takes place at weekends, and guides in period costume show visitors round. (*Open*: 10–5, mid-June to Labor Day, weekends 1–5; then 1–4, weekends only until Columbus Day.)

Out of town, the **Matthews Museum** at Union comprises a collection of bygones, including a schoolroom, a horse-drawn hearse, a cooper's shop, a colonial kitchen, spinning and weaving items, and farm tools.

The Federal-style Blaine House (1833) in Augusta is the official residence of the state's governors

The birth of Moxie
The locally popular soft drink known as Moxie began life at Union, near Augusta, in 1885. Its inventor, Dr Augustin Thompson, originally sold it as Moxie Nerve Food. The Matthews Museum in the village has an interesting collection of memorabilia.

FORT WESTERN MUSEUM · 1754 · ON THE KENNEBEC

MAINE

Above and below right: ships' figureheads and marine art feature among the indoor displays at Bath's maritime museum

King of Bangor
Stephen King, the author, lives in West Broadway, Bangor, and his fans frequently track him down. Many of his novels and films have a local setting. Betts Bookstore in Main Street specialises in Stephen King books and memorabilia.

Lumber capital
In the 19th century Bangor was the world's largest lumber-exporting centre. The industry peaked in 1872, when 2,200 ships entered Bangor via the Penobscot river in a year, but the timber supply waned and ship-building declined as paper-making assumed an important role in the state. Between Milford and Brewer, off Route 178, the Maine Logging Museum at Orono stands on the site of Leonard's Mills (1790). It features a working water-powered sawmill, a sawing demonstration, a trapper's cabin and more. For hours, tel: 207/581 2871.

Bangor   108B2

Bangor is more a commercial centre than a visitor destination. Although victim of a fire in 1911 and much redeveloped in the 1960s, the city retains some fine buildings, notably along Broadway, High Street and the streets leading off. The **Thomas Hill Standpipe** in Summit Park is a unique contribution to Bangor's skyline. Built in 1897, this water-tower observation point is floodlit at night. During weekday afternoons, the **Historical Society** operates a museum in a Greek Revival house at 159 Union Street, and runs bus tours of the city's sights on Thursdays at 10:30am.

Bangor's heyday is chronicled in the **Old Town Museum** on North 4th Street (*open*: 1–5pm, Wednesday to Sunday; free). At the I–95 and I–395 intersection, the **Cole Land Transportation Museum** boasts over 200 vehicles, including snow-ploughs and logging trucks from old Maine.

▶▶   Bath   108A1

Bath's **Maine Maritime Museum and Shipyard▶▶**, at 243 Washington Street, is the most ambitious of its kind in the state. It occupies the last surviving wooden shipbuilding yard in the nation, used by Percy & Small from 1897 to 1920. The *Wyoming*, the largest ever sail vessel used in the country, was built here. Inside the Maritime History Building, a museum display tells the story of Maine's seafaring past from the days of the early explorers to 20th-century tourism and fishing. The museum possesses over 200 paintings and drawings, 250 models and 100 boats.

In the Percy & Small shipyard you can see apprentices at work restoring and building wooden boats on weekdays. Five of the original buildings survive; displays include small craft and the story of lobstering. Tours of the shipyard, available at no extra cost, are highly recommended.

Special cruises usually take place on Tuesdays, in addition to a regular programme of 50-minute narrated boat trips on *Hardy II*. The latter pass the Bath Iron Works, the state's largest industrial employer, and a major shipyard. It is usually possible to board vessels by the museum piers, including the *Sherman Zwicker*, where you can get an idea of the tough life endured by the Great Banks cod fishermen.

▶▶▶ Baxter State Park 108B3

The park is one of the more accessible parts of Maine's unpopulated mountains and forests. Wild flowers, hiking, geology, whitewater rafting, cross-country skiing, moose-spotting, hunting, canoeing and fishing are among its attractions.

Baxter Peak (5,267 feet) is the summit of **Mount Katahdin**▶▶▶ and marks the northern end of the 2,100-mile Appalachian Trail to Georgia. It is the highest point in Maine and probably the only mountain in the state to have remained bare of trees since glaciation. Several trails lead to the top, including the famous **Knife Edge Trail**, which edges its way along a sharp glacial ridge, or arête. Two cirques (glacial hollows) flank the Knife Edge, which is just 3 feet wide in places and with dizzy drops on either side of up to 2,000 feet. The trail is strictly for experienced walkers in calm weather conditions.

Great Basin is the finest of seven cirques on the mountain; the Chimney Pond Trail from Roaring Brook campsite gives access. Outstanding for its arctic wildflowers, the Tableland has abundant evidence of freeze-thaw weathering processes on the rocks scattered over it.

Other notable trails include **Doubletop Mountain**, **South Turner**, the **Owl** and **The Brothers**. Moose may often be seen at **Big** and **Little Niagara Falls**.

Southwest of Baxter State Park, the West Branch of the Penobscot river has its moment of glory as it gushes though **Ripogenus Gorge**▶▶ (access by unpaved road). Over a mile long, the gorge has almost vertical sides up to 200 feet high, with the rock strata exposed like a school textbook diagram. It can be seen on foot or by whitewater rafting or canoeing.

Further south, near Brownville Junction, is **Gulf Hagas**▶▶, another magnificent canyon best reached from Lloyd Pond. Here, the West Branch of the Pleasant river tumbles over five waterfalls, a memorable sight when in full spate in spring. Allow six hours for the hike.

The Lumberman's Museum (*open*: summer except July and August), at **Patten**, has 10 buildings that tell the story of the state's lumber industry. There is also a museum of bygones at the paper-producing town of **Millinocket**.

An industrial ghost town
Gulf Hagas canyon can be included in a visit to the site of the Katahdin Iron Works, signposted off Route 11 south of Millinocket. Now a state memorial park, it retains kilns and a stone furnace as reminders of a mining town which in the 19th century produced almost 2,000 tons of raw iron per year and employed nearly 200 men.

Camping at Baxter
For information about camping in Baxter State Park, contact Baxter State Park Authority, 64 Balsam Drive, Millinocket, ME 04462 (tel: 207/723 5140). Reservations are advisable in summer as the numbers of campsites and lean-tos (simple shelters) are deliberately restricted.

Baxter State Park is easily accessible and is one of the best places in Maine for moose-spotting

Sunrise canoeing
A lovely way to enjoy the wildlife and scenery of the Western Lakes area is to take a dawn canoe trip. Look for advertisements in Rangeley, for instance, for a guided trip that offers the chance to watch beavers and moose, and be serenaded by birdsong as the mists rise.

Moss garden
A few minutes' walk from Moose Cave in Grafton Notch State Park (signposted from the lay-by on Route 26) is this little fairy-tale clearing. A silvery carpet of reindeer moss (*Cladonia rangifera*), an exquisite erect ferny lichen, is interspersed with other mosses, some cool green and smooth, others darker and upright. With the tiny pine seedlings, it looks like a miniature forest.

One of Bethel's many pretty houses

▶▶   **Bethel and the Western Lakes**   108A2

The Western Lakes Region, stretching north from Sebago Lake up to the lakes and mountains around Rangeley, includes some of New England's most beautiful countryside, with forested hills rolling down to crystal lakes and rivers. The further north you go, the more remote and wild it all becomes. It's a paradise for the lover of the great outdoors, with wonderful opportunities for walking, camping, fishing, golfing, sketching and moose-spotting. In summer there is boating of all sorts on the lakes and rivers, in winter every type of snow-sport and in autumn, of course, the brilliant foliage.

At the heart of the region is **Bethel**▶▶, a classic New England small town with a handful of crafts shops, inns and restaurants. Near by is the burgeoning Sunday River ski resort (see page 229). Alongside the road that passes the resort from Newry is one of Maine's most photographed covered bridges, **Sunday River Bridge**, built in 1870. Northwest of Newry is **Grafton Notch State Park**▶▶, an area of gorges, waterfalls and mountains, where walks range from short hikes marked from easy access points, such as Screw Augur Falls Gorge and Mother Walker Falls Gorge, to challenging trails up Table Rock or Old Speck Mountain. Those interested in Maine's economy will find **Rumford** worth a look for its all-encompassing paper mills, one of several in this important lumbering area.

Rangeley▶ is the hub of the Rangeley Lakes region, which offers over 450 square miles of canoeing, sailing, swimming, fishing and walking. The town has hotels, restaurants, campsites and sports shops (for rentals and licences), and a spectacularly sited golf course. The Rangeley State Park has chalets, picnicking and boat-launching areas, and nearby Saddleback Mountain is excellent for winter sports.

South of Bethel is **Fryeburg**, a canoeing centre (with hire shops) famed for its agricultural fair in October. **Harrison**, set between Long Lake and Crystal Lake, is a another good centre for the outdoor enthusiast. Famous for its trout and land-locked salmon fishing, **Sebago Lake**▶▶ is ringed with small towns offering every facility for the watersports enthusiast.

Boothbay Harbor is a busy boating resort as well as an active fishing port

Visiting Monhegan Island
In 1614 Captain John Smith landed here, and settlers followed 11 years later. The island then became an artists' haunt: Rockwell Kent and Edward Hopper were among those who visited and painted the cliffs and the great ocean panoramas.

Trips are offered from Boothbay Harbor by Balmy Days Cruises (tel: 207/633 2284), from New Harbor by Hardy Boat Cruises (tel: 207/677 2026) and by Laura B from Port Clyde (tel: 207/372 8848).

Rafting
New England Whitewater Center operates raft trips on the Kennebec, Dead and Penobscot rivers between April and October: Box 21, Caratunk, ME 04925 (tel: 1-800/766 7238).

▶ **Boothbay Harbor**   *108B1*

Settled in the 17th century and developed for tourism from the 1870s, Boothbay Harbor is the largest boating harbour northeast of Boston, as well as a busy resort town packed with boutiques and galleries. The self-proclaimed 'boating capital of New England' offers over 50 daily cruises, the best choice in Maine – including seal-, whale- and puffin-watching trips, deep-sea fishing expeditions and tours of the coast and islands. By the Lobsterman's Co-op, the Sea Pier Aquarium is stocked by local fishermen and contains a good variety of species from the Gulf of Maine.

Out of town along Route 27 is **Miss Daisy Farm**, a petting zoo with llamas, goats, sheep and rabbits. On the east side of Route 27, near its intersection with Route 1, **Boothbay Railway Village** is a village theme park encompassed by a narrow-gauge railway, where an original narrow-guage train hauls you through woods inhabited by garden gnomes. There is a collection of re-erected buildings to explore (a blacksmith's shop, an old fire station, a village school and more). For the most part, you can only look inside the buildings from the entrance.

Some 10 miles offshore, **Monhegan Island**▶▶ is only 1½ miles across at its widest, but has surprising variety, including some 400 species of wildflowers. The Cliff Trail runs the length of the island and there are fine walks in the balsam-scented Cathedral Woods, as well as 160-foot cliffs on the east side. The island is partly developed for visitors, with shops and restaurants.

Across the inlet east of Boothbay Harbor is one of the loveliest parts of Maine's seaboard, **Pemaquid Point**▶▶, which is graced by wave-sculpted rocks and wind-battered ledges. Pemaquid Point Light (1827) presides over the scene, while the former lighthouse-keeper's cottage functions as a museum of commercial fishing and a small art gallery, open in summer. At nearby **Pemaquid Beach**▶, a sand beach rare for these parts, is the Colonial Pemaquid Restoration, the excavated site of an early 17th-century mariners' settlement, with an adjacent museum. Fort William Henry is a replica of a 1692 fort and forms part of a state park.

A local lobsterman with his catch

Massachusetts Hall, Bowdoin's oldest building, dates from 1799

▶ **Brunswick**   *108A1*

Bowdoin College▶, in the centre of Brunswick, was founded in 1794 and counts among its former students the writers Henry Wadsworth Longfellow and Nathaniel Hawthorne, and President Franklin Pierce. Two fine museums (both free) flank the attractive campus green. Hubbard Hall, a tall and prominent tower, houses the Peary-MacMillan Arctic Museum, which tells the story of these two former students, who made the first successful expedition to the North Pole in 1909. Displays feature three rooms of sleighs, guns, equipment and writings. To the right of Hubbard Hall, the Art Museum has American colonial and federal portraits (among them Gilbert Stuart's painting of Thomas Jefferson), paintings by Winslow Homer and classical antiquities.

In town, the Pejepscot Historical Society maintains three museum properties. The Italianate **Skolfield-Whittier House** at 161 Park Row (*open:* summer 10–3, Tuesday to Friday; 1–4, Saturday), was closed up and forgotten about from 1925 until 1982, and inhabited by a sea-captain. It contains exotic items he brought back from his voyages and family possessions spanning three generations. Its north side houses the free **Pejepscot Museum** (local history and genealogy). The **Joshua L Chamberlain Museum** (*open:* summer, 1–4, Tuesday to Saturday) commemorates the college professor who achieved fame as the hero of Little Round Top in the Civil War Battle of Gettysburg.

▶ **Bucksport**   *108B2*

This small port on the Penobscot river is busy with tankers off-loading petroleum products and picking up coated paper manufactured locally. Route 1 crosses the Penobscot by Waldo-Hancock Bridge, affording a spectacular view of the formidable **Fort Knox▶▶**. Not to be confused with its more famous namesake in Kentucky, the fort was built between 1844 and 1869, originally because of the British threat from Canada. It was never completed but saw activity in the Civil War and Spanish American War of 1898. An annual Civil War encampment, with costumed actors and cannon firing, enlivens the fort on two weekends in July and August. Take a torch for exploring the inside of the structure.

►► **Campobello Island**
(New Brunswick, Canada) *108C2*

Franklin D Roosevelt's 'beloved island', where he found
rest and freedom from care, is just over the Canadian border, but his family summer house is jointly maintained as
an International Park by the US and Canada. The park
comprises 2,800 acres of deep forest, bogs, stone and
sand beaches, ocean-side trails and viewpoints in addition
to the house. Maps are available from the visitors' centre
near International Bridge. (See also panel, page 122.)

The **Roosevelt Cottage**►► is in Dutch colonial style,
and retains the original furniture. The atmosphere is comfortable and personal rather than grand, with the president's umbrellas and books put out as if the great man
had just stepped outside. The adjacent **visitor centre**
shows a film on Campobello and the Roosevelts (cottage
and visitor's centre *open*: daily, May to October; free).
Next door, the opulent **Hubbard Cottage** was home to
Gorham and Sara Hubbard, an insurance businessman
and a concert pianist who became friends of the
Roosevelts. The cottage is open to the public.

Roosevelt spent his boyhood summers at a cottage on
the adjacent site, which his father built in 1885 (demol-
ished in 1951). His family later made the existing building
the summer home.

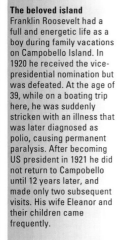

The beloved island
Franklin Roosevelt had a
full and energetic life as a
boy during family vacations
on Campobello Island. In
1920 he received the vice-
presidential nomination but
was defeated. At the age of
39, while on a boating trip
here, he was suddenly
stricken with an illness that
was later diagnosed as
polio, causing permanent
paralysis. After becoming
US president in 1921 he did
not return to Campobello
until 12 years later, and
made only two subsequent
visits. His wife Eleanor and
their children came
frequently.

123

*Roosevelt's house on
Campobello Island*

*One of New
England's most
familiar light-
houses,
West
Quoddy
Light*

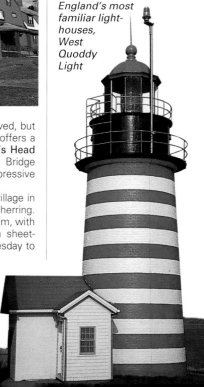

Many roads on the 9-mile-long island are unpaved, but
are passable in dry conditions. The northern tip offers a
fine view, and whales can often be seen. **Friar's Head
Outlook**►► (signposted between International Bridge
and the Roosevelt Cottage) commands an impressive
view of Passamaquoddy Bay.

On the way to Campobello, **Lubec** is the last village in
Maine, and is noted for sardines and smoked herring.
Aptly, it is home to the Old Sardine Village Museum, with
displays including canning equipment, boats, a sheet-
metal shop and a company store. (*Open*: Wednesday to
Sunday afternoons in July and August; weekends only in June and September).

To the south, **Quoddy Head**► marks the
easternmost point of the US mainland. **West
Quoddy Light**, built in 1858, sends out a 20-
mile beam. A 4-mile trail along high cliffs
provides opportunities for spotting whales.

■ 'In 1492 Native Americans discovered Columbus lost at sea!', reads the T-shirt slogan. And not long afterwards these so-called 'American Indians' met the first European colonists on the shores of New England. This was a meeting of two cultures, which to this day are as different as chalk from cheese.....■

A proud tradition
Keeping the tradition of basket-making alive is seen as important to the preservation of Indian culture. The Maine Arts Commission has developed a programme through which basket-makers pass on their skills to apprentices. These works of exquisite craftsmanship may be bought at crafts festivals and through co-operatives or shops.

A Passamaquoddy native of Maine

124

Windsong, a Massachusetts Wampanoag who does no live on an Indian reservation, is a deeply spiritual man. Fo his traditional, sacred rituals he needs eagle feathers. Bu the eagle is a protected bird and only Native American living on registered land are entitled to their feathers. This lack of awareness of the spiritual needs of another culture is, he says, typical of a white man's society brought up or images of peace-pipe-smoking Indians who raise one hand and call out 'How!', images that have more to do with Hollywood than real life.

Cultural and social issues For hundreds of years the Native People of the eastern United States have mixed with other elements in society – with blacks and, in more recent decades, with whites. There is a degree of inte gration that does not exist in the western states, where reservations are often dispirit ing enclaves of poverty and social disintegration.

Yet the Native Americans o New England still have a bitte sense of discrimination. In the workplace, for instance, a Harvard graduate who wanted to teach high-school children i given a kindergarten post, while in the town hall a Native American member of staff is repeatedly overlooked for pro motion. If there is a clash of cu tures, however, the white would argue that there is also a clash of work motivation. The archetypal conscientious and diligent Yankee may find the Native American frustratingl casual and slow.

The Native Americans have also socially suffered unde the white-dominated society Drying-out programmes fo alcoholics have been set up both on and off the reserva tions, but otherwise the suppor that now exists in plenty fo whites and blacks in social nee is conspicuously lacking for the Native Americans.

Staking a claim

Since the 1970s there has been a certain amount of political and legal action by Native Americans aimed at achieving equal status as citizens. The Penobscots and the Passamaquoddy of Maine have fought for legal control of fishing, mineral and forest rights on their lands. The Abenakis people have threatened to make legal claims

on much of the land in Vermont. But the hottest of local issues concerns the Mashantucket Pequots in Connecticut.

In 1992 the Pequots, a tribe that had all but died out, opened Foxwoods High Stakes Bingo and Casino (see panel). It currently brings in more than $1 million daily on slot machines alone. It is the largest casino in the western hemisphere, a vast operation through whose ever-open doors pass 40,000 Americans a day, some bussed in for two hours from New York and Boston. Awaiting them are the 1,500 clattering slot machines, the bingo rooms and the blackjack, craps, baccarat, roulette, acey-deucey, money wheel, pai gow poker and chuck-a-luck, to name but a few of the table games. In an area of dire unemployment, Foxwoods is now one of the biggest employers. Moreover, Connecticut's coffers are fatter by well over $100 million per year, as a result of a deal with the governor whereby 25 per cent of slot machines takings are handed over in exchange for a monopoly control of all gaming machines in the state.

Foxwoods looks after its employees well, but along with jobs it brings traffic, noise and, potentially at least, some of the less desirable members of society to the neighbourhood. Now its owners plan to buy more land, annexing it into sovereign Indian land and thereby removing it from local control and tax rolls. The villagers of Ledyard, Preston and Stonington are worried; the cards are in Pequot hands.

*Top: spinning the wheel at Foxwoods
Left: a Connecticut Algonquin*

Sovereignty of land

A tribe that is federally recognised can assume responsibility for its own internal control. The Pequots, for instance, have established their own police force, housing authority, ambulance and fire service, as well as their own court system. They also have their own water supply and sewage system. No federally recognised tribe pays state or federal taxes. This means that cigarettes and alcohol can be sold more cheaply in a reservation than elsewhere.

Playing the game

Federal law allows recognised Indian tribes to conduct gambling if the state in which they live allows gambling. Connecticut allows fund-raising, non-profit 'casino nights' (for example church bingo evenings) and the Pequots took advantage of this, opening Foxwoods Bingo in 1986. It began to make a profit and the state of Connecticut sued them. The case went to the Supreme Court, where the state lost. The Pequots obtained investment capital from Malaysia and opened the casino. In 1993 Rhode Island, not liking the possibility of a similar temple to gambling, repealed its law allowing fund-raising bingo.

Almost extinct 100 years ago, the puffin has recently been making a come-back in the Gulf of Maine

Wildlife sanctuary
Moosehorn National Wildlife Refuge, 5 miles north of Calais (pronounced 'Callous', itself north of Eastport on Route 1) on the Charlotte Road, consists of 23,000 acres of bogs, woods and marshes, inhabited by 216 species of birds, plus moose, deer, bear, beaver, mink and woodchuck (groundhog). Some 50 miles of roads and trails are open to hikers.

Revolutionary memorabilia is displayed in the Burnham Tavern, Machias

► **Eastport** *108C2*

This is small-town Maine at its most seductively peaceful, far removed from the crafts-designer shops and tourist crowds of the more frequented parts of the coast. Eastport's population numbers under 2,000 but is rated important enough to have its own city hall. High, Ray, Washington and Water streets contain an attractive mixture of architectural styles, from colonial to Victorian.

In the town itself, seek out Raye's Mustard, the last stone-ground mustard mill in America, a legacy of the days when mustard was used as a preservative. In the summer months (afternoons only), you can visit the local history museum, which is housed within the old Sullivan Barracks (1809). The garrison surrendered to the British in the War of 1812 without a shot being fired.

The town, sited on Moose Island and linked by causeway to the mainland, is a sardine, granite, timber and processed-paper port. It lies on **Passamaquoddy Bay►►**, site of the world's largest lobster pound, and notorious for treacherous waters that include fast incoming tides and great changes in water levels. Old Sow, the world's second largest whirlpool, can be seen from the car ferry to Deer Island. The curious tidal phenomenon of **Reversing Falls**, where the current goes in the contrary direction to the tide at certain times of day, occurs near Pembroke (see panel opposite).

A little further south, **Cobscook Bay State Park** has two trails, one leading to the coast, the other along the creek.

There are ferry connections to **Deer Island**, connecting with another ferry for **Campobello Island►►** (see page 123). At the far end of Deer Island a free ferry crosses to L'Etete on the Canadian mainland.

In the former lumber town of **Machias**, the **Burnham Tavern►** on High Street (dating from 1770) is eastern Maine's oldest building. Here patriots planned the capture of the British schooner *Margaretta* on 12 June 1775, after the British captain had ordered locals to take down their liberty pole. This was the first naval battle of the Revolution, the 'Lexington of the Sea'. Open to the public, the tavern has Revolutionary-era furnishings and items from the British vessel. On Route 92, half a mile from town, the Maine Wild Blueberry Company produces around 20 million pounds of berries a year; free tours (weekdays in summer, best by appointment; tel: 207/255 8364) show the processes of cleaning, freezing and grading the berries.

Route 191 leads through the town of Cutler, where the lobster hatchery is open to the public in summer (tel: 207/259 3693). Route 187 reaches

Jonesport, a typical Downeast fishing village, linked by bridge to Beal Island, where clams are raised. A causeway gives access to the Mud Hole Trail (from Black Duck Cove), with good views across to the islands.

Ellsworth
108B2

An unassuming small town on the way to Bar Harbor, Ellsworth has a fine First Congregational Church (1846), thought to be Maine's best example of a Greek Revival church. The steeple is a faithful fibreglass replica. The Old Hancock County Buildings, on Cross Street, are in similar style. The Big Chicken Barn, on Route 3 in town, is Maine's largest antiquarian bookstore and antique shop.

Just out of town is the **Black House▶** (*open*: June to mid-October), built in 1824–8 by land agent Colonel John Black. This charming Georgian home has original furnishings, a fine circular staircase and delightful formal gardens. The old carriage house contains old sleighs and carriages.

Out on Route 3, the **Birdsacre Sanctuary** covers 100 acres, with trails leading past ponds and nesting areas. The Stanwood Homestead Museum here is dedicated to pioneer ornithologist Cordelia Stanwood.

Lamoine State Park▶, on Route 184, has excellent views of Mount Desert Island and a safe beach. At Columbia Falls, just off Route 1, is **Ruggles House▶** (*open*: 1 June to October), which dates from 1818 and was inhabited until 1920. The house is noted for its 'flying' staircase (supported only at the top and bottom); the woodcarving on the staircase was executed with a penknife over a three-year period.

The 1817 Tisdale House, now Ellsworth's City Library

Granite mementoes
On Route 1 between Calais and Robbinston are 12 granite milestones erected by James Shepherd Pike in 1870. Pike, a Calais lumberman, writer, abolitionist and later US ambassador to the Netherlands, had a summer residence in Robbinston. After making careful measurements using the circumference of his cartwheels, he placed the stones to check the speed of his horses.

Reversing Falls
The 'Falls' take some finding. Turn off Route 1 at Pembroke, taking the road to the right of the post office. Turn right and then left (signposted to the shore), then, after 3.2 miles, turn right past a cemetery. Bear left at a T-junction with a dirt track. Continue for 1.4 miles, then fork left beyond a covered picnic bench up on the left: the car park is just beyond.

LL Bean

LL Bean's started as a humble one-man mail-order operation and has since boomed. In 1912 Leonwood Bean marketed his invention, the Maine Hunting Shoe: 'designed by a hunter who has tramped the Maine Woods for the past 18 years. They are as light as a pair of moccasins with the protection of a heavy hunting boot.' Today the store sells over 6,000 products. It is still largely mail-order, but there are factory outlets at Ellsworth, ME, and North Conway, NH.

Above: Freeport is home to the popular mail-order clothing company, LL Bean

Penobscot Bay has long been busy with boats, both large and small

▶▶ **Freeport** *108A1*

Freeport, Maine's biggest visitor attraction along with Acadia National Park, consists of a main street lined wall-to-wall with factory shopping outlets. There are over 100, and most of the time sale prices are offered somewhere. Serious shoppers journey up here from New York and even further to make Christmas purchases.

It is a matter of dispute whether Freeport is really such good value (compared to North Conway for instance), but the choice (candles, kids' clothes, maps and guides, crafts, sports equipment, soap and so on) is impressive. Although village-sized, Freeport is crammed with shoppers transporting bulging carrier bags, and the traffic and car parks are on an urban scale. Maps showing locations of the stores are given away at Bean's and other shops. Freeport has inns, motels and B&Bs as well as a beach, and is the starting point for ocean cruises.

Outside Freeport, the **Desert of Maine▶** is a curiosity. This really is a small desert, an eye-opening example of 18th-century bad farming practice, where the soil was depleted and massive erosion followed. Entire farm buildings and trees were engulfed in the dunes, and tell-tale tree-tops still protrude like small bushes. From May to Columbus Day a tour is provided of this odd tribute to human failure.

The **North American Wildlife Expo**, 2 miles south of Freeport, is an all-year museum of stuffed animals. Also south of town, live osprey and seals may be spotted from **Wolf Neck Woods State Park▶**, which has trails and wooded shores as well as some curious rock formations. At **Bradbury Mountain State Park▶** a 20-minute trail to the summit leads to views over Casco Bay, while other paths head along the bay and Harraseeket river.

▶▶ **Penobscot Bay** *108B2*

The biggest indentation in Maine's coast, Penobscot Bay and its islands offer some of the loveliest panoramas along New England's seaboard. Boating has been big here for centuries. The Penobscot river once supplied over 20 towns with timber for ship-building, and today the ports are busy with pleasure and commercial craft. Rockland and Camden are the busiest boating areas; Camden is much prettier and more of a

resort. Be warned, though: the sprawl along Route 1 is unsightly, and in summer driving along it is no pleasure.

The west side Port Clyde, on the west side of the bay, is the departure point for ferries to **Monhegan Island**►► (see page 121). On the way to the town you pass through Tenants Harbor, a typical fishing village with lobster boats in the harbour.

Further north, **Owls Head Transportation Museum**► opens year-round, and displays New England's largest collection of pioneer vehicles from the early 20th century. A schedule of events features airshows, and motorcycle and tractor meets.

Nearby **Rockland**, New England's biggest distribution centre for the lobster industry and a major sardine port, has a workaday atmosphere. The local processing of seaweed gives the place a wholesome whiff.

The **Old Conway Homestead and Museum**, Route 1 and Conway Road, (open: 10–4, Tuesday to Friday) is an atmospheric 1770s farmhouse and barn with farm tools, a blacksmith shop and a maple-sugar house (with sugaring demonstrations in spring).

On the move at Owls Head Transportation Museum

The Beans of Egypt, Maine
No relation to the Beans of Freeport, the Bean family of Egypt was a fictitious invention of novelist Carolyn Chute. Her book *The Beans of Egypt, Maine* (1985) is the saga of a violent and primitive family, prisoners of rural poverty in the woods of Maine. Despite its bleak setting, the novel has moments of black humour.

Bay islands
Penobscot Bay's main islands make attractive hiking or cycling country. Vinalhaven, the largest at 14 miles long, and Islesboro (12 miles long) have accommodation but no camping is allowed. North Haven and Matinicus both have accommodation and camping by permission. Isle au Haut is part of Acadia National Park (see pages 112–13). For Monhegan Island, see page 121. Islesboro is reached by ferry from Lincolnville Beach; North Haven, Vinalhaven and Matinicus from a car ferry at Rockland. For details, call the Maine State Ferry Service (tel: 207/596 2203).

Map: Penobscot Bay region

Freedom · Brooks · Fort Knox State Park · **Bucksport** · Orland · Surry
347m · Penobscot · **Penobscot Marine Museum** · Fort Point St Park · Searsport · Penobscot · 306m · Blue Hill
Liberty · 3 · Moose Point State Park · **Belfast** · **Maine Maritime Academy** · Castine · Brooksville · Long Island
Searsmont · Northport · Pripet · **Islesboro Island** · Islesboro · Little Deer Isle · Sedgwick · Brooklin
Appleton · Lincolnville · Camden Hills State Park · Warren Island · Deer Isle
Hope · **Camden** · Penobscot Bay · Deer Isle · Sunshine
Union · Rockport · Pulpit Harbor · North Haven Island · **Crockett Cove Woods** · Jericho Bay
Rockville · Glen Cove · North Haven · Stonington
Warren · **Rockland** · Vinalhaven Island · Marshall Island
Thomaston · Owls Head · Vinalhaven
Cushing · St George · Acadia National Park · Isle au Haut
Friendship · Spruce Head
Tenants Harbor · Martinsville
Port Clyde · Matinicus Island · Seal Island
Monhegan Island · Ragged Island

0 · 1 · 2 km
0 · 1 mile

MAINE

Castine's military past
Castine had a strategic importance and was fought over by the French, Dutch, British and Americans for nearly two centuries. Above the Maine Maritime Academy are the grassy ramparts of Fort George, built by the British in 1779 to protect Canadian interests and the last fort they abandoned at the end of the Revolutionary War. It retains its moat and earthworks.

Crammed into the **Shore Village Museum**►►, at 104 Limerock Street, Rockland, is the largest collection of light-house lenses and lighthouse paraphernalia in the US, plus coastguard buoys, bells, ship models, navigational instruments, Civil War memorabilia and 19th-century costume dolls. (*Open*: daily 10–4, 1 June to 15 October; donations requested.) Also in Rockland is an outstanding art collection at the **Farnsworth Art Museum and Homestead**►► (*open*: daily 10–5, except Sunday, 1–5). The display of art is rotated and features Maine and New England art and artists, including the three generations of the Wyeth family. Winslow Homer's *Girl in a Punt* is one of the best-known works. The 19th-century Greek Revival homestead of William A Farnsworth, the lime baron who endowed the museum, has period décor in its 12 small rooms.

Andrew Wyeth had a studio at the **Olson House** on Hathorn Point Road, Cushing (*open*: 11–4, Wednesday to Sunday, June to September). He depicted the owner,

The bold and bright Romance of Autumn by George Bellows (1882–1925), on display at the Farnsworth Art Museum in Rockland

Christina Olson, in front of the house in *Christina's World*, one of the most evocative of all American paintings.

Rockport► has a charming village centre, little changed from the 19th century, which overlooks a marina, old lime kiln and oceanside park. The best of **Camden**► lies off busy Route 1: Chestnut and Bayview streets are conspicuously attractive. Crafts shops and traffic jams are the norm in summer, with window-shoppers spilling off the sidewalks. The village keeps going all year, with events, a community theatre, an opera house and a winter carnival.

Mount Battie is the crowning glory of **Camden Hills State Park**►►► (*open*: 1 May to 1 November), where a toll road winds up to the top for a glorious view of the bay and towards Acadia, and over the strikingly empty hinterland. Hikers can walk 25 miles of park trails; it takes 1–1½ hours to ascend the mountain on foot.

Searsport is Maine's 'antiques capital', well endowed with shops and flea markets. **Penobscot Marine Museum►►** in town (*open*: Memorial Day weekend to 15 October) chronicles the maritime history of Penobscot Bay. Searsport once specialised in building trading ships, and several captains' houses (including the Fowler-True-Ross House) survive from those times. The museum is on several neighbouring sites; one ticket covers cham all. The main building has a notable collection of maritime art, a remarkable film of a 1929 voyage around Cape Horn in a hurricane and a quaint assemblage of 200 butter dishes collected by a captain's wife. Other buildings display small craft, whaling and scrimshaw, and ship-building.

The east side By complete contrast this side of Penobscot Bay has few attractions but has a quiet charm of its own by virtue of its inaccessibility. A causeway links Deer Isle to the mainland, with the sleepy fishing village of Stonington at its southern tip, where ferries leave for Isle au Haut in Acadia National Park (see pages 112–13). **Blue Hill►►** rises to 934 feet just north of the village of the same name: from the village take Route 15 north, then turn right into Mountain Road; the trail starts on the left-hand side and ascends for a view over Acadia and Penobscot Bay. An easier viewpoint to reach is the Caterpillar Hill picnic area a mile south of the junction of Routes 15 and 175.

Castine►►, one of the most attractive villages in the state, has some gracious early 19th-century homes, with plaques recording their history, in Main and Perkins streets. By the common is the First Parish Church, begun in 1790 and eastern Maine's oldest church. At shore level, lawns slope to the water's edge and there are two museums. The entire village has been designated a National Historic Site (see panel opposite). Berthed here is the *State of Maine*, a former troopship used by the adjacent Maine Maritime Academy for training merchant midshipmen. Ship tours are on the hour, 10–4.

Crockett Cove Woods Preserve is a 100-acre site maintained by the Nature Conservancy and comprising coastal spruce woods and a miniature bog. A self-guided trail leads visitors around the preserve, and brochures are available from the entrance registration box.

A nostalgic side-trip
At Belfast, the Belfast & Moosehead Lake Railroad (tel: 207/338 2330) runs narrated two-hour trips to Brook in 1920s Pullman cars. This is a 25-mile round trip (it is extended to 33 miles in the autumn), and you get 'ambushed' by comic bandits on the way. A critically acclaimed theatre shares the train station, located near the water's edge. The railroad operates at weekends in spring, daily except Monday in summer; there are autumn foliage specials on Friday and at weekends.

Windjammer vacations
Companies in Penobscot Bay offer vacations on schooners known as windjammers (see picture below). Participants stay for the week and can enjoy sailing trips lasting from two hours to several days on tall-masted wooden sailing ships (some are magnificent 19th-century restorations). You can hoist the sails, take a turn at the wheel and help navigate. Anyone sailing alone in the Boothbay or Penobscot Bay areas should have plenty of experience and be able to read a nautical chart.

131

Camden has the largest fleet of windjammers

■ **For lovers of the great outdoors, New England has something for everyone, whether lone fishermen or families, adventurous young or 'active seniors'. From spring to autumn there is first-rate hiking, cycling, fishing and hunting. There are watersports from sailing and windsurfing to canoeing and whitewater rafting.....■**

Canoeing

The Appalachian Mountain Club (AMC) publishes the *Quiet Water Canoe Guide, New Hampshire/Vermont.* Their *River Guide, Central/Southern New England* is also full of information on. Contact AMC, PO Box 298, Gorham, NH 03581 (tel: 603/466 2727).

Canoes can be hired and trips operate from dozens of locations, including the Rangeley Lakes area, Maine; the Lamoille and Batten Kill rivers, Vermont; the Saco river at Conway, and the Connecticut river at Hanover and Balloch's Crossing (all in NH).

Hiking and biking Walking, or as Americans call it, hiking, is on marked trails (see page 257). All state parks have clearly signed trails, and notice-boards often indicate length and difficulty. Trails range from easy to extremely challenging, but with vast areas of New England covered in forest, the terrain is not always particularly varied.

New Hampshire's White Mountains make superb hiking territory (see page 208). The lakes and forests of Maine's Kennebec Valley and the Western Lakes and Mountains are popular for both hiking and biking. There are thousands of miles of quiet, secondary roads to explore, and bicycles can be hired in many places. Naturalists will enjoy the trails in the wilds of Baxter State Park. Like some of the ski resort towns in Vermont and New Hampshire, Sunday River in Maine has a network of mountain-bike trails using the ski-lifts. In Massachusetts, the Cape Cod National Seashore has 40 miles·of hiking and cycling trails; the Berkshires is another favourite area. Nantucket, MA, and Block Island, RI, have miles of easy, attractive biking paths.

Fishing and shooting Big-game hunting (shooting) is very popular in the autumn months, mainly for white-tailed deer but also for black bear, wild turkey and moose (in Maine this is for one week in October; permits available only through lottery; apply January to April). Game birds include grouse and woodcock.

Anglers can find excellent fishing opportunities throughout New England. Lake Champlain, 100 miles long, has dozens of public access points (with no closed season) for fishing for lake trout, land-locked salmon, bass, walleye and the brightly coloured, tasty pumpkinseed. The lake is also superb for ice-fishing, an increasingly popular winter sport.

From mid-April to the end of October there is excellent fishing for landlocked salmon and trout in the lakes and ponds of New Hampshire and areas of Maine such as Bethel and Rangeley, the Winthrop Lakes, and around The Forks and Jackman in the north. Vermont's Northeast Kingdom region is especially popular for lake trout and

Anywhere in New England, fishing provides beautiful scenery: above, near the Mohawk Trail

land-locked salmon. The region also has numerous 'back-woods' ponds, remote and lovely beaver ponds teeming with brown trout and needing a map and maybe a compass to reach them. The 397-mile-long Connecticut river is a scenic, peaceful waterway, a delight for anglers in search of such fish as yellow perch, bass, and brown and rainbow trout.

Watersports There is good sailing from many places around the coast. Newport, Rhode Island, former home of the America's Cup, and the Penobscot Bay section of the Maine coast are the best-known areas (but beware, much of the Maine coast has odd currents and is not for the novice). Inland, Lake Champlain and the bigger lakes in New Hampshire and Maine are popular for sailing, sail-boarding, canoeing and windsurfing, and most have launching ramps and boats for hire. The Connecticut river and the Housatonic in the Berkshires provide plenty of opportunities for gentle, easy canoeing. Canoeing is a wonderfully peaceful way to explore the remoter areas of northern New England, offering intimate encounters with beaver, moose and other wildlife (see panels, opposite page and page 120)

Whitewater rafters await the spring run-off, when the rivers start to swirl and swell. Mecca is The Forks, in Maine, where several companies organise trips down the Kennebec, Dead and Penobscot rivers. In the far north, experts relish the challenges of the Allagash Wilderness Waterway. In Vermont, whitewater rafting trips operate on West river. There is rafting on seven rivers from Conway, New Hampshire, and in western Massachusetts there are rafting centres on the Deerfield river.

Fishing and hunting
Licences are necessary for hunting; resident and non-resident licences may be obtained from town clerk offices, local sporting shops or the state Fish and Wildlife Office (see below). To get a hunting licence you must show a previous or current hunting licence or a hunter safety course certificate from any state.

Vermont Fish and Wildlife Department, 103 South Main Street, Waterbury, VT 05676, publishes *Guide to Hunting* and *Guide to Fishing* leaflets.

Other useful addresses for further information on fishing and hunting:
● Connecticut Department of Environmental Protection, State Office Building, Hartford, CT 06106.
● Maine Department of Inland Fisheries and Wildlife, 284 State Street, Augusta, ME 04333.
● Massachusetts Division of Marine Fisheries, 100 Cambridge Street, Boston MA 02202.
● New Hampshire Fish and Game Department, 2 Hazen Drive, Concord, NH 03301.
● Rhode Island Division of Fish and Wildlife, Government Center, Tower Hill Road, Wakefield, RI 02879.

The Appalachian Trail
The Appalachian Trail (2,144 miles) stretches from Maine, through New Hampshire, Vermont, Massachusetts and Connecticut, continuing south to Georgia. Road access makes it easy to cover short stretches.

MAINE

Casco Bay
Casco Bay is the largest deep-water haven on the Atlantic coast; the islands that protect the bay are said to number 365. The first secret war conference between Churchill and Roosevelt took place in a battleship off Long Island in the bay, when the Atlantic Pact was signed. Several fortifications can be spotted on the islands, including forts Scammel, McKinley and Gorges. South Portland is the water terminal for the Portland–Montreal pipeline. Crude oil super-tankers from South America and the Middle East are common sights.

Brewed in Portland

Cruises from Portland
Casco Bay Lines' mailboat run is the longest such operating service in the US, stopping at the islands of Cliff, Chebeague, Long, Little and Great Diamond. The company also provides cruises to Bailey Island (tel: 207/774 7871). Eagle Tours (tel: 207/774 6498) offer seal-watching and fishing trips, as well as cruises to Eagle Island.

►► **Portland** *108A1*

Maine's largest city prospered as a port on the basis of its accessibility to Europe. Its decline after World War II was reversed by a revival in fortunes, spearheaded by the revitalisation of the Old Port Exchange district, with its uniform grid of red-brick streets rebuilt in the 1860s after a disastrous fire. This part of the city is pleasant for walking, and has restaurants and speciality and antiquarian shops. Portland's face is unmistakably urban, but the city has good cultural attractions. Commercial Street runs along the harbour, where you can join cruises (see panel).

The **Portland Museum of Art**►►, in Congress Square, houses one of New England's finest art collections. The American collection includes Maine scenes by Winslow Homer, Andrew Wyeth, Marsden Hartley and Rockwell Kent. European art features sculpture by Henry Moore and Rodin, and Impressionist and Cubist works. The museum is closed Monday, open late night on Thursday; gallery tours are at 11 and 2 daily (for current opening hours, tel: 207/775 6148). The museum building itself is a mixture of 1911 Beaux Arts and 1983 post-modernism.

Next door, the **Children's Museum of Maine**►, 142 Free Street (*open*: daily; until 8pm on Friday; free admission 5–7pm Friday), ranks among the best of its kind in New England.

At 485–9 Congress Street is the **Wadsworth-Longfellow House**►, the childhood home of Henry Wadsworth Longfellow, America's most popular 19th-century poet. His family was comfortably well off but not wealthy, and in the house are numerous family possessions and portraits. (*Open*: 10–4, Tuesday to Saturday, June to Columbus Day.)

Portland Observatory, at 138 Congress Street, was built in 1807, and is a rare example of a signal tower on which signal flags would be flown to identify incoming vessels. Steps lead to the top of the observatory for a view of the bay.

Victoria Mansion►►, on the corner of Danforth and Park streets, is an ornate Italianate brownstone house, built 1858–60 and reflecting northern European taste. The interior is a lavish showpiece, with plasterwork made to resemble wood, an eye-catching chandelier, painted walls and ceilings, and a Moorish-style smoking room. (*Open*: Memorial to Labor Day, then weekends only to Columbus Day; closed Monday.)

Tate House, 1270 Westbrook Street (*open*: 1 July to 15 September, except Monday) is a fine colonial-period house with a riverside setting and 18th-century herb garden. A worthwhile free visit is the **Neal Dow Memorial**, at 714 Congress Street, a Federal mansion of 1829 which belonged to a leading figure in the temperance cause.

Fort Williams Park► occupies a fine section of rocky coast south of the city. Adjacent to the fort, Portland Head Light (1791) is the oldest lighthouse in Maine and inspired Longfellow. A museum in the lighthouse-keeper's quarters tells its story. (*Open*: June to October; weekends only in November, December, April and May; tours at 11 and 2.) Lighthouse devotees may also like to visit nearby **Two Lights State Park**. Not far away, artist Winslow Homer made his home at Prout's Neck (also open).

► **Wiscasset** 108B1

On the Sheepscot river at Wiscasset is one of the most evocative sights on Route 1: the two huge wrecks of the *Hesper* and *Luther Little*, the world's last four-masted schooners, here since the 1930s. Every 4 July they are set alight, and their eventual demise seems on the cards.

Fort Edgecomb► (*open*: in daylight hours), reached by turning off Route 1 on the east side of the river bridge, is a well-preserved octagonal wooden blockhouse of 1808–9. It was one of four defensive forts on the Lincoln County coast. Although there is nothing to see inside, the riverside setting is superb.

In town, at Lee and High streets, is **Castle Tucker** (*open*: Tuesday to Saturday, July and August) a grand house built in 1807 by Judge Silas Lee and later modified, and now displaying 19th-century furnishings. In Federal Street, the **Old Lincoln County Jail** (*open*: daily except Monday in summer), was built in 1811 and in use until 1953. Visitors can see the cells and jailer's house.

Rail and sail excursions run from Wiscasset (see panel below)

135

Rail and sail
Combined rail and sail excursions from Wiscasset from May to October are offered by Maine Coast Railroad (tel: 207/882 8000). The excursion train features restored 1920s and 1930s carriages, and the cruise explores the Sheepscot river and passes Fort Edgecomb.

Longfellow's tragedy
On Longfellow's marriage to his cousin, Fanny Appleton, in 1843, her father presented the house in Cambridge, Massachusetts (see page 75) to the couple as a wedding present. She died 18 years later when her hoop skirt caught fire while melting sealing-wax to preserve locks of her children's hair. Henry grew a beard to cover the physical scars incurred while trying to save her, but remained emotionally scarred.

The wrecks in the river at Wiscasset

Hancock Warehouse, York, dates from the mid-1700s and is still used as a boathouse today

Blowing Cave

Located between Walker Point and Cape Arundel, just east of Kennebunkport, this sea cave is a curious phenomenon. As waves enter it, air is trapped and compressed; as the water recedes, the trapped air is released, sometimes sending out a spray of sea-water. Unfortunately it is difficult to see this happen as the cave is only really accessible at low tide, but it is fun to explore just the same.

In love with the past

Elizabeth Perkins and her mother fell in love with their house in York and spent their summers there. Proud of their New England heritage and ancestors, the Perkins crammed the house with antiques and furniture, creating a comfortable rather than historically accurate house for entertaining and holidaying. Elizabeth took an interest in preserving York and was responsible for saving the schoolhouse and wooden bridge. She loved collecting antiques, and installed old-fashioned beams and panelling for effect in the dining room. Both women's ashes are in the garden.

Elizabeth Perkins House, York

►► **York and Kennebunkport**   108A1

York is a composite place: just off Route 1 lies historic York Village, alone worth at least half a day to explore. Along the shoreline are Long Sands Beach (popular for surfing) and the famous Nubble Lighthouse (also known as Cape Neddick Lighthouse), built in 1789 on York Beach, which itself retains a graceful 19th-century air. York Harbor is a small area between the old village and the beaches. An hourly trolley service connects the sites and intermediate points.

The Old York Historical Society sites These include a number of buildings, some with tours conducted by interpreters, others self-guided. Tours start on the hour; the last are at 4pm. **Jefferds Tavern** (1754), where you buy your ticket, features displays about York and is often filled with the aroma of hearth-side cooking. Next door, the **Old Schoolhouse** (1745) has a small exhibit on schooling and apprenticeship in Maine.

Made from two colonial houses put together, the **Emerson Wilcox House►** is presented in a variety of periods, from the 1765 parlour to the 1930s dining room. The bedroom possesses the oldest known complete set of American bed-hangings, done in crewel work in 1746 and in pristine condition (with the original spelling mistakes in the words of a hymn worked into the design).

The **Old Gaol►**, in use from 1719–1860, took in about 14 prisoners per year; interpreters fill in the facts and legends. Jail quarters and the jailer's chambers are on show.

The **Hancock Warehouse►**, once owned

by John Hancock, occupies a charming spot on an unspoilt creek, near a wooden bridge. A replica of an 1880s gundalow (a flat-bottomed boat) is often on the river here. The warehouse is the last commercial colonial building in town, and is still used as a working boathouse. It houses a small exhibition on ship-building, timber, shipping, farming and lobstering.

By the York river, the **Elizabeth Perkins House►►** is a fascinating example of the Colonial Revival style – a colonial house kitted out during the 1920s to 1940s in an idealised conception of the colonial style itself. Its transformation began in 1898 when the Perkins bought the (then four-roomed) 18th-century farmhouse (see panel).

Elsewhere along the coast The yachting and fishing village of **Kennebunkport** is the home and former Summer White House of ex-President George Bush, who used to jog along the beach (often with scores of red-faced reporters and photographers in tow). His house at Walker's Point can be seen from the sea-front, otherwise memorable for its swing-bridge. On Route 9A/35, the Wedding Cake House is a particularly fetching yellow and white confection.

The **Brick Store Museum►**, at 117 Main Street, Kennebunk (*open*: Tuesday to Saturday; closed Saturday in winter), is a fine local history museum with rotating exhibits on both maritime and social history, and on the decorative arts. Three miles north of Kennebunkport, the **Seashore Trolley Museum►** (*open*: May to November) has the world's largest collection of trolleys (trams), and offers a chance to take a nostalgic ride.

Route 1 in this area is packaged-fun country. At York itself is York's **Wild Kingdom** (see page 245). The **Wells Auto Museum** has over 70 vehicles and is open in summer. Saco is home to **Funtown**, the **Maine Aquarium** and **Aquaboggan Water Park**. **Old Orchard Beach**, on the coast, has a sandy shoreline and is densely developed with fast-food outlets and amusements; **Palace Playland** is a major attraction whose seaside rides are reminiscent of New York's Coney Island.

Ogunquit is an upmarket resort village, and was once an artists' colony. Cove views are available from a pretty swing-bridge leading to Perkins Cove, and from a mile-long coastal path known as Rustic Way. Ogunquit's Museum of Art is open in the summer months, and there is a summer theatre season.

Kittery► has similar factory shopping outlets to Freeport (see page 128); there are over 100 such discount stores along Kittery's 'miracle mile', offering savings of up to 70 per cent.

137

Travel through time at the Trolley Museum near Kennebunkport

MASSACHUSETTS

Map of western Massachusetts showing:

VERMONT · **NEW HAMPSHIRE** · **NEW YORK** · **CONNECTICUT** · **RHODE ISLAND**

Williamstown · Clarksburg · North Adams · Mohawk Trail · Charlemont · Turners Falls · Winchendon · Townsend · LOWELL
Taconic Mts · 1064m Mt Greylock · Adams · Shelburne Falls · Greenfield · Athol · Gardner · Fitchburg · Aver
Hoosic Ra · Cummington · Deerfield · North New Salem · Petersham · Leominster · Fruitlands Museums · Concord · Clinton
Hancock Shaker Village · Pittsfield · Dalton · Goshen · Pioneer · Quabbin Reservoir · Barre · Paxton · Shrewsbury · Sudbury
Lenox · Becket · Northampton · Amherst · Winsor Dam · WORCESTER · Framingham
Tanglewood · Lee · Dinosaur Footprints Reservation · 366m Mt Tom · South Hadley · Belchertown · Spencer · Grafton
Stockbridge · Huntington · Holyoke · Brimfield · Old Sturbridge Village · Auburn · Milford
Great Barrington · Otis · Chicopee · Southbridge · Bellingham
South Egremont · 800m Mt Everett · Monterey · Westfield · SPRINGFIELD · Webster
Sheffield · New Boston · West Springfield
Ashley Falls · Housatonic · Berkshire Hills · Connecticut

Scale: 0 — 20 — 40 — 60 km / 0 — 10 — 20 — 30 — 40 miles

A · B · C

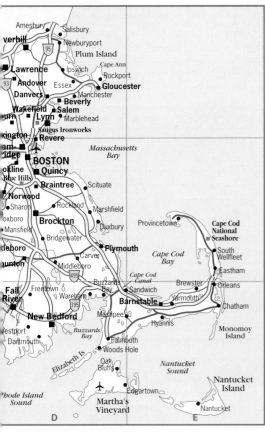

Massachusetts Even apart from the attractions of Boston (see pages 48–73), there is plenty in the rest of Massachusetts to excite the curious traveller. The state is the cradle of modern America and as such is packed with history. In 1620 the Pilgrim Fathers landed at Provincetown, some 600 miles further north than they had intended (they were bound for Jamestown in Virginia) before finally establishing themselves at Plymouth. In 1775 the first shots of the American Revolution sounded at Lexington and Concord. In the 19th century the first large-scale textile mills appeared in Lowell, heralding the birth of industrial America. Massachusetts is seen as a centre of political and intellectual thought: great names associated with the state include Ralph Waldo Emerson (1803–82), Henry David Thoreau (1817–62), Herman Melville (1819–91), Emily Dickinson (1830–86), Louisa May Alcott (1832–88), Edith Wharton (1862–1937) and John F Kennedy (1917–63).

Along the coast Early settlers ensconced themselves along the coast, often referred to as the North Shore and the South Shore, with Boston at the pivot. Today the coast is a place for summer relaxation, though the sheer

Autumn colour on the Mohawk Trail

numbers of visitors trying to get away from it all can be self-defeating. North Shore towns are select and picturesque, notably Salem, Marblehead, Rockport (on Cape Ann) and Newburyport. Each makes a feasible day trip from Boston, with good public transport links. Of these, Salem has the most to see, with its gruesome episode of the witches persecution told at a number of venues in a variety of styles.

On the South Shore, Plymouth is a pleasant town with several mementoes of the pioneer days, most notably the re-created Pilgrim village at Plimoth Plantation and the *Mayflower II*. Cape Cod needs time to appreciate fully, although quirky Provincetown is an entertaining day out by ferry from Boston. Ideally, Cape Cod should be seen out of high summer, and the trip should include visits to the islands of Martha's Vineyard and Nantucket, both haunts of the rich but remarkably different in character; in particular the towns of Oak Bluffs and Nantucket have their very own, inimitable period atmospheres. New Bedford, the whaling port that succeeded Nantucket, looks unappetising as you speed through its industrial outskirts on the I-195, but its old centre has atmosphere and a good whaling museum.

The harbour at Rockport, Cape Ann

Heading inland Concord and Lexington lie just beyond the western suburbs of Boston; in addition to the Revolutionary battle sites, there is a rich literary heritage to explore at Concord. Worcester, a large industrial city, deserves a look for its Armory and art museum.

Of much more mainstream appeal is the evocation of 1830s New England at Old Sturbridge Village – sheer pastiche, but convincingly done and atmospheric when not too crowded. Even the farm animals resemble authentic early 19th-century breeds.

Up to the late 18th century New England extended only as far west as the Connecticut river (known here as Pioneer Valley), where you will find an academic centre, the so-called Five Colleges Area, plus the industrial centres of Holyoke and Springfield. There are some good walks along the river, with abrupt cliff edges in places. Historic Deerfield is the best sight in the valley. Here the

'Listen to the surf, really lend it your ears, and you will hear in it a world of sound: hollow boomings and heavy roarings, great watery tumblings and tramplings, long hissing seethes, sharp rifle-shot reports, splashes, whispers, the grinding undertone of stones, and sometimes vocal sounds that might be the half-heard talk of people in the sea.'
– Henry Beston, *The Outermost House* (1927), written in a coastal shack on Cape Cod.

mile-long village street has none of the period-clad actors found in Old Sturbridge, but some will find the uncommercialised and slow-going atmosphere appealing.

The far west Massachusetts now extends west of the Connecticut river into Berkshire County, which borders New York state. This hilly and predominantly rural region has much to offer in the arts: Tanglewood hosts the premier summer musical event in Massachusetts, and is the summer base of the Boston Symphony Orchestra (see page 79). Artist Norman Rockwell is remembered near Stockbridge by an excellent museum, and at Chesterwood the house and studio of sculptor Daniel Chester French makes an absorbing visit. Hancock Shaker Village gives a fascinating insight into the virtually vanished lifestyle of the Shaker sect.

Trustees of Reservations A useful source of information for exploring the further-flung sights of Massachusetts is the handbook published by The Trustees of Reservations. Established in 1891, this is the world's oldest preservation society. It owns over 70 houses and areas of countryside, including woodlands, gorges, waterfalls and wildlife refuges throughout Massachusetts. Members are admitted to most properties free of charge and to the remaining few at reduced rates. Information and membership details can be obtained from 572 Essex Street, Beverly, MA 01915-1530 (tel: 508/921 1944).

Events

The precise dates of festivals vary from year to year. Advance booking is advised for popular events, such as the Tanglewood summer concerts. For further information contact the state tourist office (see page 266) or chambers of commerce.

April
Daffodil Festival, Nantucket: flower show and vintage cars.
Re-enactment of the Battle of Lexington and Concord.

May
Brimfield Antique Flea Market, Brimfield: New England's prime antiques event (also held in June and September).
Salem Seaport Festival, Salem: celebration of the town's maritime past, with crafts, walks, exhibitions and children's activities.

June
ACC Craft Fair, West Springfield: 500 of the nation's highest calibre artists and craftsmen show and sell their work.

Plymouth Rock, the stone on to which the Pilgrim Fathers are supposed to have stepped when they came ashore from the Mayflower

Blessing of the Fleet, Provincetown: dancing, parade and crafts.
St Peter's Fiesta, Gloucester: Blessing of the Fleet.

July
Barnstable County Fair, East Falmouth: the major (and long-established) event on Cape Cod's calendar.
Jacob's Pillow Dance Festival, Becket: oldest dance festival in America (until September).
Mashpee Pow Wow: Native American festivities, contests and food.
Tanglewood Music Festival, Lenox: concerts by the Boston Symphony Orchestra (until end August).

August
Eastham Originals Arts and Crafts Show: the major event of its kind on Cape Cod.
Fall River Celebrates America, Fall River: parade of ships, boat races, fireworks and more.
Feast of Blessed Sacrament, New Bedford: the country's largest Portuguese festival, with the Blessing of the Fleet, food, dance and a parade.
Martha's Vineyard Agricultural Fair.
Pilgrim Progress Procession, Plymouth (Fridays).

September
Bourne Scallopfest, Buzzards Bay.
Harwich Cranberry Festival, Harwich: country and western music, fireworks and parade spread over 10 days.
The Big E, West Springfield: New England's great state fair.

October
Haunted Happenings, Salem: magic, witches, costume parade and candlelight tours at Halloween.
Nantucket Cranberry Harvest.

November
Thanksgiving Day Celebration, Plymouth: Pilgrims' procession, Thanksgiving service and dinner.

December
Christmas Shoppers' Stroll, Nantucket: carol-singing, theatre, house tours.
First Night Celebration, Cape Cod, Lowell, Newburyport, New Bedford, Northampton, Pittsfield, Salem, Springfield and Worcester: New Year fun and frivolity.

▶▶▶ Berkshire Hills   *138A2*

The Berkshires is the hilliest and western-most part of Massachusetts and was a fashionable summer resort area for wealthy urbanites in the late-19th century. Summer nowadays is busy with arts events, with some 300,000 people attracted to Tanglewood (see page 146) for the Boston Symphony Orchestra summer concert series alone. The area's autumn foliage brings in more crowds later on in the year, and there are opportunities for downhill and cross-country skiing enthusiasts in winter. Compulsive antique-shop browsers may like to head for the area around Route 7 between South Egremont and Ashley Falls. Many of the museums and houses close between mid-October and late May.

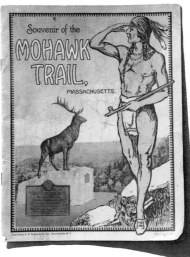

The Mohawk Trail and the northern Berkshires The Mohawk Trail▶, the

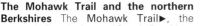

country's first designated Scenic Road (opened 1914), fol-lows Route 2 for 63 miles from the Pioneer Valley to the New York state border. The trail dates back to 1663 when the Pocumtuck tribe invaded Mohawk Territory by creat-ing this route over the mountains from Deerfield, MA, to Troy, NY. Today motels and 'Indian trading posts' (with racks of plastic totem poles, spears and the like) straggle the highway.

The Mohawk Trail passes through some spectacularly rugged scenery – and there are plenty of reminders of its origins
Left: the 'Hail to Sunrise' memorial at the entrance to the Mohawk Trail State Forest

  French King Bridge▶ is a scenic crossing of the Connecticut river, the first point worth stopping for; the river is 140 feet below. Further west, **Shelburne Falls**▶

is known for its Bridge of Flowers, an old trol-ley bridge graced with colourful blooms. Near the Salmon Falls weir, jagged rocks in the river attract swimmers and picnickers. The road passes the **Hail to the Sunrise Monument**, erected in 1932 by tribes and councils of the Approved Order of Red Men, showing a Mohawk with arms out-stretched.

  Signs soon begin to announce 4 miles of steep gradients and sharp curves, culmin-ating spectacularly at **Hairpin Turn**▶▶, a fine outlook. Go north along Route 8 towards Clarks-burg for **Natural Bridge State Park**. Waters tumble through a small chasm gouged out by glacial meltwater and spanned by a natural bridge. Adjacent is an aban-doned white marble quarry.

Information for the Berkshire Hills
For further information contact the Berkshire Visitors' Bureau, Berkshire Common, Plaza Level, Dept MT, Pittsfield, MA 01201 (tel: 413/443 9186, or toll-free 1-800/BERKSHR). *Berkshires Week* is a free weekly listings magazine containing information on state parks, campgrounds, sights, children's activities, shopping and events; it is available at all chambers of commerce.

Aerial view of Williamstown in the Berkshires

Trails in the Berkshires
October Mountain State Forest, off Route 20 near Lee, is Massachusetts's largest state forest, with 50 campsites and many trails, including the walk to Schermerhorn Gorge. To the south of Tyringham Center are good hill walks on Tyringham Cobble and the McLennan Reservation, the occasional haunts of coyotes, bob cats, black bears and wild turkeys.

The 2,035-mile Appalachian Trail, from Georgia to Maine, crosses the length of the Berkshire Hills south to north.

Mount Greylock►►►, the highest peak in Massachusetts at 3,491 feet, was named after Chief Grey Lock who hunted here. A road climbs to the top for a grand view over three states. Church spires dominate **North Adams**, a red-brick mill town. The museum at Western Gateway Heritage State Park narrates the history of the Hoosac Railroad Tunnel (see panel). Away from the Mohawk Trail, the cotton-mill town of **Adams** has legacies of the 18th century, most significantly the atmospheric Quaker Meeting House of 1782 on Friend Street.

Founded as West Hoosac in 1750, elegant **Williamstown►►** owes its name to Ephraim Williams, who left money for the founding of an academy, stipulating that the town must take his name; the academy opened in 1791, becoming Williams College two years later. Today it is among the top liberal arts institutions in America. The **Sterling and Francine Clark Art Institute►►►** (*open*: Tuesday to Sunday; free) is noted for French Impressionist and American paintings, as well as British silverware. The **Williams College Museum of Art►** (*open*: Tuesday to Sunday; free) possesses 11,000 works ranging from 9th-century Assyrian stone reliefs to Andy Warhol's last self-portrait. The **Hopkins Observatory** contains a museum and planetarium, open during term time and on occasions during the summer.

The town of **Pittsfield** has been a paper-mill centre since the 19th century and is the largest town in the Berkshires region. Art galleries exhibiting local work include Pittsfield Arts League (2 South Street), Radius Gallery (137 North Street) and Berkshire Artisans (28 Renne Avenue). **Berkshire Museum►** (39 South Street) includes art of the Hudson River school, dolls, early electric inventions of the Stanley Electric Company and domestic bygones. The Crane Paper Company's **Wahconah Mill** manufactures paper on which the American currency is printed. At Dalton, east of Pittsfield, the **Crane Museum**, within the 1844 Old Stone Mill, tells the story of American paper-making (*open*: 2–5 summer weekdays; free). On the outskirts of Pittsfield, off Holmes Road, **Arrowhead** (tours 10–4:30; closed Tuesday and Wednesday in autumn) was the home of Herman Melville and family from 1850–63. The furniture is not original but is contemporary. The house contains the room where Melville wrote *Moby Dick* (1851).

Renoir and Degas, part of the notable French collection in the Sterling and Francine Clark Art Institute

The region's best-preserved Shaker village, active from 1783 to 1960, **Hancock Shaker Village►►►** is today a living museum, well worth a full day's visit if you want to catch the various events held here (*open*: daily 9:30–5, May to October, 10–3 November to March; tel: 413/443 0188). Originally called the 'City of Peace', the village is noted for its famous round stone barn, built before 1830. The museum's craftsmen and craftswomen continue to live out the Shaker lifestyle (see pages 148–9), tending historic livestock breeds, maintaining an authentic herb garden and giving demonstrations of Shaker cooking.

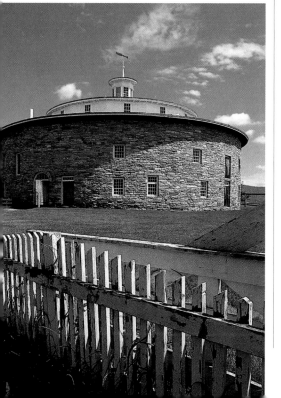

The Hoosac Railroad Tunnel
This 4.7-mile tunnel near Adams, in the northwest corner of the Berkshires, was constructed in 1851–75 and was the first project of its kind to use nitroglycerine for blasting out the rock. The project was costly, both in terms of money ($24 million) and lives (195 workers perished). It gained the nickname of the 'Bloody Pit' and, not surprisingly, is alleged to be haunted.

The round barn at Hancock Shaker Village. People came from far and wide to study its ingenious design

Music at Tanglewood
The Tanglewood Music Center, a training centre for musicians, is the summer home of the Boston Symphony Orchestra (see page 79). The open-sided Music Shed is the main concert hall; it is cheapest to sit on the adjoining lawn for concerts (the sound does carry). Open rehearsals take place at 10:30am on Saturdays; you can eavesdrop from the lawn at other times, since members of the public are admitted into the grounds. Whilst there you can visit the Little Red House, a reconstruction of the house in which Nathaniel Hawthorne wrote *The House of the Seven Gables* (1851) and *Tanglewood Tales* (1852–3); inside is a free museum, open in summer.

Stockbridge walks
Just south of Stockbridge, off Park Street, boulder-strewn Ice Glen is so called because of the presence of ice crystals well into summer; a trail climbs up to Laura's Tower for a three-state view.
   Three miles south of Stockbridge, on Route 7, the Monument Mountain Reservation overlooks the southern Berkshires, with trails encountering rock outcrops, caves and a hillside strewn with quartzite boulders. William Cullen Bryant waxed lyrical in a poem about the mountain: 'the beauty and the majesty of the earth, spread wide beneath'.

The southern Berkshires An amiable small-town atmosphere envelopes **Lenox▶**, well located as a base for exploring the southern Berkshires. In the late-19th century the estates formed rural summer retreats for the wealthy; one such was **Tanglewood** (see panel), near Lenox, originally owned by the Tappan family. Another was **The Mount▶**, in Lenox, summer residence of the writer Edith Wharton (see page 46) from 1902 to 1911. A sledding accident at Lenox was the basis of her novel *Ethan Frome* (1911). The restored **Lenox railway station** (1902) also evokes the period; the Berkshire Scenic Railway maintains a model railway, a short section of track and a shop.
   Norman Rockwell (see page 150) put **Stockbridge▶▶** on the map with his depiction of Main Street. At the heart of the village is the Red Lion Inn, dating from 1773 and sporting the sign of George III. Even older is the **Mission House▶** (*open*: 11–4 Tuesday to Sunday Memorial Day weekend to Columbus Day and holidays; closed Tuesday after holidays), the only elegant house in a wilderness when built in 1739 for a Congregationalist minister; its furniture is original and there is a display on the Native

Chesterwood, the summer home of sculptor Daniel Chester French

American community of Stockbridge. Across the street, **Merwin House▶** (*open*: summer, 12–5, Tuesday, Thursday, Saturday and Sunday; owned and operated by SPNEA – see page 68) is a Federal-style brick house built around 1825, furnished in turn-of-the-century style.

Located just outside town, the **Norman Rockwell Museum▶▶▶** holds the world's largest collection of original works by America's best-loved artist. About a quarter of the works are on display at any one time. The reconstructed studio has Rockwell's art books, easel and many props familiar from his paintings.

Chesterwood▶▶ (*open*: daily May to October; sign-posted from the west end of Main Street, Stockbridge), was the summer home of sculptor Daniel Chester French from 1898 ('I live here six months of the year – in heaven. The other six months I live, well – in New York'). Tours take in his studio and house (see panel).

The best opportunity to glimpse inside a fashionable summerhouse in the Berkshires is at **Naumkeag▶▶** (*open*: Tuesday to Sunday late May to Labor Day; weekends in winter). Built in 1885 by Stanford White for the Choates, it retains the family's eclectic possessions. Fletcher Steele modified the gardens to create terraces with a stepped waterfall.

The **Berkshire Botanical Garden▶** (*open*: May to October; Route 102 west of the intersection with Route 183) is compact but varied, with a herbarium of dyer's and medicinal herbs, rock garden, lily pond, day-lilies, shrubs and wildflowers. July and August are the best months to visit.

Bidwell House▶, in Monterey (*open*: 11–4 Tuesday to Sunday and holidays, Memorial Day to mid-October), is a Georgian house built for a minister; it has original features and is furnished according to an inventory of 1784.

At Great Barrington the **Albert Schweitzer Center** is a museum and library dedicated to the humanitarian and winner of the 1953 Nobel Peace Prize.

Colonel John Ashley House▶, Ashley Falls (*open*: 1–5, Wednesday to Sunday and holidays, late May to mid-October; free), is a quintessential Colonial house of 1735 where Ashley and others drafted the petition against Britain in 1773 known as the Sheffield Declaration. In 1781 Ashley's slave, Mum Bett, was the first slave to win her freedom, doing so under the new constitution.

The pools below **Bash Bish Falls▶▶**, a very fine waterfall cascading over huge rocks, are excellent for swimming. They can be reached from the lower car park (beyond the New York State sign). Near by is **Mount Everett State Forest▶**, with a road leading to its summit.

147

Daniel Chester French
America's most prolific sculptor, French produced some works of worldwide renown, including his first commission, the *Minute Man* (completed in 1875 and made from 10 army cannons melted down for the purpose) at Concord, the John Harvard statue at Harvard University and the Lincoln statue in Washington, DC.

The Shakers

■ **The Shaker religious sect is now almost extinct but, in today's complex world, the purity of its followers' way of life, the simple, functional design of their architecture and furniture, and their herbal medicines and organic farming methods have an increasing appeal.....■**

Shaker your plate

In the summer and autumn, visitors to Hancock Shaker Village can partake of a candlelight dinner. The Shaker practice of silence during meals is not observed, and the sexes may mix, but the dishes are taken from Shaker cookbooks. Guests should note an extract from Rules for Visitors: 'At the table we wish all to be as free as at home, but we dislike the wasteful habit of leaving food on the plate'. Hence the American expression 'shaker your plate'.

The kitchen at Hancock, efficient and elegant

Named because of the trembling some members experienced during worship, the Shakers were a persecuted offshoot of the Quakers in England. In 1774 their founder, Ann Lee, led eight followers from Manchester, England, to America, where religious liberty was firmly upheld, and settled near Albany, New York. Their beliefs and practices soon attracted interest and converts, and by the mid-19th century there were 18 Shaker communities in New England, New York and the Midwest, with about 6,000 members in all.

The Shakers were originally called the United Society of Believers in Christ's Second Appearing and believed that the millennium, a thousand years of heaven on earth, had arrived with Mother Ann. The fundamental principles laid down by Mother Ann were communal living, separate from 'the world', and celibacy. In the belief that Mother Ann was the female aspect of God, her followers shared leadership and work equally between men and women. Tasks indoors and out were put on a rota so that no one had to endure the unpopular jobs for too long (such as looking after the small boys sent by their parents to learn a trade in the Shaker community).

'Hands to work and hearts to God' The Shakers aimed for perfection in all they turned their hands to. Adapting the Yankee work ethic to fit their religious ideals, they became renowned for their industry and ingenuity. Their numerous inventions include the circular saw, a rotary harrow, a threshing machine, an automatic hay-seeding device, a non-drip paint can and the flat broom.

The Shakers were also immensely practical and kept the house very clean (this was heaven on earth, and there is no dust in heaven). This explains the ubiquitous wooden peg rails for hanging clothes, kitchen utensils, mops and their ladder-backed chairs; the built-in, floor-to-ceiling wardrobes (no need to sweep underneath or dust on top) and the beds on rollers for ease of sweeping; it also accounts for the striking efficiency of their kitchens, and the famously progressive round barn at Hancock, Massachusetts (see page 145).

In the belief that a sound soul needs a healthy body, the Shakers ate well (their recipes are famous); they also made a wide range of herbal medicines. Assiduous gardeners, they were the first to market seeds, an enterprise which developed into a most successful industry.

Villages such as Hancock (left) are preserved for posterity

Shaker artefacts

Oval boxes, baskets and furniture, in particular the chair, exemplify the clean, simple lines of Shaker design and their perfect craftsmanship. Everything was made purely to serve its function, without any embellishment. The chair is sturdy, but light – so it could be hung up out of the way – with a straight ladder-back. The chairs' back legs were fitted with a 'button tilter', a swivel device designed to prevent wear on floors. The reproduction of Shaker artefacts is a burgeoning industry and the Shaker villages sell beautiful examples.

The gift of song

Singing and dancing was, and is, an integral part of the Shaker service of worship and 10,000 or more of their songs have been collected. Many are based on English and early American folk tunes. Aaron Copland borrowed the Shaker 'Simple Gifts' melody for his *Appalachian Spring*, scored for a Martha Graham ballet in 1944:
''Tis the gift to be simple,
'tis the gift to be free,
'Tis the gift to come down
   where we ought to be,
And when we find
   ourselves in the place
   just right,
'Twill be in the valley of
   love and delight.'

Shakers and 'the world' The Shaker communities adopted orphans. They also took in children indentured to the society by their parents in order to learn a trade, many of whom later joined the communities. Converts were also made from the many visitors who came to the villages, for while separation from the world was a basic principle, Shakers were happy to sell their goods to the 'world's people' – brooms, chairs, boxes, baskets, seeds and cloaks (specially woven in bright colours for society ladies to wear to the opera).

Numbers peaked in the 1840s but, in the decades that followed, began to decline; restrictions were put into force on adoption, and the pacifism Shakerism stood for and which had attracted converts, went out of favour. Celibacy began to take its toll in falling numbers and communities could not compete with mass-production of goods.

Today, only a handful of Shakers are left, living in the town of Sabbathday Lake, Maine. They generally continue to live the traditional Shaker life, worshipping devoutly, selling their goods at fairs, farming their land (though they are more likely to be seen wearing Levis for hoeing the vegetables than the long skirts or white shirts and black waistcoats still worn for services). Tours can be taken around the village, but most buildings may be seen from the outside only. At Canterbury and Lower Shaker villages in New Hampshire (see pages 192 and 195), and at Hancock village in Massachusetts (see page 145), the old buildings are preserved in recognition of the purity and ingenuity of the Shaker contribution.

■ **'Without thinking too much about it in specific terms, I was showing the America I knew and observed to others who might not have noticed.'** Norman Rockwell's portrayal of scenes from everyday life touched the nation's soul and made him America's best-loved illustrator..... ■

Top: Triple Self-Portrait (1960)
Above: 'Freedom from Want'

Where to see his work
The largest collection of Rockwell originals is in a museum at Stockbridge, Massachusetts (see page 147). The old carriage house he converted to a studio has been moved to this site from his Stockbridge home. In Vermont, Rockwell's hometown of Arlington has a display of prints in a 19th-century church, and in Rutland the Norman Rockwell Museum has an exhibition covering his career (open all year).

Born in New York in 1894, Norman Rockwell was given his first freelance commission by the magazine publishers Condé Nast, at the age of 17. In 1916 he took some paintings to the art editor of the *Saturday Evening Post*, the most widely circulated magazine in America, and thus began a partnership that was to turn Norman Rockwell into a household name, and his works into national treasures. Over the next 47 years he illustrated 317 covers for the *Post*, each one eagerly awaited by its readers.

The American dream In almost photographic detail Rockwell depicted childhood, scenes family scenes and small-town scenes, each tinged with affection and gentle humour: the family outing in the car, the boy who discovers his father's Santa Claus costume, a visit to the optician, the signing of a marriage licence. When he moved with his wife Mary Barstow and their three sons to Arlington, Vermont in 1939, the neighbours were 'exactly the models I need for my purpose – the sincere, honest, homespun types that I love to paint.' And it was just these people that he depicted in the famous wartime series of posters – 'Freedom of Speech', 'Freedom of Worship', 'Freedom from Want' and 'Freedom from Fear' – inspired by President Roosevelt's Four Freedoms Proclamation of 1941.

In 1953 the family moved to Stockbridge in Massachusetts, where Rockwell lived and worked right up to his death in 1978. His works include illustrations for calendars, such as the Boy Scout Calendar, covers for other magazines, advertisements and greetings cards, as well as oil paintings and portraits.

Rockwell's work has always been a touch too sentimental for the fine art buffs, but among ordinary people for whom he captures American life as it was always meant to be, Norman Rockwell remains as popular as ever.

► ► Cape Ann 139D3

Abutting the northern extremity of Massachusetts Bay, Cape Ann harbours many charming fishing ports, as well as idiosyncratic historic buildings and coastal views much depicted by artists. There are good bathing beaches and shops for browsing. Weekend traffic winds slowly along Routes 127 and 127A, and parking can be very difficult, particularly in Rockport. A rail service from Boston's North Station and Monday to Saturday bus services provide feasible alternatives.

Manchester has an attractive harbour and clean sands at Singing Beach (the rail station is a short walk away).

Gloucester► is a starting point for whale-watching trips and is also a working fishing port – founded in 1623 it is America's oldest. Fine beaches draw crowds at summer weekends. Artist Fitz Hugh Lane (1804–65) lived in the three-gabled granite house on the waterfront, and the nation's largest collection of his work is exhibited with fishing industry displays at the **Cape Ann Historical Society►**. Living artists' work can be seen in the thriving **Rocky Neck Art Colony** and at the North Shore Arts Association's exhibition centre.

Hammond Castle Museum►► in Gloucester (*open*: 10–6 summer, some winter weekends; for details, tel: 508/283 7673) is a sham medieval folly perched just above the shore; home of the inventor John Hays Hammond Jr, the eye-catching edifice was built around the Hammond organ in the Great Hall (see panel). The castle comprises a labyrinth of small rooms and passages adorned with Renaissance treasures, a library with a 'whispering ceiling' that picks up the slightest sounds, and a courtyard graced by a Roman sarcophagus.

Birdseye's frozen foods
Clarence 'Bob' Birdseye (1886–1956) created the frozen-food business from Gloucester after observing, on an expedition to Labrador in 1914–17, that local people ate fish, meat and vegetables that they had frozen months before. In 1925 he developed a quick-freezing system for commercial use and helped to found the General Seafoods Company in Gloucester, selling frozen foods to consumers in Springfield, Massachusetts. Birds Eye is now a household name and the original plant in Commercial Street is still in operation.

The mighty Hammond
The massive 8,200-pipe Hammond organ at Hammond Castle was built to play automatically because, ironically, Dr Hammond, the inventor, was not musical enough to play the instrument himself. The immense sound of Bach's *Toccata and Fugue*, often played to tour groups, is astonishingly powerful. There is a programme of concerts given here.

The Gloucester Fisherman *by Leonard Craske looks out to sea*

Harbour scenes at Rockport

The Paper House
North of Rockport, off Route 127 at Pigeon Cove, is this endearingly eccentric all-paper building constructed between 1922 and 1942 by Elis F Stenman as an experiment. Stenman invented a special paste for the purpose and used some 100,000 newspapers: the furniture (made from hollow tubes) included a piano, a clock, a radio cabinet, a fireplace mantel, a standard lamp, chairs and a desk. The walls are made of diamond-shaped blocks, with the headlines still legible. Stenman's wife created the bead curtains from old magazines.

A short drive southwards along the coast, though still in Gloucester, is the fantasy retreat of **Beauport►** with its warren of 40 rooms, many of them devoted to historical themes (*open*: Monday to Friday, mid-May to mid-October, plus weekends September and October; owned and operated by SPNEA – see page 68). The house was built, and periodically enlarged, between 1907 and 1934 by interior designer Henry Davis Sleeper. It is full of quirky visual effects, windows with coloured glass, and bottles, antiquites and curiosities – including a secret staircase. The Pine Kitchen, recalling the simple homes of the colonial era, contrasts with the Octagon Room, elegantly French in spirit, or the Belfy Bedroom, which is sheer chinoiserie. The road continues southwards to **Eastern Point Lighthouse** at the east side of Gloucester Harbor.

Picturesque **Rockport►►** is the most visited place on Cape Ann. The harbour scene epitomises coastal New England and includes the fishing shack known as 'Motif No 1', one of the most photographed and painted buildings in all America. **Bearskin Neck**, the heart of the old village, is a mixture of craft shops and toytown-scale fishing huts turned into homes with tiny front gardens.

Within the 54 acres of **Halibut Point State Park►►** is a fine panorama where a dwarf forest gives way to heathland and scrub, with drops to a rocky shore.

Essex stakes a claim as 'king of the clam'. It has lobster shacks, seafood restaurants, fishing-tackle shops and over 60 antique shops. The Shipbuilding Museum expounds on 300 years of the industry in Essex. Boat trips up the Essex river give opportunities for bird-watching, while Crane's Beach at **Ipswich** ranks among the North Shore's finest.

Lighthouses

■ **All the way up the coast, lighthouses stand as symbols of New England's maritime history. The Coast Guard has now automated the light stations, but they remain a unique and cherished part of New England's heritage.....■**

One of the earliest acts of Congress, signed by George Washington in 1789, provided for a programme of construction and maintenance of lighthouses, beacons, buoys and public piers. Both immigrants and traders from Europe were vital to the early development of the American nation and the safe navigation of their ships was crucial.

Unique landmarks Constructed of anything from wood or granite to concrete or iron, every lighthouse is different. The tall New London Harbor Light was built in simple colonial style by the British, while Portland Breakwater Light was built in 1855 in the Greek Revival style, its height typical of the shorter lighthouses found in ports. Portland Head Light, probably the most painted and photographed on the coast of New England, stands 80 feet high above the cliffs. Owls Head and Pemaquid Point in Maine are also very photogenic. The red and white stripes of West Quoddy Head will also be familiar to many. At Fort Point the wooden fog-bell house still stands, one of the last of its kind. Anyone interested in lighthouses should visit the Shore Village Museum in Rockland, Maine (see page 130).

Keeping the lights shining The heroic keepers have passed into history, and today many lighthouses are in poor repair. There is, however, mounting interest in preserving them and lighthouse cruises operate from Bath's Maritime Museum and Portsmouth, New Hampshire.

Get-away
For a 'unique romantic adventure' – and a taste of what life was like for the keeper and his family – you can book bed and breakfast at Rose Island Lighthouse in Narragansett Bay (also available for longer spells, with record-keeping and maintenance chores). Contact Rose Island Lighthouse Foundation, PO Box 1419, Newport, RI 02840 (tel: 401/847 4242). Similarly, you can spend the night in the lightkeeper's quarters on the Monomoy Islands, a wildlife refuge (Cape Cod Museum of Natural History, PO Box 1710, Brewster, MA 02631; tel: 508/896 3867), or in Isle au Haut lighthouse, Acadia National Park (Keeper's House, PO Box 26, Isle au Haut, ME 04645).

Tales of heroism
Most famous of all New England's keepers was Ida Lewis (1842–1911) who took over from her father at Lime Rock Light in Newport, Rhode Island, when he was paralysed by a stroke. She became an expert oarswoman and over half a century saved dozens of lives.

Winter comes to Nobska Light, Falmouth, Cape Cod

MASSACHUSETTS

Cameos of nature
Cape Cod has several nesting areas for plovers and terns. Diamond-back terrapins, an endangered species, lay eggs in Sandy Neck Beach, Barnstaple. Some 90 per cent of the rare Plymouth gentian, found by ponds, grow on Cape Cod. Much of the hinterland between the two coasts consists of infertile dwarf forest, characterised by pitch pine and scrub oak: coyotes have moved in since the late 1980s. Wild cranberries proliferate. Bog plants, such as bladderwort, pitcher plant and sundew, thrive on the salt marsh.

Hyannis, for shops, ferries to the islands and round-the-harbour cruises

▶▶▶ Cape Cod and the Islands   *139E1*

Cape Cod▶▶ is a busy vacation resort. Off season you may have the beaches more or less to yourself, but in July and August traffic grinds along the roads, the beach car parks fill up early in the day and accommodation prices are high. It's emphatically not touring territory and there are only a few major sights. So is it worth it? The answer is maybe – if you are a nature-lover, or like a stay-put holiday with some boat trips and mild sightseeing thrown in.

Physically the Cape is low-lying, covered with dwarf forest and cranberry bogs, and edged by marshes and sandy beaches. It is often likened to a bent arm: severed at the shoulder by the Cape Canal, with most of the population around the biceps portion (or Upper Cape); as it turns north (the Lower Cape) the peninsula narrows to curve round at Provincetown. The towns on the south side virtually roll into one anonymous mass. The waters on the Atlantic side are cool but often good for surfing; the bay side (facing south and west) is calmer and warmer.

The Upper Cape: south coast Family-style attractions (see page 245) are abundant on the much-developed south coast. Routes 6 and 28 cross the **Cape Cod Canal**. For a longer look at this waterway, completed in 1914 and possessing a rare vertical rail lift (for hoisting the railroad up to allow shipping through), look out at water level from the largely reconstructed **Aptucxet Trading Post Museum** in Bourne. Also on site are reconstructed 18th-century salt works and a railway station specially built for President Grover Cleveland who summered here.

Although much expanded, **Falmouth▶** preserves its old village centre and green. The Falmouth Historical Society maintain a handsome 1790 house, subsequently home to Elijah Swift, who pioneered the local whaling industry. A

The Glass Museum at Sandwich displays items from the town's 19th-century factory

museum in the grounds honours local lady Catherine Lee Bates, author of *America the Beautiful* (1893).

Like Falmouth, **Woods Hole►** is a ferry port for Martha's Vineyard and Nantucket (see pages 160–3). The National Marine Fisheries Aquarium is stocked with local species, while Woods Hole Oceanographic Institution museum has displays on the wrecks of the *Titanic* and *Bismarck*.

At the Old Town Hall in Main Street, Hyannis, the **JF Kennedy Museum** has displays of JFK's vacation days on the Cape with family and friends; the Kennedy summer home was at Hyannis Port.

The Upper Cape: north coast The north shore is more genteel and historic; Route 6A is the Cape's 'antiques road'. **Pairpoint Glass Works** on Sandwich Road, Sagamore Bridge, is the oldest glass-manufacturer in America, with glass-blowing demonstrations on weekdays.

Sandwich► has an attractive centre, with a church and pond. Dexter Grist Mill (1640) still produces corn meal for sale and Hoxie House is a 1675 saltbox; both are open and stand by Shawme Pond, a haunt of waterfowl. The 1641 Wing Fort House has heirlooms and period pieces, and is the oldest house in America continuously lived in and owned by the same family. The **Glass Museum►** has items made by the defunct Boston Sandwich Glass Company. Yesteryears Doll Museum is one of the largest collections of its kind in New England. Thornton W Burgess Museum commemorates the creator of the children's stories *Peter Cottontail* and *Old Mother Westwind*.

The **Heritage Plantation►►** (*open*: daily mid-May to late October) is a delightful museum of Americana displaying custom-made cars, model soldiers, Currier-and-Ives pictures, toys and old tools. The setting is enchanting: the extensive grounds are planted with over 125 varieties of rhododendron, which bloom in May.

At **Brewster►** the Cape Cod Natural History Museum has hands-on exhibits for children and runs outings (including trips to the Monomoy Islands; tel: 1-800/ 479 3867). Close by, the Fire and History Museum has a gleaming array of over 30 vintage fire-fighting devices.

Continued on page 158.

Visitors may join an oceanographic cruise from Woods Hole

155

Marine research
Since the 1870s the pleasant shoreside village of Woods Hole has been home to two important marine research establishments: the National Marine Fisheries Science Center and Aquarium and the Woods Hole Oceanographic Institution (WHOI). The latter exists to study rivers, coasts, sea beds, marine life, currents, pollutants and other aspects of the oceans. In season daily oceanographic cruises are run from here on the *Oceanquest* (tel: 1-800/37 OCEAN). This is an excellent introduction to the study of the sea, enabling participants to use plankton nets and microscopes under the guidance of a scientist.

MASSACHUSETTS

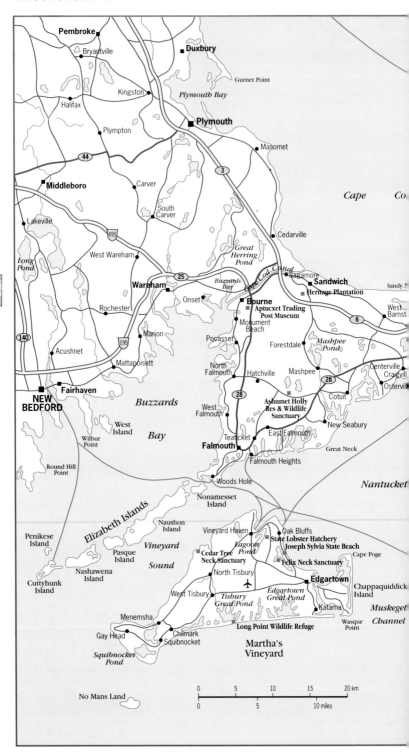

Pembroke
Bryantville
Duxbury
Gurnet Point
Kingston
Plymouth Bay
Halifax
Plympton
Plymouth
Manomet
44
Middleboro
Carver
Cape Co
South Carver
Lakeville
Cedarville
495
Great Herring Pond
Long Pond
West Wareham
Cape Cod Canal
Sagamore
Sandwich
Sandy N
25
Buzzards Bay
Wareham
Heritage Plantation
Rochester
Onset
Bourne
140
Marion
Aptucset Trading Post Museum
Monument Beach
West Barnst
6
Acushnet
Pocasset
Forestdale
Mashpee Pond
195
Mattapoisett
North Falmouth
Hatchville
Mashpee
Centerville Craigvill
Fairhaven
28
Cotuit
Osterville
NEW BEDFORD
Buzzards
West Falmouth
Ashumet Holly Res & Wildlife Sanctuary
28
New Seabury
West Island
Bay
East Falmouth
Great Neck
Wilbur Point
Teaticket
Falmouth
Round Hill Point
Falmouth Heights
Woods Hole
Nantucket
Nonamesset Island
Penikese Island
Elizabeth Islands
Naushon Island
Vineyard Haven
Oak Bluffs
State Lobster Hatchery
Joseph Sylvia State Beach
Pasque Island
Vineyard
Lagoon Pond
Cape Poge
Cedar Tree Neck Sanctuary
Cuttyhunk Island
Nashawena Island
Sound
North Tisbury
Felix Neck Sanctuary
Edgartown
Chappaquiddick Island
West Tisbury
Tisbury Great Pond
Edgartown Great Pond
Muskeget
Menemsha
Katama
Channel
Gay Head
Chilmark
Squibnocket
Long Point Wildlife Refuge
Wasque Point
Squibnocket Pond
Martha's Vineyard

No Mans Land

| 0 | 5 | 10 | 15 | 20 km |
| 0 | 5 | | 10 miles | |

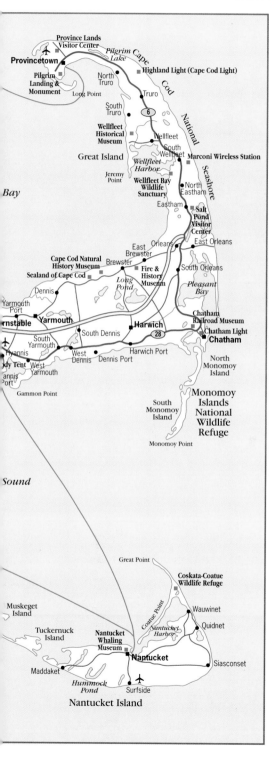

*Cape Cod National
Seashore*

MASSACHUSETTS

Provincetown, overlooked by the belfry of the 1861 Center Methodist Church

Continued from page 155.

The Lower Cape The best scenery on the Cape is found here, especially along the 40-mile **National Seashore►►** with its superb beaches and cliff-like dunes. The area is famous for its plant and bird life.

Salt Pond Visitor Center► is useful for information on natural history, trails and ranger-led walks; it is also the start of the **Nauset Marsh Trail►**. The **Rail Trail,** an inland course of some 20 miles, passes ponds, salt marshes, pine woods and cranberry bogs; it is open to cyclists, horse-riders and hikers.

The site of **Marconi Wireless Station** was abandoned in 1920 and only concrete foundations now remain, though a model explains how the first overseas radio message was transmitted from here in 1901 to Cornwall, England. **Cape Cod Light,** the Cape's oldest lighthouse, dates from 1857 and sends out a 20-mile beam.

On the west coast, **Wellfleet►** is prettily sited overlooking an intricate pattern of marshy creeks and a marina. To its west, the trail along the sandy spit known as Great Island (4 miles each way) has remote beauty.

At **Province Lands Visitor Center►** (tel: 508/487 1256), an observation platform gives a panorama of the invasive dunes resulting from the removal of trees, overgrazing and the subsequent loss of topsoil.

Provincetown Sand spills on to the road and is whipped up by the wind as you approach **Provincetown►►**. On 11 November the Pilgrim Fathers first touched American soil here in 1620. The Pilgrims' arrival, and the signing of the Mayflower Compact, are commemorated by the **Pilgrim Monument►►** (modelled on the belltower of the

Beaches

The National Seashore beaches are all suitable for families; a pass covers admission to all six of them (free out of season or after 5pm). To reach Coast Guard Beach it is best to take the free shuttle bus from the car park signposted for that beach; car parks are often full in July and August. There are numerous town beaches (fee payable). Le Count Hollow and White Crest are known for surfing, Cahoon Hollow for surfing and partying. Newcomb Hollow and Longnook are quiet family beaches. First Encounter Beach at Eastham is where the *Mayflower* landed, to be greeted by friendly Native Americans.

The Monomoy Islands

Nature-lovers should not miss a visit to the Monomoy Islands, formed of a barrier beach south of the elbow of Cape Cod. North Monomoy has dunes, beach grass, migrating birds and a large summer population of eastern shore birds, while South Monomoy is much larger and has a wide range of flora and fauna, including deer and seals. Other sites for observing nature include Falmouth Ponds, Ashumet Holly and Wildlife Sanctuary (Falmouth), Sandy Neck (Barnstable), the beech forest at Provincetown and West Harwich Conservation Area.

town hall in Siena, Italy), 252 feet high and the nation's tallest granite structure. From the top the Cape seems spread out like a map and Boston's towers can be seen on a clear day. The adjacent museum (entry covers both sites) exhibits scrimshaw, toys, a fire engine and items relating to the Arctic explorer Admiral Donald MacMillan.

Provincetown itself (known as 'P-town') is commercialised and touristy but great fun, with shops ranging from the tastefully arty to the outrageous. The subtle lighting effects of sun and water have drawn innumerable artists, including Edward Hopper, Jackson Pollock, Robert Motherwell and Mark Rothko. The town's galleries include the Provincetown Art Association Museum, the Fine Arts Work Center and the Provincetown Gallery Guild. Provincetown also has a strong theatrical heritage: Eugene O'Neill had his first plays performed here, and Richard Gere, Marlon Brando and Al Pacino have all acted at P-town. The artistic and theatrical ethos has gone hand in hand with the establishment of one of the East Coast's largest gay communities.

Accommodation is plentiful, and the town is easy to walk around. Trolleys tour the sights, and horse and trap tours leave from the town hall.

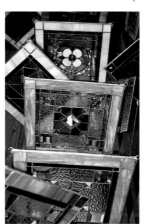

Cruises and trips
Whales can be seen near Provincetown – boats from all over the Cape, and from Boston, Plymouth and the North Shore, head over here. Passenger-only ferries connect Provincetown with Plymouth (tel: 1-800/242 2469) and Boston (tel: 617/723 7800). Scenic flights can be made on a classic 1930 Stinson Detroiter plane (tel: 508/487 0240). Fishing and sightseeing cruises leave from Hyannis, Provincetown, Falmouth and elsewhere. Cape Cod Canal Cruises depart from Onset (tel: 508/295 3883), while Water Safaris at West Dennis offer the only river cruise on the Cape (tel: 508/362 5557).

Stained-glass shop in Provincetown

Joseph Sylvia State Beach

Getting around
Cycle hire is available at ferry ports. A public bus network connects most places, and tour buses meet the ferries. Adamcab (tel: 508/627 4462) offers minibus tours at 10:30am and 2pm. Petrol is expensive: fill up on the mainland.

Wildlife sanctuaries
● Cape Poge Reservation – salt marsh, ponds and red cedar uplands with a range of wildlife (entry is via the adjoining Wasque Reservation).
● Felix Neck Wildlife Sanctuary – trails, wildfowl ponds, salt marshes and an interpretation centre.
● Cedar Tree Neck Sanctuary – good for wildlife spotting from trails and has coastal views.
● Long Point Wildlife Refuge – butterflies and moths, spring and fall bird migrations and birds of prey.

Martha's Vineyard The English explorers, John Brereton and Bartholomew Gosnold, landed on **Martha's Vineyard►►** in 1602, and Gosnold named the island after his daughter, Martha. Brereton remarked on the 'incredible store of vines and the beautie and delicacie of this sweet soil'.

The East Coast's largest warm-water resort island is about three times the size of neighbouring Nantucket (see page 162). The rich and famous have summered here for many years: President Clinton recently took his vacation here and singers Billy Joel, Carly Simon and James Taylor are among those owning houses on the Vineyard.

Variety is a key feature in the island's places, architecture, people, weather and scenery. The north shore is craggy, the south shore sandy with a heathy hinterland speckled with ponds. Inland a dwarf forest of scrub oak blankets much of the scene. Weather is remarkably localised; often one part of the island can be basking in bright sunshine while another is cloaked in a hot, humid mist (a 'smoky sou'wester').

Most of the island's beaches are privately owned. The main public beaches are Joseph Sylvia State Beach, between Edgartown and Vineyard Haven (no surf, ideal for families); Katama (facing the Atlantic, good surf, strong swimmers only); Moshpu (by Gay Head cliffs, with surf); Oak Bluffs Town Beach (convenient, though often crowded, family beach); and Menemsha (small and quiet).

Around the Vineyard At the western extremity of the island, the village of **Gay Head** has a sizeable Wampanoag community (hence the Native American crafts shops). **Gay Head cliffs►►** are a tumbled mass of multi-coloured clay, a spectacular natural landform of great geological interest with an excellent beach at the base accessible by road. The fishing village of **Menemsha▶** has retained a weather-beaten character, with little hint of gentrification. An excellent fishmarket is found among the tiny shacks in the harbour. You can take the ferry from here to Cuttyhunk in the Elizabeth Islands, where a monolith commemorates the first European settlement in America.

Immaculately preserved **Edgartown▶▶**, haunt of millionaires, gained its prosperous look when sea-captains from the whaling days built handsome Federal-style homes. The Old Whaling Church of 1843, an outstanding example of Greek Revival architecture, has been converted into a performing arts centre; walking tours begin from here (for details, tel: 508/627 8619). Vincent House (open to the public) dates from 1672 and is the oldest building on the island. The town centre is usually busy with window-shoppers, admiring the jewellery stores and upmarket boutiques.

Endowed with the longest beach on the Vineyard (scenes from the movie *Jaws* were filmed here), **Oak Bluffs▶▶** is a period-piece resort where the Methodists held their first summer camp in 1835. By 1850 some 12,000 people were attending the Sabbath meetings at the open-sided tabernacle. Tents were replaced by charming 'carpenter Gothic' gingerbread houses, each adorned with ornate filigree work. There are now more than 300, with no two quite alike. One house is open as a museum.

Vineyard Haven (Tisbury)▶ is a big yachting and boat-building centre, and possesses a state lobster hatchery. A fire destroyed much of the town in 1883 but Greek Revival houses survived along William Street. Ritter House Museum expounds upon times past. Crafts such as scrimshaw are exhibited in the Old School House Museum. The Seaman's Bethel (1892) was the place of refuge for seamen; gifts from those who survived storms and shipwrecks are displayed.

Getting to the islands
● The Steamship Authority (tel: 508/540 2022) runs ferries from Woods Hole to Vineyard Haven and Hyannis to Nantucket, plus inter-island services.
● Hy-Line Cruises run from Hyannis to Oak Bluffs (tel: 508/778 2600).
● Cape Island Express Lines operate from New Bedford to Vineyard Haven and Nantucket (tel: 508/997 1688).
● Island Commuter Corporation runs a summer service to Oak Bluffs, taking about 35 minutes to the Vineyard and 2 hours 15 minutes to Nantucket.
● Cape Air (tel: 1-800/352 0714) is among several airlines serving the islands.

Victorian gingerbread cottages at Oak Bluffs

MASSACHUSETTS

Lighthouse guarding the entrance to Nantucket town's harbour

Nantucket The island of Nantucket►►►, 30 miles off the Massachusetts mainland, deserves the accolade 'a step back in time'. The town (also called Nantucket) is preserved down to the last paving stone, and the handsome houses evoke the prosperity of the whaling days. Like Martha's Vineyard, this is a millionaires' vacationland, but while the larger island is considered the territory of the newly rich, Nantucket is more the haunt of rich Yankees who choose not to flaunt their wealth, and is certainly less developed.

Nantucket►►► town preserves an air of genteel perfection. In Main Street the oldest houses include the Three Bricks, built in 1836–8 by Captain Joseph Starbuck for his sons. The tower of the Congregational Church offers a good view of the island. Shops tend towards artiness and good taste (although at a price), antique shops abound and there are weekend antique auctions. Center Street's shops have traditionally been run by women (dating back to the time when captains' wives had time on their hands). A local speciality is the Nantucket Lightship, a woven basket into which is inserted a scrimshaw disc.

One ticket gets you into all Nantucket's museums, though apart from the Whaling Museum these are modest in scale. Housed in a former whale oil refinery, the **Whaling Museum►►** displays artefacts related to past whaling days, including the ship's logs of the *Essex* (the vessel immortalised in *Moby Dick*), sailors' souvenirs, a finback whale skeleton and scrimshaws.

Local history collections forms the basis of the P Foulger Museum. The **Museum of Nantucket History►** covers the complete timescale from the distant geological past to the present day; a model shows how the island's coastline is changing. **Hadwen House►**, built in imposing Greek Revival style in 1845, belonged to the same man who owned the refinery that is now the Whale Museum; it has Federal, Empire and Victorian furnishings. A four-vane **windmill** (1746) still grinds corn today.

The little **Life Saving Museum** covers the work of the United States Life Saving Service. Both the **Old Firecart House** (vintage fire-fighting equipment) and the **Old Gaol** are open free of charge. The **Quaker Meeting House** was built in 1838, though Quaker worship on the island goes back to 1690. Simply furnished, the **Jethro Coffin House**

Touring Nantucket
Ferry boats (see panel on page 160) bring you directly into Nantucket town where there are plenty of taxis. In addition to public bus services, Gail's Tour runs a 1 hour 45 minute bus tour from Federal Street Visitor Center at 10am, 1pm and 3pm (tel: 508/257 6557). Bicycles can be hired; cycling the island's quiet roads and cycle paths is a pleasure. Numerous boat trips depart from the wharves in Nantucket town. Walking tours (tel: 508/228 5585) start from the Atheneum Library Garden in India Street at 11am and 4pm.

of 1686 is the oldest on the island and gives a good idea of an early settler's home.

Beaches At its maximum dimensions, Nantucket is 14½ miles long by 3½ miles wide. The northern beaches are sheltered and the waves usually gentle, while the south-facing ones have plenty of surf and are strictly for strong swimmers.

Smaller beaches in and around Nantucket town have shallow waters and are suitable for children. Jetties Beach, good for watching boats and migrating birds, is an easy walk from the town (or take a shuttle bus), past the lighthouse on Brant Point; sailboards can be rented at the beach. Further west, Dionis is a family beach.

On the south side are Surfside (public bus service) and Nobadeer beaches (the latter popular with teenagers). Madaket Beach, at the western tip, has stunning sunsets. Siasconset Beach, served by bus, has some surf.

Further afield The former fishing village of Siasconset▶ (pronounced 'Sconset') has tiny shacks with names such as Doll's House and La Petite Cottage, though house prices are astronomical. In the 1930s Hollywood stars, such as Clark Gable and Carole Lombard, summered here. Near by, Sankety Head Golf Course has a 15-year waiting list for membership!

The **Coskata-Coatue Wildlife Refuge▶**, at the northeastern end of the island, is shaped like a fish-hook and formed of a huge barrier beach. Wind and sea have sculpted a remote and wild place; the Refuge includes around 10 miles of shoreline, as well as salt marsh, ponds, forest and tidal creeks.

Surfside beach

163

The inland scene
Nantucket's hinterland is mostly scrub oak, with patches of heath and cranberry bogs. Altar Rock (111 feet) is the island's highest point. The lack of mammalian predators makes the island suitable for ground-nesting birds such as northern harriers, short-eared owls, least terns and piping plovers.

A whaling tradition
Settled by the English in 1659, Nantucket rapidly took off as the New World's premier whaling centre, and by 1775 the export of whale oil, ambergris and whalebone meant that Nantucketers accounted for over a third of the hard currency earned in New England. The demise in Nantucket's whaling industry after 1842 was hastened by the emergence of the whaling port of New Bedford (see page 172), and by the collapse of the British market for whale oil with the advent of gas lighting.

Waterfront scene, Nantucket town

Coastal wildlife

■ From the rocky inlets and myriad islands of the north through sandy beaches and salt marshes southwards to the dunes of Cape Cod, the coast of New England supports an exceptionally rich and diverse plant and animal life. Opportunities abound for visitors to observe it all at close hand.....■

Top: dolphins may well join in a whale-watch cruise

Whale-watching cruises
In the 19th century the hunting of whales was a principal source of revenue for New England; nowadays whale-watch cruises have taken over as a burgeoning industry. In summer, boats leave from many ports, including Barnstable Harbor and Provincetown (Cape Cod); Boston, Plymouth, Gloucester, Newburyport (MA); Portsmouth (NH); Kennebunkport and Bar Harbor (ME). Qualified naturalists give commentaries while furthering research. Trips usually take half a day and go well out to sea. You may need warm clothes – and seasick pills.

Marine studies
A number of excellent aquaria are listed on pages 244–6 where visitors can get a close-up view of many of the creatures of the deep. For more serious naturalists, the Oceanographic Institute at Woods Hole, Cape Cod, is an international centre for marine research offering study cruises. Similar cruises also run from Mystic, CT. The Shoals Marine Laboratory on Appledore Island in the Isles of Shoals, NH, offers courses for naturalists (details from Shoals Marine Laboratory, G-14Y Stimson Hall, Cornell University, Ithaca, NY 14853-7101).

Whales and dolphins In the Gulf of Maine is a chain of rocky ledges and underwater sandbanks. Tidal currents around their edges are constantly churning up the plentiful nutrient-rich algae. The tiny crustaceans that feed on this green-algae soup are in turn the diet of the slim, silvery, 6-inch sand eel (or sand lance), the primary food source for several species of whale. Every summer hundreds of humpbacks come up from the Caribbean to feast in these rich feeding grounds. And every summer thousands of people go out to sea for a close-up look at these captivating creatures.

There is a good chance of seeing the massive but sleek and speedy fin (or finback) whale (they grow to over 65 feet) and the smaller (less than 30 feet) minke whale. The most commonly seen, and the most fascinating in its behaviour, however, is the humpback. Anything up to 50 feet in length and over 40 tons in weight, humpbacks will be seen raising their flukes, or tails, out of the water and then lobbing them down with a splash. They will roll on to their sides for a bit of flipper-slapping and, most exciting of all, will 'breach' or jump vertically out of the water. Each humpback has a distinctive black-and-white pattern on its fluke, enabling researchers to identify and name individuals.

Just as engaging as the antics of the whales is the sight of a school of white-sided (and occasionally white-beaked) dolphins surfing the waves alongside the boat. Porpoises too are sometimes spotted, while the harbor seal is fairly common near port. Seabirds to look for during the May to September whale-watching season include Wilson's petrel, great shearwater, gannet, herring gull and cormorant.

The American lobster *Homarus americanus* differs from the common or European lobster in the fearsome size of its claws. The cutter claw is used to grab and cut food (some lobsters being right-handed, some left-handed) while the broader, crusher claw is used to crush it. A nocturnal creature, of mottled green, yellow and black (it turns red only when cooked), the lobster lives on the floor of the ocean feeding mainly on clams, sea urchins and fish. Several times a year it outgrows and sheds its shell.

Bog and marsh life The New England coast has several areas of salt marsh. Hampton Harbor and marshes are New Hampshire's largest salt marsh, rich in birdlife. Look out for piping plover, whimbrel, short-billed dowitcher, black skimmer, least sandpiper, sanderling, snowy egret, osprey and great blue heron. In Maine, the Wells National

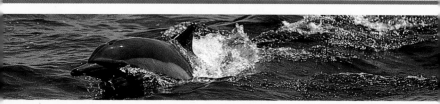

Estuarine Sanctuary at Laudholm Farm has marked nature trails along the marsh, while Scarborough Marsh Nature Center, just outside Portland, runs guided nature walks and canoe tours (summer only). From Essex, Massachusetts, you can glide up the Essex river saltwater estuary in a glass-bottomed boat. Two-thirds of the fish caught off this coast have fed on the insects, larvae and other rich pickings of the salt marsh 'pantry'.

Plants thriving in salt marsh habitats include sea lavender, sea aster, seaside and grass-leaved golden rod, cockleburr, beach grass (or 'compass grass', because it sways in the wind) and 'salt marsh hay', used by early colonists for cattle food, and the protected salt reed grass (*Spartina cynosuroides*).

Another plant that thrives on a combination of peat and sand is the cranberry. In September/October the extensive cranberry bogs of Cape Cod, Nantucket and the Plymouth area are flooded and the berries are shaken loose to float to the surface in a most spectacular sea of red. One of the trails from the Cape Cod Natural History Museum at Brewster winds through a cranberry bog.

Blowing bubbles
One humpback whale eats up to 2 tons of food per day (about 250,000 sand eels). Uniquely among whales, humpbacks blow a 'bubble net' below and round a shoal of fish, then rise to the surface with mouth open wide to swallow hundreds of fish in one gulp.

165

Left: a great blue heron keeps a beady look-out

A look at puffins
Hunted for their meat, eggs and feathers for over 300 years, puffins were virtually extinct in Maine by the late 1800s. Since the 1970s the National Audubon Society has successfully encouraged the re-establishment of colonies in the Gulf of Maine. Boat trips may be taken from Rockland, Boothbay Harbor and other Maine ports to nesting colonies on Eastern Egg Rock, Matinicus Rock and Machias Seal Island, in the Gulf of Maine. The best time is during June and July or the beginning of August.

Salt reed grass, found in Cape Cod's salt marshes, is now a protected species

MASSACHUSETTS

The sun goes down on Columbia Street, Fall River

Fruitlands persona
Others at the Fruitlands community included Joseph Palmer, persecuted for his unfashionable beard: he was picked on in a scuffle and refused to pay a $10 fine so went to jail for a year. Samuel Bower was an Adamite (a nudist), while Samuel Larned allegedly lived one year entirely on a diet of crackers, the next on nothing but apples.

The Borden mystery
The mystery of who killed Andrew and Abby Borden has never been solved. Lizzie (their daughter) was tried but acquitted for lack of evidence. This did not stop the nation drawing its own conclusions, which were expressed in satirical verse:
'Lizzie Borden took an axe,
And gave her mother forty whacks,
When she saw what she had done
She gave her father forty-one.'

The Con-Sociate Family
The Fruitlands community attempted to create a new Eden. Property was owned in common, and technology and animal products were shunned (ploughing had to be done by hand). A leading member was Bronson Alcott, whose daughter Louisa (author of *Little Women*) was only 10 when she was exposed to the regime's cold-bath rigours. A conflict between Charles Lane – who urged Bronson Alcott to become celibate – and Mrs Alcott may well have contributed to the decline of the community.

▶ **Fall River** 139D1

In its heyday Fall River was one of the great textile producing centres of the world. Today many mills survive, some empty, some as sewing-machine sweatshops and some as factory-shopping outlets. Though not picturesque, the town is set dramatically beneath the I-95 viaduct over the Taunton river.

The town's waterfront attractions begin with the **Fall River Heritage State Park** (*closed*: Monday in winter; free) which charts the chequered mill history of the town, its labour disputes and its demise, and includes a film show on Fall River's social history. The tower gives a view over the harbour and its ships. Free paddleboats are available in summer; competent sailors have free use of sailboats too. Adjacent is an old-time carousel, now housed under cover.

Close by, **Battleship Cove▶** features historic battleships which you can board and explore at will, and there is a 1960 replica of HMS *Bounty*, used in the film *Mutiny on the Bounty* starring Marlon Brando; a uniformed Captain Bligh tells the tale and shows you below deck. Walk under the I-95 viaduct for the **Marine Museum**, which presents a history of steamers and steam power as well as a model of the ill-fated *Titanic*, used by Twentieth Century Fox for the 1953 movie.

The **Fall River Historical Society▶** (*open*: 9–3 Tuesday to Friday, plus 1–4 summer weekends) maintains a Greek Revival granite mansion at 451 Rock Street, moved in 1869 to its present location and redecorated in French Empire style. Exhibits include art, toys, china, glassware and material on the mysterious and much publicised murder of Andrew Jackson Borden and his wife Abby in 1892 (see panel).

▶▶ **Fruitlands Museums** 138C3

Fruitlands (in the town of Harvard, northwest of Boston) owes its present form to Clara Endicott Sears who lived in a house (now gone) by the road and who created the museums between 1914 and 1947. The site comprises four buildings. The **Fruitlands Farmhouse** was used by the Con-Sociate Family, a utopian transcendentalist community which existed for seven months in 1843 (see panel). The rural retreat was chosen for its contemplative setting overlooking mounts Monadnock and Wachusetts. Thoreau manuscripts are on display.

Shaker House (1794), used as an office by Harvard Shakers (extant 1791–1919), is now furnished with Shaker items. The **American Indian Museum** displays head-dresses, pottery, painted leather, baskets and clothing. The **Picture Gallery** features Hudson River School artists and portraiture. (*Open:* Tuesday to Sunday, and Monday during holidays).

▶▶▶ Lexington and Concord *138–9C3/D3*

The names of Lexington and Concord are inextricably linked with the events that sparked off the American Revolution in 1775 (see pages 32–3 and 55). The historic sites where these events took place are all marked along the 4-mile road that links the two towns (see below).

In the 19th century Thoreau, Emerson, Hawthorne and Louisa and Bronson Alcott all lived at Concord, and their homes give a fascinating insight into a remarkable circle of intellectual and literary talent (see also page 46).

The Revolution Road At Lexington, a flagpole stands on the triangular Green near the statue of Captain Parker. Guides sporting hats in Minute Man style give tours on the Green (tips appreciated). On Patriots Day (the Monday nearest to 19 April) you can witness battle re-enactments, both here and at Concord's North Bridge. Behind the church the Burying Ground contains 17th-century gravestones.

The Lexington Historical Society (*open:* 10–5 daily, 1–5 Sunday; Munroe Tavern open Friday to Monday) maintains three historic buildings . At **Buckman Tavern▶** the American militia gathered before dawn prior to the battle on the Common. A bullet hole is visible in the front door. The **Hancock-Clarke House▶** was in the parsonage of the Reverend Jonas Clarke in 1775. Patriots John Hancock (Clarke's cousin) and Samuel Adams were staying here on the eve of the battle, when Revere and Dawes alerted them of the British approach. The house contains the drum which William Diamond sounded to rally men to assemble in two lines on the Green prior to the firing of the first shot. The **Munroe Tavern▶**, a mile from the centre of town, was used by the British as a field hospital on their retreat.

The first shot
On 19 April 1775 the British marched into Lexington on their way to Concord where they planned to seize a store of arms and ammunition. Revere and Dawes rode to Lexington to alert the colonial militia. By the time the 700 British – under Lieutenant-Colonel Francis Smith and Major John Pitcairn – had arrived, Captain John Parker and 77 American militia were waiting in two lines on Lexington Common. It will never be known who fired the first shot in the confusion, but the British ignored orders not to return fire and they shot at the fleeing Americans, killing eight.

167

Fruitlands Farm, an early, short-lived commune, is now a museum dedicated to the idealists who set it up

The advance to Concord
After the skirmish at Lexington, the British advanced to Concord where they started to burn military supplies. The American militia saw the smoke and hastened to save their town. The opposing ranks met at North Bridge and the British fired. With Major Buttrick's words 'Fire, fellow soldiers, for God's sake, fire!' the Americans returned a volley and forced the British to retreat. At Lexington, Lord Percy met the British with reinforcements and the fighting intensified.

'By the rude bridge that arched the flood
Their flag to April's breeze unfurled,
Here once the embattled farmers stood
And fired the shot heard round the world.'
– Written for the dedication of the 1836 monument at Concord by Ralph Waldo Emerson.

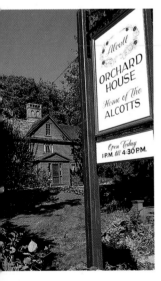

Orchard House, home to novelist Louisa May Alcott

On the way out of Lexington, the **Museum of Our National Heritage**▶ on Route 2A (open: daily; free) has permanent and changing exhibits on American history; Lexington is featured in the display entitled 'Let it Begin Here'.

A self-guided historical trail begins from the **Fiske House** site, explaining how the silence was shattered at Ebenezer Fiske's Farm that fateful day. Part of the original Lexington–Concord road here is an unpaved track, giving an idea of its appearance in 1775. Virtually adjacent, the **Battle Road Visitor Center**▶▶ has guided walks and talks, and an excellent film dramatisation re-creating the events leading up to the battle. The **Paul Revere Capture Site** is marked by a memorial. The **Captain William Smith House** was the residence of the captain of the Lincoln Minutemen. **Hartwell Tavern** has been restored to its appearance in 1775, when it played the role of the community meeting-place; here volunteers now re-create colonial life (open: Wednesday to Sunday).

At **Concord**, an obelisk marks the spot where the first British soldier fell on 19 April 1775 at the **Old North Bridge Battle Site**▶▶. Adjacent is the famous Minuteman statue sculpted by Daniel Chester French (see page 147). Ranger talks and activities are scheduled in summer through the nearby National Historical Park Visitor Center (open: all year; free), which has historical displays, a video and a diorama of the Lexington–Concord road.

Concord Founded in 1635, Concord has numerous 17th- and 18th-century houses, many with date plaques. In the 1850s Concord was a stop on the underground railroad for escaping slaves. One-hour walking tours at weekends and holidays begin at 12:45pm from the information booth. Canoeing on the Concord river is also popular.

At the **Concord Museum**▶▶ Revolutionary exhibits include the lantern from Old North Church and a diorama of the battle at Old North Bridge. Ralph Waldo Emerson's study has been installed here, complete with his books

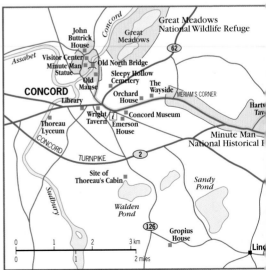

and rocking chair, and there is a Henry Thoreau collection. Archaeological finds, communion silver, samplers and costumes are also displayed.

Literary Concord The Ralph Waldo Emerson House▶ (*open*: Thursday to Saturday 10–4:30, Sunday 2–4:30), has been restored and is furnished very much as it was in the time when the author lived here, from 1835 to 1882.

Orchard House▶▶ (*open*: daily April to October, weekends March and November) was the home of the Alcotts; the six members of the family feature in Louisa May Alcott's novel, *Little Women* (1868), written and set here. The Alcotts used to host an 'at home' every week, with music, singing and acting. They were then a poor family and the present comfortable appearance of the house owes much to Louisa's writing income. Mary's room contains several of her sketches, some drawn on the walls. Next door, the former Concord Summer School of Philosophy, extant 1880–8, was established by Louisa's father, the transcendentalist Bronson Alcott.

Nathaniel Hawthorne lived for a period near Orchard House at **The Wayside**▶ (*open*: April to October; closed Monday), which he purchased from the Alcotts.

Minute Men relive the Revolution at North Bridge, Concord

'To outsiders, the five energetic women seemed to rule the house, and so they did in many things; but the quiet scholar, sitting among his books, was still the head of the family, the household conscience, anchor, and comforter, for to him the busy, anxious women always turned in troublous times, finding him, in the truest sense of those sacred words, husband and father.'
– Louisa May Alcott, *Little Women* (1868).

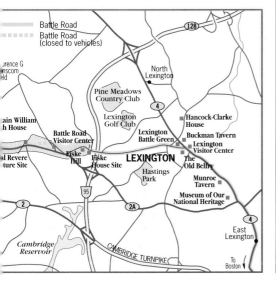

Battle Road
Battle Road (closed to vehicles)

128

urence G nscom eld

North Lexington

Pine Meadows Country Club

4

ain William h House

Lexington Golf Club

Hancock-Clarke House

Battle Road Visitor Center

Lexington Battle Green

Buckman Tavern

Lexington Visitor Center

l Revere ture Site

Fiske Hill

Fiske House Site

LEXINGTON

The Old Belfry

Hastings Park

Munroe Tavern

95

Museum of Our National Heritage

2

2A

East Lexington

4

Cambridge Reservoir

CAMBRIDGE TURNPIKE

To Boston

The **Thoreau Lyceum**, headquarters of the Thoreau Society, gives lectures and classes. A furnished replica of his famous cabin at Walden stands in the grounds.

The Old Manse▶▶, next to North Bridge (*open*: 10–4:30 daily, 1–4:30 Sunday; closed Tuesday), was built by William Emerson in 1769 or 1770. His grandson, Ralph Waldo Emerson, wrote *Nature* (1836) while living here. The house was also rented out to Nathaniel Hawthorne and his wife, Sophia, for three years. All the possessions are original, including Hawthorne's tiny desk and nearly 3,000 books. Sophia loved to paint in the dining room, and she etched the writing and the dates on the windows.

Sleepy Hollow Cemetery lies off Route 62 (Bedford Street). At Author's Ridge are buried Emerson, Thoreau, Hawthorne, Louisa May Alcott and Daniel Chester French.

Thoreau made regular visits to **Great Meadows**, now a designated National Wildlife Refuge with headquarters at Weir Hill. This wetland is an important wildlife habitat, with well over 200 migratory and nesting bird species recorded.

At **Walden Pond Reservation**▶ Thoreau observed nature and faithfully recorded 'the progress of the seasons' in a journal he kept while living in a cabin. Pieces of the cabin have long since been turned into letter-openers and other souvenir items for devoted admirers. Visitors in the 19th century used to sign stones and leave them on a cairn on the site of the structure. There is a trail around the edge of the lake.

Further afield, the **Gropius House**▶ (*open*: Friday to Sunday, 1 June to 15 October, plus first full weekend of each month November to May; tours: 12, 1, 3 and 4pm; 68 Baker Bridge Road, Lincoln; owned and operated by SPNEA – see page 68) was designed by the architect Walter Gropius (1883–1969), founder of the Bauhaus School of Design. Built in 1938, this house is a remarkable synthesis of tradition and innovation, ahead of its time in the use of acoustical plaster, chrome, welded steel, glass blocks and other modern materials.

At Framingham, south of Concord, **The Garden in the Woods** (*open*: Tuesday to Sunday, 15 April to 31 October; last admission 4pm, May 7pm) is the botanical garden of the New England Wildflower Society. It covers 45 acres and is planted with a mixture of wild native flowers, shrubs, ferns and trees.

The Old Manse, Concord, where writers Ralph Waldo Emerson and, later, Nathaniel Hawthorne lived and worked

'I went to the woods because I wished to live deliberately, to front only the essential facts of life, and see if I could not learn what it had to teach and not, when I came to die, discover that I had not lived.'
– Henry David Thoreau, *Walden* (1854).

▶▶ **Lowell** *138C3*

When they were first built in the 19th century, Lowell's textile mills were the wonder of the age and a landmark in the early industrialisation of America (see pages 36–7). Today, after a long decline, Lowell has cleaned up its 6 miles of canal and its mills to become a much-cited example of successful urban regeneration.

The **Lowell National Historical Park Visitor Center**▶ (free) explains Lowell's social and industrial history through audio-visuals and exhibits. The park itself offers free ranger-led tours lasting 90 minutes and also operates a free trolley shuttle to the Boott Cotton Mills Museum (see below). An inexpensive 2½-hour **canal and trolley bus tour**▶▶ (eight times daily) heads along the Pawtucket Canal, past guard locks where the water levels were measured, to the **Pawtucket Falls**, a 32-foot drop in the Merrimack river which provided power for all the mills; now it generates hydroelectric power, supplying electricity to 120,000 homes. Those wishing to explore on foot should pick up the booklet for the Lowell Waterpower Trail. The Mack Building has a Water Power Exhibit.

The fully restored Boott Cotton Mills at Lowell offer an excellent insight into the life of a major textile manufacturing town

171

At **Boott Cotton Mills Museum**▶▶ earplugs are provided to counter the deafening clatter of the 88 looms. An excellent exhibition includes a model of the mill, plus videos of the 1912 strike and the reminiscences of mill workers. The **Boott Gallery** has changing exhibits of paintings and photographs, and chronicles Lowell in the Civil War.

By Boott Mill the **Working People Exhibit**▶ (*open*: 10–4, Wednesday to Sunday; free) shows the life of the first mill girls, who were well looked after, and of the bleaker conditions of the immigrants who followed. Near by, the mills at Lawrence were the largest in the world when built; the **Lawrence Heritage State Park** (tours May to November) merits a two-hour visit.

MASSACHUSETTS

Newburyport's eccentric Former resident Timothy Dexter proclaimed himself 'the Greatest Man in the East'. He wrote a book entitled *A Pickle for the Knowing Ones*, nicknamed 'the Foe of Grammar' by its detractors because it was so illiterate. One critic said it would be read 'when Shakespeare and Milton are forgot… but not until'. Dexter arranged a mock funeral for himself, then caned his wife because she did not shed sufficient tears. In the early 1800s, his Newburyport garden was adorned with statues of great men, allegorical figures and Native American chiefs. These he transformed with paint into new characters when the old ones fell from fashion.

The harbour at New Bedford

► **New Bedford** *139D1*

The fishing and manufacturing town of New Bedford retains an attractive old town at its heart, recalling its hey-day as America's greatest whaling port. The whaling industry began in 1765 and by the 1840s there were some 10,000 seamen working here, pushing rival Nantucket into second place in the whaling league. Melville enthused about the town and some of the patrician houses he referred to in his whaling epic, *Moby Dick* (1851), can still be seen along County Street (for example the Rotch-Jones-Duff House and Garden Museum). The decline in whaling was sparked by the loss of numerous whaling ships at sea and by the discovery of petroleum, which gradually superceded whale oil as a fuel for use in oil lamps. The town remains the nation's busiest fishing port.

The **Seamen's Bethel**, with its boat-shaped pulpit, was frequently visited by mariners before they set out on a perilous voyage; it was also the setting for a chapter in *Moby Dick*. Close by, the **Whaling Museum►►** (*open: daily*) occupies an 1821 mansion. Among a fine array of model ships is the world's largest: an 89-foot-long half-size replica of the New Bedford whaling bark *Lagoda*. Scrimshaw, fishing gear, figureheads, harpoons and paintings are exhibited; William Bradford's huge 19th-century canvas, *Sealers Crushed by Icebergs*, was the first to depict the harsh reality of the life of seal-hunters. Toys, samplers, dolls and glassware are also displayed.

Opposite the Whaling Museum is the **Glass Museum**, showing locally made glassware. The **Fire Museum** (Bedford and South Sixth streets) has antique fire-fighting

equipment. Two vessels open to the public are the retired **Lightship** on State Pier (*open*: July and August) and the schooner *Ernestina*, an 1894 fishing vessel once used for Arctic expeditions (30 Union Street; free).

The village shoe-maker at work in Old Sturbridge

▶ **Newburyport**
139D3

Newburyport, pleasantly situated on the Merrimack estuary, is one of the most popular day-trip destinations on the North Shore. It is a centre for fishing and whale-watching trips as well as for excursions along the Merrimack itself. It also has a seductive selection of antique shops and boutiques. The **Custom House Maritime Museum▶** (*open*: April to December), located within the granite Custom House, has displays covering 300 years of nautical history. Much of the town was rebuilt in brick after a fire. **High Street** has the finest architectural survivals, including the **Cushing House Museum▶** (*open*: Tuesday to Saturday; tours 10–3), a three-storey brick house of 1808 that has many reminders of the town's maritime heyday.

Out of town, **Plum Island Beach** has 10 miles of sands and incorporates Parker River Wildlife Refuge, prolific in birdlife; in high season, this peninsula often fills to capacity quite early in the day.

▶▶▶ **Old Sturbridge Village**
138B2

Old Sturbridge Village opened 1946 and is arguably New England's most memorable re-creation of yesteryear. Actors in period dress play the part of the villagers and craftsmen who would have inhabited a typical New England settlement of the 1830s. The village green is flanked by several venerable buildings brought from all over New England and re-erected here. There is a bank, meeting-house, shops, a saw mill and more; ramshackle outbuildings, 19th-century cattle breeds and roaming chickens help compound the time-warp illusion (*closed*: Monday in winter; for details of special events, tel: 508/347 3362).

173

A trip from Newburyport
From the Custom House Maritime Museum you can take a boat trip to Lowell's Boatshop at Amesbury, where boat-building has been carried out since 1793 and where the flat-bottomed dory was invented. Paint encrustations, hanging like stalactites from the ceiling in the paintroom, are testimony to the long history of the site, which is very prettily located and recalls the early seafaring days of New England.

174

► **Pioneer Valley** *138B3*

In pioneer days the Connecticut river in Massachusetts marked the western frontier of New England. Until west-ward expansion began in the 19th century this was stock-farming country, and many trees were felled to feed the kilns making bricks to build the mills in Holyoke and South Hadley. The valley today is broad and tame but some drama comes from the basalt ridges, where vertical splits in the rock have formed exciting cliffs and slopes. The val-ley's sedimentary rocks have also preserved same 200-million-year-old dinosaur footprints. These, along with fossil plants and petrified ripple marks of a prehistoric pool, can be seen at the **Dinosaur Footprints Reservation** on the west bank of the Connecticut river near Holyoke (Route 5).

The campus of Amherst College, founded in 1821

Holyoke itself is reached by driving north from Springfield (see page 187). Here, a modest Volleyball Hall of Fame (free) commemorates the birthplace of the sport. At **South Hadley** the Mount Holyoke College **Art Museum►** is one of the oldest collegiate museums in the country and contains classical and Egyptian artefacts as well as American paintings. The summer festival features student theatre and concerts by student and visiting artists.

Hadley Farm Museum (*open*: May to October; closed Monday; free) houses rural bygones, including the first broom-making machine, and offers teas on the porch on Saturday afternoons.

The main entrance for **Holyoke Range Park►►** and **Skinner State Park►►** is off Route 47 at Hadley. From here the park road winds up to a famous viewpoint over a loop in the river, painted by Hudson River School artist Thomas Cole as *The Oxbow* in the 1830s. Basalt columns known as Titan's Piazza add to the drama, and mounts Monadnock and Tom are in sight. Folk, jazz and classical concerts are given at the summit cabin in summer.

Mount Tom, south of Northampton, is equipped for year-round activity, with skiing, a 4,000-foot alpine slide, a wave pool and a chair-lift to the summit. **Northampton►** itself is a lively college town. **Smith College** has an arts museum begun in 1879 featuring European masters, the Hudson River School, and 20th-century sculpture (*open*: Tuesday to Sunday; Wednesday and weekends only June to July). **The Words and Pictures Museum►** in Main Street pays tribute to comic-book art, including that of the local co-creators of Teenage Mutant Ninja Turtles (*closed*: Monday; free)

Amherst The attractive college town of **Amherst►**, built around a sloping common, makes one of the best bases for explaining the Pioneer Valley. The **Emily Dickinson Homestead►** (280 Main Street; *open*: 1:30–3:45, Wednesday to Saturday, May to October; advance booking essential, tel: 413/542 8161) was the home of the poet (see page 176). The world's largest collection of Dickinson memorabilia forms a display and archive in the Jones Library and is open free of charge when the archivist is there (tel: 413/256 4090); it also incorporates a large collection of material relating to Robert Frost. Next door, the **Strong House** (1740) has rooms in a range of styles including Colonial and Victorian (*open*: 2–4, Wednesday and Saturday, May to October).

In Amherst College, the **Pratt Museum** exhibits natural history while the **Mead Art Museum►** shows ancient art, European sculpture and paintings, and works by American masters. Just outside town, the University of Massachusetts has concert offerings during the academic year.

Continuing north The architectural highlight of the Pioneer Valley, **Historic Deerfield►►** is a beautifully preserved historic village displaying a variety of domestic buildings from early colonial times. First settled in 1669, the village grew rich on beef farming. Today it is still a living village but, thanks to its residents, it is one of the best documented places in the country. Currently 13 houses are open for 30-minute tours. Combined entry tickets last two days and opening times are staggered; guided walking tours and horse-and-carriage tours are also available.

Near by, off Route 116, **Mount Sugarloaf State Reservation►** has a road to the top where fine views extend from a rocky cliff.

On and in the water
Twelve-mile cruises along the Connecticut river are offered on *Quinnetukut II* from the Riverview Picnic Area on Route 63 (tel: 413/659 3714). For canoeing, kayaking and whitewater rafting, try the stretch from Cheapside Bridge to the Route 116 Bridge near Deerfield, or from Turners Fall Dam to Vernon Dam in Vermont. Beginners can sample the stretch from Holyoke Dam to the Northeast Utilities Power Dam in Turners Falls. The Deerfield river has mild whitewater conditions from Shelburne to Route 5 Bridge in Greenfield. Lake swimming is feasible in the Upper Highland Lake at DAR State Forest on Route 112 in Goshen

175

Dwight House, an early 18th-century house which, like others in Deerfield that are open to the public, displays a fine collection of furniture

■ In 1886 Emily Dickinson died in the house in which she had been born, in the village of Amherst in Massachusetts, a lyric poet unknown and unpublished. Her sister found 1,775 poems and numerous letters that revealed an original and exceptional talent. Equally extraordinary is the life led by this 'New England mystic'.....■

'There's a certain slant of
   light
On winter afternoons,
That oppresses, like the
   weight
Of cathedral tunes.

Heavenly hurt it gives us;
We can find no scar,
But internal difference
Where the meanings are.

None may teach it
   anything,
'Tis the seal, despair,
An imperial affliction
Sent us of the air.

When it comes, the
   landscape listens,
Shadows hold their breath;
When it goes, 'tis like the
   distance
On the look of death.'

'It's all I have to bring to-
   day,
This, and my heart beside,
This, and my heart, and all
   the fields,
And all the meadows wide.
Be sure you count, should I
   forget,
Someone the sum could
   tell,
This, and my heart, and all
   the bees
Which in the clover dwell.'

The recluse Emily Dickinson was born in 1830 into a household dominated by her puritanical father, a lawyer and treasurer of Amherst College. Described by a schoolfriend as demure and shy but witty, she began to write poems when she was in her 20s, sewing them into little booklets. During her most productive year, 1862 (the height of the Civil War), she wrote 356. She tried unsuccessfully to interest a newpaper editor, Samuel Bowles, in her work, and in 1862 she asked a young man of letters, TW Higginson, for an opinion. He did not recommend publishing, although they remained correspondents, and from then on she refused to consider publication.

After the mid-1860s Dickinsons's output waned and she began to withdraw from the world, seeing few friends. By the late 1860s she had become known as an eccentric recluse, always dressed in white, who never left the grounds of her home (see page 175). From the mid-1870s she was increasingly saddened by the deaths of many dear to her.

The poetry Emily Dickinson's themes of love, death and nature are treated with an intensity and a sensitivity surprising for one who led such a secluded life. The poems and letters of the late 1850s and early 1860s reveal intense emotions, probably focused on a married Philadelphia clergyman, Charles Wadsworth. In her years of retreat, one person she did see was Otis Lord, an old family friend, and drafts of letters from these latter years suggest a tender and passionate relationship. Her poems, like her letters, are composed with scrupulous artistry: words are pared down to an epigrammatic minimum, rhythms are often irregular to assist expression of thought, and the rhymes themselves are sometimes imperfect.

Right: the young recluse

176

▶▶▶ **Plymouth**

139D2

Hallowed as the birthplace of modern America, where the Pilgrim Fathers first established themselves, Plymouth preserves the spirit of the early years. Apart from Plimoth Plantation (see page 179), the attractions are small-scale, but the town has become a place of historic pilgrimage and the **Pilgrim's Path**, a designated walking route, will lead you around the town's historic sites.

Given pomp by its classical canopy, insignificant-looking **Plymouth Rock▶** is very probably where the Pilgrims alighted in 1620 and is, in any event, nicely symbolic of a nation that likes to think of itself as built upon a rock. *Mayflower II▶*, close by, is a faithful replica of the 104-foot-long ship in which the Pilgrims crossed the Atlantic, with period-clad actors telling the story of the 66-day voyage. The cramped conditions leave you wondering how the 102 Pilgrims dealt with frayed tempers on their long journey. The original *Mayflower* returned to England in 1621 and was broken up a few years later.

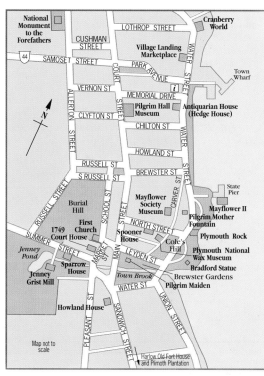

Across the street, on Cole's Hill, a sarcophagus of 1921 contains the remains of some of the Pilgrims while a monument honours Chief Massasoit of the Wampanoag tribe, who befriended the Pilgrims. Adjacent, the **Plymouth National Wax Museum** (*closed*: winter) has 26 tableaux and 120 characters telling the story of Plymouth's beginnings.

North Street leads away from the sea from here and has some fine houses. Most notable is the **Mayflower Society Museum▶** (*open*: daily in summer, Friday to Sunday in spring and autumn), high-ceilinged and with a magnificent flying staircase that is supported only at top and bottom. Edward Winslow, a Pilgrim descendant, built the house in 1754 and Lydia Jackson married Ralph Waldo Emerson in the east front parlour in 1835. **Spooner House** at 27 North Street has five generations of family possessions. **Antiquarian House▶** (1809), opposite Town Wharf, is a Federal-style home of a 19th-century merchant shipowner, one Thomas Hedge, and displays China trade porcelain, dolls, costumes, quilts and toys.

The Mayflower Society Museum, Plymouth

177

Pilgrims and Native Americans share an authenticated 17th-century meal at Plimoth Plantation

The **Pilgrim Hall Museum▶** (*open*: daily), designed by Alexander Parris (architect of Boston's Quincy Market) focuses on the Pilgrims and their voyage. Paintings show their embarkation and landing, and there are items thought to have been brought to America as part of the *Mayflower*'s cargo, including the cradle of Peregrine White, born on the voyage. The Lower Hall contains artefacts relating to the Plymouth Colony, featuring paintings, furniture, tools and clothes.

The 1749 **Court House and Museum** (*open*: summer; free) is notable as America's oldest wooden courthouse. The reconstructed court room was saved from demolition during major redevelopment in the 1950s. A vintage piece of 1828 fire-fighting equipment is displayed. **Sparrow House** is the oldest surviving dwelling in Plymouth (*closed*: Wednesday). The house dates from 1640 and has characteristic leaded window panes and period furnishings; pottery demonstrations are given inside.

Howland House▶ (*open*: daily Memorial Day to Columbus Day, then weekends until Thanksgiving) is the only Pilgrim house remaining; *Mayflower* passengers John and Elizabeth Tilley Howland resided here and had 10 children. The building was enlarged in 1750. A path along the river leads to the **Jenney Grist Mill**, America's first public utility, set up by the Pilgrims in 1636. The exterior is very picturesque, with a waterwheel still churning over the water. Along Sandwich Street is **Harlow Old Fort House** of 1677, with a museum devoted to Plymouth's 17th-century settlers.

The **National Monument to the Forefathers▶** is an outstanding example of 19th-century statuary, commemorating the Pilgrims. A gigantic central figure of Faith flanked by Law, Education, Liberty and Morality stands high on elevated ground. Bas reliefs depict the Departure from Delfthaven, the Landing of the Pilgrims, the Treaty with Massasoit and the Signing of the Mayflower Compact. Etched in granite are the names of the 102 *Mayflower* passengers.

Ocean Spray, makers of cranberry juice (exported worldwide), shows its wares at **Cranberry World▶** (*open*: 9:30–5, daily, 1 April to 30 November, plus 5–9pm July and August; free). Displays explain cranberry growing and harvesting, and there are vintage Ocean Spray TV commercials. Free samples of a range of cranberry-based juices await at the end. This is one of New England's greatest freebies, especially on a thirst-inducing summer's day!

Plimoth Plantation▶▶▶ is a reconstruction of the original Pilgrims' village, 3 miles north of the landing site (*open*: 9–5 April to November, 5–6:30 June to Labor Day). The '1627 Village' has all the authentic elements: partly thatched wooden dwellings, straw on the ground, woodsmoke, cow dung, blankets hung out to dry in a yard. Dressed in period costume, interpreters answer visitors' questions as if they were Pilgrims, not tourist guides, and the authenticity extends to the carefully researched 17th-century accents. One woman talks of midwifery as she spins wool, a man tells of his voyage and another explains the schisms in the Church of England. Even the chickens resemble the breeds the settlers would have had.

Also re-created here is the homesite of a native Wampanoag who acted as counsellor to the new settlers. The gentle, peaceloving Wampanoags traded with the Pilgrims but some were later taken as slaves.

'Down to the Plymouth Rock, that had been to their feet as a doorstep Into a world unknown – the corner-stone of a nation.'
– Longfellow, *The Courtship of Miles Standish* (1858).

'Neither do I acknowledge the right of Plymouth to the whole rock. No, the rock underlies all America: it only crops out here.'
– Wendell Phillips, Speech at dinner of the Pilgrim Society at Plymouth, 21 December 1855.

179

Plymouth cranberries
Plymouth County has some 12,000 acres of cranberry bogs, set within impermeable clay-lined kettleholes and dependent on supporting wetlands for their survival. In spring the bogs look like a sea of light pink flowers. The petals fall off in mid-July, leaving a green berry which ripens spectacularly to a brilliant red and is harvested a few weeks after Labor Day. Plymouth Colony Winery, near Plymouth, claims to be New England's original cranberry winery. Cranberry juice and vodka are mixed to create the 'Cape Codder' cocktail.

Visit Cranberry World to learn about cranberry growing and harvesting

The Pilgrim Fathers

■ **Weak and weary from an uncomfortable nine-week voyage, an intrepid band of 102 English men and women arrived in Plymouth in the winter of 1620. About one-third had been driven out by their radical Puritan faith. All had hopes set high on a new life .....■**

Blown off course?...

Tradition has it that the Pilgrims, who set off heading for the Hudson river in Virginia, were blown off course and ended up in the Cape Cod area. However, the chances of an experienced mariner such as Christopher Jones not knowing he was 120 nautical miles too far north are remote. First, he would certainly have known the latitudes of all American east coast landmarks; secondly, the astrolobe, a forerunner of the sextant, enabled navigators at that time to calculate all north and south distances with precision.

...or a change of mind?

Descendants of David Thomson have claimed that when the *Speedwell* needed repair work and she and the *Mayflower* unexpectedly called at Plymouth, the Pilgrim leaders spoke there with David Thomson about New England. The indications are that Thomson, who had been there more than once but never further south than Cape Cod, might have recommended the Plymouth area, where his friend Squanto lived. Did the Pilgrims then change their minds about Virginia?

Puritans and Separatists At a time when the English monarch was also head of the Church in more than just name, dissenting from the Anglican Church was a treasonable offence. While some Puritans attempted to reform the Church of England, one group decided in 1608 to flee to Leiden in Holland, a centre of Protestantism, to escape persecution. These Protestant Separatists lived rather discontentedly in Holland for some 12 years before deciding to start a new life in America. They managed to secure finance from a group of London investors for a pilgrimage that would take them to a land where, according to all reports (and there had been many by then), they could find a better life as well as religious freedom.

The Leiden Separatists bought a small ship, the *Speedwell*, in which they sailed from Holland to Southampton, England, where they met up with the *Mayflower*. Some of the *Mayflower*'s passengers were also Puritan Separatists, but the majority were sent by the London stock company to ensure the venture's success, men such as the military officer Miles Standish (hero of Longfellow's long poem *The Courtship of Miles Standish*). Both ships set sail from Southampton, but the

The Mayflower, *an English merchant ship before she was hired to transport the Pilgrims*

Speedwell proved unseaworthy and had to be abandoned at Plymouth in Devon, and her passengers crammed on to an already crowded *Mayflower*, which set sail once again on 6 September 1620.

Arrival in America Amazingly, the ship and her passengers survived a 66-day journey that was not without storms or near-disasters, and land was sighted on 9 November. On the 11th, the *Mayflower* dropped anchor at what is now Provincetown on Cape Cod. A meeting was held on board and a famous document, the 'Mayflower Compact', was drawn up by the Pilgrim Fathers (as they were only much later called) under the leadership of William Bradford. Under the terms of this agreement, the settlers promised obedience to the minority of Pilgrim leaders and, despite its one-sidedness, it remained in force until the settlement joined with Massachusetts Bay Colony in 1691.

A reconnaissance party then sailed along the coast to Plymouth, with its safe harbour, running water and corn-fields already cleared by the Wampanoag. It also had high ground from which the colonists could defend them-selves against possible attacks from Native Americans, Spanish and French traders or fishermen. On Christmas Day the men began to build their new homes.

Settling in By the end of that first winter, half of the *Mayflower*'s passengers had died. The weather was harsh, the colonists were weak from the journey, food supplies were low and crops not yet established. It was a tough time, until the spring came and, with it, friendly contact with members of the Wampanoag people. Like so many other Native Americans, the Wampanoag had been decimated by epidemics of European disease that had come with the traders, but one of the survivors was a man named Squanto. Squanto had been to England (see panel opposite) and was prepared to help the colonists.

The Pilgrims and their fellow settlers had come with a diversity of skills and interests, but most were craftsmen and not used to making a living from the land. Nevertheless, with guidance from the Wampanoag and the arrival of more goats, cattle and other goods with fur-ther colonists from England, the Plymouth settlers became self-sufficient within a few years, and by 1640 their numbers had swelled to about 3,000.

181

Top: Miles Standish makes a treaty with the Native Americans Above: the Pilgrim Fathers give thanks after landing

Squanto
In 1605 an English captain, George Weymouth, captured five Wampanoag men, including Squanto, and took them back to Plymouth in England. Here they became friendly with David Thomson, an appren-tice to a ship's doctor. In 1607 the doctor, Thomson and the five Wampanoag joined Sir John Popham's expedition to Sagadahoc, the men acting as interme-diaries between the Native Americans and the English. Squanto made several more similar trips.

► **Quabbin Reservoir** 138B3

One of America's largest reservoirs, Quabbin supplies water to half of Massachusetts and its zigzag form effectively divides the state into eastern and western halves. The reservoir has a 118-mile shoreline and many islands. Some 2,500 homes were lost when it was built and 7,500 bodies from 34 cemeteries were reinterred. For the tourist its scenic attributes make it worth a detour: an excellent view is from **Quabbin Summit►►** at the southern end, where a tower looks to Mounts Tom, Lincoln, Monadnock and Wachusett. To locate the tower follow signposts past Winsor Dam. The reservoir offers outstanding freshwater fishing (boat hire is available for anglers) and there are nine trails, including the ¾-mile summit trail from Quabbin Hill Lookout.

North of the reservoir, at North New Salem, the Swift river's middle branch roars along **Bear's Den►**, a gorge with rushing waterfalls embraced by granite cliffs which are cloaked with hemlock trees. Supposedly this was a Native American haunt in 1675 during the wars against the white settlers.

A calm evening on Quabbin

► **Quincy** 139D2

Quincy (pronounced 'Quinzee') is known as the 'City of Presidents' because John Adams (America's second president) and his son, John Quincy Adams (America's sixth) were both born here, in 1735 and 1767 respectively. The **Adams Mansion►**, a large clapboard house, was home to four generations of the Adams family and now displays family pieces and paintings. In the garden, the 1870 Stone Library contains presidential books and manuscripts. Both John and John Quincy Adams were born in 17th-century saltbox farmhouses near by, forming, with the mansion, the **Adams National Historical Site**, the earliest surviving presidential birthplace. The **Adams Academy**, built on the site of John Hancock's birthplace, is now the home of the Quincy Historical Society. The National Park Service Visitor Center (opposite City Hall on Hancock Street) has brochures on historic Quincy, with information about the Quincy Homestead, the Josiah Quincy House, the Quarry Museum, and the United First Parish Church and Crypt, where two presidents and their wives are buried. Quincy can be reached from Boston by the Red Line to Quincy Center.

The Salem witches

■ **In 1692 the village of Salem, in the Massachusetts Bay Colony, suddenly found itself in the grip of an infamous witchcraft hysteria. It was a brush with the devil that that would leave its mark for ever.....■**

Tituba's secret Reverend Samuel Parris came to Salem after working as a merchant in the Caribbean. He brought back a slavegirl, Tituba, who was put in charge of Parris's daughter Betty and her cousin Abigail Williams, girls at the impressionable ages of nine and 11. Innocently, Tituba would tell them stories of her own voodoo culture, so very different from the starchy Puritan ethic the girls were brought up on. They were gripped. Soon they were bringing others into Tituba's 'circle' – but for fear of eternal damnation they had to keep it all secret. Betty, however, could not cope with the divided loyalties, and it began to show in her behaviour. Abigail, jealous of all the fuss now being made of Betty, mimicked her 'fits' and one by one the other girls began to writhe and scream similarly.

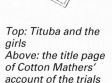

'Spectral evidence' In 1692 most of the world believed in witchcraft, and to the Puritans of Salem this was the only explanation for the girls' behaviour. But who was it who was bewitching them? The hunt was on. Tituba and others were put under pressure, false confessions were made, innocents incriminated. Things got out of control. Prisons were bursting with suspects (even the wife of the governor of Massachusetts, William Phips, was accused), and 19 'witches' were actually hanged. But everything hinged on 'spectral evidence', the evidence given by the bewitched girls that they were afflicted by a spectre, or the devil, in the image of someone else.

Eventually, in October, Increase Mathers and his son Cotton, leading Puritans, and others protested that this meant that it was on the testimony of the devil that justices were condemning people to death. Governor Phips brought the trials to an end, prisoners were released and convictions annulled. The girls were discredited – and Tituba was able to renounce her confession.

Top: Tituba and the girls
Above: the title page of Cotton Mathers' account of the trials

The Crucible
The names of Tituba, Abigail and many of the other personalities involved will be familiar from American playwright Arthur Miller's play *The Crucible* (1953), based on the Salem witch trials. A French film, *Les Sorcières de Salem*, was made of the play.

An all-too-common sight in 1692: a 'witch' is arrested

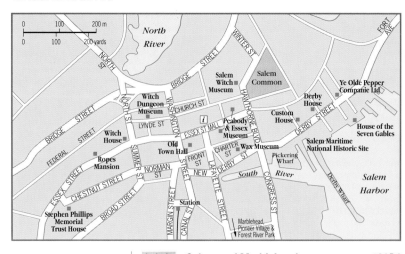

Map of Salem showing: North River, North St, Bridge Street, Federal Street, Essex Street, Chestnut Street, Broad Street, Winter St, Church St, Lynde St, Washington St, Summer St, Norman St, Margin Street, Canal St, Lafayette Street, New Derby St, Front St, Charter St, Essex St Mall, Hawthorne Blvd, Congress St, Derby Street, Fort Ave. Locations: Salem Witch Museum, Salem Common, Ye Olde Pepper Companie Ltd, Derby House, Witch Dungeon Museum, Custom House, House of the Seven Gables, Witch House, Peabody & Essex Museum, Old Town Hall, Wax Museum, Salem Maritime National Historic Site, Ropes Mansion, Pickering Wharf, South River, Salem Harbor, Station, Marblehead, Pioneer Village & Forest River Park, Stephen Phillips Memorial Trust House, Salem Wharf, Derby Wharf.

The Puritan Roger Conant founded Salem in 1626; his statue can be found in front of Salem Witch Museum

►►► Salem and Marblehead 139D3

Salem's notorious witch-hunts of the past are only one aspect of the town. Its prosperity, brought about by trading (in particular with China), has left the town with a rich architectural legacy and a particular wealth of Federal-style houses.

That the witch trials (see page 183) amounted to a puritanical persecution of innocent women is hardly remembered here in the ghoulish array of trinkets and souvenirs, all featuring witches in pointed hats. At least the museum-type attractions aim for rather more authenticity.

History Alive! Cry Innocent – The People Versus Bridget Bishop► is worth catching (tours daily at 11:30, 1:30 and 3pm only, June to October); this theatrical reconstruction of a witch trial is set in the Old Town Hall, with its faded classical grandeur and courtroom atmosphere. The audience plays the role of a 17th-century Puritan jury asked to judge the woman's guilt. The **Witch Dungeon Museum** also starts with a short two-person theatrical presentation, setting the scene for the persecutions, before embarking on a brisk tour of the reconstructed dungeons.

The **Witch House►** is a fine example of a mid-17th-century house, with period furniture. It belonged to Jonathan Corwin, one of the witchcraft trial judges. It was here that witches were examined for bodily defects. In the **Salem Witch Museum** (presentations every half-hour), 13 tableaux are lit to spin the witchcraft yarn; the dummies are not particularly lifelike and the commentary is over-sensationalised in tone, but the story is gripping.

Trading and maritime legacies Founded in 1626, Salem was once America's sixth largest city. So widely was the name of Salem known at the peak of its trading activity (1790–1807) that many overseas merchants thought Salem was a country and America just a part of it. At the **Salem Maritime National Historic Site▶** (free) you can see three surviving wharves (there were once over 50). Elias Hesketh Derby, America's first millionaire, established Derby Wharf (1762), and his brick Georgian home, Derby House, can be visited along with the unfurnished Narbonne-Hale House. In the 1840s Nathaniel Hawthorne worked as a surveyor in the Custom House (1819): you can peer into his 'cobwebbed and dingy' office, still used up to 1937. Behind is the Scale House (1829) where goods were weighed and taxed.

While Hawthorne worked here observing the life of Salem, he lived in a house in the grounds of his cousin's 17th-century mansion, **The House of the Seven Gables▶▶**. A secret staircase, a look-out window for observing ships in the harbour, and numerous odd corners and narrow passages

Above: The House of the Seven Gables, inspiration for Hawthorne's novel Left: ship's figurehead in Salem's Peabody Essex Museum

185

add to the romance of the house that inspired Hawthorne to write his famous novel (1851) of the same name. Hawthorne's birthplace, the Retire Becket House of 1655, and the Hooper-Hathasay House of 1682 are on the same site.

The **Peabody Essex Museum▶▶▶** (tours at 11am and 2pm) celebrates three centuries of Salem trade with an outstanding collection of model ships and maritime art, as well as period rooms, pictures of old Salem, witchcraft exhibits and a splendid array of ships' figureheads. Outside are an 1830s shoe shop and the 1684 John Ward House.

The adjacent Andrew-Safford House (1819) was, in its day, the most expensive house ever built (not open).

Chestnut Street▶▶ has been called America's finest street. The Stephen Phillips Memorial Trust House at number 34 and the Ropes Mansion (1727), around the corner at 318 Essex Street, are both open in summer. Salem Common was a pasture and drill ground.

Pioneer Village, a short drive to the west (*open*: late May to mid-October), is a re-creation of old Salem, with gardens, farm animals and crafts as well as costumed actors playing the roles of 17th-century Puritans and acting scenes from Hawthorne's *The Scarlet Letter* (1850).

Getting around
Salem is easily reached from Boston's North Station; trains are frequent and inexpensive (with discounts for round trips) and take 30 minutes. Trolley buses tour Salem every half hour and there is also a free shuttle bus. However, the sights can easily be taken in on foot, and Salem is a delightful town for walking. A red line marks the walking route linking the historic sights (but omits Chestnut Street); free brochures are available from the National Park Visitor Center in Museum Place or from the Chamber of Commerce in the Old Town Hall.

Marblehead, once a busy trading port, is today popular with yachtsmen

Trade with China
The China trade began when Derby's ship, the *Grand Turk*, dropped anchor at Whampoa in 1786. By 1800, traders from Salem and Marblehead were a common sight in Canton, the only Chinese port open to them. All sorts of exotic items turned up in America as a result of this trade. From East Africa came ivory, gold, ostrich feathers and hippopotamus teeth; from the West Pacific appeared semi-precious corals and mother-of-pearl; from the Far East, ceramics, text-iles, tea, coffee, spices, sugar and Japanese arte-facts were landed.

Marblehead▶▶ This handsome coastal town is located just to the east of Salem and can be reached by bus 441 from Boston or Salem. Like Salem, it prospered on trade. Its tightly knit, irregular 18th-century streets have a salty charm that evokes coastal England. Today it is a wealthy commuter satellite, known for boating, antique shops and boutiques.

At **Public Landing** you can join cruises around the harbour and buy lobster, sea bass and stripers off the boats. Fort Sewell, a small fortification built for the War of 1812, Fountain Park and Crocker Park all overlook the bay. Some 600 Revolutionary War soldiers are buried in the **Old Burial Ground**. In **Abbot Hall** (the town hall) hangs Archibald Willard's famous painting, *Spirit of '76*, epitomising the patriotic spirit of the Revolution. The **Jeremiah Lee Mansion▶** (*open*: summer) has altered little since it was built in 1768; its wooden exterior was made to resemble stone in an attempt to look English.

A causeway road links **Marblehead Neck**, skirted by a loop road; affluent New Yorkers have built summer houses here in various styles such as French château and English Tudor. Chandler Hovey Park is at the northern tip of the Neck and overlooks the bay at Marblehead Light. The best sandy beaches are at Beverly; West Beach has 3 miles of sand while Dane Street Beach is smaller.

► **Springfield** *138B2*

This major industrial city sits at the southern end of the Pioneer Valley (see pages 174–5) and deserves a visit for its museums (*open*: 12–4 Tuesday to Sunday; free Friday). Combined entry to four of them, all situated by the Quadrangle, is available.

The **Connecticut Valley Historical Museum** details the history of the valley from 1636. Dinosaur exhibits, an aquarium, a planetarium and the story of early aviation in Springfield are attractions at the **Springfield Science Museum**. The **George Walter Vincent Smith Art Museum** is an excellent collection of Victoriana, armour, Hudson River School paintings and an outstanding collection of Chinese *cloisonné*. The **Museum of Fine Arts** features French Impressionist works among its European paintings.

At **Springfield Armory National Historic Site**► Washington set up the first arsenal in America. In 1873 the 'Trapdoor' Springfield Rifle was invented here (the

model 1903 was used by the US Army in World War I). The arsenal closed in 1968 and now contains perhaps the nation's finest collection of firearms.

In 1891 Dr James Naismith devised the game of basketball in Springfield. At 1150 West Columbus Avenue the **Naismith Memorial Basketball Hall of Fame**► pays homage to the sport's great players, teams and coaches with reverent displays of photos and mementoes. Interactive exhibits include the chance to participate in a shoot-out.

► **Worcester** *138C2*

A busy industrial and commercial centre, and New England's second largest city, Worcester has two notable museums. The **Worcester Art Museum**►► (*closed*: Monday; 55 Salisbury Street) boasts works from the ancient world, European art from the Renaissance to the 20th century, and American masters including Whistler, Homer, Copley, Sargent and Edward Hick. The **Higgins Armory Museum**►► (open: 9–4 weekdays, 12–4 weekends; 100 Barber Avenue) is spectacularly housed in a gallery modelled on the hall of a medieval Austrian castle, and displays a collection of weapons and armour from all over the world.

Industrial legacy
The Blackstone River Valley close to Worcester was a busy mill district in the 19th century. Mill owners provided jobs, schools, housing, churches and stores for their workers, who included refugees from Europe seeking religious and personal freedom. Industrial competition from the South eventually spelt economic decline. Some old mill villages survive, such as Hopedale and Whitinsville, while the Willard House and Clock Museum at Grafton honours the Willard brothers, clock-makers in the 18th century.

187

Worcester: museum visitors can choose between armoury (left) or fine art (below)

Welcome to the Worcester Art Museum

NEW HAMPSHIRE

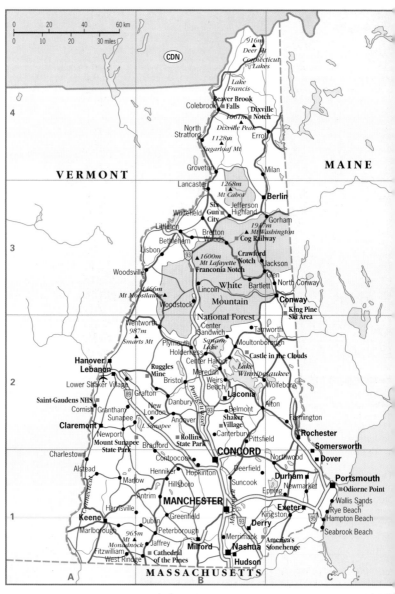

Map legend and locations:

VERMONT

MAINE

MASSACHUSETTS

CDN

916m
Deer Mt
Connecticut
Lakes

Lake
Francis

Beaver Brook
Falls

Colebrook

Dixville
Notch

1001m
Dixville Peak

North
Stratford

1128m
Sugarloaf Mt

Errol

Groveton

Milan

Lancaster

1268m
Mt Cabot

Berlin

Whitefield

Six
Gun
City

Jefferson
Highland

Gorham

1917m
Mt Washington

Cog Railway

Littleton

Bretton
Woods

Bethlehem

Crawford
Notch

Lisbon

1600m
Mt Lafayette
Franconia Notch

Jackson

Woodsville

Lincoln

Glen

Bartlett

North Conway

1466m
Mt Moosilauke

White

Mountain

Conway

Woodstock

King Pine
Ski Area

National Forest

Center
Sandwich

Tamworth

Wentworth

987m
Smarts Mt

Plymouth
Holderness

Squam
Lake

Moultonborough

Castle in the Clouds

Center Harbor

Lake
Winnipesaukee

Hanover
Lebanon

Ruggles
Mine

Meredith

Weirs
Beach

Wolfeboro

Lower Shaker Village

Bristol

Laconia

Alton

Saint-Gaudens NHS

Grafton

Danbury

Belmont

Farmington

Cornish
Grantham

New
London

Andover

Shaker
Village

Claremont

Sunapee

L Sunapee

Canterbury

Pittsfield

Rochester

Newport

Rollins
State Park

CONCORD

Somersworth

Mount Sunapee
State Park

Bradford

Northwood

Dover

Charlestown

Contoocook

Deerfield

Alstead

Henniker

Hopkinton

Suncook

Durham

Portsmouth

Marlow

Hillsboro

Newmarket

Odiorne Point

Antrim

MANCHESTER

Epping

Wallis Sands

Harrisville

Greenfield

Kingston

Exeter

Rye Beach
Hampton Beach

Keene

Dublin

Peterborough

Derry

Seabrook Beach

Marlborough

965m
Mt
Monadnock

Merrimack

America's
Stonehenge

Jaffrey

Milford

Nashua

Fitzwilliam

Cathedral
of the Pines

Hudson

West Ridge

Scale:
0   20   40   60 km
0   10   20   30 miles

*The Union Church
and covered bridge
at Stark (both 1850s)
in northern New
Hampshire*

Fall foliage in the White Mountains

New Hampshire The state's triangular form extends 168 miles north to south and 90 miles west to east at its maximum dimensions. In shape and size, it is an inverted form of Vermont, although its population, nudging a million, is almost twice as high.

The land and people By repute, New Hampshire inhabitants are independent, hardworking, conservative and proud of their state and its history. They are also thrifty, and somewhat suspicious of government. One typical manifestation of this die-hard New Hampshire attitude is that there are no income or sales taxes: much state revenue comes instead from 'sin tax' on liquor (hence you can only purchase alcohol at state liquor stores), and from tobacco and gambling. Another is that the state is unique in the Union in that any resident has the right to raise an issue at the state capitol for discussion. 'Live free or die', words first uttered in the Revolution by Colonel John Stark, form the most cut-and-thrust of all state mottos. New Hampshire was the first state to vote in favour of the Declaration of Independence.

Despite its nickname 'The Granite State', New Hampshire does have areas of good, fertile land, particularly in the river valleys. Agriculture, together with forestry, ranks third in the state's economy after manufacturing and tourism. With a decline in the number of dairy farms in recent years have come changes in farming methods, including the replacement of animal-feed crops with strawberries, flowers and other produce.

NEW HAMPSHIRE

Ask a New Hampshire native if he's lived there all his life and he'll reply 'not yet'

Industry, however, is New Hampshire's economic mainstay, and its factories employ a higher proportion of the population than those in New York. Textiles have declined drastically in New Hampshire since their economic heyday in the 19th century. Machinery, paper, pulp, plastics and electronics are now important in the industrial heartland in the southern part of the state centred on the Merrimack Valley.

Tourism is another state money-earner. Locals will tell you that New Hampshire has better maple syrup than Vermont and the best autumn foliage in New England. It certainly does have the distinction of possessing New England's tallest mountains, and the merit of having lakes, uplands, forests and the coast all within an hour or two's drive.

Visitor highlights The **White Mountains** in the north are New England's tallest and finest uplands. This prime territory for leaf-peeping, scenic drives and hiking has attracted artists, writers and intellectuals since the early 1800s. Today it is busier than ever, and shopping outlets, motels and theme parks have sprung up around its edges. Many of the visitor attractions, however, are only open in the May to October season.

The scenic Kancamagus Highway

Summer crowds also head for the Seacoast and Lakes regions of New Hampshire. The state's first colonial settlers came to the **coast** in 1623 and eked out a living supplying timber to the English. In 1679 New Hampshire became a separate royal colony from Massachusetts. Today, **Portsmouth** continues as a commercial port, where craft still ply one of the world's fastest-flowing navigable rivers. The town itself has the state's biggest concentration of historic houses.

Elsewhere the 18-mile seaboard is given over to pleasure-seeking. Apart from a short, empty stretch at its northern end it is almost entirely developed, with summer cottages, motels, fast-food outlets and motels culminating in the 3-mile boardwalk at Hampton Beach.

The lakes number about 1,300 in all, including the smaller 'ponds'. **Lake Winnipesaukee** is the largest and the most obviously commercialised, but is still very attractive with abundant islands and tempting boat excursions.

The **Mount Monadnock region** in the southwest has a bucolic charm belying its nearness to the urbanised parts of New England. Bumpy backroads set a slow pace in the vicinity of Mount Monadnock itself, where the sleepy villages are quintessential white clapboard and trim greens. The mountain itself gives a view over six states and has long attracted visitors; in 1860 there was a 'half-way house' and a 'summit house'.

'...New Hampshire has One each of everything as in a show-case.'
– Robert Frost, *New Hampshire* (1937).

Events

For further information contact the state tourist office (see page 266) or local chambers of commerce.

January
Loon Mountain Independence Day Weekend, Lincoln.
New London Winterfest Week, New London.

February
Great Rotary Fishing Derby, Meredith.
Dartmouth Winter Carnival, Hanover.
World Championship Sled Dog Derby, Laconia.

March
Christa McAuliffe Ski Invitational, Waterville Valley.
Spring Fling Weekend, Loon Mountain, Lincoln.

April
Aprilfest, Cannon Mountain, Franconia.
Spring Mania, Attitash Mountain, Bartlett.

May
Sheep and Wool Festival, New Boston.
New Hampshire Lilac Festival, Lisbon.

June
Market Square Celebration, Portsmouth.
Old Time Fiddlers Contests, Lincoln and Stark.
Seacoast Jazz Weekend, Portsmouth.

July
Nascar Winston Cup Race, at NH International Speedway, Loudon.
Wolfeboro Antique Fair, Wolfeboro.
Northeast Antique and Classic Boat Show, Laconia.

August
League of NH Craftsmen's Fair, Mount Sunapee State Park.
Monadnock Balloon Festival, at Keene Airport, Swanzey.
Attitash Equine Festival, Bartlett.
Candlelight Tour of Historic Homes, Portsmouth.

September
Riverfest Celebration, Manchester.
Seafood Festival, Hampton Beach.
NH Highland Games, Loon Mountain, Lincoln.

October
Harvest Day, Canterbury Shaker Village, Canterbury.
Warner Fall Foliage Festival, Warner.
Sandwich Fair, Sandwich.

November
Traditionally Yours, Jackson.

December
Dickens of a Christmas, Hanover.
Candlelight Stroll, Strawbery Banke, Portsmouth.
First Night Celebrations, Concord, Portsmouth and Keene.

On the shores of Lake Sunapee, an all year round resort

Canterbury Shaker Village, immaculately preserved

A prehistoric mystery
Also known as Mystery Hill, America's Stonehenge comprises chambers with massive capstones, stone walls, standing stones, a sacrificial table and a 'speaking tube'. Various monoliths align with the pole star and the summer solstice. What connection all this had to solar and lunar events is uncertain, but its purpose may well have been astronomical and/or ceremonial.

► ◼ **America's Stonehenge** *188B1*

This enigmatic 4,000-year-old site at North Salem may not quite emulate its more famous English namesake but is a genuine prehistoric relic (see panel). From Boston leave I-93 at Exit 3 and take Route 111 east to Island Pond and Haverhill Road. Go south on Haverhill Road to the entrance on the right. (*Open*: weather permitting, daily, May to October; weekends only in winter.)

►► **Canterbury Shaker Village** *188B2*

Just north of Concord, this pristine example of a Shaker community, established in the 1780s, is the sixth of 18 such villages in order of founding. The last surviving female inhabitant, or sister, died in 1992, but the village has been preserved intact, with a meeting-house (note the separate entrances for men and women), fire station, schoolhouse, herb garden, dwelling house (with a bell cast by Paul Revere) and a remarkably preserved steam-powered laundry. The Shakers here were progressive in outlook: they had the first telephone and first car in the area, and converted to electricity in 1910, five years before the state house in Concord.

The guided tour takes a look at Shaker inventions, which include the wide-headed brush, an early washing-machine, knitting-machines, an automatic hayseeding device and a self-sealing front door. Craft workshops, including herbal crafts, broom-making and box-making, are held in season. For more on the Shaker way of life see pages 148–9. (*Open*: daily, May to October, from Friday to Sunday in April, November and December. Tours last 90 minutes, starting on the hour.)

A broom-maker keeps a Shaker tradition alive

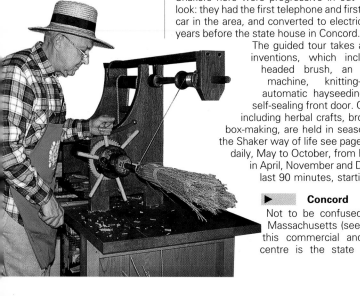

► ◼ **Concord** *188B1*

Not to be confused with Concord, Massachusetts (see pages 168–70), this commercial and administrative centre is the state capital of New

Hampshire. Visitors are most likely to come for the **Christa McAuliffe Planetarium**►► (for times and reservations (tel: 603/271 STAR), named after the Concord astronaut and schoolteacher who died instantly in the ill-fated take-off of the *Challenger* space mission. The planetarium is currently the world's most technologically advanced. It offers a number of programmes, in which you may see our galaxy from inside and outside in a simulated voyage through space, and home in on close-ups of the moon and the planets.

One of a number of granite public buildings downtown, the **State House**► was erected by prisoner labour in 1819 and much enlarged subsequently, although the legislature still meets in the original chambers. With 400 representatives it is the fourth largest such assembly in the world (after the government assemblies of Britain and India, and the US Congress). Murals and some 200 portraits of New Hampshire dignitaries adorn the inside, as well as 88 tattered Civil War flags in the entrance hall. There are free weekend tours on the hour between 10am and 2pm; during the week you guide yourself with the aid of a leaflet available at the desk.

In Eagle Square, close by the State House, the **New Hampshire Historical Society** (free) maintains changing displays on the state's past and exhibits an 1852 Concord stage-coach (see panel). The **Coach and Eagle Trail** is a self-guided walk taking in points of interest in the city centre (free pamphlets available from the State House and from the Chamber of Commerce, 244 North Main Street). The **League of New Hampshire Craftsmen**, a state-wide handicraft association, has its headquarters and a gallery at 205 North Main Street.

Out of the downtown area at 14 Penacook Street at the end of North Main Street, the **Franklin Pierce Manse** (*open*: 11–3, Monday to Friday, mid-June to Labor Day) was the home from 1842 of the 14th president and contains numerous family pieces.

Pierce had a somewhat nondescript political life, and a tragic family one: two of his children died in infancy, then his third was killed in a railway accident aged 13, two months before his inauguration in 1853. As a consequence of this his wife could not face public appearances and his cousin had to stand in as first lady.

West of Concord, at 38 Flanders Road in Henniker, the **New England Winery**, the oldest in New England and the only one in the state, opens its doors daily for tours and tastings.

Concord's up-to-the-minute planetarium

The Concord coach
Concord's history of coach-making dates from 1827 when J Stephen Abbot, coach-builder and wheelwright, completed the first Concord coach. He forged a partnership with Lewis Downing, and together they created 14 types of Concord coach, as well as numerous kinds of other recreational and commercial vehicles. Their company produced 3,000 coaches, some of which were used by the Wells Fargo Company in the pioneering days of the West.

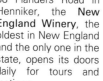

Pick your own fruit in Canterbury – and in many other places

■ **Winter, with deep snow in much of the region, is very different in New England from summer. Christmas and First Night, a New Year's Eve festival that originated in Boston's bi-centennial Independence celebrations of 1976, are very special times.....■**

194

*Top: Christmas at Faneuil Hall, Boston
Above: snow and a welcoming wreath on the door – all part of the spirit of a New England Christmas*

Christmas wreaths
One small but thriving industry in the economically impoverished area of northern Maine is the making of decorative Christmas wreaths. Based on a particular type of balsam fir, they are sold all over eastern America.

First Night Buttons – passport to Boston's New Year's Eve celebrations

Christmas As soon as Thanksgiving Day is over, Christmas trees, lights, wreaths and garlands start going up all over the towns and villages. The month of December is filled with festivities, from lantern-lit sleigh rides to readings of Dickens. To highlight just three: in Portsmouth, New Hampshire, there is a Candlelight Stroll round the houses of Strawbery Banke Museum, each decorated in its own period style; lantern-bearing guides in 19th-century costume lead evening tours in Mystic Seaport Village, Connecticut; and Old Sturbridge Village, Massachusetts, celebrates a colonial-period Christmas.

Summer visitors who want to see what a New England Christmas is like should be sure to look inside one of the dozens of Christmas shops that stay open all year round. Plastic trees hung heavy with colour-co-ordinated bows, baubles, enamelled cut-outs and crystal Santas glitter against the fake snow and piped carols. There are rolls of ribbon by the dozen, tiny stars by the yard, garlands and wreaths ready-made or in kits. Displayed amongst it all are little groups of 'Snowbabies', 'Carolers', Annalee dolls (see panel on page 196), nutcrackers and miniature Christmas villages – collections to build up and arrange under the tree or on the mantlepiece. There may even be a Nativity scene.

First Night This colourful and exciting, non-alcoholic community festival has become a well-established tradition that is spreading rapidly to dozens of towns throughout New England and elsewhere. Between the afternoon carnival procession and the midnight fireworks on New Year's Eve, there are scores of different indoor and outdoor 'happenings'. For the cost of a First Night Button (badge), families and friends, often wearing masks or fancy dress, wander the streets imbibing jazz, dance, theatre, puppets, ice carvings, storefront tableaux and many other entertainments.

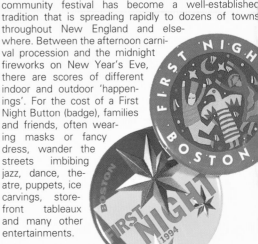

Dartmouth College, the only Ivy League college in northern New England

Dartmouth's beginnings
Dartmouth College was founded in 1769 when the Congregational minister, Eleazar Wheelock, gained a charter from the governor of New Hampshire to educate Native Americans in a log hut. The college's first sponsor was the 2nd Earl of Dartmouth, the secretary of state for the colonies under George III.

195

▶ **Hanover** *188A2*

In Hanover, on the Connecticut river, the town centre is dominated by the 265-acre campus of prestigious **Dartmouth College**▶, an Ivy League establishment (see pages 22–3). Notable among the college buildings grouped around the maple-shaded green are the colonial-style **Baker Library** (1928) and **Dartmouth Hall** (1784). The **Hood Museum** has a small but choice art collection (*open*: 11–5 Tuesday to Friday, 9:30–5 Saturday and Sunday). The **Hopkins Center** features year-round music performances, plays, movies and other cultural events.

South of town towards Windsor, the **Saint-Gaudens National Historic Site**▶▶, off route 12A at Cornish, marks the summer home of Augustus Saint-Gaudens (1848–1907), one of America's foremost sculptors. Many of his works are on show, both in the garden that was his passion and in his studio. Pieces include copies of the *Shaw Memorial*, which stands on Boston Common opposite the State House, and the *Adams Memorial,* installed in Washington, DC. (*Open*: last weekend in May to end of October; small fee.)

East from Hanover, by Mascoma Lake, the **Lower Shaker Village** retains 13 Shaker buildings of the former nearby Enfield community (1781–1923) and includes a craft shop and a small museum of Shaker artefacts (*open*: 1 June to 15 October). The nearby feast ground on Mount Assurance was chosen for its view of the lake. Further on, at Grafton Center, a signpost points up a bumpy road to the **Ruggles Mine**▶. This abandoned mica, feldspar, beryl and uranium mine (see panel) is an expensive visit for what is offered, but the site is dramatic. Entrance is through a rock tunnel into a huge open-cast mine, from which a number of man-made caverns and underground ponds can be explored (a torch is advisable). (*Open*: 9–5, weekends mid-May to mid-June, then daily until mid-October.)

Mica at the Ruggles Mine
The flexible, flaky material known as mica, which is found abundantly in the Ruggles Mine, has high resistance to heat. It was formerly used to glaze stove-fronts and lanterns, and to carry wires in electric toasters. The owners claim over 150 types of minerals have been found at the mine. Visitors can rent hammers and take home souvenir chunks of rock.

Annalee's dolls, a cult

Annalee's dolls
Back in 1934 Annalee Thorndike made her first doll, the first of many thousands of felt and wire creations, which with their hand-painted faces and rosy cheeks, have gained something of a cult status. Near Meredith in the Winnipesaukee region is the Annalee Doll Museum and shop, on the original manufacturing site. The museum exhibits some pre-World War II specimens, including the first doll ever produced (in 1934; early examples can fetch $2,000 nowadays). The gift shop sells a variety of mice in top hats, Christmas shepherds, baseball players and fishing boys.

Boating on Lake Sunapee

▶▶ **Lake Sunapee**   188B2

The Sunapee area offers unspoilt lake and mountain scenery, and a good alternative for those who find Lake Winnipesaukee too commercialised. The state beach on Lake Sunapee is a narrow sandy strip, ideal for families with small children as the water is shallow and the beach shelves very gently. The M/V *Mt Sunapee II* cruises the lake, with two narrated tours daily (tel: 603/763 4030).

Mount Sunapee▶▶ towers over the lake. Its ski-lift operates all year, and the summit café offers a spectacular panorama encompassing Mad River Glen (73 miles) and Mount Washington (75 miles). Walks from the top include the 1,000-yard trail to a cliff high above spectacularly sited Lake Solitude. The area around the base of the chair-lift is the site of the League of New Hampshire Craftsmen's Craft Fair in August.

Mount Kearsarge▶ (2,937 feet), in Rollins State Park, has a straightforward trail up its south side (reached by road from Warner). The walk up takes 20–30 minutes; the view from the top takes in the White Mountains. **Mount Kearsarge Indian Museum** (Exit 8 off Route 89 near Warner) explores the world of the North American Indians with exhibits of baskets, fishing artefacts, canoes and quiltwork.

▶▶ **Lake Winnipesaukee**   188B2

New Hampshire's largest lake is the centre of a busy vacation area whose fortunes were boosted considerably by the movie *On Golden Pond*, filmed at adjacent Squam Lake. Its shoreline is very irregular and the charming views ever-changing, although the small Victorian resort communities that fringe it are of limited interest. The best way to appreciate it is to take a cruise on the M/S *Mount Washington* (May to October; tel: 603/366 5531).

Ellacoya State Beach is suitable for families, with a narrow sandy strip; the water is clean and there is a boat launch for lightweights. **Weirs Beach**, with the main steamer pier, is the most commercialised point on the lake. It is a far from sedate boardwalk village thick with fast-food stands, motels and family-oriented action (see

Speedway
New Hampshire International Speedway (tel: 603/783 4931) is a big state revenue earner on Route 106 north of Canterbury. Races take place in the 60,000-seater stadium.

Aerial view of Moultonborough in the Lakes Region

Family fun at Weirs Beach
The Winnipesaukee Railroad runs diesel trains along the lakeside from here, with dinner specials in the evening. There are also two open-air water parks, one called simply Water Slide; pay for a batch of rides, or for two hours, or for the whole day. The Surf Coaster lies away from the beach and is pricier, but also has a wave-machine surf coaster. The latter also runs a crazy-golf course. Across the road, another company operates go-karts and a baseball pitching machine.

Seaplane rides are a popular way of enjoying the autumn foliage

panel), but retaining a quaintly antique array of 1950s home-made slush kiosks and amusement arcades. One of New England's last drive-in movie theatres (an endangered species) is here too. **Meredith Bay** hosts a summer theatre, while **Center Harbor** has a Children's Museum for ages two to ten.

The **Science Center of New Hampshire▶** (*open*: 1 May to 1 November) , off Route 113 near Holderness, is a wildlife sanctuary for rescued animals of New Hampshire. It is nicely done, with a ¾-mile trail leading past enclosures. Live animal demonstrations, with a naturalist, take place twice daily, and there are lots of hands-on activities for children, including microscopes and quizzes. In addition to the main trail, there is a 1-mile trail up to Mount Fayal which offers a view of **Squam Lake**. The Center also runs nature cruises on the lake for sightings of loons and other wildlife (for details, tel: 603/968 7194). Cruises are also operated by Squam Lake Tours (tel: 603/968 7577).

Quieter, traditional towns include **Center Sandwich** and **Wolfeboro▶**. Both have crafts shops and historical museums. Devotees of old-style country stores should look in at the store at Moultonborough. The nearby **Castle in the Clouds▶**, built in 1911–14 for millionaire Thomas Plant, is a turreted hilltop house with whimsical interior features, including an octagonal elm-panelled dining room. However, it is the setting that is most memorable. The shuttle bus which takes you up also visits the Castle Springs mineral-water bottling plant. Be prepared for crowds: the rooms in the house are small, and this is a frequent coach-tour visit.

At **Tamworth** is the Barnstormers Theater, New Hampshire's oldest professional summer theatre. Tamworth itself glimpses Chocorua Lake, while nearby **White Lake State Park** has a beach with canoe and rowing-boat rentals.

SEAPLANE RIDES
FOLIAGE FLIGHTS

NEW HAMPSHIRE

► **Manchester** *188B1*

In the 19th century the thriving Amoskeag Mill made Manchester the world's largest cotton cloth-producing centre. Today it is a commercial and manufacturing city, but the **Currier Gallery of Art►►** makes the city worth a visit. The collection includes European and American masters, with paintings, sculpture and decorative art from the 13th to 20th centuries (*open*: 10–4 Tuesday to Saturday, 10–10 Thursday, 2–5 Sunday). The gallery also organises tours of the 1950 Usonian home, designed by Frank Lloyd Wright (Thursday to Sunday; advance booking only, tel: 603/669 6144).

South of town, the **Robert Frost Farm►** at Derry was the poet's home from 1900–11 (see page 209). Here he 'wrote more than half of my first book, much more than half of my second and even quite a little of my third'. He later visited it to find it a scrap yard, and it was only after his death that his daughter Lesley Frost Ballantine restored it. The locality was the setting for Frost's 'Stopping by Woods on a Snowy Evening'. (*Open*: daily in summer, weekends in spring and autumn.)

Andrew Wyeth is one of several artists with New England connections on show at the Currier Gallery

►► **Mount Monadnock Region** *188A1*

Mount Monadnock►►►, America's most climbed peak, rises to a modest 3,165 feet, but by virtue of its isolation from New England's other high spots it gets one of the grandest views in the Northeast. The surroundings are relatively unfrequented and make a good getaway from the Boston area for those seeking accessible, low-key relaxation. Walking, kayaking, canoeing, covered-bridge spotting, leaf-peeping, skiing and antique-hunting lead the pursuits.

Only accessible on foot, the mountain demands a substantial walk to the top (see panel). Rock formations to look for include the Imp, the Sarcophagus (a boulder transported and dumped on Pumpelly Ridge by glaciers in the Ice Age) and the Doric Temple (a set of composite stone blocks). The summit view on a clear day extends to the White Mountains, to the Boston skyscrapers and over every New England state.

Peterborough is home to the MacDowell Colony, begun by composer Edward MacDowell. It offers artistic seclusion to artists, composers and writers, but only a small part is open to the public. Those attracted here have included Leonard Bernstein, Thornton Wilder, Aaron

---

Monadnock checklists
Because the forest on Mount Monadnock was burned off around 1810, the views from the upper trails are particularly fine. The open terrain here gives rise to some rare semi-alpine flora, including mountain cranberry, mountain golden rod, mountain sandwort and cinquefoil. Fauna includes moose, black bear, white-tailed deer, grey fox, red fox, woodchuck, porcupine, opossum and raccoon.

Routes up Mount Monadnock
Numerous routes lead up the mountain from Monadnock State Park headquarters at Jaffrey, where free maps are available. The most popular and easiest are the White Cross and White Arrow trails (3–4 hours there and back). The Pumpelly Trail is the longest at about 5 hours' walking time. The Spelman Trail, which heads up a breathtaking series of schist rock ledges to reach Pumpelly Ridge, ascends 1,000 feet in half a mile and is the steepest. The Red Spot Trail is perhaps the most scenic. For a very full but rewarding day's walking, make a circuit by taking any trail via Bald Rock to the summit and return via Pumpelly Ridge.

Copland and Virgil Thomson. Wilder's play, *Our Town*, was set in Peterborough and became one of the cornerstones of American drama. Theatrical traditions are maintained by the Peterborough Players with their summer theatre, and the Marionette Theater (tel: 603/924 7585), which specialises, most unusually, in opera performed by marionettes. Fans of vintage diners should seek out the Peterborough Diner in Depot Street. **Miller State Park▶▶**, off Route 101 east of Peterborough, has road access for vehicles to the summit of Pack Monadnock (2,300 feet), plus picnic sites and a summit loop trail. You can walk up (nearly 1½ miles) by following the Wapack Trail from Route 101.

Blink and you'll miss **Dublin**. Along its sleepy main street is the headquarters of the *Yankee Magazine* and *Farmers' Almanac*, two famous New England-based publications; tours of the premises are given on weekdays. West of town, Dublin Pond is the haunt of blue herons and offers a town beach with water-slides, sailing, windsurfing and swimming. Close by, Friendly Farm (*open*: daily in summer, weekends in autumn) operates a petting farm for children, with a range of farmyard animals and milking demonstrations. Near by, **Harrisville▶** has a pretty pond and a cluster of old mill cottages; Harrisville Designs demonstrate old weaving methods (*open*: Tuesday to Saturday; free).

Keene is a commercial centre rather than a tourist town, but has some dignified 19th-century homes. The Horatio Colony House Museum, at 199 Main Street, is a pleasing Federal-style house of 1806. The Children's Museum has displays on different parts of New England, including colonial life and a 'typical' village.

Further south, **Rhododendron State Park▶**, at Fitzwilliam, comes into spectacular bloom in mid-July and has views of Mount Monadnock. **Fitzwilliam itself** has a concentration of antique shops, while at **West Rindge** Ed's Country Auction offers rural antiques, domestic junk and copious local colour (Saturdays in summer at 10am; winter at 6pm). Near Rindge is the **Cathedral of the Pines▶** (*open*: 1 May to 1 November; see panel).

The Wapack Trail
A 21-mile hiking trail leads from the base of Mount Watatic, near Ashburnham, MA, to the slope of North Pack Monadnock in Greenfield, NH. The trail takes a skyline route over the summits of Watatic, New Ipswich, Barrett and Temple mountains, with views of Boston, the White Mountains and Vermont on the way. Yellow triangle markers and cairns show the route.

Cathedral of the Pines
Begun to commemorate Lieutenant Sanderson Sloane, shot down over Germany in 1944, this outdoor interdenominational place of worship became a national memorial in 1957. With its charming backdrop of Mount Monadnock, it focuses on a 2,000-seat 'cathedral' shaded by tall white pines. The altar contains stones donated by every president since Truman, and the stone lectern contains sand and rock from every battlefield where Americans have fought. The Memorial Bell Tower, with bas-reliefs designed by Norman Rockwell, was the first memorial in the US devoted to womankind.

199

Mt Monadnock, seen from Dublin

■ **Over 80 per cent of New England is covered in forest. The woods, a mixture of hardwoods and softwoods, are home to an exciting variety of wildlife species. Seeing moose or beaver can be a holiday highlight, and in summer the sound of songbirds is sensational. There are also areas of enchanting alpine flora.....■**

'Brake for moose...'
'...It could save your life'. So read the road signs in New Hampshire. Every year there are scores of collisions between moose and cars on forest roads. A moose can severely damage not only the car but, quite possibly, the driver too. If you see a moose at the side of the road, try not to startle it and go carefully – moose are unpredictable. Dark brown in colour, they are difficult to see in the dark.

Poison ivy
Poison ivy is common throughout eastern North America and is poisonous to touch. Its leaves have three leaflets, green turning to red/purple, and it has white berries. If you so much as brush against the plant, its poison causes blistering and great discomfort (it can even rub off from a dog's coat on to your leg). Clothes worn a year after contact can cause poisoning. Don't go into undergrowth and always wear socks and long trousers if you are going near wild vegetation.

200

New England has two National Forests: the White Mountains National Forest, which covers much of New Hampshire and creeps over the border into Maine, and the Green Mountain National Forest, in Vermont. Both are laced with trails. Away from the coastal strip, Maine too is heavily forested – and dotted with thousands of lakes. Its most northerly areas are predominantly softwood, managed by timber companies. The softwoods are mainly pine, spruce and fir, while sugar maple, yellow birch, aspen and paper birch are New England's dominant hardwoods.

Forest fauna The largest of the forest animals are moose, black bear and white-tailed deer. The deer are ubiquitous and hunting them is an autumn ritual. The black bear stands almost 3 feet high and is fairly frequently seen making its clumsy way through the woods of Maine, New Hampshire and, occasionally, Vermont. They are usually harmless (but see panel). The animal that attracts most attention, however, is the moose. There are numerous organised moose-watching trips (information available locally) and you may well see one as you drive around (they like the salt that runs off the roads), particularly in northern Maine, the most northerly parts of the White Mountains and along the Kancamagus Highway. Baxter State Park is one of the best places in New England for moose. The most likely time of day to spot moose is at dawn or dusk, especially near ponds or marshes. A full-grown male moose can be 6 feet tall at its shoulders, weighing over half a ton, and has huge antlers to boot – give such an animal a wide berth. Moose are most ungainly creatures, with a long, pendulous snout

White-tailed deer are a fairly common sight

and a hairy dewlap. They eat grasses and often stand in lakes.

Smaller forest animals include raccoon, chipmunk, marten, woodchuck and porcupine. Red squirrel, coyote, red fox, lynx, muskrat, skunk and snowshoe hare are fairly common. Beaver activity in rivers and lakes is always fascinating. Their lodges (houses of sticks and mud) are up to 6 feet high, and the dams, similarly built, are amazing constructions. The beaver's favourite food is bark – look out for sticks that have been neatly stripped and gnawed. The beavers themselves are usually seen at dusk or dawn, giving themselves away with a slap of their tails as they dive.

Mountain birds Even if you cannot identify all the songbirds, you will enjoy the songs that fill the woods in spring and summer. Many of the birds are migratory. The most common include blackpoll and Nashville warblers, ruby- and golden-crowned kinglets, pine siskin, raven, blue jay and chickadee, Maine's state bird and familiar to Europeans as a member of the tit family. The loon, a diver sometimes heard calling from the lakes of New Hampshire, is reputedly the oldest bird species on earth.

Alpine flora There are over 8 square miles of alpine zone in the White Mountains. On Mount Washington the treeline occurs exceptionally low, at 1,400 feet. Climb it (see page 208) and you will notice the trees become more and more stunted. Dense mats of vegetation called *krummholz* (German for 'twisted tree') cover the ground.

Above the treeline, in the alpine zone, 100 different alpine flowers that are unique to Mount Washington, Labrador and the Arctic grow among lichens, sedges and mosses. The dwarf cinquefoil (*Potentilla robbinsiana*) is endemic to Mount Washington. Other alpine flowers that may be found here and in the alpine areas of the Katahdin range in Maine's Baxter State Park include mountain aster, alpine violet, alpine bearberry, moss plant, mountain brook saxifrage and goldthread.

A young moose

Bear essentials
Black bears are shy, preferring to stay away from people and unlikely to do any harm. Nevertheless, it is wise to be careful with food as the smell attracts them and this is when injuries may occur.
● Never feed bears.
● Don't leave food scraps lying around and never throw them into a camp fire.
● Store food (and any clothes soiled with food) in sealed containers in the boot of the car or in a tree (so the bears can't damage your car).

Fragile flora
The ecology of the alpine zones is extremely fragile. Remember that some of the flowers that have adapted to the biting winter winds and the poor soil take up to 25 years to flower for the first time, so mind where you put your feet. The best time to see them is from mid-June to August.

Buildings in Strawbery Banke

Strawbery Banke
Settled in the 1630s and named for its abundance of wild strawberries, Strawbery Banke became a prosperous merchants' centre. Later, the Puritans came and, in 1653, changed the name to Portsmouth, which sounded less frivolous. Having escaped an urban renewal plan in 1958, the grid of old streets of the 1690s has been restored. The 42 houses show the lifestyles of its inhabitants through the ages.

New Hampshire cruises
Cruises to the nine islands constituting the Isles of Shoals and whale-watching trips are popular excursions. Operators around Portsmouth include:
● Portsmouth Harbor Cruises (tel: 1-800/776 0915).
● The Isles of Shoals Steamship Co (tel: 1-800/441 4620).
● New Hampshire Seacoast Cruises (tel: 603/964 5545)
● The Atlantic Fishing Fleet, which operates the *Atlantic Queen II* (at Rye Harbor; tel: 603/964 5220).

►► **Portsmouth** 188C1

Occupying the northern end of New Hampshire's short coastline, Portsmouth was the most important colonial town north of Boston. It has an English look, with a fine legacy of red-brick 18th- and 19th-century houses, many built for prosperous sea-captains. Along the waterfront you can see one of the swiftest flowing navigable rivers in the world.

The original colonial settlement in the harbour was **Strawbery Banke►►**, one of New Hampshire's leading historic attractions (see panel). All but one of the houses, plus a re-erected four-seater privy, stand on their original sites. (*Open*: May to October for self-guided tours, and two weekends in December for Candlelight Strolls, which also take place one night in August.)

Portsmouth Historical Society, with the Society for the Preservation of New England Antiquities, maintains a number of 18th-century houses scattered around town (the Portsmouth Trail connects each of these historic sites). If you intend to visit more than one, pick up a Portsmouth Passport for reduced admission.

In 1962 the **Warner House►►** (*c* 1716) became the first house in the US to be registered as a National Historic Landmark (following the restoration of the White House in Washington, DC, an action that promoted an awareness of house preservation). It was Portsmouth's first brick house, the work of John Drew, an English builder. The house retains numerous English features in its panelling and furniture. Folk-art murals date back to the time of construction; one of them (once covered up) shows English patriotic sentiment with its portrayal of a redcoat. Outstanding among the furnishings is a Portsmouth-made high chest on the upstairs landing.

The **Moffat Ladd House►** (*open*: daily), a three-storey blue and white building of 1763, stands amid pretty English-style gardens with grass steps. In them William Whipple, a signatory of the Declaration of Independence, planted what is now the state's tallest horse-chestnut tree. The house has fine Portsmouth furniture, eye-catching wallpaper that was hand-painted in Paris in 1819 and a tunnel in its kitchen that supposedly led to the wharf! Its spacious entrance hall is modelled on the

English style. The **Wentworth Gardner House**, located at 50 Mechanic Street (*open*: Tuesday to Sunday, 1–4), is a Georgian structure of 1760, and is noted for the quality of its interior carved woodwork, tiled fireplaces and painted wallpaper.

Two other houses have historical connections: the **Tobias Lear House** (*open*: Wednesday, 1–4) was the birthplace of George Washington's private secretary, Colonel Tobias Lear, while the **John Paul Jones House** was Jones's lodging while his frigate *Ranger* was being refitted in the port.

A state-of-the-art interior of 1807 is found in the **Rundlet-May House** (owned and operated by SPNEA – see page 68), featuring a contemporary roasting oven, Portsmouth furniture and foreign wallpaper, while the **Governor John Langdon House** of 1784 (also an SPNEA property) has fine carving, Portsmouth furniture and landscaped grounds.

On display in Albacore Park, Market Street, is the **USS Albacore** (*open*: 1 May to Columbus Day), a navy submarine that was in service from 1953 to 1972 but never fired a weapon.

Horse-and-carriage tours of the old town start from the church. The **Children's Museum** at 280 Marcy Street provides a variety of hands-on activities for youngsters of all ages (*open*: daily, except Monday out of summer and school vacations).

Just out of town, **Odiorne Point State Park►** covers 350 acres of duneland, the largest tract of undeveloped land on the 18-mile New Hampshire coast, and provides views of the harbour. The World War II fort here is one of a number of historic harbour defences. The Science Center (free) features aquariums showing tide-pool and salt-marsh ecology. There is also a fine drive on Route 1B to **New Castle Island►** (also known as Great Island), which has old homes, forts and lighthouses. The remainder of the coast is almost entirely built up, except for a few patches of marshy hinterland, but there are good state beaches at **Wallis Sands, Jenness** and **North Hampton. Hampton Beach** has a long sandy beach but is very commercialised with a long boardwalk, amusements and fast-food outlets. **Water Country**, New England's biggest water park, is on Route 1 some 3 miles south of Portsmouth.

Portsmouth furniture
Portsmouth's proximity to vast stands of inland timber and its ice-free harbour made it a major centre of ship-building, house construction and furniture-making in the 18th century. The town prospered, the ships' captains built grand mansions, and a market for quality furniture was born. Foreign influences moulded taste and fashion in furniture, notably through the skills of immigrant craftsmen from England. New styles were born; reversed curves, scrolled pediments and cabriole legs appeared. Black walnut was the rage; stained maple was a simulation. John Gaines III and Joseph Davis led the way with flamboyant styles, Gothic and Chinese caprices appearing in the 1760s.

203

Portsmouth's waterfront: boats have taken visitors to the Isles of Shoals from here since the mid-19th century

NEW HAMPSHIRE

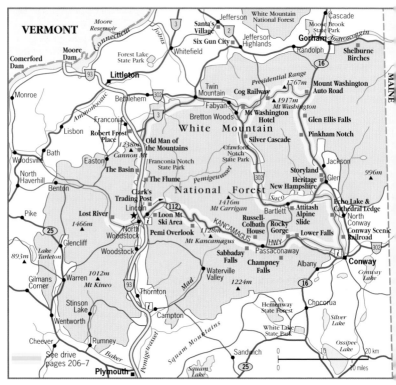

See drive
pages 206–7

▶▶▶ The White Mountains   188B3

The White Mountains are the highest and most dramatic uplands in New England. This is the region's finest area for mountain walking, and in season draws crowds to its ski slopes and fall foliage display. The main accommodation areas are the purely functional resort towns around the White Mountains proper. These places are well geared to tourism but not strong on character.

North Conway is highly rated by many for its outlet shopping malls, which get particularly busy on rainy days in high season. **Woodstock** and **Lincoln** are best placed

Early conservation days
The Weeks Act was passed in 1911 and introduced the National Forest system. The White Mountains were the first such forest area to be designated, affording protection after the removal of many trees in the region. The soil erosion and washdown that had occurred had worried politicians who spent vacations here, and political pressure for change followed.

Winter in the White Mountains: Echo Lake

The Mount Washington Cog Railway puffs its way up an uncomfortable but scenic 1¼-hour ascent over fragile-looking viaducts and up 37-degree gradients

for exploring the Kancamagus and Franconia areas. **Bethlehem** in the far northwest is particularly noted for its architectural gems.

White Mountain sights Mount Washington▶▶▶, New England's tallest (6,288 feet) and extremely windswept mountain, soars high above the rest of the Presidential Range. Numerous hiking routes lead up the slopes, but the most popular ways up are by the toll road (guided tours by van available) and the **Mount Washington Cog Railway▶▶**, the world's oldest tourist railway. At the summit the view extends to Boston and the Atlantic Ocean. There was once a succession of grand hotels at the top; today only the Tip Top House survives (preserved as a museum; free), while the rest is a stark miscellany of masts and huts, together with an observatory and a small museum. Visitors making the trip by railway only have 20 minutes at the summit to ensure a seat on the return; you can descend later, but you will probably have to stand.

The **Robert Frost Place▶**, in a remote spot near Franconia, is the humble 50-acre farmstead where the New England poet (see page 209) dreamt he 'could live cheap and get Yankier and Yankier'. The tiny house contains original manuscripts and Frost's own writing table.

Clark's Trading Post▶, near Lincoln, was set up by a family of avid collectors in the 1920s. The complex includes a reconstructed New England Street, the museum (with working musical boxes, vintage slot machines and peep-shows), and a topsy-turvy 'haunted house'. Black bears perform three times daily, while the railroad around the grounds gets held up by 'bandits'.

At Glen, **Heritage New Hampshire**, a look at the state's past using tableaux of selected historical titbits, is like walking through a huge stage set. Actors explain their lives – one as a trapper, another in a mock-up of 18th-century Portsmouth. It finishes with a simulated train ride. Next door, **Storyland** is a well thought out children's theme park. There is a Mexican village, and rides that include flying clogs and a log-boat trip down water-slides.

Two other theme parks, both at Jefferson, are **Santa's Village**, including 'Santa's summer home' with similar rides to Storyland, and **Six Gun City**, with a water-slide and Wild West adventure. **Whale's Tail** (Route 3, North Woodstock) is a water park. **Attitash Alpine Slide**, at Bartlett, features 'wet and wild water-slides', plus a scenic chair-lift, horseback riding and a golf-driving range.

Continued on page 208.

'Men hang out their signs indicative of their respective trades; shoe makers hang out a gigantic shoe; jewelers, a monster watch; and the dentist hangs out a gold tooth; but up in the mountains of New Hampshire God Almighty has hung out a sign to show that there He makes men.'
– Attributed to Daniel Webster, on the Old Man of the Mountain, Franconia Notch.

205

The world's worst weather Because of a funnel effect, Mount Washington gets the full brunt of three continental storm systems. The fastest winds ever recorded (231mph) have occurred here: a 10mph breeze further down becomes an 80mph blast at the top. Some 175 feet down, the ground is permanently frozen. These unusual conditions give rise to 63 alpine flower species. The mountain has claimed many lives: below the summit, on the right of the railway, a wooden sign and cairn mark the spot where 23-year-old walker Lizzie Bourne died of exhaustion in 1855.

Drive The White Mountains

See map on page 204.

This 94-mile loop tour is perhaps the most scenic mountain drive in New England. It takes in the Kancamagus Highway and Franconia Notch, and provides opportunities to drive up to the magnificent viewpoints on Cathedral Ledge and Mount Washington. Watch out for moose, which often stray on to the roads, and keep the petrol tank topped up.

From North Woodstock take Route 112, the **Kancamagus Highway▶▶▶**, famous for its fall foliage and with choice but scattered views. Beyond **Loon Mountain ski area**, with its gondolas and outdoor activities, there are particularly fine roadside panoramas from the **Pemi Overlook** (with its view of mounts Kancamagus, Osceola and Loon) and from **Kancamagus Pass Overlook** (with Mount Kancamagus prominent). Numerous trails start from the road, including a short path to **Sabbaday**

Covered bridge over The Flume in Franconia Notch

Falls▶, a trio of waterfalls tumbling and twisting into a deep chasm, and another to **Champney Falls▶**.

Passaconaway Historic Site: Russell-Colbath House (*open*: July and August, 9–4:30, but may vary; free) is a tiny cottage formerly occupied by Ruth Colbath, the 'hermit woman' postmistress whose husband walked out without explanation one night. She waited 39 years for him and left a light burning each night, but died in 1933 before his return. The Swift river flows over great boulders at **Rocky Gorge**, where a short loop trail leads to Falls Pond. A short distance east, also by the road, Lower Falls is designated for swimming and picnicking. At the next left turn take Dugway Road, leaving Route 112 to dodge the traffic jams of North Conway. **Conway** has a pair of covered bridges.

Turn left to Echo Lake and **Cathedral Ledge▶▶▶**. The small lake (a state park with a small, roped-off swimming area) is magnificently sited beneath the huge granite outcrop of Cathedral Ledge, a popular cliff for rock-climbing. A road ascends

the top of the ledge, and a path leads out to a dizzy view.

Further north, via Glen, the Summit of **Mount Washington**▶▶▶ is approached on foot, by toll road or by cog railway.Retrace your drive to Glen then follow Route 302 to the **Mount Washington Hotel,** New England's largest wooden building, the last surviving of 15 grand hotels in the White Mountains and still laced with period atmosphere (see pages 40–1).

To the west, the **Franconia Notch road (I-93)** ▶▶▶ carves its way through awesome scenery. The drama unfolds fully from above: take the cable-car up **Cannon Mountain**▶▶, where the ½-mile Rim Trail looks down 2,500 feet into the valley and into New York State. By the cable-car station, the **New England Ski Museum** (*open*: 12–5, daily except Wednesdays; free) has displays of archive photographs and equipment of various periods, plus a multi-screen slide show about skiing history.

From I-93 you can glimpse the famous **Old Man of the Mountains**, a rock outcrop some 40 feet tall which displays the uncanny profile of a human face. There is roadside parking for northbound traffic, and a short trail from a parking lot to Profile Lake for southbound traffic. **The Basin**▶, a 30-foot-wide pothole, was gouged out by glacial meltwater and is one of a number of attractive features passed on the popular Cascade Brook Trail. Better known still is **The Flume**▶▶, a dark, steep-sided chasm that keeps cool on the hottest of summer days and becomes laden with 30–40 feet of ice in winter, when the wooden walkways are dismantled. A fine waterfall tumbles into its far end.

At North Woodstock, it is worth diverting west on Route 112 to **Lost River**▶▶ (closed winter). The boardwalk trail, through caves created by tumbled boulders and along a series of waterfalls, is tortuous and exciting, and requires good footwear. The river disappears at points into the caves, which can be explored by ladder. This

Take a diversion on a cable-car for bird's-eye views

Glorious colour is guaranteed in the autumn

remote spot was discovered by two brothers on a fishing trip when one fell into the top entrance of a cave and had to be rescued.

NEW HAMPSHIRE

Hikers consider that the most difficult part of the Appalachian Trail is in 'The Whites'

Continued from page 205.

White Mountain walks The White Mountains are amply laced with trails of all degrees of difficulty. The Presidential Range (so called because some of the peaks are named after presidents) has the highest summits. **Mount Washington** is an obvious objective and has some outstanding features, such as Tuckerman's Ravine. Another rewarding hike is the **Zealand Trail** to the Zealand Falls Appalachian Mountain Club (AMC) hut (3–3½ hours there and back). From the AMC building at Crawford rail depot on Route 302, an easy climb up **Mount Willard** follows a well-graded trail, an old carriage road, which takes in ledges and cliffs above Crawford Notch Zealand Campground (allow 2–2½ hours).

Along the Kancamagus Highway, photogenic **Mount Chocorua** can be approached from the trailhead leading to **Champney Falls**. The less demanding 3-mile **Boulder Loop Trail**, starting at Covered Bridge Campground, offers views from high rock ledges. Easier still is the Lincoln Woods Trail from Hancock Campground, which follows the course of an old railroad and gives river views before reaching Franconia Falls (allow 4 hours).

Northeast of Glen, Town Hall Road leads into Slippery Brook and becomes a dirt road. Further on is the trail encircling lonely **Mountain Pond**, set beneath Slope Mountain. One of the best ridge walks above the tree-line is along the **Franconia Ridge Trail**, reached from Lafayette Campground on I-93 (allow 5 hours). Ascend via the Falling Waters Trail and climb Mount Lincoln (5,089 feet); descend via the Bridal Path. **Mount Kearsarge North** (3,268 feet) is a 2,700-foot climb, north of North Conway, taking roughly 3 hours each way.

For a very arduous day's walking (for experienced and fit hikers only) an exceptionally fine route is from Route 16 south of Gorham up **Mount Jefferson**.

Further ideas for short walks are covered in the drive on pages 206–7.

Robert Frost

■ The poet Robert Frost is best known for his simple everyday themes, his language and his rhythms. His appeal lies in his sharp observation of daily rural scenes, which he describes in conversational language, but with delicacy and a hint at deeper meanings. In setting and in character, his poetry is deeply rooted in New England.....■

ROBERT LEE FROST
MAR. 26. 1874 — JAN. 29. 1963
HAD A LOVERS QUARREL WITH THE WO
HIS WIFE
ELINOR MIRIAM WHITE
OCT. 25. 1873 — MAR. 20. 1938
TOGETHER WING TO WING AND OAR T

Early days Robert Frost's father, William, a teacher and newspaper editor, was a New Englander. His mother, Isabell Moodie, also a teacher, was born in Scotland, of Orkneyan origin. Robert was born on 26 March 1874 in San Francisco, where his father was working on a newspaper, but after his father's death he was taken back to New England, aged 10.

Frost's mother was to exert a strong influence, teaching him and his sister and encouraging the enjoyment of literature. He briefly attended both Dartmouth College in Vermont and, later, Harvard, but gave up to teach and to write poetry. In 1900 he began working on a farm in Derry, New Hampshire, given him by his grandfather (see page 198). Farming was to be a recurring theme of his life, one never taken very seriously as a living, but something that brought him close to nature and, in particular, botany.

'The voice of New England' Some of Frost's best-known poetry was written in Derry, but he received no recognition there. In 1912 he moved with his wife, Elinor Miriam White, and their children to Britain, to live in Beaconsfield, Buckinghamshire. During this time, two collections of poems written in Derry, *A Boy's Will* and *North of Boston*, were published in Britain, and to great acclaim.

After the outbreak of World War II, Frost returned with his family to America, unexpectedly famous. He bought another farm, in Franconia, New Hampshire (see page 205), and began a long association as teacher and poet-in-residence with several academic institutions, including Amherst College in Massachusetts.

Four times Pulitzer Prizewinner, Robert Frost died in Boston in 1963, almost 90 years of age.

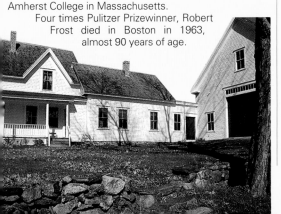

Top: the poet's grave in Bennington
Above: Robert Frost on his 85th birthday
Below: the Robert Frost Farm in Derry

'I'd like to get away from earth awhile
And then come back to it and begin over.
I'd like to go by climbing a birch tree,
And climb black branches up a snow-white trunk
Toward heaven, till the tree could bear no more,
But dipped its top and set me down again.
That would be good both going and coming back.
One could do worse than be a swinger of birches.'
– From 'Birches'

Yachting is big in Rhode Island, and Newport in particular

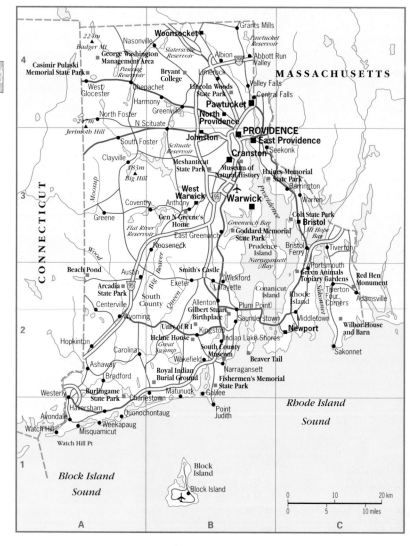

MASSACHUSETTS

CONNECTICUT

Grants Mills
224m
Badger Mt
Nasonville
Woonsocket
Pawtucket Reservoir
George Washington
Management Area
Slatersville Reservoir
Albion
Abbott Run
Valley
Casimir Pulaski
Memorial State Park
295
West
Glocester
Pascoag Reservoir
Chepachet
Bryant
College
Lincoln Woods
State Park
Valley Falls
Central Falls
Limerock
Harmony
Greenville
Pawtucket
North Foster
247m
Jerimoth Hill
N Scituate
North
Providence
PROVIDENCE
South Foster
Scituate Reservoir
Johnston
East Providence
Seekonk
Clayville
183m
Big Hill
Cranston
Meshanticut
State Park
Museum of
Natural History
Haines Memorial
State Park
West
Warwick
Warwick
Barrington
Coventry
Anthony
95
Warren
Greene
Gen N Greene's
Home
Flat River Reservoir
East Greenwich
Greenwich Bay
Colt State Park
Bristol
Mt Hope Bay
Nooseneck
Goddard Memorial
State Park
Prudence
Island
Bristol
Ferry
Tiverton
Narragansett Bay
Beach Pond
Austin
Smith's Castle
Wickford
Portsmouth
Green Animals
Topiary Gardens
Red Hen
Monument
Arcadia
State Park
95
Exeter
Lafayette
Conanicut
Island
Rhode
Island
Tiverton
Four
Corners
Adamsville
Centerville
South
County
Queen
Allenton
Plum Point
Saunderstown
Middletown
Wilbor House
and Barn
Wyoming
Gilbert Stuart
Birthplace
Univ of R I
Kingston
Newport
Hopkinton
Helme House
Great Swamp
Indian Lake Shores
Sakonnet
Carolina
South County
Museum
Beaver Tail
Ashaway
Bradford
Wakefield
Narragansett
Fishermen's Memorial
State Park
Westerly
Burlingame
State Park
Royal Indian
Burial Ground
Matunuck
Galilee
Rhode Island
Sound
Haversham
Charlestown
Avondale
Quonochontaug
Point
Judith
Watch Hill
Weekapaug
Misquamicut
Watch Hill Pt

*Block Island
Sound*

Block
Island

Block Island

0   10   20 km
0   5   10 miles

A   B   C

Rhode Island Officially this is Rhode Island and Providence Plantations, the state with the longest name but the smallest area, roughly 48 miles by 37 miles at its maximum dimensions. The state capital, Providence, lies at the northern end of Narragansett Bay, a scenic 28-mile inlet which is speckled with islands and which almost splits the state in two. The hinterland is low lying. To the east it is densely urbanised and industrialised, while to the west it is more rural, with pockets of solitude such as the 2,600-acre Great Swamp. But it is the intricate coastline, measuring 419 miles, that most attracts visitors. Rhode Island is one of the finest sailing areas on the East Coast, and the state proudly proclaims itself as 'America's first resort'. Its major island, Block Island, has an open terrain with cliffs and a rolling countryside that remind some visitors of Scotland.

The state's remarkable architectural legacy includes 20 per cent of all the nation's Registered National Historic Landmarks. Most famous of all are the Newport mansions, the summer 'cottages' of magnates of the coal and railroad age, but there are also fine earlier survivors. Both Newport and Providence have impressively intact colonial districts.

Early days Rhode Island began as a haven in a time of religious intolerance. Roger Williams, a clergyman, founded the state in 1636 after being expelled from the Puritans' Massachusetts Bay Colony for his heretical views. A few years previously, Reverend William Blackstone, a hermit from the Shawmut Peninsula and also a Puritan refugee, had been the first to arrive.

Williams and his followers established a settlement on the banks of the Moshassuck river and named the place Providence, as God's providence was thought to have led them there. In 1644 he travelled to England and gained a charter, reinforced in 1663, uniting the various settlements in the area as the Colony of Rhode Island and Providence Plantations. The charter gave the inhabitants a degree of independence and 'full liberty in religious commencements'. Hence the state became a sanctuary for religious refugees. Jews and Quakers came to Newport, and their presence made a significant contribution to the town's success. The Native American population declined after 1676 when an unsuccessful attempt by Philip, king of the Wampanoags, led his people, the Narragansetts and Nipmucks, in a war against the English colonists.

Rhode Island was the first colony to declare its independence from Britain (May 1776) but the last to become a state (1790); it celebrates 4 May as well as 4 July. Providence became a commercial centre with the boom in shipping and trade. The China trade, pioneered by John Brown of Providence, and the notorious Triangle Trade (see page 34) enhanced the state's prosperity. In 1793, the opening of Slater's Mill at Pawtucket lit the touchpaper for the mass-production of textiles, a landmark in America's industrialisation.

Events

For further information contact the state tourist office (see page 266) or chambers of commerce.

April
Spring Antique and Craft Marketplace, Wakefield.
Spring Bulb Display, Blithewold: in the house grounds.

May
Bank of Newport Memorial Day Regatta, Newport: J24, Shields and 110 Class Sailboats.
May Breakfasts: over 100 statewide.
Shad Festival, Block Island: picnics and antique cars.
Westerly Antique Show and Sale, Westerly.

May–June
Gaspee Days, Cranston and Warwick.

June
Block Island Race Week: boat races.
Chowder Cook-Off, Newport.
Festival of Historic Houses, Providence: private houses and gardens specially open for tours.
Lobsterman's Festival, Narragansett.
Newport Outdoor Art Festival.
Newport–Bermuda Race (even years), Newport.
Quonset Air Show, North Kingstown.
Secret Gardens Tour of Colonial and Victorian Homes, Newport.
Snug Harbor Shark Tournament, Narragansett.
Wooden Boat Show, Newport.

July
Black Ships Festival, Newport: Japanese festival.
Blessing of the Fleet, Galilee.
Fourth of July Parade, Bristol: one of the country's biggest, and the oldest.
Newport Music Festival: two weeks

of classical music in the mansions.
Seafood Festival, Wakefield.
South County Hot-Air Balloon Festival, Kingston.
Miller Lite International Tennis Hall of Fame Championships, Newport: professional grass-court tournament.
Wickford Art Festival: largest art festival in New England.

August
Block Island House and Garden Tour.
Jazz Festival, Newport: hugely popular event at Fort Adams, with big names.
Newport Folk Festival: the best and biggest in the country.
Seafood Festival, Charlestown: lobster, chowder, clams, hot-air balloons, vintage cars and more.

September
Cajun and Bluegrass Music-Dance-Food Festival, Eschoheag, Labor Day weekend.
Heritage Festival, Providence.
International Boat Show, Newport.
Rhode Island Tuna Tournament, Galilee.
Taste of Rhode Island, Newport.
Waterfront Festival, Providence: food, entertainment, tours, boat races, crafts.

October
Autumnfest, Woonsocket.
Octoberfest, Pawtucket.
Quahog Festival, Wickford.

December
Christmas at Newport: much of the town and several mansions lavishly decorated, candlelight tours, concerts.
Festival of Lights, Wickford Village.
First Night, Providence: concert, dance, alcohol-free celebrations.

Fishing boats on their moorings in Galilee

▶▶ **Block Island** *210B1*

Block Island is something of an under-rated getaway. Formed of rock debris dumped by two glaciers in the Ice Age, the island has 200-foot clay cliffs, 365 glacial ponds and an open terrain. Known by Indians as Manisses ('Island of the little God') and mentioned by the Italian explorer Giovanni da Verrazano in 1524, the island was explored by and named after the Dutchman Adriaen Block before being settled by the English in 1661.

In the 19th century Block Island became a weekend pleasure resort, but by the 1960s much of it was boarded up and its Victorian charm lay crumbling and forgotten. Today it has been spruced up, but not overdone; the Victorian character is jealously preserved and nightlife is distinctly sleepy. There are more bicycles than cars outside the main town, and its attractions are deliberately low key. In fact, the island is nowhere near as busy as Martha's Vineyard or Nantucket. The authorities are promoting the island for 'green' tourism as it has appeal for naturalists and for walkers, with coastal and inland trails; but beware of the deer ticks, for Lyme Disease (see page 263) is prevalent.

The island is 7 miles by 3 miles at its maximum dimensions, and is small enough to cycle round at leisure (bicycles can be hired at the port). Alternatively, taxi-drivers will give a tour for about $20 (the older drivers tend to have the best anecdotes), or you can see the island on horseback. **Black Rock Point**, at the island's southern tip, and **Clay Head** (with trails), at the northeastern end, have fine cliffs. The Greenway Trails are recommended for flora and fauna and there are guided nature walks for visitors during the summer.

The main town is officially called **New Shoreham**, but is usually known as Block Island, and has a small beach. Beaches on the south coast have no undertow (unlike those on the mainland) and are ideal for families. **Corn Neck**, at the north end, has the longest beach. Surfers should head for the south coast, while **Chaqum Pond** is the place for windsurfing.

Getting to Block Island
The fastest ferry crossing is from Galilee (1 hour 10 minutes); for car reservations, tel: 401/783 4613. Other ferries operate from Providence, New London (Connecticut) and Montauk (Long Island). Flights can be made from Westerly (New England Airlines, tel: 401/596 2460).

Block Island wildlife
In 1991 the Nature Conservancy listed Block Island among the 12 'Last Great Places' in the Americas, and 23 per cent of the island is now held for nature conservation. The island is the home of the rare northern harrier and is one of only two habitats in the US for burying beetles and regal fritillary butterflies. May brings out the snow-white flowers of the shad bush, while autumn sees a spectacular bird migration of some 150 over-wintering species.

A freak view
West Side Baptist Church on Block Island is the only church in the US where you can see the sun both rise and set over the Atlantic Ocean.

A view along the dramatic Mohegan Bluffs towards Southeast Lighthouse, at the southern end of Block Island

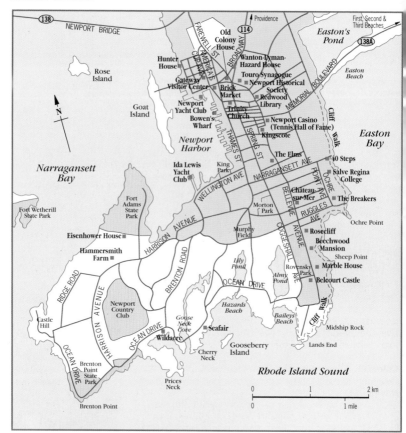

RHODE ISLAND

Newport Bridge

138 NEWPORT BRIDGE

138 114 → Providence

First, Second & Third Beaches

Easton's Pond

138A

Old Colony House

FAREWELL ST

AMERICA'S

CRESCENT ST

BROADWAY

Easton Beach

Rose Island

Hunter House

Wanton-Lyman-Hazard House

Touro Synagogue

Newport Historical Society

MEMORIAL BOULEVARD

Gateway Visitor Center

Brick Market

Redwood Library

Goat Island

Newport Yacht Club

Trinity Church

CLIFF Walk

Easton Bay

Bowen's Wharf

Newport Harbor

THAMES ST

SPRING ST

Newport Casino (Tennis Hall of Fame)

Kingscote

The Elms

40 Steps

Narragansett Bay

Ida Lewis Yacht Club

King Park

NARRAGANSETT AVE

POINT AVE

OCHRE

Salve Regina College

Easton Bay

Fort Wetherill State Park

Fort Adams State Park

WELLINGTON AVE

BELLEVUE

Morton Park

Château-sur-Mer

RUGGLES AVE

The Breakers

Ochre Point

Eisenhower House

HARRISON AVENUE

BRENTON ROAD

Murphy Field

Rosecliff

Beechwood Mansion

Hammersmith Farm

Lily Pond

COGGESHALL AVENUE

Sheep Point

Almy Pond

Rovensky Park

Marble House

RIDGE ROAD

HARRISON AVENUE

OCEAN AVENUE

OCEAN DRIVE

Newport Country Club

Goose Neck Cove

Seafair

Wildacre

Cherry Neck

Hazards Beach

Baileys Beach

CLIFF Walk

Beleourt Castle

OCEAN DRIVE

Gooseberry Island

Lands End

Midship Rock

Castle Hill

Brenton Point State Park

Prices Neck

Rhode Island Sound

Brenton Point

0 ____ 1 ____ 2 km

0 ____ 1 mile

Newport Bridge, leading over Narragansett Bay

▶▶▶ Newport

210C2

With the combined attractions of its historic summer mansions and colonial architecture, its jazz festival, its sailing and regattas, its golf, its beaches and its nightlife, Newport has a lot to offer visitors. Although the town gets busy at summer weekends, accommodation is plentiful with a large concentration of B&Bs.

Newport is an important lobster town; lobsters can be bought fresh off the boats at Aquidneck Lobster Co in Bowe's Wharf near the harbour, at the hub of the town's crafts and gift shops. The three main beaches are called, unsurprisingly, First Beach, Second Beach and Third Beach. Additionally, there are a couple of small beaches off Ocean Drive. Parking fees at the beaches are expensive, but it is only a mile or so to cycle out from the town centre. Good views of the ocean can be had from the 3½-mile **Cliff Walk▶▶**, which snakes above rocky shores and beaches, and offers fascinating glimpses of some mansion back gardens. Good shoes are needed to walk it in its entirety. Just outside town is a major naval base. Allied navies come to the Naval War College to carry out both war games and the real thing (much of the 1990 Gulf War was planned here).

Newport in its early days was a centre for religious tolerance, thanks to the liberal attitude of Roger Williams

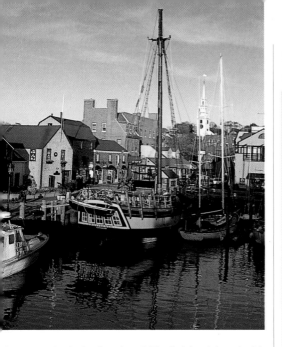

Enigma variations

The provenance of the curious building in Newport's Touro Park is obscure. Various explanations claim that it has Viking origins, that it was built in conjunction with the solstice, that it was a beacon, that privateers stored their booty in it, that giants with green eyes and red hair erected it, or that it was a windmill. However, carbon-dating in 1993 indicated that the structure dates from either the 16th or early 17th centuries.

America's oldest tavern

Threatened with demolition in the 1950s, Newport's White Horse Tavern, dating from the 17th century, was fortunately rescued and still survives as the oldest tavern in the US. Churches on either side had objected to the renewal of its liquor licence; to get round this, a state law was specially passed to the effect that only taverns built before 1700 with a church on either side can obtain a new licence!

A foresighted plea

'These old houses and old doorways are a stock-in-trade for Newport, and there is a decided question whether the so-called march of progress, which prompts the tearing down or extensive remodelling of old structures, will in the long run pay the owners as well as if they were put in repair and their features preserved, so that in years to come they may continue to attract strangers who are interested in the old and quaint.'
– *Newport Daily News,* 15 April 1910.

(see page 211), the founder of Rhode Island. In colonial times Jews and Quakers made it their home, and this cultural diversity was instrumental in the town's success.

Colonial Newport Despite devastation in the Revolutionary War and a long period of neglect, colonial Newport still survives to a remarkable extent: there are 200 buildings over 200 years old (the biggest such concentration in the country). Until the late 1960s, the town looked drab and many houses were tar-covered. Although many buildings were torn down, 60 were saved by Operation Clapboard, a campaign to encourage people to buy and renovate a historic house, and Newport's dreamed-of face-lift became a reality. Pineapple motifs are found on many of Newport's older buildings. The fruit being a symbol of hospitality in the state (sailors returning from the tropics used to display a pineapple in their windows to show they had returned safely and were receiving visitors).

Today, **Town Green** looks a typically timeless New England green, dominated by **Trinity Church▶** (1726), which still has box pews and a galleried interior. In fact, the green was a 20th-century beautification scheme: houses were moved here after buildings were cleared.

In **Touro Park** is the town's most celebrated enigma, an open-sided stone structure in the centre of a green (see panel). Near by is the library, opened in 1748 and the oldest in the US. It is a classical, wooden building, designed to resemble stone.

The **Touro Synagogue▶▶** is the oldest Jewish place of worship in the country, and dates from 1763. A century earlier, Portuguese and Spanish Jews, fleeing religious persecution, found sanctuary in Newport. The elegant interior is a real surprise and contains the famous letter from George Washington to warden Moses Seixas extolling religious tolerance.

*Aerial view of The
Breakers, showing
the cliff walk that
skirts its ground*

Newport Casino
This American
Renaissance period-piece
began in 1880 as a social
and residential club, gain-
ing popularity with old-
money families as lawn
tennis boomed. The
Newport Casino hosted the
US National Tennis
Championships (later to
become the US Open) from
1881 to 1914, and is still the
venue for major competi-
tions as well as court tennis (real tennis) and bowls
tournaments. The 13 grass
courts are the only ones in
the nation available for
public use. Tournaments
held today include tennis,
sumo, bowls and croquet.
For more information, tel:
401/849 3990.

At 54 Washington Street is **Hunter House** (1748) a
colonial-era house open to the public. It has period furniture made locally and a charming old-world garden.

At 17 Broadway, the restored **Wanton-Lyman-Hazard
House** (1675) is Newport's oldest colonial house (*open:*
Tuesday to Saturday in summer). In Thames Street, the
Brick Market Museum▶ is a recently opened treasure-
house commemorating Newport's remarkable past, with
exhibits on fishing, crafts, religion and social history. The
Doll Museum, at 520 Thames Street, has over 600
antique and modern dolls (*closed:* Tuesday).

The **Newport Casino**▶▶ has never had anything to do
with gambling, taking its name from the Italian for 'little
house' (see panel). Inside the Casino is the **Tennis Hall of
Fame**▶▶, the world's largest tennis museum and a
shrine to the tennis greats, where new additions undergo
an induction ceremony. In addition to the displays of
vintage tennis equipment, there are entertaining interactive videos featuring quizzes and comparisons of the
game techniques of the stars.

The mansions In the 19th century Newport became a
summer playground for the élite. Mansions modelled on
Italian *palazzi*, French châteaux and English stately homes
appeared along **Bellevue Avenue**▶▶▶ and **Ocean
Drive**▶▶▶. No expense was spared as European craftsmen were employed and the rooms packed with costly
objets d'art. First came the old-money families; later, the
new-guard Vanderbilts and others added flamboyance
and entertained in their fabulous 'summer cottages'.

Today, numerous mansions are open to the public. It is
best to select a few contrasting types, then drive or cycle

along Bellevue Avenue and along the 9½-mile Ocean Drive to enjoy the scenery. The Preservation Society of Newport County maintains nine properties (*open:* daily in summer, with several also open on weekends in winter; reduced admission if visiting more than one property, including the five mansions on Bellevue Avenue). For further details, tel: 401/847 6543.

Kingscote►, a grey clapboard Victorian Gothic house of 1839, is notable as being Newport's first 'cottage', and is more modest than its successors. The house contains family pieces of William Henry King, a China trade merchant. McKim, Mead and White, architects of the Newport Casino, added the dining room.

The Elms►► (1901), a French Renaissance château built by Horace Trumbauer for a Pennsylvania coal magnate, was modelled on the Château d'Asnières near Paris.

Château-sur-Mer►► (1852) was the first truly grand cottage, with its French-style mansard roof. Inside, a wall-painting of the Tree of Life accompanies the staircase, with overhead paintings of sky, birds and foliage. This was a year-round rather than a summer residence and was enlarged by Richard Morris Hunt in the 1870s, his first commission in the High Victorian grand manner although he later reverted to French and Italian styles.

The Breakers►►►, on Ochre Point Avenue, was designed by Richard Morris Hunt for Cornelius Vanderbilt and took 2,500 workers two years to complete in 1895. It was modelled on a 16th-century Italian *palazzo*, with French additions, and no expense was spared. The music room was constructed in Paris and shipped over, and there is a huge hall of Caen marble. The grandest gesture in an architectural medley of styles is the formal dining room, festooned with gilded garlands of fruit and cherubs, decorated with wall-paintings and alabaster pillars, and lit by chandeliers. It is perhaps testament to the Vanderbilts' wealth that the house was only seen as the 'summer cottage', used for about 10 weeks each year, and that, accordingly, the youngest daughter inherited it.

Rosecliff►►, a graceful building of 1902, was modelled by Stanford White on the Grand Trianon palace at Versailles and features a Court of Love and a heart-shaped staircase. *The Great Gatsby* was filmed here.

Newport practicalities
In the Newport Gateway Visitor Center there is a free direct-dial service connecting with hotels. Walking tours of colonial Newport also begin here. Bicycle rental and tours are available from Ten Speed Spokes at 18 Elm Street (tel: 401/847 5609), and two-seater electric cars (by the hour) from Cart-Aways of Newport (tel: 401/849 0010). Some of the best views of Newport are from the water, and cruises tour the harbour offering excellent views. Viking Cruises operate from Goat Island (tel: 401/847 6921) and M/V *Amazing Grace* from near Newport Harbor Hotel (tel: 401/847 9109).

The Ballroom at Rosecliff, the grandest of all ballrooms in Newport, where leading socialites were entertained and many dazzling soirées were held

The Astors' **Beechwood Mansion▶** (1856) is presented by costumed guides, who treat visitors as if attending a dinner party with the Astors in the 1890s, and who play the part of servants and debutantes. Special events include tea-dance tours, coming-out parties and murder mystery tours. The house lacks the physical glamour of many of the others, but many visitors prefer this livened-up approach.

Marble House▶▶▶ (1892) was the first of the 'gilded era' houses and was modelled on the Grand and Petit Trianons at Versailles. Although smaller than The Breakers it is even more ornate. It was built for William Vanderbilt by Richard Morris Hunt, who was also involved in designing the pedestal of the Statue of Liberty and New York Public Library. A whimsical Chinese Tea House stands close to the Cliff Walk.

Belcourt Castle▶▶ (1891), modelled on the Louis XIII hunting lodge at Versailles, has an intimate half-timbered courtyard, and 60 rooms filled with European treasures, including 13th-century stained glass and a 13,000-piece crystal chandelier from Imperial Russia.

The coal man's retreat
In 1894 Pennsylvania coal magnate Augustus van Wickle gave his wife Bessie a steam yacht for her birthday. They cruised into Narragansett Bay and set their hearts on owning a summer retreat at Bristol, north of Newport. Their first house burned down in 1906, but their new 45-room 'cottage', Blithewold, survives and is open to the public. It is a delightful amalgam of English manor, colonial and Dutch styles. Bessie filled the grounds with exotic trees and flora.

Hammersmith Farm, a 'mansion' of interest for its links with JFK

Newport firsts
● In 1803 Newport was the first town in the US to have its streets installed with gas lighting.
● A Newport man was the first person brave enough to eat a tomato (the fruit was previously thought to be poisonous).
● The town's synagogue was America's first (1763), as was its ferry (1657), open golf tournament (1895) and free public school (1640).

Hammersmith Farm▶, on Ocean Drive, can be reached by taking a Viking Cruises tour (see panel on page 217), or by a short drive or cycle ride. Built in 1887–9, it gained worldwide prominence in the 1950s when Jacqueline Bouvier and John F Kennedy had their wedding reception here. It later functioned as the Summer White House, and Kennedy's presidential desk can be seen. Compared to the other mansions it is somewhat a return to normality, its décor having a luxurious 1940s and 1950s look. It is still a working farm, the only one in Newport, and is rated the top wedding venue in the whole of the US.

Along **Ocean Drive▶▶▶** are the America's Cup Museum and the summer home of the New York Yacht Club, where hundreds of regattas are held each year. Apart from Hammersmith Farm, the mansions here are private; look for 'Normandy', designed in the style of a Normandy farmhouse.

North of town, at Portsmouth, **Green Animals▶▶** is a bewitching topiary garden featuring 21 animal creations ingeniously formed from privet and yew, and numerous other geometrical boxwood figures, as well as a toy museum.

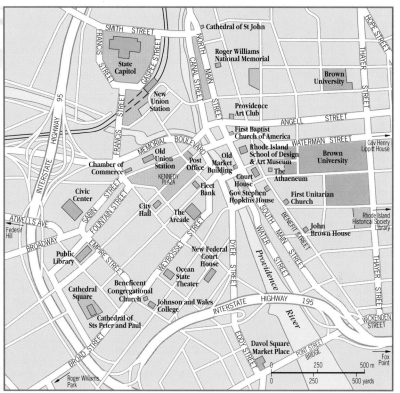

Map labels:
SMITH STREET · Cathedral of St John · Roger Williams National Memorial · Brown University · HOPE STREET · THAYER STREET · State Capitol · FRANCIS STREET · CASPEE STREET · NORTH MAIN STREET · CANAL STREET · New Union Station · Providence Art Club · ANGELL STREET · HIGHWAY 95 · FRANCIS STREET · MEMORIAL BOULEVARD · First Baptist Church of America · Rhode Island School of Design & Art Museum · WATERMAN STREET · Gov Henry Lippitt House · Brown University · INTERSTATE · Chamber of Commerce · Old Union Station · Post Office · Old Market Building · Court House · The Athaeneum · KENNEDY PLAZA · Civic Center · Fleet Bank · Gov Stephen Hopkins House · First Unitarian Church · Rhode Island Historical Society Library · SABIN STREET · FOUNTAIN STREET · City Hall · The Arcade · SOUTH MAIN STREET · BENEFIT STREET · WATER STREET · John Brown House · ATWELLS AVE · Federal Hill · BROADWAY · EMPIRE STREET · WEYBOSSET STREET · Public Library · New Federal Court House · DYER STREET · Providence River · THAYER STREET · Cathedral Square · Beneficent Congregational Church · Ocean State Theater · Johnson and Wales College · INTERSTATE HIGHWAY 195 · EDDY STREET · WICKENDEN STREET · Cathedral of Sts Peter and Paul · BROAD STREET · Davol Square Market Place · PONT STREET BRIDGE · Fox Point · Roger Williams Park · 0 250 500 m · 0 250 500 yards

219

►► Providence
210B3

Providence is increasingly becoming an agreeable place around which to walk, with its major museums, State House, dignified commercial quarter and old colonial centre all within easy reach. Founded by Roger Williams in 1636, the city prospered as a China trade and Triangle Trade seaport and spread over several hills. Although the city sprawls, its downtown has considerable presence, with the State House, the **First Baptist Church of America**► (1775) and the **Fleet Bank** (the art deco mini-skyscraper known locally as the Superman Building) prominent on the city skyline.

The **State House**►► (free tours: 9:30–3:30, Monday to Friday), built of Georgia marble, was modelled on the Capitol at Washington, DC, and boasts the world's second largest self-supporting marble dome (smaller than that of St Peter's in Rome but larger than the Taj Mahal's in Delhi). Gilbert Stuart's famous portrait of George Washington hangs in the Executive Chamber, while the 1663 charter granted by Charles II is displayed at the entrance to the Senate.

In the downtown shopping area at 65 Weybosset Street, **The Arcade**►, the nation's oldest covered shopping mall (1828), is a smaller version of Boston's Quincy

Rhode Island State Capitol

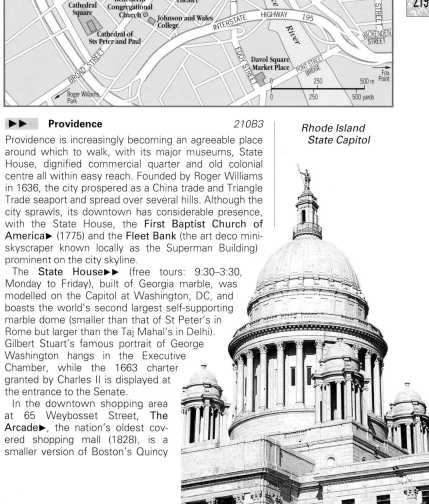

The Carrie Tower, a landmark of Brown University's campus

Birth of a boom

North of Providence the Blackstone River Valley was once a hive of textile mills and the cradle of the American Industrial Revolution – the catalyst for huge social change later in the 19th century. The nation's first mass-production of cotton yarn using water-powered machines took place in 1793 at Slater Mill in Pawtucket. Samuel Slater had been a manager at Arkwright Mills in Derbyshire, England, and brought technical know-how with him. The mill now functions as a museum, and gives demonstrations.

Tours

Self-guided cassette walking tours are available from the old schoolhouse at 21 Meeting Street, while trolley tours start from Kennedy Plaza. Cruises on the *Bay Queen* start from Warren and take in Narragansett Bay (tel: 410/245 1350).

Market, a three-tier Greek Revival structure with food stalls and shops. Well worth a visit are the **Rhode Island Historical Society Museum** and the **Culinary Museum**. The latter, part of Johnson and Wales University, includes the huge personal collection of everything connected with gastronomyaccumulated by Chicago chef Louis Szathmary.

Set on College Hill close to downtown, historic **East Side▶▶** formed the town's original centre, and retains lovely colonial clapboard homes and steep, cobbled streets. **Benefit Street**, the city's 'Mile of History', is its pride and joy. Restoration began in the 1950s with the founding of the Providence Preservation Society, which bought up houses and pushed for conservation laws. A fine view extends from **Prospect Terrace**, a park where Roger Williams is buried on Congdon Street.

The presence of both **Brown University**, an eminent Ivy League establishment (see pages 22–3) founded in 1764 and centred on College Green, and the **Rhode Island School of Design** lend the East Side a college-life air, with plenty of cafés, boutiques and bookshops along Thayer and Wickenden streets.

At 224 Benefit Street, the School of Design's **Art Museum▶▶** has an outstanding collection which includes paintings by US masters (Homer, Bierstadt and Cole among them), French Impressionists and modern artists. Highlights among artefacts of the ancient world are a wooden Buddha (*c.*1150) from Japan and a 4th-century Roman mosaic. (*Open*: 12–5pm, Wednesday to Saturday in July and August, and Tuesday, Wednesday, Friday and Saturday for the rest of the year; free on Saturday.)

Foremost among the historic houses open to view is the **John Brown House▶▶**, built at 52 Power Street in 1786 for a wealthy China trade merchant, and later extended. It contains period wallpaper, a Gilbert Stuart portrait, silverware, toys and a turn-of-the-century bathroom with risqué tiled murals of water nymphs. By contrast, the **Governor Henry Lippitt House▶** (1865) at 199 Hope Street is pure Renaissance Revival, with plentiful stained glass and false marble in its rich interior. At the corner of Hopkins and Benefit streets is the **Governor Stephen Hopkins House** (1743), home of the Rhode Island signatory of the Declaration of Independence, a Quaker and civic leader who was also the first chancellor of Brown University.

Federal Hill is the Italian quarter, with lively festivals, authentic groceries and good restaurants, at its most animated around Atwells Avenue. Discreet gentrificiation is taking place as the preservation effort gathers momentum. Further evidence of Providence's ethnic mix is found in the Portuguese community of **Fox Point**.

South of downtown, **Roger Williams Park** is a Victorian creation with bandstand concerts and lakes. It contains a natural history museum and planetarium, as well as a zoo with over 600 animals, including a wetlands area with native New England species.

▶ South County   210A2

South County makes up Rhode Island's southwestern corner. Bathing and beaches are the main draw of the coast itself, although wildlife reserves here and in numerous inland wetlands attract naturalists.

Sedate **Watch Hill** is both a fishing port and resort town, with long beaches, and shopping opportunities for antiques and jewellery. Its Flying Horse Carousel, built in 1867, is the oldest in America. Lively family fun is provided at Misquamicut, where **Atlantic Beach Park** offers amusements, miniature golf, a giant water-slide and a roller rink. There are several beaches between the resort towns of **Charlestown** and **Narragansett**. Near the latter, the **South County Museum▶** displays reconstructed New England buildings, including an old-time store and a cobbler's shop (*open*: May to October, Wednesday to Sunday).

The old community of **Wickford▶,** off scenic Route 1A, has a pretty view of the harbour and abounds in antique, craft and speciality shops. John Updike set his novel *The Witches of Eastwick* here. Signposted off Route 1A, the **Gilbert Stuart Birthplace,** near Saunderstown (*open*: April to November, closed Friday), was the home of the artist who created the portrait of George Washington seen on dollar bills. At Wakefield, the **Washington County Jail** (1792) has changing local history exhibits and original jail cells and rooms (*open*: 1–4pm, May to October, Tuesday, Thursday and Saturday; free).

Native American monument, Narragansett

221

Galilee: fishing is important all along Rhode Island's coastline

A marine feast
Bargain-priced fresh lobsters can be bought at Galilee, near Point Judith, when the boats come in at around 4–5pm. Take a plastic bag.

VERMONT

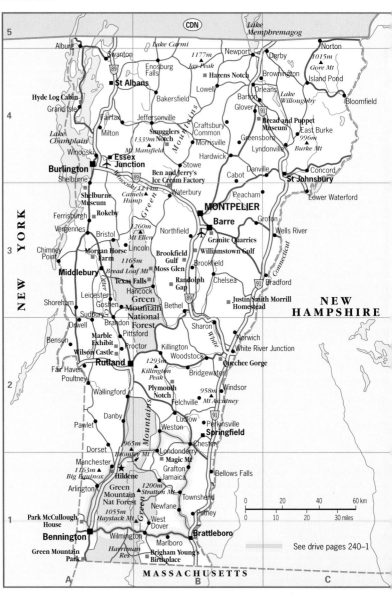

CDN

Lake Memphremagog

Lake Carmi

Alburg
Swanton
Enosburg Falls
1177m
Jay Peak
Newport
Derby
Norton
1015m
Gore Mt
Island Pond

Hazens Notch
Brownington
Bloomfield

89
St Albans
Bakersfield
Lowell
Barton
Glover
Orleans
Lake Willoughby

Hyde Log Cabin
Grand Isle
Fairfax
Jeffersonville
Craftsbury Common
Greensboro
91
Bread and Puppet Museum
East Burke
996m
Burke Mt

Milton
1339m
Smugglers Notch
Morrisville
Lyndonville

Lake Champlain
Winooski
Mt Mansfield
Hardwick
Danville
Concord

Essex Junction
Stowe
Cabot
St Johnsbury

Burlington
Shelburne
Ben and Jerry's Ice Cream Factory
Waterbury
89
1241m
Camels Hump
MONTPELIER
Peacham
Lower Waterford

Shelburne Museum
Rokeby
Barre
Groton
Wells River

Ferrisburgh
260m
Mt Ellen
Northfield
Granite Quarries
Williamstown Gulf

Vergennes
Bristol
Lincoln
Brookfield Gulf
Brookfield

Chimney Point
Morgan Horse Farm
1165m
Bread Loaf Mt
Moss Glen
Chelsea
91
Bradford

Middlebury
Texas Falls
Hancock
Randolph Gap

Shoreham
Leicester
Goshen
Bethel
89
Justin Smith Morrill Homestead

Sudbury
Brandon
Green Mountain National Forest
Sharon
Norwich

Orwell
Benson
Marble Exhibit
Pittsford
Proctor
Killington
Woodstock
White River Junction

Wilson Castle
1293m
Killington Peak
Quechee Gorge

Fair Haven
Poultney
Rutland
Bridgewater
958m
Mt Ascutney
Windsor

Wallingford
Plymouth Notch
Felchville

Danby
Ludlow
Perkinsville
91
Springfield

Pawlet
Weston
Chester

Dorset
965m
Bromley Mt
Londonderry
Magic Mt
Grafton
Bellows Falls

Manchester
1163m
Big Equinox
Hildene
Jamaica

Arlington
Green Mountain Nat Forest
1200m
Stratton Mt
Townshend

1055m
Haystack Mt
Newfane
West Dover
Putney

Park McCullough House
Wilmington
Marlboro
Brattleboro

Bennington
Harriman Res
Brigham Young's Birthplace

Green Mountain Park

NEW YORK

NEW HAMPSHIRE

MASSACHUSETTS

0   20   40   60 km
0 10   20   30 miles

See drive pages 240–1

A rural retreat in Vermont

The Northeast Kingdom in the autumn

Vermont Vermont is a survivor, a rural state of mountains and forests, much of it quite unspoilt. The landscape is folded; its very name, derived from the French words for green mountain, is descriptive enough for much of the year (although the forests you see today have taken over after cleared farmland was abandoned a century or so ago). Towns are distinctly on the small side; even Burlington is far from being a buzzing metropolis, and Montpelier, the state capital, has a village-like quietness at night. A few days' driving around the state will leave memories of quiet, winding roads and huge red barns, of hand-painted signs pointing out automatic bank cash machines and home-made maple syrup outlets, of smart designer shops and country stores. Vermonters thrive on crafts, music and literature, and are strongly involved in the visual arts of painting and sculpture. The events calendar always looks busy.

The rural heritage In the second quarter of the 19th century, Vermont was the wool capital of the world. Spain had been forced to sell off a large part of its herds of sheep in 1811 to pay off Napoleonic War debts, and many of the sheep came here. Wool production only declined in Vermont after the Civil War, when the railroads in the West allowed sheep from Wyoming and Montana to dominate the wool trade. Foreign competition from Australia accompanied this downturn.

VERMONT

Right: red barns and silos are a common sight

'They hewed this state out of the wilderness, they held it against a foreign foe, they laid deep and stable the foundation of our state life because they sought not the life of ease but the life of effort for a worthy end.'
– President Theodore Roosevelt, 1902.

Firsts in the nation
Vermont was the first state in the USA:
● to manufacture a postage stamp (at Brattleboro, 1846).
● to offer troops in the Civil War.
● to found a Boy Scout Club (at Barre, 1909).
● to install a chair-lift (at Mount Mansfield 1940).
● to file a US patent for making potash from wood ash (1790).

The first pumpkins of the season: they must be picked before the frosts arrive

Today, cows and sheep no longer outnumber the inhabitants, but dairy farming is by far the largest agricultural industry. Fruit and vegetable farming, producing hardy crops which can survive the harsh winters, also takes place. Other industries are granite and marble extraction, and the state's products include timber, maple syrup, clay, paper, furniture, machine tools, carpeting, gemstones and cast-iron wood-burning stoves.

The fragile character of 'Vermontness' has been preserved, but only just. Proximity to the Big Apple and to Boston might change all that, although large advertising signs are banned in this last bastion of rural perfection. A state law lays down 10 tough environmental conditions to be met by all new large developments, including a requirement that new structures should not adversely affect the 'aesthetics, scenic beauty, historic sites or natural areas' of the vicinity. In 1993 the National Trust for Historic Preservation put the whole state of Vermont at the head of its annually published list of endangered historic places. The Trust feared that the state was about to succumb to megastores and anonymous shopping malls when the Wal-Mart chain, ensconced in every other state, sought approval for two sites in northern Vermont.

Vermont for visitors The southern part of Vermont, with its relatively affluent communities of Bennington, Manchester and Woodstock, is seductive vacation territory. Northern Vermont is appreciably quieter and emptier, except for the area around Burlington and Shelburne. The Northeast Kingdom (the northeast corner of the state) is less sophisticated, ideal for those who like to make their own discoveries.

For hikers, the 260-mile Long Trail crosses the state from the Massachusetts line to the Canadian border, via the Green Mountains and Mount Mansfield (4,393 feet), the highest peak in Vermont.

For further information contact the state tourist office (see page 266) or chambers of commerce.

January
Ice Harvest, Brookfield.
Winter Carnival, Stowe: top winter event.
Winterfest, Newport: week-long event.

February
Snowflake Festival Winter Carnival, Lyndonville and Burke.
Winter Carnival, Brattleboro.

March
Maple Festival, Woodstock.

April
Festival of Quilts, Rutland.
Vermont Maple Festival, St Albans.

May
Champlain Valley Quilt Show, Shelburne.
Spring Farm Festival, Woodstock.

June
Balloon Festival and Crafts Fair, Quechee.
Discover Jazz Festival, Burlington.
Lake Champlain Balloon and Craft Festival, Champlain Valley/Essex Junction.

July
Antiques and Uniques Festival, Craftsbury Common.
Bennington Museum Antiques Show.
Fiddlers' Contest, Hardwick.
Marlboro Music Festival, Marlboro College (ends Aug).
Old Time Farm Day and Grand Old Fourth Celebration, Shelburne.
Vermont Mozart Festival, various locations (ends Aug).
Vermont Quilt Festival, Northfield.

August
Antique and Classic Car Rally, Stowe.
Bennington Battle Day Celebration.
Domestic Resurrection Day Circus, Bread and Puppet Theater, Glover.
Vermont Antique Dealers' Association Antiques Show, Stratton.
Vermont Craft Fair, Manchester.

Autumn colour comes to the Northeast Kingdom

Vermont State Fair, Rutland (ends Sept).

September
Antique and Classic Car Show, Bennington.
Champlain Valley Exposition, Burlington.
Harvest Festival, Shelburne.
National Traditional Old-Time Fiddlers' Contest, Barre.
Northeast Kingdom Fall Foliage Festival, various locations (ends Oct).
Stratton Arts Festival, Stratton Mountain (ends Oct).

October
Apples and Crafts Fair, Woodstock.
Festival of Vermont Crafts, Montpelier.
Foliage Craft Fair, Stowe.
Mount Snow Craft Fair, West Dover.
Renaissance Art and Craft Fair, Bennington.

November
Thanksgiving Weekend Craft Show, Killington.
Vermont Hand Crafters Craft Show, Burlington.

December
Wassail Christmas Festival, Woodstock.

VERMONT

The archetypal New England clapboard church, Bennington's Old First Church

The Battle of Bennington

On 16 August 1777, British General Burgoyne sent Hessian and Indian troops to capture military supplies stored in Bennington as part of his attempt to split the colonies in two in an advance down the Hudson river. Brigadier-General John Stark countered by sending two detachments to head off the British. The battle actually took place at Walloomsac Heights (now in New York State) 5 miles from Bennington; it began at 3pm, and two hours later the British were forced on the retreat. The British failure to procure supplies resulted in defeat at Saratoga two months later, and in surrender on 7 October.

Grandma Moses (1860–1961)

Born in New York State, Grandma Moses lived in Virginia and later in Bennington. As an artist she was self-taught, and her primitive, even child-like style, which captured the public imagination, is immediately identifiable. Typically her work shows village scenes or hill landscapes with tiny figures. She was perhaps more significant for recording a particular time and region in America's past than for her gifts as an artist.

► Barre
222B3

Pronounced 'Barry', this is a blue-collar town adjacent to the **Rock of Ages►**, the world's largest granite quarry, which covers a 50-acre site. Self-guided tours from the visitors' centre (Monday to Friday) give a view of the quarry, where huge blocks are lifted by derricks, and of the manufacturing division and the finished products. **Hope Cemetery**, established in 1895, has choice examples of memorials crafted from Barre granite.

►► Bennington
222A1

Tucked into Vermont's southwest corner, Bennington is doubly famous for its college and for the Battle of Bennington, a turning point in the Revolution (see panel). A bronze panther marks the site of the Catamount Tavern where Ethan Allen and the Green Mountain Boys plotted against the British for the capture of Fort Ticonderoga. Allen's house was beside the **Old First Church** (1805), whose magnificent steeple dominates the old village, up the hill from the modern town. The beautifully sited churchyard has a good number of fine carved tombstones. Among these are the graves of Revolutionary War soldiers from both sides, as well as the resting place (follow the arrows) of the poet Robert Frost (see page 209), whose epitaph records 'I had a lover's quarrel with the world'.

The entire district of Old Bennington is worth taking in for its crisp examples of Federal-style homes. At the far end, the **Bennington Battle Monument**, a 306-foot memorial tower, rises close to the site of the storehouse that sparked the battle. An elevator whisks you up Vermont's tallest structure for a view over three states.

Bennington Museum► has a collection of Grandma Moses paintings (see panel), as well as numerous examples of Bennington glassware and pottery, plus musical instruments, Revolutionary War exhibits and the oldest Stars and Stripes flag in existence.

Route 67A passes the **Park McCullough House►** (hourly tours), in West Street, North Bennington, a cheerful yellow 35-room Second Empire Victorian mansion. Built as a summer cottage in 1875, and occupied by four generations of one family up to 1965, it retains original furnishings and even the owners' clothing, diaries and 37,000 documents. It hosts regular music recitals.

Also on Route 67A, **Bennington College** is an exclusive, liberal and progressive institution where plays, readings and an August music festival are presented. South of town, **Southern Vermont College** is the home, from June to December, of the professional Oldcastle Theatre Company (tel: 802/447 0564).

Joseph Cerniglia Winery, New England's largest, is on scenic Route 103 and offers free tastings.

► ■ **Burlington**   222A4

Set beside Lake Champlain on the state's western border, Burlington is a university town whose population increases drastically in the autumn, and which hosts numerous arts and music events. Apart from the considerable attractions of Lake Champlain, the largest city in Vermont is a place worth stopping at for its shops. It has a range of 'environmental' stores, sidewalk cafés and the pedestrianised area of Church Street Marketplace. Of the town's four beaches, North Beach is the best.

Lake Champlain►►, 128 miles long and up to 12 miles wide, and the largest body of fresh water in the US outside the Great Lakes, lies between the Hudson river and New York to the south, and the Richelieu river and Montreal to the north. Lake views can be enjoyed from a number of points on the shore, notably Red Rocks Park in South Burlington and Sand Bar State Park at Milton (where there are windsurf and boat rentals). To appreciate the lake's shoreline and sunsets, try a cruise on the *Spirit of Ethan Allen* from Burlington (tel: 802/862 9685).

The **Lake Champlain Maritime Museum►**, near Vergennes (*open*: May to October) has historical and maritime displays, boat-building demonstrations and a working forge. On Grand Isle, **Hyde Log Cabin** dates from 1783 and is one of the country's oldest log cabins. Built by surveyor Jedediah Hyde Jr, whose family stayed here for 150 years, the interior houses maps and bygones.

Champ
Lake Champlain has its own version of Scotland's Loch Ness Monster, known as Champ. This creature gets occasional 'sightings'. In 1982 the Vermont House of Representatives passed a resolution to protect the beast from 'any wilful act resulting in death, injury or harassment'.

Across the lake
The ferry from Burlington to Port Kent, NY, is handy for visits to Ausable Chasm (*open*: mid-May to early October). This sandstone gorge with its rapids and whirlpools surging beneath 200-foot cliffs, can be seen from a boat ride and a ¾-mile walkway. Further south, on Route 74, a ferry gives access to the New York side at Fort Ticonderoga, begun in 1755 by the French to block the British, and now mostly reconstructed and marketed for the heritage industry. Between mid-May and mid-October costumed guides explain the history, and cannon firing and period music supply the background atmosphere.

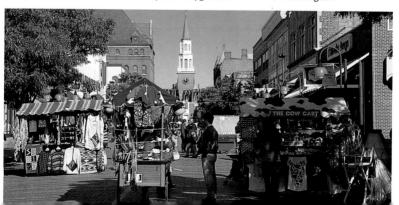

The lively Church Street Marketplace, Burlington

■ **New England gets plenty of snow and New Englanders certainly know how to make the most of it. The skiing is renowned, with resorts ranging from world-class to family. But that is not all, for there is also cross-country skiing, snowmobiling, snowboarding, snowshoeing – and even dog sledding.....■**

Useful addresses
Contact the Forest Supervisor, Green Mountain National Forest, 231 North Main Street, Rutland, VT 05701 (tel: 802/747 6700), for a copy of *Winter Recreation in the Green Mountain National Forest*).
   The Appalachian Mountain Club (information on hiking and winter sports), Box 298, Gorham, NH 03581 (tel: 603/466 2727).

Guided tours
Several areas offer cross-country ski tours led by registered instructors. See local advertisements. For those who do not own a snowmobile there are operators hiring out vehicles and offering tours: in Vermont at Killington, Wells and Post Mills; in New Hampshire at Bartlett, Colebrook, East Conway Littleton and Tamworth; and in Maine at Rangeley.

There's skiing for all in New England

Downhill and cross-country skiing The skiing season in New England is a long one; some resorts are open from October until May. Snow-making and snow-grooming is highly efficient. Vermont, New Hampshire, Maine and the Berkshires in Massachusetts all have excellent skiing but it is Vermont that claims to be 'the East's premier ski state', the heart of its ski country being just three hours from Boston or Montreal and five hours from New York. Snow-making covers an average 70 per cent of terrain.
   Killington is Vermont's number one resort. Vast, varied and glitzy, it encompasses six mountains, 18 lifts, 76 miles of trails (the longest being 10 miles) and accommodation for nearly 5,000 at the base. Elsewhere in Vermont, Stowe is a classic, with an extensive choice of both downhill and cross-country trails. Its neighbour, Smugglers' Notch, offers large areas of advanced terrain and specialises in children's programmes. Bolton Valley, too, is good for families. Jay Peak, close to the Canadian border, has a strong Quebec flavour and stunning views. Mount Snow is the most southerly of Vermont's resorts, large and varied, with 127 trails and 24 lifts. Sugarbush has some challenging runs, and excellent restaurants. Pico, not without justification, calls itself 'Vermont's friendly mountain'. Stratton is an upmarket resort town clustered at the base of the slopes, with classy shops and 12 lifts, and is best for beginners and intermediates. Snowboarding, available at all the resorts, is very popular here (this is where it began).
   The largest of New Hampshire's 24 alpine ski areas are Loon Mountain (41 trails, 9 lifts) and Waterville Valley (53 trails, 13 lifts). Both are good for children and beginners, although there is a variety of runs for all levels. Black

Mountain, Jackson and Bretton Woods are good-value family resorts. Of the 29 touring centres, Bretton Woods, Waterville Valley, Jackson, Mount Washington Valley and Franconia have the most extensive cross-country trail networks.

Sunday River in northern Maine has burst on to the ski scene with six mountain peaks, 72 trails, super-efficient lift systems, the world's largest high-pressure snow-making system (covering 95 per cent of the terrain) and accommodation for 4,400 close to the runs. In 1993–4 it opened a snowboard park complete with half-pipe. Maine Handicapped Skiing runs an acclaimed programme here for skiers who are physically disabled. There are four cross-country touring centres in the area. Saddleback, in the Rangeley area, has long uncrowded runs of all levels and 31 miles of cross-country trails ranging from gentle tours around the lake to exciting mountain slopes.

The main alpine ski areas in the Berkshires, Massachusetts, are Jiminy Peak (25 trails, 5 lifts) and the Catamount area (23 trails, 6 lifts), both of which welcome snowboarding, and the beautiful Butternut Basin. Cross-country skiers are well catered for with several touring centres.

Snowmobiles, snowshoes and sleighs
Riding racy little motorised 'snowmobiles' around the mountains has become a highly popular pastime. In Vermont alone there are about 2,800 miles of well-signed and main-tained trails. The State of New Hampshire and various clubs maintain 360 miles of trails, while Maine's best snowmobiling is in the Rangeley area, where there is a groomed network of over 135 miles of lake and moun-tain riding. The January 'Snodeo' is a popular event here, with 600 machines taking part. Snowmobiling is allowed in many of the state parks in the Berkshires, Massa-chusetts (but you cannot rent, so you must have your own). See panel for snowmobiling rules and regulations.

At a somewhat slower pace, snow-shoeing is the latest (but also one of the oldest) ways of exploring the winter countryside, whether your shoes and bindings are of the traditional type or the latest high-tech. Always check the weather report before setting out.

Rules and regulations
Owners of snowmobiles must register their vehicle with the state in which they will be using it. Ask locally about state tax.

Horse-sleighs
For a gentle, romantic ride through the snowy landscape, take one of the horse-drawn sleigh rides offered at many resorts and especially popular around Christmas time.

The thrills and spills of a dog-sledding race

► **Manchester** 222A1

Pristine-looking old Manchester Village, with its white houses and marble sidewalks, has been a pleasure resort and spa since the 1850s. Nowadays the village merges into Manchester Center, often something of a traffic jam owing to the popularity of its outlet shopping and crafts and country stores.

On the southern fringes of the village is **Hildene►►** (*open*: mid-May to October), a 24-room Georgian Revival mansion, the home of Robert Todd Lincoln, son of Abraham and Mary Lincoln. Mary discovered this élite mountain village retreat and the Lincolns spent the summer here in 1863 to recuperate in the midst of the Civil War. Robert made Hildene his home, and his descendants lived here until 1975. Today, the house, with its family furnishings and memorabilia, offers an informative insight into the lives and times of the Lincolns. Highlights include landscaped grounds and a self-playing Aeolian organ. Also in Manchester is the **American Museum of Fly Fishing** (*open*: May to October), with rods and reels of President Eisenhower, Bing Crosby and other celebrities.

Manchester lies beneath the commanding peak of **Mount Equinox►►** at 3,835 feet the highest point in the

230

Covered bridges
Spanning rivers and streams all over the region, wooden covered bridges, built from the 1830s onwards, are now recognised as historic landmarks. Pretty structures, often painted in reds, greens and blues, and by the nature of their setting almost inevitably highly picturesque, they are collected by photographers (particularly in the fall foliage season). Their *raison d'être* seems to be to protect the wooden bridge from the weather, particularly snow – though some say they prevented horses from taking fright. They are usually named after their builder or the river they cross.

Manchester, with its upmarket shops (right), is popular as a base for fishing and other outdoor sports

Taconic Mountains, it is reached by the Skyline Drive toll road and has a mountain-top inn. On the way up the views unfold spectacularly; you pass Little Equinox Mountain and a Carthusian monastery, built in 1960.

At Arlington, south of Manchester, the **Norman Rockwell Exhibition** comprises reproductions of the famous illustrator's work (see page 150). A 15-minute film show is included. Northwest on Route 30, **Dorset** is a showcase village in a conspicuously attractive setting and with a summer playhouse.

▶ Middlebury and the Green Mountains
222A3

Middlebury is a small but bustling college town, picturesque and unfussy, dominated by the four-tiered wedding-cake steeple of its Congregational Church. Crafts are thick on the ground here, with the non-profit-making Vermont State Craft Center based with other craft outlets in the old mill complex in Frog Hollow. On Park Street, the Sheldon Museum (displaying furniture and decorative arts) has been open since 1882.

Out of town on Route 23, past a rare two-way covered bridge, the **Morgan Horse Farm** (*open*: May to October) still breeds the famous Morgan horses and gives tours of its stables (see panel). Further north, **Vergennes** has over 100 craft and other shops in its Factory Marketplace. At Ferrisburgh is **Rokeby▶** (*open*: Thursday to Saturday, May to October), a fascinating 11-room Quaker family home that was once a focus of abolitionist activity, and a stop on the Underground Railroad.

West of **Orwell** is a relic of the Revolutionary War: Mount Independence, a peninsula jutting into Lake Champlain which was fortified to defend against a British attack from Canada. The visitors' centre fleshes out the historical background, and trails lead past blockhouses, a stockade and the remains of batteries.

The **Green Mountain National Forest** describes an area of densely wooded, rounded hills covering much of western Vermont. Much of it is unspoilt and offers countless opportunities for walking. On Route 125, the 1-mile **Robert Frost Trail** begins close to the site of his summer cabin: Frost's verses are placed along the route, which crosses bilberry bogs and passes through scrub and woodland. **Silver Lake**, east of Leicester, has a 2½-mile shoreline interpretive nature trail, and there is a shorter circuit around the nearby **Falls of Llana** (both in Branbury State Park). More dramatic hikes include the hour-long walk to **Sunset Ledge** from Lincoln Gap, east of Lincoln. **Bristol Ledges** (1,825 feet) is the highlight of a 1-mile trail above the pleasant town of Bristol, and provides views of the village and of Lake Champlain. More ambitious is the 3–4 hour walk on the Long Trail to **Mount Abraham** from Lincoln Gap, with its rocky 4,006-foot summit rising above the timberline.

Kingsland Bay, on Lake Champlain northwest of Vergennes, and **Lake Dunmore** in Branbury State Park are good for swimming.

Morgan horses
In the 18th century, a Massachusetts school-teacher named Justin Morgan came to Vermont and created the country's first horse breed. He was second owner of a rough-coated, hardy colt born in 1793 called Figure, which had attributes of both draft and riding horse, and was muscular and compact with plenty of stamina but a gentle disposition. Figure, renamed Justin Morgan, was first used as a working horse, then for breeding in Woodstock. From 1878 Colonel Joseph Battell Hardy continued the stock line. Morgans seen at the Morgan Horse Farm and elsewhere look much now as they did then, and they commonly live to 30 years.

Visitors to Morgan Horse Farm can see where these sturdy working horses are trained

VERMONT

The golden dome of the State House, Montpelier, seen against the early autumn sky

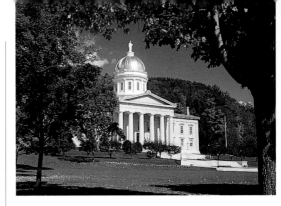

Mountain greenery
As you ascend Mount Mansfield, notice the changes in vegetation as the climate gets harsher. The typical New England trees are found lower down (sugar maple, yellow birch and beech). Further up the slope are pine, white birch, red spruce and balsam fir, and finally tundra. At the summit is the largest community of arctic-alpine flora in Vermont.

'Vermont's Finest' is a Ben & Jerry's ice-cream

► ▬▬▬ **Montpelier** *222B3*

Vermont's state capital is scarcely more than a country town graced by the golden dome of the State House. A good local view of the town can be obtained by climbing from Elm Street to Winter Street and up into Hubbard Park, where a stone tower in the woods affords an all-round panorama. Life continues at an amiable pace in a town small enough to make a relaxing base. Alongside the alternative lifestyle of the Horn of the Moon Café, on Langdon Street, Montpelier has the New England Culinary Institute, a large insurance industry and a high proportion of lawyers.

The **State House►** (*open*: weekdays; free) has been restored to its original 1859 appearance internally and is the third building on its site. The first State House became too cramped, while its 1838 successor was the victim of an exploding stove. Brochures for self-guided tours are available. Next door, the **Vermont Museum** (*closed*: Monday), run by the Vermont Historical Society, has well-displayed, changing exhibitions about various aspects of state life.

Ben & Jerry's Ice-Cream Factory►► (see also page 234), near Waterbury on Route 100 north of I-89, has become Vermont's biggest visitor attraction. The free samples are the lure; although the tour omits the factory on Sundays, the samples are larger. The tours are very popular: you may have to wait hours, but there are kids' activities (face-painting and the like) and ice-cream to be eaten. Cow souvenirs of the wackiest kind proliferate in the gift shop. There is also a Hall of Fame, featuring the biro-scrawled napkin used by former school-friends, Ben Cohen and Jerry Greenfield, to plan their ice-cream pick-ups on their marathon promotion journey ('Scoopathon') across the US, giving free samples of their super-premium ice-cream as they went. It proved a hugely successful public relations venture. From humble beginnings in an abandoned filling station in Burlington in 1978 on an $8,000 investment, their ice-cream business has soared.

Other Vermont specialities are produced at the Morse Farm maple sugar plant, outside Montpelier, and the Cold Hallow Cider Mill, on Route 100.

▶▶ **Mount Mansfield and Stowe** *222B4*

Vermont's highest peak, **Mount Mansfield** (4,393 feet) rises amid some of the state's grandest scenery. At the Stowe Mountain Resort, on Route 108 some 6 miles north of Stowe, are the toll road and gondola up the mountain. The toll road winds up the slopes for 4½ miles (bicycles are not allowed) and is open from May to October. Further north along Route 108, at Spruce Peak on the right, a chair-lift gives access to the Alpine Slide, a summer sled ride. At **Smugglers Notch**, the road rises to 2,162 feet, with 1,000-foot cliffs on either side. During the War of 1812, when trade with Canada was forbidden, much cattle smuggling took place here.

Stowe, the main skiing and recreation centre for the area, has a wide choice of high-class dining and lodging. Many of its hotels have an Austrian appearance, including the Trapp Family Lodge, still owned by the Trapps of *The Sound of Music* fame. Other local attractions include the 5,000-seat outdoor amphitheatre of Stowe Mountain Performing Arts Center.

> **Mount Mansfield**
> The remarkable resemblance the mountain has to an upwards-facing head has meant that each protuberance is named accordingly on the map: the Forehead, the Adam's Apple, the Chin and the Nose. Native American folklore speaks of the mountain as a sleeping giant. The Chin, reached by a 1¼-mile trail, is the true summit.

233

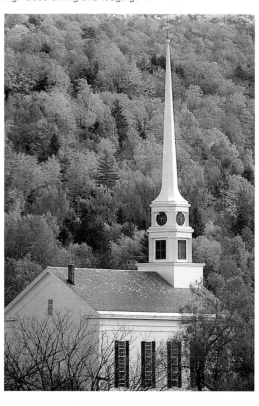

▶ **Plymouth Notch** *222B2*

This tiny and remote hamlet was the birthplace and home of 'silent Cal', Calvin Coolidge (1872–1933), president of the United States between 1923 and 1929. Today the hamlet is part museum, and one ticket covers all the sites. The modest homestead that was the **Coolidge Birthplace** is much as it was, with a quilt and a miniature chest of drawers he made himself; the **Coolidge Homestead** is the family's later home. The visitors' centre tells of the president's life, while the (still-functioning) store displays a 'Drink Moxie' sign – a memento of his favourite drink. Upstairs in the latter building, the **Coolidge Hall** served as the Summer White House: it is quite remarkable that the nation's affairs were conducted with a staff of two from this humble place. The huge barn next to the visitors' centre houses a collection of family carriages.

The village **cheese factory**, built in 1892, offers handmade cheddar-like products, including an extra-sharp cheese matured for two years. Cheese-making takes place from Monday to Wednesday, when visitors are welcome to watch the process.

Stowe: a classic landmark

> **Silent Cal**
> A dinner party guest once jested, 'Mr President, I have made a bet with my friends that I can get more than two words out of you this evening.' Coolidge replied 'You lose.'

■ **Out of Vermont's rolling hills and lush valleys come a range of distinctive products. There are the famous traditional cheeses (including cheddar, colby and Monterey jack); there are McIntosh apples and there is cider; there is honey, chocolates and hams. And then there is maple syrup, and Ben & Jerry's.....■**

Liquid gold

Maple syrup is sold in a variety of grades: Fancy, or Grade A Light Amber (delicate flavour, light colour); Grade A Medium Amber (the most popular); Grade A Dark Amber (stronger flavour, dark colour); and Grade B (robust colour and flavour, good for cooking). You can sample them all at the New England Maple Museum in Pittsford (see page 235) or the Maple Grove Maple Museum and Factory in St Johnsbury (see page 236). During the maple-sugaring season (March and April) visitors are welcome at farms listed in the brochure *Maple Sugarhouses Open to Visitors*, available from Vermont Department of Agriculture, 116 State Street, Montpelier, VT 05620-2901 (tel: 802/828 2416).

Vermont farm produce includes maple syrup (below) and cider (right)

234

Vermont's finest All over Vermont there are black-and-white cows. A good many are the Holstein (Holstein-Friesian) cows grazing in the fields; others are Woody Jackson's Holy Cows. Woody Jackson is an artist and his famous symbols of Vermont appear on anything from mugs and boxer shorts to the T-shirts produced for Ben & Jerry's.

Ben & Jerry's makes Vermont's Finest All Natural Ice-Cream, in over 30 'euphoric flavors'. But making great ice-cream (and frozen yoghurt) is only part of the Ben & Jerry's story that has so captured the public imagination. For Ben Cohen and Jerry Greenfield, serving the community is just as important as making a profit: 7.5 per cent of pre-tax profits go to non-profit organisations working for progressive social change, and half the proceeds of the Waterbury factory tours (see page 232) go to Vermont charities. So popular have Ben and Jerry found their ice-creams to be, that they have now taken them abroad, notably to Britain.

Maple syrup See steam billowing up from the sugar houses that dot the Vermont landscape and you know spring has arrived. Ideally the temperature will be about 40°F in the daytime but there will still be a light frost at night. Under these conditions sap rises up the sugar maple tree (*Acer saccharum*) and the sugar farmer gets 'a good run' – any warmer and the tree bursts into bud and the sap stops rising.

The farmer drills holes in the trunk, into which he fits spouts through which the sap drains, either into galvanised buckets or into long plastic pipes that feed directly into a holding tank in the sugar house. The buckets (up to three per tree) take several hours to fill and about 40 gallons of sap will have to be boiled down to make one gallon of syrup.

► **Proctor**   *222A2*

Proctor and its larger neighbour Rutland are at the heart of Vermont's marble-producing district (see panel). The **Marble Exhibit** displays the virtues of marble here in the form of a marble chapel (complete with Leonardo da Vinci's *Last Supper*, also in marble) and a series of bas-reliefs depicting every US president.

Wilson Castle►, south of Proctor, was built in 1874 by Dr Robert Johnson for his wife Sarah, who had set her heart on living in a castle in the Green Mountains. Unfortunately, the marriage broke up just as the 32-room castle was being completed. It is still lived in and feels like it, with a welcome lack of roping off. Despite being an architectural hotchpotch, with Dutch gables and French Renaissance-style mansards and turrets, it is a good example of an opulent Victorian status symbol, designed to impress, with stained glass and painted ceilings. Far Eastern and European antiques adorn an interior dramatically bathed in golden light. (*Open*: 9–6, daily, late May to mid-October.)

North of Pittsford on Route 7, the **New England Maple Museum** is at the back of a huge gift shop selling syrups by the gallon, maple candy and numerous other Vermont specialities. The exhibition shows maple sugar-making methods through the ages, with murals, utensils and the most complete collection of old sugar-making equipment known to be in existence; there is also a short film and free samples of the various grades of syrup are offered.

The **Pico ski area and resort** on Route 4 has an alpine slide, mountain bikes, miniature golf and a summit that is accessible by chair-lift (for information, tel: 1-800/848 7325).

One of dozens of Victorian stained-glass windows in Wilson Castle

Vermont marble
Vermont marble is extracted from Dorset Mountain near Danby, the largest underground marble quarry in the world. The qualities of the 400-million-year-old rock are advertised in an extravagant marble bridge in Proctor. More famous examples of its use are at the Beinecke Rare Book and Manuscript Library at Yale University in New Haven, the US Supreme Court in Washington, DC, and the UN Building in New York City.

A sculptor works in Vermont marble

►► **St Johnsbury and the Northeast Kingdom** *222C4*

The modestly sized town of **St Johnsbury►**, known locally as St Jay, harbours a few surprises. One is its main street itself, a fetching Victorian survival, with its brick mansions and granite churches. Another is the room at the back of town library housing the celebrated **Athenaeum►►** art museum (*open*: during library hours; free; see panel). Also on the main street, the **Fairbanks Museum and Planetarium** is yet another Victorian period piece; the museum houses natural history exhibits, tribal artefacts and dolls in its old-fashioned barrel-vaulted hall. The tiny **Maple Grove Maple Museum and Factory** is a sweet-smelling, sticky place where you can watch the sugar-making process and see maple candies being packed – and find your shoes sticking to the floor.

St Johnsbury is well placed for excursions into the three northeastern counties that comprise the remote-feeling **Northeast Kingdom►►**. North of the town **Burke Mountain** (3,267 feet) is accessible by toll road and affords 120-mile panoramic views. **Lake Willoughby►**, beside Route 5A, is popular for windsurfing, boating and fishing, and swimming for those hardy enough. Hikers can take the 7-mile circular route up adjacent **Mount Pisgah** (2,751 feet). Adventurous naturalists might care to seek out **Victory Bog**, a huge wetland preserve harbouring rare plants, as well as moose and black bears. The rural character of the area is exemplified by the **Bread and Puppet Museum►**, south of Glover on Route 122 (see panel). There is also the farmers' **Co-operative Creamery** (*closed*: Wednesday and Sunday in winter) at Cabot which makes a renowned sharp cheddar cheese.

Craftsbury Common►, conspicuously attractive and high up on a ridge road (part of a planned military route to Canada built in the 1780s), was painted white for the filming of Alfred Hitchcock's 1955 movie *The Trouble with Harry* and has stayed that way ever since. Route 14 north of here and the unclassified road southwest to Route 15 give a good idea of the quiet beauty of the Northeast Kingdom. Willey's General Store at nearby **Greensboro** is one of the best stocked in Vermont; its outside wall serves as the local notice-board.

St Johnsbury and the forests, hills and valleys of the Northeast Kindom that surround it

The SS Ticonderoga *is preserved at the Shelburne Museum*

Bread and Puppet
Glover is the home of the Bread and Puppet Theater troupe, founded in New York in 1974. Its rickety looking barn, a free 'museum', displays the giant Expressionist-style puppets, masks and props used in previous shows and pageants. Sourdough bread is given to audiences, symbolising that theatre is as much a necessity as bread. Performances in the field across the road attract 20,000-strong audiences. Some camp out the night before. The troupe regularly tours the US and Europe.

'I did not want to create a village...I was anxious to create something in arrangement and conception that had not been tried.'
– Electra Havemeyer Webb, founder of the Shelburne Museum.

A farm of the future
Shelburne Farms was founded in the late-19th century by Dr William Seward Webb and Lila Vanderbilt Webb as a grand agricultural experiment. Dr Webb purchased 32 farms and hired the services of landscape architect Frederick Law Olmsted, designer of Central Park in New York City, and forester Gifford Pinchot, known in the US today as the father of forestry. Architect Robert H Robertson designed the three main buildings on the property. The Shelburne House, once the Webb's family residence, is now a comfortable inn and restaurant (*open*: mid-May to mid-October).

At **Brownington**, a back-of-beyond hamlet in the far north where the paved road turns to a dirt one, is the **Old Stone House**, the former county grammar school built by Reverend Alexander Twilight, a black minister, in the 1830s. The building now houses a local history museum (*open*: Friday to Tuesday, mid-May to mid-October; daily, July and August), which is run on a shoestring with everything donated by locals. Across the road, a path to the right of the church leads to an excellent viewpoint.

►►► Shelburne   222A4
Of most interest to visitors at Shelburne is the remarkable **Shelburne Museum►►►**, an astonishing collection of buildings, re-assembled and packed with Americana and American folk art, which was the creation of Mrs Electra Havemeyer Webb. Her love of everyday objects started as a hobby, the collection being housed in a public museum when the first building, a schoolhouse, was moved here in 1947. Other structures then followed, including a general store, jail, inn and covered bridge. The wide-ranging collection of objects – over 80,000 items in nearly 40 buildings – means there is something for most tastes. Allow a full day to see it properly (tickets are valid for two consecutive days). Do not miss the comprehensive .quilt collection, the 1890 private rail car, the *Ticonderoga* (America's last-surviving vertical beam sidewheel steamboat, once in service on Lake Champlain) and the Electra Havemeyer Webb Building (a stylish New York apartment adorned with Impressionist paintings).

To the north, **Shelburne Farms►** was an agricultural experiment set up with Vanderbilt money (see panel). Today it plays a semi-educational role in demonstrating stewardship and farm animals, with a family-oriented hands-on activity area, cheese-making, a farm trail, 90-minute tours and farm animals.

Also of interest are the **Vermont Teddy Bear Co**, on Route 7, and **Vermont Wildflower Farm**, in Charlotte.

■ **Quilts and rugs, weather-vanes and whirligigs, trade signs and decoy ducks, baskets, boxes and wooden toys – New England's myriad antique shops, its dozens of crafts shops and many of its museums are stuffed with examples, old and new, of these folk crafts.....■**

Stencilling
Kitchen utensils, containers, walls and pieces of furniture were commonly painted and decorated with motifs. Some of these patterns were applied with stencils, and itinerant stencillers would work from pattern books, using milk-based paints in dusky shades.

Do-it-yourself
Visitors interested in patchwork and quilting will enjoy a browse in the many shops that sell everything needed. Keepsake Quilting (Senter's Marketplace, Center Harbor, New Hampshire; catalogue available) claims to be America's largest quilt shop, with thousands of small prints as well as plains. Paints for stencilling may be found in crafts supply shops but are also readily available in many hardware shops.

Right: a spinner practises an ancient craft
Top: crazy quilting

Spruce gum boxes
Lumbermen whiling away the evenings in the logging camps of Maine, New Hampshire and Vermont used to carve little wooden boxes for a wife or sweetheart to hold a gift of spruce gum. These were often in the shape of books and fitted with a slide at one end, and typically carved with hearts and a cross.

Quilts and coverlets Winters have always been hard in New England and the early colonials certainly needed the quilted bed coverings that had long been traditional in Europe. Fabric was in short supply, so the tradition of piecing scraps of left-over fabric together was an economic necessity. Some patchwork designs crossed the Atlantic with the early settlers: 'Log Wood,' used in the north of England, for instance, became known as 'Log Cabin'; and some Pennsylvania quilts, made by settlers from Germany, used designs known in Europe since the Renaissance. Other patterns, such as 'Bear's Paw', were clearly inspired by new experiences. As material became more available, small pieces were appliquéd on to larger areas, often representing the farmhouse, its occupants and animals, so that the quilt was a personal journal of its creator's life. Old quilts are collectors' items, while modern ones are sold widely across New England.

The colonial coverlet, woven in cotton in overshot patterns, traditionally in blue and cream, is another craft that dates back hundreds of years. Popular as throw-overs, modern versions of these cotton rugs in various, usually pastel colours may be found in numerous crafts outlets.

Baskets and boxes Market baskets, half-bushel and bushel baskets, fish baskets, berry baskets, clothes baskets, sewing baskets, feather baskets (in which to collect feathers until you had enough to stuff a pillow) – in the days before containers were made of mass-produced material, the Native Americans made baskets in dozens of shapes and sizes, traditionally using the brown ash (*Fraxinus nigra*). The Native Americans are still noted for their basketry, though now it is made for the tourist trade. Glass beads may have been replaced by plastic, and coloured strips are no longer dyed with berries, but basketry is an unbroken tradition, passed from generation to generation. The Shakers, who made a unique contribution

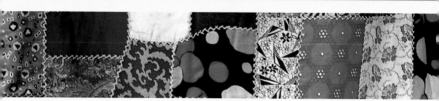

Scrimshaw jagging wheels or pie-crimpers

Scrimshaw

Dating from the whaling boom of the early 19th century is the type of carving called scrimshaw. Using a sail needle or jack-knife, sailors out at sea carved exquisitely detailed designs on whale-bone or teeth, which they then etched in black. There are many examples of scrimshaw in maritime museums and the old captains' houses.

239

Cigar store figures

The Shelburne Museum in Vermont (see page 237) has a room full of these carved figures. Anything up to 6 feet high, they normally depicted Native Americans, wearing or carrying the tobacco leaves that they introduced to the colonials.

to American crafts, were also famed for their baskets as well as their oval boxes and furniture (see pages 148–9).

Carving Native Americans introduced the early colonials to the use of duck decoys in hunting. Made at first of skin and feathers, they were later made from wood carved and painted more and more realistically until the decoy became a traditional art form. The Shelburne Museum in Vermont has the largest decoy collection in the world.

New England's was a seafaring and a farming community, dependent on the weather, and many buildings would have a weather-vane on the roof, cut from metal or carved in wood in a variety of shapes. Along the coast, fish, mermaids or ships were popular designs, while a farm building would often be topped by a cow or sheep. A variant, the 'whirligig', had paddles that kept it turning in a wind; the noise it made, they say, kept the moles at bay. So sought after are these traditional pieces of folk art now that thieves have been known to go to the extent of dropping a line from a helicopter to grab an antique off a roof. Reproductions are popular, decorative items.

Boat-builders turned their skills to woodcarving too, and some made magnificent figure-heads for the ships they built. Woodcarvers produced signs to hang outside shops, painted to advertise their speciality. They also made little models of subjects dear to them: a maple-sugaring scene, a team of working horses, or farmers chain-sawing.

Weathervanes are now more decorative than functional

Wooden dishes for sale at the Weston Bowl Mill

Drive Southern Vermont

See map on page 222.

This is a tour of southern Vermont's choicest rural retreats. Allow a very full day to sample the crafts shops and village atmosphere, and maybe to take in a walk in Townshend State Park.

Start from **Manchester** (page 230). A few miles east, **Bromley Ski Area** stays open all year round and operates an alpine slide and a chair-lift up to a 360-degree lookout with views stretching over five states. There are a number of hiking trails from the summit.

Then stop off at **Weston▶**, home to the Vermont Country Store, to browse in its quintessentially

Vermont-style crafts shops, of the homespun rather than the designer variety. Clustered around the green and village bandstand are the old sawmill, now housing a tinsmith's workshop and a display of antique tools, and the Weston Playhouse, Vermont's oldest professional summer theatre (tel: 802/824 5288). Just to the north, in an appealingly ramshackle old sawmill which began life in 1902, the Weston Bowl Mill carries inexpensive wooden products, while southwards the Toy Works stocks wooden toys, marionettes and more. The Farrar-Mansur House (*open*: Memorial Day to Columbus Day) is a former colonial tavern.

Chester▶ is quiet and prosperous looking, with some classic old-fashioned shops, including a drugstore with an enamel sign and the famously offbeat Inn at Long Last along its main street. The National Survey Charthouse ('Clear, correct, complete' boasts its motto) has a stock of world maps and excellent local hiking maps, as well as art supplies. A rare group of stone houses are found a mile out of Chester by turning off the main street by the Jiffy Mart.

Covered bridge at Brattleboro

Rising from a bridge, immaculate **Grafton**►►, a former woollen and soapstone-quarrying village, was rescued from part dereliction and is now one of Vermont's best-looking villages. It makes a point of having plenty of nothing to do, though there are a historical society and natural history museums. Crafts-watchers can observe a smithy at work and watch cheddar cheese being made at the Grafton Village Cheese Company. A covered bridge can be seen in Townshend Road.

administrative and manufacturing town, is more of a cultural than a rural centre. The Museum and Art Center in Union Railroad Station opens May to October. Connecticut River Tours offer cruises on the *Belle of Brattleboro* (Wednesday to Sunday in summer and foliage time).

Maple-syrup stalls accompany Route 9 west. **Marlboro College**, a liberal arts establishment that is one of America's smallest colleges with just 260 students, hosts a major summer chamber music festival, founded

The Old Tavern Inn, in the pristine village of Grafton

On Route 35 to Townshend, the road is briefly unpaved. Continue 2 miles west of Townshend on Route 30, past the **Scott Covered Bridge**► on the left, then turn left across the dam to **Townshend State Park**► (fee payable). Here you can walk 1,100 feet up Bald Mountain, which rises above the treeline and affords fine views of Mount Monadnock and West River Valley. The 1.8-mile trail has both steep and gentler routes. Near by, Townshend Dam (free entry) offers swimming and canoeing from a man-made sand beach.

Newfane offers a touch of grandeur around its green, with its county courthouse, Congregational Church and old inns. **Brattleboro**, a red-brick

in 1951 by the legendary Rudolf Serkin, which attracts big names. Its Tyler Gallery is a showcase of regional artistic talent (*open*: Monday to Friday during the school year; free).

Westward, the road climbs to **Hogback Mountain**►, giving an extensive view south, with the prominently pointed Haystack Mountain (3,420 feet) visible to the northwest. Close by, the slopes of Mount Olga offer pleasant walks in Molly Stark State Park. **Wilmington** is a small resort town on the main road; but there are quieter accommodation options near by in the Mount Snow resort area to the north.

Continue west to **Bennington** before turning north to explore **Arlington** and enjoy the spectacular scenic drive up **Mount Equinox** on the way back to Manchester.

Skiing superlatives
● The Suicide Six ski area near Woodstock was the site of the world's first rope tow, installed in 1934.
● Killington ski area has the most extensive snow-making system in the world: skiing is certainly reliable here. There are also more than 100 ski trails.

▶ **Windsor** *222B2*

Windsor has the longest covered bridge in New England, spanning 460 feet over the Connecticut river and the border with New Hampshire. On Main Street are the Vermont State Craft Center and the former Elijah West tavern, known as the **Old Constitution House** (*open*: Wednesday to Sunday in summer). Vermont's constitution was signed here in 1777, and a historical display relating to this accompanies period furnishings, toys and artefacts. In the autumn a train runs from Bellows Falls to the Chester area for leaf-peeping. On South Main Street, the American Precision Museum, housed in an 1846 armoury and machine shop, is a tribute to historic technical innovations.

North of Windsor, **White River Junction**, once a busy railroad junction with 50 passenger trains daily and an eight-track crossing, has tours of Catamount Brewery. Southwest of Windsor, **Mount Ascutney▶** (3,144 feet) can be ascended by following hiking trails from Routes 44, 44A and 131, or by taking the 3.8-mile toll road. Its summit, a ½-mile walk from the car park, looks over the Green and White Mountains, as well as Mount Monadnock and Lake Sunapee in New Hampshire.

You get a good idea of the rural feel of Windsor County by taking Route 106 through Felchville, with its miniature-looking buildings, then along the flat valley bottom, past cornfields and maple-syrup outlets. Stoughton Pond lies

A fisherman faces the challenges of the Quechee Gorge

Along the river
The Connecticut river flows 250 miles along the Vermont–New Hampshire border. The river was the waterway along which numerous early settlers came to these parts. North Star Canoe Rentals (tel: 603/542 5802) offer canoeing to the covered bridge and to the Sumner Falls from Cornish, NH, as well as winter sleigh rides.

just off the main road, and offers swimming, a picnic site and a nature trail in very pretty surroundings. Perkinsville is grander but quite unspoilt, with white chainlink fencing around its green.

▶▶ **Woodstock** *222B2*

A self-consciously pretty village at the heart of Vermont, with its own covered bridge and numerous handsome Federal-style homes, Woodstock has captured the public imagination as epitomising that elusive quality called 'Vermontness'. However, the crowds of visitors and the concentration of boutiques, galleries and designer shops have also given it the veneer of a sophisticated all-year resort. Money was poured into Woodstock and the overhead wires buried by the Rockefellers, who had family ties with the Billings Farm and Woodstock Inn. The **Dana House Museum** in Elm Street offers a glimpse inside one of Woodstock's many well-preserved Federal-style architectural gems.

To get to the **Billings Farm and Museum►** (*open*: 1 May to 31 October) follow Elm Street out of the village and turn right past the bridge on River Road. This premier local attraction provides a rare chance to look around a working farm, with butter-making, crafts and milking demonstrations. Established in 1871, the farm has had an outstanding Jersey herd since the 1880s, and in the pristine milking parlour each cow's name, birthday, pedigree and honours are recorded above its stall. The museum offers preserved bygones and a film show, while a renovated 1890s farmhouse gives a glimpse of a well-to-do farming household. The **Vermont Raptor Center**, 1½ miles from town on Church Hill Road, displays around 26 species of owls, hawks and eagles which, owing to their injuries, cannot survive in the wild.

Route 4 east of Woodstock crosses the **Quechee Gorge►►**, dubbed the 'Little Grand Canyon' of the Ottauquechee river. The 165-foot chasm can be looked into from the road bridge itself or from the half-mile trail to the bottom. An old riverside mill in the former textile village of **Quechee** is home to Simon Pearce Glass, where you can watch glass-blowers and potters at work. The Theron Boyd House, very much a survival of the pre-electric era, is open to the public and worth a visit as it is the state's oldest unaltered dwelling.

West of Woodstock lie **Bridgewater**, offering tours of the Mountain Brewery, makers of Long Trail Ale, and **Killington**, the largest ski area in Vermont. Summer attractions at the latter include tennis, golf, a playhouse (tel: 802/422 9795) and a music festival. Easily accessible by chair-lift, 4,241-foot Killington Peak has a nature trail, enabling study of its mountain plants, and views extending to the Adirondacks and White Mountains.

Woodstock offers chic shopping (below) and a look at 19th-century agriculture (above)

243

Eureka: a school
At Springfield, Eureka Schoolhouse stands next to an 1870 covered bridge and is Vermont's oldest one-room schoolhouse. Completed in 1790, it was abandoned in 1900 and underwent wholesale restoration in 1968. It is now open to public view.

The great outdoors In summer, take a whale-watching cruise or lobster-trapping outing (see pages 164 and 116); join an organised moose search or a sunrise beaver-spotting canoe trip (see pages 200–1); go for a swim, a sail in a lake, or take a picnic on a walk in a forest park. There are hire facilities on many rivers for canoeing, rafting (for over-12s) and (for over-10s) river tubing (see pages 132–3).

In the mountains and forests of the northern states there is excellent mountain-biking (ski-lifts carry the bikes to the mountain top), and there are miles of cycle trails on Cape Cod National Seashore (see pages 132–3). At many ski resorts you can take a cable-car to the top of the mountain for a spectacular view (especially in the autumn). In some places (such as Pico in Vermont, and Mount Tom and Jiminy Peak in Massachusetts) you can take a chair-lift up and a slide down. In the winter, there is the whole gamut of snow sports (see pages 228–9) from skiing to snowshoeing, and as spectator sports, there are baseball and basketball matches galore to watch. And why not try jai alai, an exciting Basque game like large-scale squash?

Museums and attractions 'Hands-on' is the buzz word. Children's museums can be found throughout the region (see panel) and many others have special rooms, exhibits or events for children. Listed below are just some of the dozens of attractions featured in official state guides. Aquaria and a selection of amusement parks are listed separately in the side panels.

Connecticut

Mystic Seaport and **Norwalk Maritime Museum** are popular with older children who like ships, history and the sea. At **Mystic Seaport Children's Museum** you can dress up, swab the deck and cook in the galley. In the Connecticut River Valley, the **Steam Train and Riverboat** combines a train ride with a riverboat cruise. You can see inside a lighthouse by visiting the **Old Lighthouse Museum** in Stonington, handle a live python

---

Children's museums
● **Connecticut** Manchester, Mystic Seaport, New Haven and Niantic.
● **Rhode Island** Pawtucket.
● **New Hampshire** Portsmouth.
● **Massachusetts** Boston; Dennis and Falmouth on Cape Cod; Acton (west of Boston) and Dartmouth, Easton and Foxboro (all in Bristol County, south of Boston); Holyoke (Springfield area).

244

Amusement parks
● **Connecticut** Quassy Amusement Park, by Lake Quassapaug, Middlebury.
● **Maine** Funtown, Saco, biggest children's park in southern Maine; Aquaboggan Water Park, Saco.
● **Massachusetts** Riverside Park, Agawam, near Springfield, largest amusement park in New England; Water Slide and Family Fun Center, Westport, near Fall River; on Cape Cod, Cartland, Wareham (buddy and indy-style carts, bumper boats); Water Wizz (wet and wild thrills and spills).
● **New Hampshire** Plenty around Weirs Beach, Lake Winnipesaukee (see panel, page 197), and at Hampton Beach on the coast. In the White Mountains, Santa's Village, Six Gun City, Whale's Tail water-slide, Attitash Alpine Slide, Storyland.

Catching supper?

in the discovery room of the **Peabody Museum**, New Haven, and take a model human body to pieces at the **South Eastern Connecticut Children's Museum** in Niantic (see page 107).

Maine

The four-level **Children's Museum** in Portland is one of the best of its kind in New England – meet Mr Bones, the cycling skeleton, and read the news on television. The **Maritime Museum** at Bath has a variety of interesting exhibitions in its restored shipyard buildings. The **Seashore Trolley Museum** at Kennebunkport, has the world's largest street and railway car collection, while at **Boothbay Railway Village** (see page 121) you can take a train ride through gnome-inhabited woods. **North American Wildlife Expo**, Freeport, is a wildlife museum with over 100 North American animals (stuffed) and **York's Wild Kingdom**, on Route 1, is a zoo and amusement park. Try to visit a lighthouse.

Massachusetts

In and around Boston The city is so visually exciting that most children will

History comes alive at Old Sturbridge Village

get a thrill out of just being there: take them up one of the skyscrapers (to the **Prudential Skywalk** or the **John Hancock Observatory**), enjoy the free entertainment of Faneuil Hall Marketplace, ride the swan boats in the **Public Garden**, take in **Harvard Square**, visit the **Mapparium, Charlestown Navy Yard** and the **Bunker Hill Pavilion**. Older children will find **Filene's Basement** fun for bargain shopping. The one and only **Computer Museum** has superb hands-on displays, while the **Children's Museum**, the **New England Aquarium** and the **Museum of Science** are all big crowd-pullers. For sports-lovers there is the **New England Sports Museum** (see panel), and if legs get tired, the 'T', as the subway system is called, is useful.

At **Salem** (see page 184) on the North Shore, you can go into a jail cell, attend a mock trial and do some gravestone rubbing at the **Salem Wax Museum**. At Plymouth, **Plimoth Plantation** (see page 179) and the *Mayflower II* make an expensive but unforgettable outing. The **New Bedford Whaling Museum** is one of the best.

The Springfield area and the Berkshires History really comes alive at **Old Sturbridge Village**, a re-creation of life in the 1830s (see page 173). Young dinosaur experts will insist on seeing the quarry of dinosaur tracks at **Dinosaur Land** in South Hadley and on meeting *Tyrannosaurus Rex* in the **Springfield Science Museum**. See page 175 for the **Words and Pictures Museum** in Northampton, in the Pioneer Valley, and see the panel for the **Basketball Hall of Fame**.

For the sports enthusiast Young basketball fans will want to try their skill at the Basketball Hall of Fame in Springfield, Massachusetts; tennis players should visit the Tennis Hall of Fame in Newport (see page 216); the action-packed New England Sports Museum in Cambridge gives a hands-on taste of everything sporty (see page 75).

Aquaria
● New England Aquarium, Boston.
● Marinelife Aquarium, Mystic, CT.
● Maine Aquarium, Saco, ME.
● Aqua Circus Aquarium and Zoo, West Yarmouth, Cape Cod, MA.
● Nantucket Aquarium, MA.

Boston Common's very famous ducklings

Holiday reading
Small children will love Robert McCloskey's 1940s classic *Make Way for Ducklings* (available in several languages), the endearing story of a mother duck looking for a home for her family by Boston's Charles river. Bring the book to life by taking a guided walk from Boston Common along the route described in the book, with readings and stops to feed the ducklings' descendants. Children love the bronze duck sculptures in the Public Garden.

Cape Cod and the islands Here are miles of sandy white beaches for windsurfing, swimming and sailing; nature trails; and fresh seafood – but beware summer traffic jams, especially at weekends. At Brewster is the excellent **Cape Cod Natural History Museum** (see page 155) and the **Bassett Wild Animal Farm**. Nantucket has a good Whaling Museum.

New Hampshire
At the **Ruggles Mine**, near Grafton, you can tap away with a hammer and explore the dramatic old mine. **Christa McAuliffe Planetarium**, Concord, is the world's most advanced, while **New Hampshire International Speedway**, near Canterbury, is the biggest venue of its kind in New England. **Clark's Trading Post** is an all-sorts museum, railroad and bear show. Not to be missed is the cog railway up **Mount Washington** (see page 205). In Portsmouth, on the coast, children can join in workshops in some of the **Strawbery Banke** buildings (see page 202).

Rhode Island
Roger Williams Park in Providence hosts a zoo, natural history museum and planetarium, and there's boating in the park. Older children will learn about the factory age at the **Slater Mill Historic Site**, birthplace of the American Industrial Revolution (see pages 36–7), at Pawtucket, while younger ones will enjoy a trip on the canal. Many of the **Newport Mansions** will impress young and old alike. For Newport's **Tennis Hall of Fame**, see panel on page 216.

Vermont
Fun is the word too at **Ben & Jerry's** ice-cream factory (see pages 232 and 234). Take in a visit to a maple syrup museum and sample the sugar candy at **New England Maple Museum**, Pittsford, or **Maple Grove Maple Factory**, St Johnsbury. Also in St Johnsbury, try the planetarium in the **Fairbanks Museum** of natural history. The **Shelburne Museum** (see page 237) is certainly one for all ages. Birds of prey are rescued and sheltered at the **Vermont Raptor Center**, near Woodstock.

A Ben & Jerry's could well be the highlight of the day

Visa formalities

Visitors to the US must have a full passport. UK citizens may arrive without a visa providing they have a return ticket and intend to stay for a period less than 90 days.

Citizens of Ireland, Australia, New Zealand and Canada, and those intending to stay longer than 90 days must obtain a visa from a US embassy before departure.

Visa extensions can be obtained in the US from the United States Immigration and Naturalisation Service offices (see the telephone book under Federal Government Offices).

Before arrival UK citizens will be given an I-94W Non-immigrant Visa Waiver form (asking you, among other things, if you are seeking entry to engage in criminal or immoral activities and if you are engaged in terrorist activities or genocide).

People arriving without a return ticket or without sufficient funds to cover their stay might not be admitted, as they might be considered to be planning to work illegally in the US. In order to show the immigration officer that you have adequate funds it is sensible to take one or two credit cards, and plenty of US-dollar traveller's cheques. Give an address where you intend to stay on your first night.

Airports

Boston's Logan Airport is the international terminal for New England, and has the usual complement of car-rental desks and currency exchange facilities (*open*: Monday to Friday 8am–9:30pm; weekends 11:30am–9:30pm) as well as a hotel reservation desk covering the whole of New England (no commission charged to customers; *open*: daily 8:30am–11:30pm).

Another possibility is to fly to New York, which has good access to southern New England, and bus and train links to Boston (reached in four to five hours). Airport tax is included in the ticket price. It is always advisable to check with your airline whether you need to re-confirm your international return flight home.

Getting into Boston

Excellent public transport gets you into downtown Boston. From Logan Airport's terminal building, leave the main exit and cross to the courtesy bus stand, where buses marked with a circled T provide a free shuttle service to Airport subway station, on the Blue Line (see pages 52–3). From here it is a few stops to the downtown area. Alternatively, the Airport Water Shuttle carries passengers to Rowes Wharf in the Financial District (last service 8pm; no service Saturdays or Sunday morning). On weekdays a non-stop Logan Link shuttle van operates from the airport to South Station in the Financial District. Taxis are available at all terminals; in 1994 fares to downtown Boston and Cambridge averaged about US$10–18 compared to 85¢ on the subway, US$8 on the water shuttle and US$5 on the Logan Link.

Customs regulations

On entering the US, visitors over 21 years of age may bring in duty-free

When it is 12 noon in Boston, it is 9am in San Francisco, 3am the next day in Sydney, 12 noon in Montreal, 5am the next day in Auckland and 5pm in London.

Daylight Saving Time alters the time by one hour from March/April to October/November.

What to take

Take a range of clothes for all temperatures, including waterproof clothing for whale-watching and hiking, and comfortable, sturdy shoes for walking around cities and along rural trails.

Take sun lotion, a first-aid box, your driving licence, a photocopy of your passport (if you lose your passport, this will make getting a replacement much easier), a photocopy of your travel insurance (leaving the original at home in case of loss), credit cards, any medicines that have been prescribed to you and an umbrella – just in case!

A ride round Faneuil Hall Marketplace provides an easy introduction to Boston

items that include 200 cigarettes or 50 cigars or 2kg of tobacco; 1 US litre of alcohol; and US$100 worth of gifts. Forbidden imports include meat, seeds, plants and fruit.

If you intend to take home tobacco, alcohol, gifts and/or perfume, check the customs allowances on leaving your country.

Time

There are four time zones within continental, or mainland USA. Boston falls within the Eastern Standard Time zone, as do New York, Washington DC, Miami and Cleveland.

249

Climate and seasonal considerations

New England's climate is characterised by warm summers, pleasant if somewhat unreliable spring and autumn seasons, and extremely cold winters. In summer, Maine has plenty of sun but few really hot days.

Spring can bring glorious weather, with warm days and cool nights; there are fewer tourists than in summer and autumn, so room rates are lower. Maple sugaring takes place in northern New England. April is 'mud season', while blackflies (whose bites are not so much painful as annoying) proliferate in late May and early June in northern New England.

More museums and houses open their doors in summer than at any other time of year. July and August see the coastal and lake resorts crowded and the roads clogged with traffic, as the temperatures soar. The events calendar is similarly packed with festivals.

Fall foliage attracts visitors from all over the world, making autumn the busiest season; hotel rates are high and the famous leaf-peeping areas, such as the Berkshires, White Mountains and Green Mountains, become very busy. Conversely, the coast sees fewer crowds after Labor Day (the first Monday in September). The days are mild, the nights cool. There are also plenty of events, such as country fairs and crafts markets, happening at this time, and the roadside produce stall is a common sight.

Winter invariably brings snow to many parts of New England

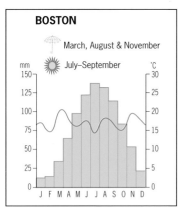

BOSTON

March, August & November

July–September

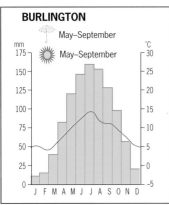

BURLINGTON

May–September

May–September

A marked lull occurs after the leaves fall in late October, but much happens at Christmas and First Night (see page 194). Winter brings enough snow to many areas to make New England a major winter sports destination (see pages 228–9), and when natural snow is lacking, the region

has the greatest snow-making capacity in the US. There are chatty TV and radio weather forecasts, well-loaded with statistics (one TV channel has non-stop weather reports).

> ❏ 'There is a sumptuous variety about the New England weather that compels the stranger's imagination – and regret...in the spring I have counted one hundred and thirty-six different kinds of weather inside four-and-twenty hours.'
> – Mark Twain, speech given in New York City, 22 December 1876. ❏

Money matters
Currency There are 100 cents (¢) in a dollar ($). Coins in general circulation are 1¢, 5¢, 10¢ and 25¢; dollar notes (always called dollar bills) come in denominations of $1, $5, $10, $20, $50 and $100. Curiously, 50¢ and $1 coins do exist but are rare. Note the terminology: a cent is also known as a penny; a 5¢ coin is a nickel; 10¢ a dime; 25¢ a quarter; 100¢ a dollar, nicknamed a buck. An amount such as $3.60 is described as 'three-sixty' or 'three dollars and sixty cents', but never 'three dollars sixty'. Always carry plenty of change, particularly for parking meters and telephones.

Credit cards These are widely accepted and essential if you want to rent a car. It is wise to take two cards, as the car-rental company may take one as a deposit in case the car is damaged or not returned.

Traveller's cheques Take US-dollar traveller's cheques, which are accepted almost everywhere as cash, and no extra commission is charged. Get $10, $20 and $50 denominations; $100 cheques may be difficult to change in shops. Keep the counterfoils separate from the cheques, in case they are lost, and make a record of those you have spent. If they go astray, contact any bank and new cheques should be issued promptly. Traveller's cheques in denominations other than US dollars are less easy to

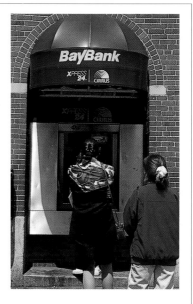

An ATM – Automatic Teller Machine

exchange and should be avoided if possible.

Banks Many banks have only one branch in each town, and often open 10–4 Monday to Thursday and 10–6 on Friday; bank cheques are rare. Nearly all banks have Automatic Teller Machines (ATMs) to dispense cash; most major credit cards can be used in these, providing you have a Personal Identity Number.

Sending money from abroad The easiest ways to get cash sent to the US are by Western Union, Thomas Cook and International Money Order.

Sales tax Except in New Hampshire, sales tax is added to certain items, including meals and lodging. A regrettable tendency among some hotels and inns is to put a 15 per cent service charge on their rates, which is then subject to tax.

Tipping The practice of tipping is universal. You are expected to tip 15 per cent for a meal, haircut, massage or taxi, and a few dollars to the bell hop who carries your bags to your room. Leave small change at a bar.

Opening times

Many museums close on Monday and on public holidays (particularly Christmas, New Year and Thanksgiving). Smaller museums, many houses and other winter attractions open in summer between Memorial Day (the last Monday of May) and Labor Day (the first Monday of September) or mid-October. In the morning, visitor attractions often open 10am–5pm (or 4pm if guided tours are given); few places open before noon on Sunday.

Offices mostly open Monday to Friday, 9–5; some open at 8am. Most shops are open on Sunday.

Information on opening times has been provided for guidance only. We have tried to ensure accuracy, but things do change and we would advise readers to check locally before planning visits.

Public holidays

Remember that roads and visitor attractions are often busy, and accommodation gets heavily booked up during New England's public-holiday weekends.

- **New Year's Day** 1 January.
- **Martin Luther King Day** 15 January (Connecticut and Massachusetts only).
- **Lincoln's Birthday** 12 February (Vermont only).
- **George Washington's Birthday** Third Monday in February.
- **Patriot's Day** Monday nearest 19 April (Massachusetts only).
- **Fast Day** Last Monday in April (New Hampshire only).
- **Memorial Day** Last Monday in May; commemorates Americans who died in wars. This long holiday weekend signals the start of the summer season.
- **Independence Day** 4 July; anniversary of independence from Great Britain in 1776.
- **Labor Day** First Monday in September; celebration in honour of the American worker, which also marks the end of summer.
- **Columbus Day** Second Monday in October.
- **Election Day** First Tuesday after the first Monday in November (New Hampshire, Rhode Island and Vermont only).
- **Thanksgiving** Fourth Thursday in November; a roast turkey dinner is traditionally cooked in tribute to the first harvest by the Pilgrim Fathers.
- **Christmas Day** 25 December.

Independence Day is celebrated with fireworks, pageants and parades

Travel insurance

Medical costs are high (until the country gets its long-awaited health service, at any rate), and travel insurance is essential and will pay directly in case of emergency. Shop around for the best value and cover, and take a copy of the policy with you (leave the original at home). Make sure your travel insurance covers the following:
● Delayed departure and baggage.
● All reasonable medical, hospital and emergency dental treatment. Expenses and flight home by air ambulance, if necessary.
● Personal liability.
● Cancelling or curtailment in the event of the illness or death of yourself, your travelling companion or a close relative; or in the event of redundancy; or in the event of being called as a witness; or in the event of your home being damaged by fire, flood or storm or being burgled; the policy should compensate the cost of the holiday.
● Belongings and money, including sufficient cover for your camera.
● Items left in a car in daytime or overnight.
● Any special risks in such activities as motorcycling, waterskiing, winter sports and rock-climbing.
  Ensure too that the policy carries a 24-hour emergency telephone number. If you should fall ill, keep receipts of all medical expenses and drugs.

Points to note:
● Contact lenses and dentures usually require special insurance cover.
● Delays under 12 hours are not normally covered.
● You usually have to pay the first given amount of any claim, and there is normally a maximum amount that can be claimed for each item.
● Cover is not normally provided for pre-existing illnesses.

Wherever you are staying in the summer months, there's usually a festival going on near by: (above) jazz in Burlington, and (below) the Maple Festival in St Albans, Vermont

A car is the most flexible way to explore New England. Rental rates are also low and driving standards good. While the public transport network is better than in much of the rest of the US, it will generally only convey you to the main centres. However, using Boston as a base, it is feasible to have a car-free holiday: Cape Cod, Newport, Providence, Cape Ann, Old Sturbridge Village, New Haven, Concord, MA, and Portsmouth, for instance, have good bus and/or rail connections. With the wide availability of bicycle hire it is possible for people with sufficient stamina to explore rural areas.

Roads

Traffic in the US drives on the right. Apart from the congested roads of downtown Boston, driving in New England is a pleasurable experience. On the whole, traffic cruises along with reasonable distance between vehicles. The speed limit is generally 55mph on country roads. On the turnpikes (toll roads) and Interstate highways (the equivalent of European motorways) the speed limits are 55mph or 65mph, although traffic tends to go 10mph faster. Overtaking on the inside is allowed; many drivers prefer to keep in the middle lane all the way as this avoids getting sucked into 'traffic must exit' lanes.

Country roads are obviously more interesting for touring, but can be slow going, with speed limits down to 25mph at some bends (look for the signs) and police radar checks enforcing the law at the most unlikely spots. Signposting is not especially good in New England, with turnings appearing without prior warning; the problem seems particularly bad in Massachusetts. Also note that interstate roads may have a local number, further adding to the confusion.

Car rental

Car rental is easy to find and, on the whole, cheaper than in Europe; discounts can often be negotiated. British travellers may, paradoxically, save money by booking in Britain. **Virgin Holidays** (tel: 0293 617181 in the UK) offer a comprehensive fly-drive package tour that includes flight to Boston, car rental from the airport and pre-booked accommodation. Typically, the 14-night itinerary would include Boston, Maine (Freeport or Acadia), the White Mountains, Vermont, Newport, Mystic and Cape Cod.

All airports have car-rental desks. Some car-rental companies offer free shuttle services to nearby airports, stations and towns. One-way rental is possible, where you can pick up and leave the car at different places; it is usually much cheaper when these places are within the same state. Choosing one of the smaller compact/sub-compact/class A cars in the range will save on fuel bills. It is also possible to rent campervans (known in the US as RVs), some of which are large enough to accommodate a family.

Take a credit card for booking and payment (it doubles as an identity document if the car goes missing or gets damaged). Collision Damage Waiver (CDW), a strongly recommended optional extra, covers you if someone else causes damage to the car. Drivers who are not covered can return home to find huge repair bills debited to their credit card. Check if taxes and mileage are included (only US$10 or so per week). Deals on longer-term rental are available and competition is cut-throat, so shop around.

LOVER$ LANE

25 M.P.H.

Even on highways, traffic moves at a slower speed than in Europe

254

Mopeds for hire on Martha's Vineyard – a good way to get around

255

Major rental companies include:
- **Alamo** (tel: 1-800/327 9633).
- **Avis** (tel: 1-800/879 2847).
- **Budget** (tel: 1-800/527 0700).
- **Dollar** (tel: 1-800/800 4000).
- **Hertz** (tel: 1-800/328 4567).
- **National** (tel: 1-800/557 7368).
- **Rent-a-Wreck** (tel: 410/581 5755).
- **Thrifty** (tel: 1-800/367 2277).

Driving licences (permits)
Holders of licences from most countries, including Australia, Canada, Ireland, New Zealand and the United Kingdom, can drive in the US without having to obtain an International Driving Licence.

Car breakdown
On Interstate highways, stay in the car (raising the bonnet will alert attention) and await police help; there are no emergency phones. Sometimes someone with a CB radio may help you. If a rental car breaks down, call the number the company has given you. It may be possible to hire a mobile phone from the car-rental company.

Driving tips
Fuel Petrol (or 'gas') is lead-free; check the recommended octane level when you hire your car. Gas pumps are activated by raising a small lever (not always obvious) on which the piston rests. Sometimes you have to pay *before* filling up. Gas is not expensive (but remember that the US gallon is about 17 per cent smaller than its British counterpart).

Hazards Snow-ploughs keep roads reasonably clear in winter, but the roads can still be treacherous; cat litter can be put down to ease the car out if stuck in the snow! Tyres with thick treads are useful in winter.

Beware of moose, which like the salt that runs off the road and are seemingly oblivious to traffic; colliding with one can cause a fatal accident. Moose are particularly prevalent in the White Mountains and inland Maine. Also keep an eye out for deer. If you collide with a skunk it may spray your car; the pungent smell is no joke.

Driving in Downtown Boston can be hair-raising for visitors and is best avoided if at all possible

Automatic cars Hire cars tend to be automatic, with cruise control enabling you to set a maximum speed (which cancels itself when you hit the brake; press 'reset' to return to your previous speed). Accordingly, you can drive along with both feet off the pedals, just steering a straight course. If you have not driven an automatic car before, ask the car-rental office to explain the controls. These are quickly mastered, providing you keep your left foot on the floor at all times (it does not activate the pedals) and start and park the car in 'park' mode. For treacherous conditions and steep downhill sections the first and second gears can be used.

Hire cars usually come with air-conditioning, which is activated by a small switch near the heater. When parked, cars tend to drizzle a pool of water out of the air-conditioning system.

Drink-driving Avoid at all costs. Keep any alcohol unopened and in the boot.

Parking You must park in the direction of the traffic. Parking is not usually allowed where traffic would have to go on to the left side of the road to get round the parked vehicles, but the roads are usually wide enough anyway. Never park by a fire hydrant. Meter-feeding is prohibited.

Red traffic lights Unless a sign says 'No turn on red' (or similar) you can turn right at a red traffic light if the road you are turning into is clear and after you have come to a full stop; in other words, you treat the light like a 'give way' sign.

Stop You must stop when a school bus (usually painted yellow) stops to unload or let on children. This rule applies even if the bus has stopped on the other side of the road.

In town areas, always give way to pedestrians on crosswalks (thick white lines painted across the road). Many intersections do not have priority markings: look around for octagonal stop signs. First arrivals at intersections have priority unless markings on signs indicate otherwise. To be on the safe side, stop and wait for the other cars to make the first move. At intersections, cars from opposite directions turning left pass in front of each other. Single flashing lights are sometimes used to indicate priority: flashing orange means go with care (you have priority), while flashing red means stop and then go if it is safe.

U-turns In town centres, do not attempt U-turns unless it is indicated that you can do so.

Cycling
New England has plenty of opportunities for the cyclist, with ready-made cycle trails on Cape Cod and in the Pioneer Valley for example, and scenic country roads in the Berkshires and northern Vermont; cycling is also a feasible option in and around Newport. Mountain biking is very popular (particularly in the White Mountains), and ski resorts often offer this facility when the snows have gone. The loop road in Acadia National Park is scenic (although traffic gets busy in summer), and there is not a lot of distance to cover. Nantucket and Block Island are excellent for exploring by bike; Martha's Vineyard has dangerous roads (too narrow to accommodate traffic safely) but some bike paths. There is no shortage of hire outlets in the region, particularly in the rural areas most frequented by visitors.

Hiking
Country walking for pleasure is mainly confined to state and forest parks, where ready-made trails are well sign-posted. There is usually an indication of the time needed, and the length and difficulty of the walk, and free maps are generally on offer. The finest areas in New England for walking are the White Mountains and Acadia National Park, although there are many smaller parks with one or two outstanding trails. Naturalists particularly enjoy the trails in the wilds of Baxter State Park in Maine.
Many of the best routes are mentioned in this book. Because of the prevalence of tree cover, good views

Left: the circled road number (11) indicates a local road, while the number enclosed in a shield (7) indicates a federal road

can be hard to find; you often see nothing until the summit. Ask locally which routes go above the tree-line. Long-distance walks include the **Appalachian Trail**, which stretches for 2,035 miles between Georgia and Maine, and Vermont's 260-mile **Long Trail** over the Green Mountains and Mount Mansfield.
A range of practical walking guidebooks covers the New England states. For further information contact the **Appalachian Mountain Club** (**AMC**), Box 298 Gorham, NH 03246 (tel: 603/528 8721) or the **White Mountain National Forest**, US Forest Service, Box 638, Laconia, NH 03246 (tel: 603/528 8721), or the **Green Mountain National Forest**, PO Box 519, Rutland, VT 05702 (tel: 802/747 6700).

Cycling is popular with holiday-makers; hire shops are common

257

Public transport

Selected train trips Commuter rail services from Boston and New Haven are inexpensive, and tickets can be bought immediately prior to travel. Long-distance Amtrak services can fill up and should be booked in advance. Some basic trips are suggested here.

● **Amtrak** (tel: 617/482 3660). Northeast Corridor: Boston South Station, Providence, Mystic, New London, Old Saybrook, New Haven, New York, Philadelphia.

● **Metro-North** (tel: 1-800/METRO INFO; in New York, tel: 212/532 4900). New York (Grand Central), Rowayton, South Norwalk, New Haven, with connections to New Canaan, Danbury and Waterbury.

● **MBTA Commuter Rail** (tel: 617/374 1234). Boston North Station to Fitchburg via Concord (MA); Rockport via Salem (for bus to Marblehead), Manchester (MA), Gloucester; Ipswich. Boston South Station to Providence.

The 'T' is useful for travelling between Boston and the North and South Shores

Selected bus trips Departures are from Boston unless indicated otherwise. Note that bus tickets cannot always be obtained in advance, and allow plenty of time at the bus station.

● **Bonanza Buses** Back Bay station (tel: 617/720 4110). Boston to Lowell; Amherst; Hyannis (ferry to Nantucket); Fall River, Newport; Falmouth, Woods Hole (ferry to Martha's Vineyard), Oak Bluffs (also

Trolleybus tours operate in Boston

from Logan Airport); Old Sturbridge; Pawtucket, Providence; Logan Airport to Providence; New York to Hyannis via Hartford and Providence, with connections to Provincetown; Providence, Hartford, Farmington, Danbury, New York; Hartford to Hyannis via Springfield, Amherst, Worcester. Providence,

● **C&J Trailways** (tel: 1-800/258 7111). Logan Airport to Dover via Newburyport and Portsmouth (NH).

● **Concord Trailways** (tel: 1-800/639 3317). Principal points in Maine, with express to Bangor via Portland, plus service to intervening points, including Searsport, Camden, Rockport, Rockland, Wiscasset, Bath and Brunswick; Concord, Manchester and other major towns in New Hampshire.

● **Greyhound International** (Peter Pan Bus Station, 555 Atlantic Avenue, Boston; opposite South Station (tel: 1-800/231 2222). Boston to Bar Harbor via Newburyport, Portsmouth (NH), Portland, Bath, Rockland, Camden, Augusta, Bangor, Ellsworth.

● **Peter Pan Buses** 555 Atlantic Avenue, opposite South Station, Boston (tel: 617/426 7838). Springfield, Amherst, North Adams, Williamstown, Bennington; Worcester, Hartford ; New Bedford (by American Eagle Coaches, address as Peter Pan Buses); New Haven (continues to Norwalk and New Rochelle, NY); New York; New York to Amherst via New Haven and Hartford; Logan Airport to Amherst, Northampton, Springfield and Worcester.

● **Plymouth and Brockton** (tel: 508/746 0378). Logan Airport and Peter Pan Terminal (see above) to Barnstable, Hyannis (Steamship Authority ferry to Nantucket), Kingston, Orleans, Plymouth, Provincetown, Rockland, Sagamore.

● **Vermont Transit Lines** (tel: 1-800/552 8737). Logan Airport and South Station (Boston) to Barre, Bellows Falls, Brattleboro, Burlington (connection to Montreal), Ludlow, Montpelier, Rutland, Springfield, St Johnsbury, White River Junction (all in VT), Nashua, Manchester (NH), Concord, Hanover. New York to White River Junction via Springfield, Brattleboro.

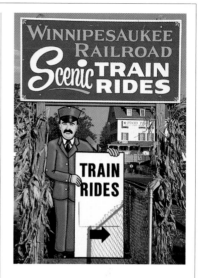

The only trains in the north of the region will be those on tourist railways

Selected ferry trips See gazetteer entries for Block Island (page 213), Martha's Vineyard (page 160), Nantucket (page 162) and Provincetown (page 159).

Domestic airlines Taking internal flights is an expensive means of getting about. Visitors from abroad can purchase a 30-day standby pass from Delta or Northwest Airlines, giving freedom of travel on standby flights or VUSAs (Visiting US Airpasses). These passes are cheap for those who wish to travel around the country, but cannot be obtained in the US.

In addition to flights from and to Logan Airport at Boston, domestic airlines serve Bangor, Bradley International Airport near Hartford, Bridgeport, Burlington (VT), Groton, Hyannis, Lebanon-Hanover (NH), Manchester (NH), Martha's Vineyard, Nantucket, New Bedford, New Haven, Portland, Providence and Worcester (MA).

Major carriers include:

● **Cape Air** (tel: 1-800/352 0714).

● **Delta** (tel: 1-800/345 3400).

● **Northwest Airlines** (tel: 1-800/225 2525).

● **USAir** (tel: 1-800/428 4322).

Language

Exposure to American films and TV has ironed out some of the differences between English and American as spoken on either side of the Atlantic, but there are numerous linguistic pitfalls awaiting the unwary traveller. Common speech features about 4,000 words used differently in the two countries. When you 'make a call' you never dial 'double-eight', it's always 'eight, eight'; when the connection is made, you are not 'through' (to Americans it means 'finished'). 'A quarter past ten' and 'quarter to ten' become 'quarter after ten' and 'quarter of ten'. A 'fortnight' makes no sense to an American.

British	American
banknote	bill
bill (for payment)	check
bonnet (of car)	hood
boot (of car)	trunk
ground-floor	first-floor
lift	elevator
nappy	diaper
pavement	sidewalk
petrol	gas
post (letter)	mail (letter)
puncture	flat
queue	line
road surface	pavement
tights	panty hose
toilet	bathroom or restroom
trousers	pants
tyre	tire
underground (train)	subway
windscreen	windshield

Media

Newspapers Apart from the national *USA Today*, the tabloid *National Enquirer* and the financial *Wall Street Journal*, newspapers are local. The *Boston Globe* and *Boston Herald* are both dailies, with listings on Thursday and Friday respectively. The *Boston Phoenix* comes out on Saturday and has listings and comments on the city's entertainments. The *Christian Science Monitor*, highly regarded for its unbiased reporting, is published on weekdays and has items of international news. International newspapers and journals can be obtained at the kiosk in Harvard Square, Cambridge.

Television There is a huge choice of channels, frequently boosted by the installation in many hotels and homes of cable TV. Chat and game shows and soaps are the norm, and there is little on minority interests, in-depth analysis or foreign news. ABC, CBS and NBC are the major three national networks, with hundreds of affiliated local stations. The Public

A newstand in Harvard Square

Broadcasting System (PBS) has some good-quality imported programmes. Many hotels have pay channels, with a range of recently released movies on offer; a free preview channel allows you to sample them.

Radio Local radio is part of the holiday experience. Flick through the channels and you will find evangelistic preaching, pop, country and western, and classical music. Public and college stations are found on FM.

Postal services

Post offices generally open Monday to Friday, 9–5. Vending machines outside dispense stamps. Stamps are also available from vending machines in hotels, supermarkets and other places for a little extra cost. Air mail takes about seven days to reach Europe.

It is cheaper to send postcards and aerogrammes than letters. Mail within the US can take a week to cross the country. Parcels can only be sent in containers bought from post offices; sea mail is appreciably cheaper than air mail and takes around six weeks.

Faxes are widely used in the US and can be transmitted or received from numerous street bureaux and hotels.

Telephones

Telephones are privately operated by various companies. Hotel telephones tend to be the most expensive (although local calls may be free). Pay telephones are found everywhere and are reliable but much more costly to use than private appliances. Pay telephones take 5¢, 10¢ and 25¢ coins, and if telephoning long-distance or non-local (anywhere in the local call area considered to be far enough away) you will need fistfuls of change. An AT&T charge card (for information, tel: 1-800/874 4000 ext 359) will make life simpler for those with a credit card or American Express card issued by a US bank. Some public telephones have a slot for credit cards. It is cheapest to telephone between 6pm and 8am.

The dialling tone is a continuous hum; long beeps denote the ringing signal, short ones mean the number is engaged, and a high-pitched noise means that the number is unobtainable. Numbers beginning with 1-800 (you usually dial 1-800) are toll-free; they are sometimes followed by a group of letters (which appear on the dial, and double up with the numbers). Local calls are either free or very cheap. For the operator dial 0. Begin direct-dial long-distance calls by dialling 1 first.

State codes Dial the following codes when phoning from a different code area (they are usually preceded by 1):
● **Boston** 617.
● **Connecticut** 203.
● **Maine** 207.
● **Massachusetts (western)** 413.
● **Massachusetts (eastern)** 508.
● **New Hampshire** 603.
● **Rhode Island** 401.
● **Vermont** 802.

Overseas call codes International calls can be made from any telephone. For the international operator, tel: 1-800/874 4000. Omit the first 0 if applicable from local area code:
● **Australia** 01161.
● **Canada** no extra code needed.
● **Ireland** 011353.
● **New Zealand** 01164.
● **United Kingdom** 01144.

Public telephone box in Boston's Chinatown

Crime

The endless production of movie and TV thrillers in the US can give the impression of a country rife with street crime. This is, of course, a far-fetched notion; most of New England is charmingly relaxed. However, it is wise to be on guard in quiet city areas, particularly at night, to lock car doors if you are driving, and to be careful about where you park. Central Boston is generally very safe in day-time. Dorchester in Boston is crime-ridden, but few visitors have reason to go there. There are other notable no-go areas in larger towns such as Hartford and Bridgeport.

If confronted by a mugger, do not resist him. A wise precaution is to carry a $20 bill separately from other valuables, in the hope that this will satisfy the attacker.

Embassies and consulates

Embassies

● **Australia** 1601 Massachusetts Avenue NW, Washington, DC 20036-2273 (tel: 202/797 3000).
● **Canada** 501 Pennsylvania Avenue NW, Washington, DC 20001 (tel: 202/682 1740).
● **Ireland** 2234 Massachusetts Avenue NW, Washington, DC 20008 (tel: 202/462 3939).

Boston is a safe city but you should take normal precautions at night

● **New Zealand** 37 Observatory Circle NW, Washington, DC 20008-3686 (tel: 202/328 4800).
● **United Kingdom** 3100 Massachusetts Avenue NW, Washington, DC 20008 (tel: 202/462 1340).

Consulates All of these are in Boston:
● **Canada** Copley Place (tel: 617/262 3760).
● **Ireland** 535 Boylston Street (tel: 617/267 9330).
● **United Kingdom** 4740 Prudential Tower (tel: 617/437 7160).

Emergency telephone numbers
Police There is no general New England emergency number. For police in Boston and Cambridge, tel: 911). For other assistance call the operator on 0.

Police

Police are armed. If they stop your car, give straight and polite answers and stay seated.

Health and insurance

Basic precautions and remedies
Travellers without health insurance should take out travel insurance (see page 253).

No special vaccinations are required to enter the US. Tap water is safe to drink. Pharmacies stock an adequate

In rural areas, watch out for poison ivy and ticks

range to cover minor ailments, although many painkillers that are normally available over the counter will require a prescription in the US.

Natural hazards Deer ticks are tiny insects that can fall on you unawares and burrow into the skin, causing **Lyme Disease**, an unpleasant condition that normally starts with a circular rash. It is followed by flu-like symptoms and lethargy, leading in some instances to numbness, tingling, arthritis, meningitis or heart failure. It is important to get treatment as soon as symptoms occur, as the condition can worsen rapidly. The highest risk areas are Connecticut, Rhode Island and Massachusetts. To reduce the chance of contracting the disease, wear light-coloured clothing (so that the dark ticks can be spotted and brushed off), tuck your trouser legs into your socks when walking in the countryside, get a companion to inspect your back and head, and wear repellents. If bitten by a tick, remove it with tweezers, and seek medical attention if the mouthpart has been lodged in the skin. Blood tests can determine whether you have been exposed to Lyme Disease.

Stream water may carry **giardia**, a bacteria causing serious intestinal problems; only drink stream water if it has been purified (iodine tablets are best), filtered or thoroughly boiled (for at least five minutes). **Poison ivy** can cause a painful rash if the skin rubs against it (see panel, page 200).

Bears frequent the northern woods of New England. Although generally timid, they can turn aggressive if you get between a mother and cub, or if they are otherwise surprised. Loud noises usually frighten them off. See also panel, page 201.

Lost property
If you lose your bags on a flight, make a report before leaving the airport building. Compensation by the airline will not amount to a great deal, so a good travel insurance policy (see page 253) should be taken out. For items lost or stolen during your travels, get a receipt from the police: this is needed for an insurance claim. Lost traveller's cheques will be replaced providing you still have the counterfoils.

Lost credit cards
● **American Express** (tel: 1-800/528 2121).
● **Diners Club/Carte Blanche** (tel: 1-800/234 6377).
● **MasterCard/Access** (tel: 1-800/826 2181).
● **Visa** (tel: 1-800/227 6811).

Lost traveller's cheques
● **American Express** (tel: 1-800/221 7282).
● **Thomas Cook** (tel: 1-800/223 7373).

Camping

New England has hundreds of camp-sites, both privately and state owned. Each state tourist office publishes lists of campsites at state parks, which are public recreation areas usually set up with hiking trails and picnic facilities. Prices are reasonable but grounds in the more frequented areas, such as Acadia National Park, tend to fill up rapidly in summer.

Campers should keep food in sealed containers, well out of the reach of bears (for example on a high, slender branch). Look out and inspect yourself regularly for ticks (see Natural hazards on page 263).

Dates

Dates are written with the month first. Hence 6/12/1950 denotes 12 June 1950.

Visitors with disabilities

Car parks all have parking spaces for the disabled; Boston's subway stations have lifts as an alternative to stairs; and public buildings are accessible to wheelchairs. Airlines and buses tend to be accommodating to the disabled. Certain hotel chains such as Holiday Inn have rooms or suites designed for guests with disabilities.

Organisations which help advise those with disabilites on travel matters include:

● **Information Center for Individuals with Disabilities** 27–43 Wormwood Street, Boston, MA (tel: 617/727 5540).
● **Mobility International USA** Box 3551, Eugene, OR 97403 (tel: 818/368 5648; also runs an exchange scheme).
● **The Society for the Advancement of Travel for the Handicapped** 26 Court Street, Brooklyn, NY 11242.
● **The Travel Industry and Disabled Exchange** 5345 Donna Avenue, Tarzana, CA 91356 (tel: 818/368 5648).

Electricity

The US electricity supply is 110 volts AC. Appliances come with two-pin plugs already fitted. Visitors with European appliances should bring an adaptor.

CONVERSION CHARTS

FROM	TO	MULTIPLY BY
Inches	Centimetres	2.54
Centimetres	Inches	0.3937
Feet	Metres	0.3048
Metres	Feet	3.2810
Yards	Metres	0.9144
Metres	Yards	1.0940
Miles	Kilometres	1.6090
Kilometres	Miles	0.6214
Acres	Hectares	0.4047
Hectares	Acres	2.4710
US Gallons	Litres	3.7854
Litres	US Gallons	0.2642

(1 US pint = 16fl oz)
(1 US gallon = 0.8 UK gallons)

FROM	TO	MULTIPLY BY
Ounces	Grams	28.35
Grams	Ounces	0.0353
Pounds	Grams	453.6
Grams	Pounds	0.0022
Pounds	Kilograms	0.4536
Kilograms	Pounds	2.205
US Tons	Tonnes	1.0160
Tonnes	US Tons	0.9842

MEN'S SUITS

UK	36	38	40	42	44	46	48
Rest of Europe	46	48	50	52	54	56	58
US	36	38	40	42	44	46	48

DRESS SIZES

UK	8	10	12	14	16	18
Rest of Europe	34	36	38	40	42	44
US	6	8	10	12	14	16

MEN'S SHIRTS

UK	14	14.5	15	15.5	16	16.5	17
Rest of Europe	36	37	38	39/40	41	42	43
US	14	14.5	15	15.5	16	16.5	17

MEN'S SHOES

UK	7	7.5	8.5	9.5	10.5	11
Rest of Europe	41	42	43	44	45	46
US	8	8.5	9.5	10.5	11.5	12

WOMEN'S SHOES

UK	4.5	5	5.5	6	6.5	7
Rest of Europe	38	38	39	39	40	41
US	6	6.5	7	7.5	8	8.5

Acadia National Park in Maine has several campsites – for more information contact the park headquarters in Bar Harbor (see page 113)

Photography

Many museums prohibit flash photography; a tripod may therefore be useful. All types of film are available but it can be hard to track down films

for colour slides (rather than prints) in smaller places. Film should be kept as cool as possible. A skylight filter helps to reduce haze and protect the lens on an SLR camera.

Places of worship

The Boston Yellow Pages lists churches in the Greater Boston area under 'Churches'; these include Baptist, Catholic, Greek Orthodox, Congregational and Evangelical.

● **Jewish Religious Information Services** 177 Tremont Street, Boston (tel: 617/426 2139).

● **The Islamic Center of New England** 470 South Street, Quincy (tel: 617/479 8341).

Smoking

Tobacco is inexpensive, but smoking is discouraged in many public places, such as restaurants. It is banned on public transport.

Toilets

Known more often as restrooms, bathrooms or comfort stations, toilets can be difficult to find in city centres, as public facilities are scarce. Restaurants and bars may allow only customers to use the facilities. Petrol stations are a good bet. Many restrooms, even those for men, have baby-changing facilities.

Many towns and villages have several places of worship
Left: Cohasset in Massachusetts

Gathering free information on an area is no problem in New England, where each state issues a free road map, as well as brochures describing its visitor attractions. In addition to the state-run tourist offices, nearly every important town has a chamber of commerce, stocked with tourist information; obviously, the chambers represent members' interests. Many inns and hotels also provide a range of leaflets about local attractions.

Discover New England, 21 Pearl Lane, East Falmouth, MA 02536 (tel: 508/540 8169; fax: 508/540 8195; UK tel: 0171 603 1213) is the international marketing arm of the six states, with an unbiased viewpoint. It produces a free colour brochure (in UK, tel: 01303 226606) and provides a wide range of information for visitors. Curiously spelt DestINNations, PO Box 1173, Osterville, MA 02655-1076 (tel: toll-free US and Canada 1-800/333 4667; toll-free UK 0800 89 8267) specialises in arranging tour itineraries, with accommodation, round New England.

State tourist offices
● **Greater Boston Convention and Visitors Bureau** PO Box 490, Prudential Plaza Tower, Suite 400, Boston, MA 02199 (tel: 617/536 4100, toll-free in US 1-800/374 7400; fax: 617/424 7644).
● **Connecticut Office of Travel and Tourism** 865 Brook Street, Rocky Hill, CT 06067 (tel: 203/258 4287; fax: 203/563 4877).
● **Maine Office of Tourism** State House, Station 59, Augusta, ME 04333 (tel: 207/289 5710 or 1-800/533 9595; fax: 207/289 2861).
● **Massachusetts Office of Travel and Tourism** 100 Cambridge Street, Boston, MA 02202 (tel: 617/727 3201 or 1-800/632 8038; fax: 617/727 6525).
● **New Hampshire Office of Vacation Travel** 172 Pembroke Road, PO Box 856, Concord, NH 03301 (tel: 603/271 2666; fax: 603/271 2629).
● **Rhode Island Tourism Division** 7 Jackson Walkway, Providence, RI 02903 (tel: 401/277 2601; fax: 401/277 2102).
● **Vermont Department of Travel and Tourism** 134 State Street, Montpelier, VT 05602 (tel: 802/828 3236; fax: 802/828 3233).

The Tourist Information Centre in Chatham, MA, is one of several providing brochures on all attractions on Cape Cod

HOTELS AND RESTAURANTS

HOTELS AND RESTAURANTS

The following recommended hotels and restaurants have been divided into three price categories:
- **budget** ($)
- **moderate** ($$)
- **expensive** ($$$)

Some establishments straddle two categories.

ACCOMMODATION

New England inns can range from genuine old-world hostelries filled with antiques and collected bits and pieces to large de luxe modern buildings. Bed and breakfasts (B&Bs) are often up-market; you pay extra for the privilege of staying in someone's home, but breakfast is included in the price. Some hotels and inns include self-catering town houses and cottages. The cheapest accommodation is generally provided by motels, which are usually adequate in comfort and facilities but not generally strong on character (although there are some in fine scenic settings).

It is often possible to negotiate cheap deals by telephone. Some motels will give you a discount over the phone if it seems that you might go elsewhere, but not if you turn up on the spot. Note that many hotels quote prices excluding state and sales tax. Some make an additional charge for service. Many hotels and inns have packages including Full American Plan (accommodation with breakfast, lunch and dinner) and/or Modified American Plan (accommodation with breakfast and dinner).

Useful state-wide organisations include:

Connecticut
- Lodging reservations can be made in Connecticut by calling toll-free 1-800/CT

BOUND. Accommodation lists can be obtained from state tourist offices (see page 266).

Massachusetts
- Telephone 1-800/447 MASS (in USA and eastern Canada) for a copy of the *Massachusetts Vacation Guide*.

Rhode Island
- Bed and Breakfast of Rhode Island (Box 3291, Newport, RI 02840; tel: 401/849 1298) and the Vermont Travel Information Service (tel: 802/276 3120).

Vermont
- Vermont Department of Travel and Tourism, distributes *Four Seasons Vacation Rentals*, a guide to cottage rentals in the state; available from 134 State Street, Montpelier, VT 05602 (tel: 802/828 3236).

Useful international organisations are:
- New England Country Homes Ltd, Grove Farm Barns, Fakenham, Norfolk, NR21 9NB (tel: 01328 856666; fax: 01328 856324) is a UK-based firm that arranges packages in self-catering accommodation throughout New England.
- US Welcome Directories, PO Box 116, Northwood, Middlesex, HA6 3BH (tel/fax: 01923 821469) also books packages or just accommodation, and publishes *Hotels & Inns* and *Country Inns and B&Bs*, which can be purchased by calling (01303) 226633 in the UK.
- House Exchange is organised by the Vacation Exchange Club, Box 820 Haleiwa, HI 96712 (tel: 1-800/638 3841).

BOSTON AND CAMBRIDGE (MASSACHUSETTS)

Agencies

B&B Agency of Boston (tel: 617/720 3540; toll-free from UK 0800 895128). The biggest bed and breakfast agency in the city, with some excellent locations, such as the Waterfront, Beacon Hill and North End.

Host Homes of Boston Box 117, Waban Branch, Boston, MA 02168 (tel: 617/244 1308).

Bed and Breakfast Cambridge & Greater Boston Box 665, Cambridge, MA 02140 (tel: 617/576 1492). Accommodation in private homes, apartments and short-term apartment rentals, with locations in Cambridge, Greater Boston and outlying towns.

Beacon Guest Houses 248 Newbury Street, Boston, MA 02116 (tel: 617/262 1771), offers furnished apartments in Back Bay.

Accommodation

Boston Harbor ($$$) 70 Rowes Wharf, Boston, MA 02110 (tel: 617/439 7000, or toll-free 1-800/752 7077). Fine site beside the harbour and aquarium, with traditional furnishings. Water shuttle to airport.

Boston International AYH Hostel ($) 12 Hemenway Street, Boston, MA 02115 (tel: 617/536 9455). Dormitory accommodation, self-service kitchens, daily activity programmes. Non-members welcome.

Boston Park Plaza ($$$) 50 Park Plaza, Arlington Street, Boston, MA 02117 (tel: 617/426 2000; toll-free in Massachusetts 1-800/462 2022; continental US 1-800/225 2008). Stylish, grand hotel built in 1927; 1,000 rooms; 82 luxurious rooms in the Towers. Adopts an 'Environmental Action Program' (through recycling and other means).

The Bostonian ($$$) Faneuil Hall Marketplace, Boston, MA 02109 (tel: 617/523 3600, or toll-free 1-800/343 0922). Excellent comfort and service; European-style hotel in building dating from 1824.

Cambridge House ($$) 2218 Massachusetts Avenue, Cambridge, MA 02140 (tel: 617/491 6300, or toll-free 1-800/232 9989). Convenient location; old-world furnishings in 1892 house and carriage house. B&B only. 12 rooms.

Copley Plaza ($$$) 138 St James Avenue, Boston, MA 02116 (tel: 617/267 5300, or toll-free 1-800/822 4200). Built in 1912, one of the grand old hotels of Boston.

Charles ($$$) 1 Bennett Street, Boston, MA 02138 (tel: 617/864 1200, or toll-free 1-800/882 1818). Modern hotel in Charles Square development.

Copley Square ($$–$$$) 47 Huntington Avenue, Boston, MA 02116 (tel: 617/536 9000, or toll-free 1-800/225 7062). Victorian hotel offering acceptable comfort at a reasonable price. Café Budapest for formal dining and an informal bar.

Eliot ($$$) 370 Commonwealth Avenue, Boston, MA 02215 (tel: 617/267 1067). Renovated with period décor; quieter rooms are at the back.

Four Seasons ($$$) 200 Boylston Street, Boston, MA 02116 (tel: 617/338 4400, or toll-free 1-800/332 3442). Looks on to the Public Garden; traditional elegance and comfort.

Hilton ($$$) 75 Service Road, Logan International Airport, East Boston, MA 02128 (tel: 617/569 9300, or toll-free 1-800/445 8667). Nearest hotel to the airport.

Hotel Le Meridien ($$$) 250 Franklin Street, Boston, MA 02110 (tel: 617/451 1900, or toll-free 1-800/543 4300). In the old Federal Reserve Building; 326 rooms; outstanding Julien restaurant.

The Inn at Harvard ($$) 1201 Massachusetts Avenue, Cambridge, MA 02138 (tel: 617/491 2222, or toll-free 1-800/528 0444). Situated by Harvard Square, and although run by Doubletree Hotels is owned by Harvard University. Pleasantly appointed, with art on loan from the Fogg Museum.

Lenox ($$–$$$) 710 Boylston Street, Boston, MA 02116 (tel: 617/536 5300, or toll-free 1-800/225 7676). Turn-of-the-century building in a good location by Copley Square.

Omni Parker House ($$$) Tremont and School streets, Boston, MA 02108 (tel: 617/227 8600, or toll-free 1-800/843 6664). Fine 1920s hotel with excellent central location.

Ritz-Carlton ($$$) Arlington and Newbury streets, Boston, MA 02117 (tel: 617/536 5700, or toll-free 1-800/241 3333). Considered by many as Boston's top hotel; overlooks Newbury Street and the Public Garden; traditional décor.

Suisse Chalet Inn ($) 211 Concord Turnpike, Boston, MA 02130 (tel: 617/661 7800, or toll-free 1-800/258 1980). Feasible budget option with access to city centre by Red Line.

CONNECTICUT
Connecticut River Valley

Bishopsgate Inn ($$$) 7 Norwich Road, Goodspeed Landing, East Haddam, CT 06423 (tel: 203/873 1677). A stone's throw from the Goodspeed Opera House. Furnished with antique and reproduction furniture.

Copper Beech Inn ($$$) 46 Main Street, Ivoryton, CT 06442 (tel: 203/767 0330). Named after the tree that shades the 19th-century main building. Period furnishings; a variety of

rooms, some in the carriage house, some with cathedral ceilings. Excellent dining. (See also *Restaurants.*)

Griswold Inn ($$) 36 Main Street, Essex, CT 06246, (tel: 203/767 1776). The earliest three-storey building in Connecticut, its structure largely unaltered over two centuries. Compact rooms, lots of character and antiques. (See also *Restaurants.*)

Inn at Chester ($$–$$$) Route 148, 318 West Main Street, Chester, CT 06412 (tel: 203/526 9541). 41 rooms, one suite; comfortable country inn with a noted dining room. (See also *Restaurants.*)

Saybrook Point Inn ($$$) 2 Bridge Street, Old Saybrook, CT 06475 (tel: 203/395 2000). Furnished with flair, more a hotel than an inn; health club. Highly recommended.

Suisse Chalet ($) 20 Waterchase Drive, Rocky Hill, CT 06067 (tel: 203/563 7877) (I-91 exit 24.) Good-value motor lodge.

Hartford
Holiday Inn Downtown ($$$) 50 Morgan Street, Hartford, CT 06120 (tel: 203/549 2400). Convenient central location.

Ramada Inn ($$) 440 Asylum Street, Hartford, CT 06103 (tel: 203/246 6591, or toll-free 1-800/228 2828). Excellent position by Bushnell Park, across from the station and capitol.

Litchfield Hills
Boulders Inn ($$$) Route 45, New Preston, CT 06777 (tel: 203/868 0541). Small inn built in 1895, with superb view of Lake Waramaug. Eclectic décor; games, waterfront, boating.

Cornwall Inn ($$) Route 7, Cornwall Bridge, Cornwall, CT 06754 (tel: 203/672

6884). A group of buildings, dating from 1810 and including a motel; restaurant on site; 17 rooms.
Ragamount Inn ($$) Main Street, Salisbury, CT 06068 (tel: 203/435 2372). Welcoming 160-year-old country inn furnished in colonial style; good restaurant. Nine rooms.
Toll Gate Hill Inn ($$$) Route 202, Litchfield, CT 06759 (tel: 203/567 4545). Out of town on the road to Torrington. Charming colonial building. (See also *Restaurants*.)

Mystic
Antiques and Accommodations ($$$) 32 Main Street, North Stonington, CT 06359 (tel: 203/535 1736, or toll-free 1-800/554 7829). Victorian B&B close to Mystic, graced with antiques, fresh flowers and creature comforts.
The Inn at Mystic ($$$) Junction Routes 1 and 27, Mystic, CT 06355 (tel: 203/536 9604, or toll-free 1-800/237 2415). Colonial style, 68 rooms, harbour views; hot spa; boating.
Randall's Ordinary ($$$) Route 2, Box 243, North Stonington, 06359 (tel: 203/599 4540). Early colonial inn, furnished simply and sympathetically. (See also *Restaurants*.)
Sea Breeze Motel ($) Route 1, Stonington, CT 06378 (tel: 203/535 2843). Modern décor; handy for Mystic's attractions; 25 rooms.

New Haven
The Inn at Chapel West ($$$) 1201 Chapel Street, New Haven, CT 06511 (tel: 203/777 1201). Victorian mansion with 10 well-appointed rooms; B&B only.
Regal Inn ($) 1605 Whalley Avenue, New Haven, 06515 (tel: 203/389 9504). On northern side of town; good value.

New London
Queene Anne Inne ($$$) 265 Williams Street, New London, CT 06320 (tel: 203/447 2600). Characterful 1903 mansion with antiques and stained-glass windows; 10 rooms.

Norwalk
Silvermine Tavern ($$–$$$) 194 Perry Avenue, New Haven, CT 06850 (tel: 203/847 4558). From Merritt Parkway, exit 39. Ten rooms, dating from 1642; lots of character. (See also *Restaurants*.)

MAINE
Acadia and Bar Harbor
Bayview ($$$) 111 Eden Street, Bar Harbor, ME 04609 (tel: 207/288 5861). Prime position by the ocean, on the edge of town. Three contrasting accommodation categories: three-storey townhouses, the modern main hotel and old-world-style inn.
Cleftstone Manor ($$$) Route 3, Eden Street, Bar Harbor, ME 04609 (tel: 207/288 4951, or toll-free 1-800/962 9762). Victorian extravaganza, ideal for a romantic retreat.

Bath
Fairhaven Inn ($–$$) RR2, Box 85, North Bath, ME 04530 (tel: 207/443 4391). Cedar-shingle house of 1790; handmade quilts and mahogany four-posters in the six rooms.

Baxter State Park
Pamola Motor Lodge ($) 973 Central Street, Millinocket, ME 04462 (tel: 207/723 9746). The nearest motel to Baxter State Park; restaurant.

Bethel, Rangeley and The Western Lakes
Bethel Inn and Country Club ($$–$$$), Village Common (Box 49), Bethel,

ME 04217 (tel: 207/824 2175, or toll-free 1-800/654 0125). The main hotel for Bethel, expanded into a sport and health resort with conference facilities; condos available.
Hunter Cove on Rangeley Lake ($$–$$$) Mingo Loop Road, Rangeley, ME 04970 (tel: 207/864 3383). Lakeside cabins sleeping 4–8, with kitchens, baths and living rooms; sand beach, swimming, boat rental, golf.
Rangeley Inn and Motor Lodge ($) Box 398, Rangeley, ME 04970 (tel: 207/864 3341 or 1-800/MOMENTS). Turn-of-the-century inn beneath Saddleback Mountain, close to the lake.

Boothbay Harbor
The Pines ($$) Sunset Road (Box 693), Boothbay Harbor, ME 04538 (tel: 207/633 4555). Quiet motel just out of town.

Eastport
Motel East ($) 23-A Water Street Eastport, ME 04631 (tel: 207/853 4747). Well-equipped rooms with kitchenette areas; views across the bay towards Canada.

Freeport
Freeport Inn ($) 335 US Route 1 South, Freeport, ME 04032 (tel: 207/865 3106, or 1-800-99-VALUE). Modern building set back from main road, a short drive from the factory outlet shops at Freeport. Also owns the nearby café where you take breakfast, and the larger Muddy Rudder restaurant.
Harraseeket Inn ($$$) 162 Main Street, Freeport, ME 04032 (tel: 207/865 9377, or toll-free 1-800/342 6423). A modern re-creation of a traditional inn, with Federal-style beds, fireplaces and a formal dining room. (See also *Restaurants*.)

Moosehead Lake

Birches Resort ($$) Box 81, Rockwood, ME 04478 (tel: 207/534 7305, or toll-free 1-800/825 9453). 17 cottages, sleeping 2–15; boating.

Chalet Moosehead ($) Box 327, Greenville Junction, ME 04442 (tel: 207/695 2950). Motel and cottages with private beach on Moosehead Lake.

Rockwood Cottages ($) Box 176, Rockwood, ME 04478 (tel: 207/534 7725). 8 cottages, sleeping 2–7, on Moosehead Lake; craft to rent; one week minimum stay in July and August.

Penobscot Bay

Blue Hill Inn ($$$) Box 403, Blue Hill, ME 04614 (tel: 207/374 2844). An inn since 1840, this charming old building has rooms with period furnishings and oriental rugs. Dinner is quite formal and is available to the public by reservation.

Castine Inn ($$–$$$) Main Street, Castine, ME 04421 (tel: 207/326 4365). Attractively sited by the harbour, with good views from the top floor. Paintings and four-poster beds in the 20 bedrooms. (See also *Restaurants*.)

Craignair Inn ($–$$) Clark's Island, Sprucehead, ME 04859 (tel: 207/594 7644). A remote backwater ideal for escaping the mainstream: this cosy inn has creaky floors, antiques and pretty rooms; there is a more modern feel to the Vestry, a former chapel. Fresh fish is served in the dining room.

East Wind Inn and Meeting House ($–$$) Box 149, Tenants Harbor, ME 04860 (tel: 207/372 6366). Simple, pleasing rooms. (See also *Restaurants*.)

Keeper's House ($$$) Isle au Haut, ME 04645 (tel: 207/367 2261). Former lighthouse keeper's house: no road leads to it and there is no electricity; lit by lanterns and candles.

Norumbega ($$$) 61 High Street, Camden, ME 04843 (tel: 207/236 4646). Spectacular 1886 castle within sight of Route 1 with lavish interiors and Empire furnishings. Garden and bay views.

Pentagoet ($$$) Main Street, Castine, ME 04421 (tel: 207/326 8616). Country-style Victorian bedrooms. (See also *Restaurants*.)

Samoset Resort ($$$) Rockport, ME 04856 (tel: 207/594 2511; outside Maine, 1-800/341 165). Large modern luxury hotel and timeshare complex with its own golf course, right by the ocean near Rockland. Formal restaurant and informal bar. Town houses available.

Whitehall Inn ($$$) Box 558, Camden, ME 04843 (tel: 207/236 3391). Former captain's house of 1843 with a later wing. American cuisine is served.

Portland

Pomegranate Inn ($$$) 49 Neal Street, Portland, ME 04102 (tel: 207/772 1006). Quiet, back-street B&B with tasteful, crisp interior.

York And Kennebunkport

Black Point Inn ($$$) 510 Black Point Road, Prout's Neck, Scarborough, ME 04074 (tel: 207/883 4126, or toll-free 1-800/258 0003). Charming inn sited at the end of a peninsula. Cottages in the grounds will particularly appeal to families.

Captain Jefferds Inn ($$–$$$) Pearl Street, Box 691, Kennebunkport, ME 04046 (tel: 207/967 2311). Clapboard sea-captain's house, built in 1804. Rooms have old dressers and chests; books, painting, ceramics and glass.

Cliff House ($$$) Bald Head Cliff, Ogunquit, ME 03907 (tel: 207/361 1000). Modern complex, a low-rise but densely developed site on low cliffs outside village of Ogunquit. Compact rooms, but the view is superb.

MASSACHUSETTS
The Berkshires

Blantyre ($$$) Off Route 7, Lenox, MA 01240 (tel: 413/637 3556). A Tudor-style castle in fine grounds, with magnificent guest rooms. Slightly less grand rooms in the carriage house and cottages.

The Orchards ($$$) 222 Adams Road, Williamstown, MA 01267 (tel: 413/458 9611). Supremely luxurious. English antiques adorn the 49 rooms.

Red Lion Inn ($$–$$$) Main Street, Stockbridge, MA 02162 (tel: 413/298 5545). Antique-laden interior befitting this celebrated old inn, sited in a village centre immortalised by artist Norman Rockwell.

River Bend Farm ($$) 643 Simonds Road, Williamstown, MA 01267 (tel: 413/458 5504). On the National Register of Historic Places; four-poster beds, washstands and spinning wheels.

Wheatleigh ($$$) Hawthorne Road, Lenox, MA 02140 (tel: 413/637 0610). Built 1893 in the style of a Florentine palace; high ceilings and some modern furnishings. Rooms vary in style and size.

Williams Inn ($$$) On the Green, Williamstown, MA 01267 (tel: 413/458 9371). Large, comfortable; in prime position at the top of the village green. (See also *Restaurants*.)

Williamsville Inn ($$) Route 41, West Stockbridge, MA 01266 (tel: 413/274 6118). Old inn by itself on a lonely country road; pretty rooms with antiques; storytelling on Sunday nights in winter.

Cape Ann

Inn on Cove Hill ($$) 37 Mount Pleasant Street, Rockport, MA 01966 (tel: 508/546 2701). Dating from 1792 and furnished with period pieces.

Old Corner Inn ($$) 2 Harbor Street, Manchester, MA 01944 (tel: 508/526 1966). Built in 1865; later a Dutch summer embassy.

Sally Webster Inn ($$) 34 Mount Pleasant Street, Rockport, MA 01966 (tel: 508/546 9251). Prettily furnished with rocking-chairs and candle lanterns.

Cape Cod

Beechwood ($$$) 2839 Main Street, Route 6A, Barnstable, MA 02630 (tel: 508/362 6618). Sympathetically furnished early Victorian house with fireplaces in some rooms and antiques; bed and (candle-lit) breakfast only.

Captain Freeman Inn ($–$$) 15 Breakwater Road, Brewster, MA 02631, (tel: 508/896 7481). Victorian sea-captain's home with pretty rooms, in village centre but a short walk from the beach; pool; B&B only; restaurant located across the road.

Captain's House Inn ($$$) 371 Old Harbor Road, Chatham, MA 02633 (tel: 508/945 0127). Charming inn, with 14 good-sized rooms in three buildings.

Chatham Bars Inn ($$$) Shore Road, Chatham, MA 02633 (tel: 508/945 0096, or toll-free 1-800/527 4484). Ocean views; main building plus cottages comprising 152 rooms.

Dan'l Webster Inn ($$) 149 Main Street, Sandwich, MA 02563 (tel: 508/888 3623). Historic inn in old-world village street, built in 1692 as a parsonage. Good-size,

well-appointed rooms and public areas. (See also *Restaurants*.)

The Inn at Fernbrook ($$) 481 Main Street, Centerville, MA 02632 (tel: 508/775 4334). Architecturally quirky Victorian house of turrets and sloping ceilings.

Mostly Hall ($$$) 27 Main Street Falmouth, MA 02540 (tel: 508/548 3786). Fine 1849 house with cupola and wrap-around veranda; stylishly furnished and in parkland setting.

Old Sea Pines Inn ($–$$) 2553 Main Street (Route 6A), Box 1026, Brewster, MA 02631 (tel: 508/896 6114). Fine old inn with wrap-around veranda, fireplaces and antiques, plus a modern building.

Penny House Inn ($) Box 238, Route 6, North Eastham, MA 02651 (tel: 508/255 6632, or toll-free 1-800/554 1751). Set back from main road; variety of rooms; B&B only.

Marblehead

Harbor Light Inn ($$$) 58 Washington Street, Marblehead, MA 01945 (tel: 617/631 2186). Old-fashioned inn with creature comforts and excellent continental breakfasts.

10 Mugford Street ($$–$$$) 10 Mugford Street, Marblehead, MA 01945 (tel: 617/639 0343). Rooms of various sizes; antiques.

Martha's Vineyard

Charlotte Inn ($$$) 27 Summer Street, Edgartown, Martha's Vineyard, MA 02539 (tel: 508/627 4751). Highly commendable inn comprising five buildings in landscaped grounds.

Daggett House ($$–$$$) 59 North Water Street, Box 1333, Edgartown, Martha's Vineyard, MA 02539 (tel: 508/627 4600). A 17th-century tavern with a secret

staircase and period interiors; fine views.

Harbor View Hotel ($$$) 131 North Water Street, Edgartown, Martha's Vineyard, MA 02539 (tel: 508/627 7000, or toll-free 1-800/225 6005). Refurbished Victorian hotel in period style, in quiet neighbourhood. Ocean views.

Oak House ($$$) Sea View Avenue, Box 299, Oak Bluffs, Martha's Vineyard, MA 02557 (tel: 508/693 4187). Victorian house with pretty rooms, near beach; quieter rooms are located at the back.

Outermost Inn ($$$) Off Lighthouse Road, RR1, Box 171, Gay Head, Martha's Vineyard, MA 02535 (tel: 508/645 3511). Civilised hideaway, with restrained décor and views of Gay Head lighthouse. Sailboat available for charter.

Nantucket

Jared Coffin House ($$–$$$) 29 Broad Street, Nantucket, MA 02554 (tel: 508/228 2405). Located in the historic heart of Nantucket town: six buildings centred on a brick mansion. Oriental carpets and antiques set the tone; other rooms have reproduction furniture. (See also *Restaurants*.)

Wauwinet Inn ($$$) 120 Wauwinet Road, Box 2580, Nantucket, MA 02584 (tel: 508/228 0145, or toll-free 1-800/426 8718). Out of town, amid fine beaches. Comfortable retreat with 25 well-appointed rooms and five cottages.

White Elephant Inn ($$$) Easton Street, Box 359, Nantucket, MA 02554 (tel: 508/228 2500, or toll-free 1-800/475 2637). Right on the harbour, with plenty of boats and boating activity. English country style in main inn; luxurious comfort in The Breakers.

New Bedford

Durant Sail Loft Inn ($$) 1 Merrill's Wharf, New Bedford, MA 02740 (tel: 508/999 2700). On the waterfront near the historic downtown area.

Newburyport

Clark Currier Inn ($$–$$$) 45 Green Street, Newburyport, MA 01950 (tel: 508/465 8363). Stylishly restored Federal-period mansion with eight rooms.

Old Sturbridge

Old Sturbridge Motor Lodge and Oliver Wight House ($$–$$$) Route 20 West, Sturbridge, MA 01566 (tel: 508/347 3327). Owned by Old Sturbridge Museum. The house dates from 1789 and has Federal-style furnishings in the 10 rooms. There are also 47 single-storey village units.

Pioneer Valley

Deerfield Inn ($$) The Street, Deerfield, MA 01342 (tel: 413/774 5587). In the heart of the historic village; 23 rooms, with antique and reproduction furnishings; country breakfasts and candlelit dinners. (See also *Restaurants*.)

Lord Jeffery Inn ($$$) 30 Boltwood Avenue, Amherst, MA 01002 (tel: 413/253 2576). A 49-room inn facing the green in the town centre, a minute's walk from the college. (See also *Restaurants*.)

Whately Inn ($$) Chestnut Plain Road, Whately Center, MA 01093 (tel: 413/665 3044, or toll-free 1-800/942 8359). Has four rooms with antiques and four-poster beds. (See also *Restaurants*.)

Plymouth

Blue Spruce ($$) 710 State Road, Plymouth, MA 02360 (tel: 508/224 3990). Modern hotel on Route 3A some 6 miles south of town.

Pilgrim Sands Motel ($$–$$$) 150 Warren Avenue, Plymouth MA 02360 (tel: 508/747 0900). South of town near Plimoth Plantation; private beach and sea views.

NEW HAMPSHIRE
Cornish

Chase House ($$) RR2, Box 909, Cornish, NH 03745 (tel: 603/675 5391). Near Cornish–Windsor covered bridge and Saint-Gaudens National Historic Site. Elegantly restored home of the man who was chief justice of America under President Lincoln. Meadow and river views.

Hanover

The Hanover Inn ($$$) Main and Wheelock Streets, Hanover, NH 03755 (tel: 603/643 4300, or toll-free 1-800/443 7024). Highly acclaimed Georgian inn, fronting the green at the hub of Dartmouth campus and adjacent to Hopkins Center for the Performing Arts. (See also *Restaurants*.)

Lake Sunapee

Dexter's Inn and Tennis Club ($$) Stagecoach Road, Sunapee, NH 03782 (tel: 603/763 5571, or toll-free 1-800/232 5571). Small, idyllically set inn above lake; tennis facilities.

English House Bed and Breakfast ($$) Main Street, Andover, NH 03216 (tel: 603/735 5987). The English owners pride themselves on their afternoon teas. Northwest of Concord.

The New London Inn ($$) Main Street, New London, NH 03257 (tel: 603/526 2791, or toll-free 1-800/526 2791). A 1792 inn on the village street.

Lake Winnipesaukee

The Inn at Mill Falls ($$–$$$) Route 3/25, Meredith, NH 03253 (tel:

603/279 7006, or toll-free 1-800/622 6455). Forms part of complex with shops and galleries around a restored linen mill, with 54 guest rooms in hotel by Lake Winnipesaukee.

Manor on Golden Pond ($$$) Route 3, Holderness, NH 03245 (tel: 603 968 3348, or toll-free 1-800/545 2141). English-style manor house beautifully sited by Squam Lake.

The Red Hill Inn ($$–$$$) Route 25B, Box 99M, Center Harbor, NH 03226 (tel: 603/279 7001). Finely sited country inn overlooking Squam Lake.

Tamworth Inn ($$–$$$) Main Street, Box 189, Tamworth, NH 03886 (tel: 603/323 7721, or toll-free 1-800/933 3902). Full of personal touches, with each room different. (See also *Restaurants*.)

The Wakefield Inn ($$) RFD 1, Box 2185 , Wakefield, NH 03872 (tel: 603/522 8272). Restored house and coaching inn of 1815.

The Wolfeboro Inn ($$–$$$) 44 North Main Street, Wolfeboro, NH 03894 (tel: 603/569 3016, or toll-free 1-800/451 2389). Expanded inn with 43 rooms by shore of Lake Winnipesaukee; old-world tavern with good-value food and remarkable beer selection.

Mount Monadnock Region

Amos Parker House ($–$$) Route 119, Box 202, Fitzwilliam, NH 03447 (tel: 603/585 6540). Attractive house just off village green.

Benjamin Prescott Inn ($) Route 124, East Jaffrey, NH 03452 (tel: 603/532 6637). Small historic inn by itself in rolling countryside; house full of artefacts and knick-knacks. 10 rooms.

The Inn at East Hill Farm ($$) Mountain Road, Troy, NH 03465 (tel: 603/242

6495, or toll-free 1-800/242 6495). Year-round farm vacation resort, good for outdoor activities.

Portsmouth and Coast

Exeter Inn ($$) 90 Front Street, Exeter, NH 03833 (tel: 603/772 5901, or toll-free 1-800/782 8444). Georgian-style inn with 50 guest-rooms.

Martin Hill Inn ($$) 404 Islington Street, Portsmouth, NH 03801(tel: 603/436 2287). Within a short walk of the historic district; antique furnishings.

Rock Ledge Manor ($$) 1413 Ocean Boulevard, Rye, NH 03870 (tel: 603/431 1413). B&B, with French owners; sea views.

Sise Inn ($$–$$$) 40 Court Street, Portsmouth, NH 03801 (tel: 603/433 1200, or toll-free 1-800/267 0525). Former merchant's house of 1881; comfortable, Victorian character.

White Mountains Region

The Balsams Grand Resort Hotel ($$$) Dixville Notch, NH 03576 (tel: 603/255 3400, or toll-free 1-800/255 0600). The last word in luxury, among the finest hotels in the state. Resort facilities, fine views. (See also *Restaurants.*)

The Bretton Arms Country Inn ($$–$$$) Route 302, Bretton Woods, NH 03575 (tel: 603/278 1500, or toll-free 1-800/258 0330). Part of the Mount Washington Hotel property chain; 34-room inn in hotel grounds with cosy atmosphere.

Bretton Woods Motor Inn ($–$$) Route 302, Bretton Woods, NH 03575 (tel: 603/278 1500, or toll-free 1-800/258 0330). Part of the Mount Washington Hotel chain; excellent location for exploring the Presidential Range (which is short on accommodation).

Christmas Farm Inn ($$–$$$) Box CC, Route 16B, Jackson, NH 03846 (tel: 603/383 4313 or toll-free 1-800/443 5837). An 18th-century inn with cottages, dairy barn suites, log cabin and 'salt box' building. (See also *Restaurants.*)

Cranmore Inn ($$) Kearsarge Street, North Conway, NH 03860 (tel: 603/356 5502, or toll-free 1-800/526 5502). A welcoming guest house.

The Darby Field Inn ($$$) Bald Hill, Conway, NH 03818 (tel: 603/447 2181). Memorable mountain views from each of the 14 rooms. (See also *Restaurants.*)

Franconia Inn ($$–$$$) Route 116, Easton Road, Franconia, NH 03580 (tel: 603/823 5542, or toll-free 1-800/473 5299). Overlooks Mount Lafayette and Franconia Notch; 35 rooms.

The Mill House Inn ($$) Main Street, PO Box 696, Lincoln, NH 03251 (tel: 603/745 6261, or toll-free 1-800/654 6183). Modern complex adjoining Millfront Marketplace, a shopping and restaurant centre in former paper mill. Close to Loon Mountain sports facilities and performing arts centre.

The Mountain Club on Loon ($$–$$$) Loon Mountain, Kancamagus Highway, Lincoln, NH 03251 (tel: 603/745 8111, or toll-free 1-800/229 STAY). Marriott-managed resort hotel; Loon Mountain facilities; golf, skiing, fitness centre.

The Mount Washington Hotel and Resort ($$$) Route 302, Bretton Woods, NH 03575 (tel: 603/278 1000, or toll-free 1-800/258 0330). Among the grandest of the White Mountains grand hotels, built in 1902: most rooms retain their

old-fashioned bathrooms; bedrooms are not luxurious but are real period pieces. Ballroom, huge veranda, golf, tennis courts; views of Mount Washington. Also owns the Bretton Woods Motor Inn and the Bretton Arms Country Inn.

RHODE ISLAND
Block Island

Manisses ($$$) Spring Street, Box 1, Block Island, RI 02807, (tel: 401/466 2063). Elegantly furnished Victorian hotel on the National Register of Historic Places. (See also *Restaurants.*)

Rose Farm Inn ($$–$$$) Roslyn Road, Block Island, RI 02807 (tel: 401/466 2021). Pretty rooms with views; outside Old Harbor village.

Surf ($–$$) Dodge Street, Block Island, RI 02807 (tel: 401/466 2241). Victorian hotel overlooking the harbour.

1661 Inn and Guesthouse ($$$) Spring Street, Block Island, RI 02807 (tel: 401/466 2421). Some of the 29 rooms have ocean views; lavish breakfasts.

Newport

Cliffside Inn ($$–$$$) 2 Seaview Avenue, Newport, RI 02840 (tel: 401/847 1811). Grand 1880s house filled with Victorian pieces; close to Cliff Walk.

Francis Malbone House ($$–$$$) 392 Thames Street, Newport, RI 02840 (tel: 401/846 0392). Harbour views are enjoyed from this grand historic inn. Polished floorboards, reproduction furniture and fireplaces.

Ivy Lodge ($$–$$$) 12 Clay Street, Newport, RI 02840 (tel: 401/849 6865). Victorian house offering the only B&B accommodation in the mansions district. Good-sized rooms.

Newport Harbor ($$–$$$) 49 Americas Cup Avenue,

Newport, RI 02840 (tel: 401/847 9000, or toll-free 1-800/955 2558). Modern building by harbour.

Victorian Ladies ($$–$$$) 63 Memorial Boulevard, Newport, RI 02840 (tel: 401/849 9960). B&B with antiques. Main-road site.

Providence

CC Ledbetter's ($$) 326 Benefit Street, Providence, RI 02903 (tel: 401/351 4699). Welcoming bed and breakfast with a homely atmosphere; most rooms share a bathroom. Choice location near Brown University.

Day's Hotel on the Harbor ($$) 220 India Street, Providence, RI 02903 (tel: 401/272 5577). Modern hotel overlooking harbour and I-95.

The Old Court ($$) 144 Benefit Street, Providence, RI 02903 (tel: 401/751 2002). A B&B in the city's prettiest quarter; Victorian décor.

Omni Biltmore ($$$) Kennedy Plaza, Providence, RI 02903 (tel: 401/421 0700, or toll-free 1-800/843 6664). A 1920s art deco building; good service and handy downtown location.

South County

Richards ($–$$) 144 Gibson Avenue, Narragansett, RI 02832 (tel: 401/789 7746). Victorian house with high ceilings and antiques, and set in a quiet residential street. B&B only, but the breakfasts are inspired.

Shelter Harbor Inn ($$–$$$) Route 1, Westerly, RI 02892 (tel: 401/322 8883). A secluded retreat with creature comforts: a cluster of buildings around a renovated 19th-century country inn. (See also *Restaurants*.)

VERMONT
Bennington

Molly Stark Inn ($–$$) 1067 East Main Street, VT 05201 (tel: 802/442 9631). An 1860

inn on road to Brattleboro; quieter rooms are at the back of the building.

South Shire Inn ($$$) 124 Elm Street, Bennington, VT 05201 (tel: 802/447 3839). Prettily decorated and furnished; near town centre.

Burlington

The Inn at Essex ($$–$$$) 70 Essex Way, off Route 15, Essex Junction, VT 05452 (tel: 802/878 1100, or toll-free 1-800/288 7613). Modern hotel and conference centre styled on a country inn. The New England Culinary Institute operates the restaurants and room service.

Radisson Hotel ($$) 60 Battery Street, Burlington, VT 05401 (tel: 802/658 6500, or toll-free 1-800/333 3333). Great views of the lake and easy access to the water, parks and downtown area.

Ramada Inn ($$) 1117 Williston Road, South Burlington, VT 05403 (tel: 802/658 0250, or toll-free 1-800/2-RAMADA, (Canada) 1-800/268 8998). Low-rise modern building on main road, handy for airport.

Sheraton Burlington ($$–$$$) 870 Williston Road, Burlington, VT 05403 (tel: 802 862 6576, or toll-free 1-800/325 3535). Close to airport; pleasant garden-style dining area.

Chester

Inn at Long Last ($$$) Box 589, Chester, VT 05143 (tel: 802/875 2444). Wonderfully idiosyncratic, all rooms in different styles; local produce; tennis and fishing.

Grafton

The Old Tavern at Grafton ($$–$$$) Route 35, Grafton, VT 05146 (tel: 802/843 2231), or toll-free 1-800/843 1801). Painstakingly restored inn of 1788 with antiques, four-posters and canopied beds in its 14

rooms. Across the street are 21 more rooms. (See also *Restaurants*.)

Manchester

Aspen Motel ($–$$) Box 548, Manchester, VT 05255 (tel: 802/362 2450).Reasonable and comfortable.

Equinox ($$$) Route 7A, Manchester Village, VT 05254 (tel: 802/362 4700, or toll-free 1-800/362 4747). Celebrated inn, much expanded; rooms at rear look towards Mount Equinox.

Hill Farm Inn ($$) RR2, Box 2015, Arlington, VT 05250 (tel: 802/375 2269, or toll-free 1-800/882 2545). Long-established inn with unspoilt river setting.

Inn at West View Farm ($$$) Route 30, Dorset, VT 05251 (tel: 802/867 5715). Ten rooms, wrap-around veranda; pampers guests.

Reluctant Panther ($$$) West Road, Box 678, Manchester Village, VT 05254 (tel: 802/362 2568, or toll-free 1-800/822 2331). Spacious and elegantly appointed rooms, most with fireplaces; jacuzzis.

West Mountain Inn ($$$) River Road (Route 313), Arlington, VT 05250 (tel: 802/375 6516). Former farmhouse, in secluded mountainside location. Hiking and ski trails within the grounds; llama ranch.

Marlboro

Whetstone Inn ($–$$) South Road, Marlboro, VT 05344 (tel: 802/254 2500). Reasonably priced inn, convenient for the Marlboro summer music festival.

Middlebury

Middlebury Inn ($$–$$$) Court House Square, Middlebury, VT 05753-0798 (tel: 802/388 4961, or toll-free 1-800/842 4666). Large village inn dating from 1827. Special programmes

HOTELS AND RESTAURANTS

include hiking and nature packages. (See also *Restaurants*.)

Swift House Inn ($$–$$$) 25 Stewart Lane, Middlebury, VT 05753 (tel: 802/388 9925). Former home of a Vermont governor comprised of three buildings, the main house dating from 1815.

Montpelier

Inn at Montpelier ($$–$$$) 147 Main Street, Montpelier, VT 05602 (tel: 802/223 2727). Variety of rooms in comfortable inn within walking distance of the town; you can eat out on the porch on fine evenings. Two Greek Revival and colonial-style buildings (early 1800s).

Proctor

Mountain Top Inn ($$) Chittenden, VT 05737 (tel: 802/483 2311, or toll-free 1-800/445 2100). Remotely situated north of Rutland, on hillside overlooking Chittenden Reservoir and the Green Mountains; games and sports activities included in room price.

St Johnsbury and The Northeast Kingdom

Inn on the Common ($$$) Main Street, Craftsbury Common, VT 05827 (tel: 802/586 9619, or toll-free 1-800/521 2233). Occupies three small buildings in pretty village; guests eat together; croquet lawn, tennis, swimming pool.

Shelburne

Shelburne House ($$–$$$) Shelburne Farms, Shelburne, VT 05482 (tel: 802/985 8498). Built in 1899 by Lila Vanderbilt Webb and William Seward; Queen Anne Revival style, with original furnishings, similar to the mansions of Newport RI. Romantic setting by Lake Champlain.

Stowe

Green Mountain Inn ($$–$$$) Main Street, Stowe, VT 05672 (tel: 802/253 7301, or toll-free 1-800/445 6629). This historic inn (*c.* 1833) has 62 fully restored rooms and suites. Two restaurants, shops and health club.

Inn at the Brass Lantern ($$) Route 100, Stowe, VT 05672 (tel: 802/253 2229, or toll-free 1-800/729 2980). Has fine views of Mount Mansfield. Its rooms are decorated with quilts and period antiques.

West Dover

Four Seasons Inn ($) West Dover, VT 05356 (tel: 802/464 8303). Pretty Victorian décor with sloping ceilings.

Snow Den Inn ($$) Route 100 PO Box 625 West Dover, VT 05356 (tel: 802/464 9355). Stylish 1885 inn in a peaceful location near Mount Snow ski area; skiing, fishing, boating.

Weston

Darling Family Inn ($$) Route 100, Weston VT 05161 (tel: 802/824 3223). Former farmhouse with hand-crafted quilts and American and English antiques; five guest rooms plus two cottages (good for families).

Woodstock

Pond Ridge Motel ($–$$), Route 4, Woodstock, VT 05091 (tel: 802/457 1667). Quiet motel with riverside setting.

Quechee Bed and Breakfast ($$–$$$) Route 4, Quechee, VT 05059 (tel: 802/295 1776). Fine cliff setting overlooking Ottauquechee river, close to village. Spacious rooms.

Quechee Inn at Marshland Farm ($$$) Clubhouse Road, Quechee, VT 05059 (tel: 802/295 3133). Historic building of 1793 with Queen Anne furniture. (See also *Restaurants.)*

Woodstock Inn ($$$) 14 The Green, Woodstock, VT 05091-1298 (tel: 802/457 1100, or toll-free 1-800/448 7900). Owned by the Rockefeller family; good comfort. Golf, antique hunting, countryside and biking packages.

RESTAURANTS

Quantities are usually generous in New England's restaurants and diners. The obvious attractions are the seafood. Prices often include a salad with a choice of dressing. For more general information about New England cuisine see pages 20–1.

It is not generally the done thing to share a table. Reservations are recommended in the most popular places, especially at the peak of the season. Casual dress is generally acceptable, although smarter restaurants may require a jacket and tie. Many places have a no-smoking policy.

You can also eat very adequately and inexpensively at diners, pizza parlours and other places. There is no problem in asking for a 'doggie bag' at most of these places. Vegetarian food is not widely available; even the more up-market establishments have a very limited choice for those who exclude fish as well as meat from their diet. State tax is normally added to the cost of a meal, and tips of 15 per cent are expected.

It is advisable to telephone ahead before arriving as many restaurants close one day or more a week, and it may be necessary to book.

BOSTON AND CAMBRIDGE

Bartley's Burger Cottage ($) 1246 Massachusetts Avenue, Cambridge (tel: 617/354 6559). Daily specials, plus over 40 hamburger varieties.

Chilis Grill and Bar ($) 114 Mount Auburn Street, Cambridge (tel: 617/876 8990). Mexican food; student haunt.

Daily Catch ($–$$) 323 Hanover Street, Boston (tel: 617/523 8567); additional branches at 261 Northern Avenue and 215 Elm Street. Informal, cramped North End oyster bar with seafood at bargain prices.

Dakota's ($$) 34 Summer Street, 101 Arch Street Building, Boston (tel: 617/737 1777). Seafood specialities; smart, classy, well patronised. Next to Filene's department store.

Durgin Park ($–$$) 340 Faneuil Hall Marketplace, Boston (tel: 617/227 2038). Crowded, but a Boston institution, opened in the 1830s; chowder, baked beans, pot roast, chunky prime ribs and more; generous portions.

East Coast Grill ($$) 1271 Cambridge Street, Cambridge (tel: 617/491 6568). Spicy American and equatorial cuisine; expect to wait at peak times.

The Gardner Café ($$) 280 The Fenway, Isabella Stewart Gardner Museum, Boston (tel: 617/566 1088). Popular for lunches.

Grendel's Den ($–$$) 89 Winthrop Street, Cambridge (tel: 617/491 1160). Wide-ranging menu, from European to Middle Eastern to Indian; informal atmosphere.

The Harvest ($$$) 44 Brattle Street, Cambridge (tel: 617/492 1115). Game and fish on a changing menu; less expensive dishes can be had in the café section.

Ho Yuen Ting ($–$$) 13a Hudson Street, Boston (tel: 617/426 2316). Well worth venturing into Chinatown for this; excellent seafood.

Il Panino ($$) 11 Parmenter Street, Boston (tel: 617/720 1336). Plain setting, but accomplished Italian cooking. In the North End. Often very busy.

Iruna ($$) 56 John F Kennedy Street, Cambridge (tel: 617/868 5633). Spanish food; salads, paella and more.

Jimmy's Harborside ($$–$$$) 242 Northern Avenue, Boston (tel: 617/423 1000). A favourite seafood restaurant in the Waterfront district; harbour views; chowder, bouillabaisse, scampi, daily specials. Jacket and tie is preferred dress after 6pm.

Joe's American Bar and Grill ($$) 279 Dartmouth Street, Boston (tel: 617/536 4200). Grills, seafood. In Back Bay.

Joyce Chen ($$) 115 Stuart Street, Boston (tel: 617/720 1331). Mandarin, Shanghai and Szechuan cuisine. Good-value lunch buffets on weekdays. In Back Bay.

L'Espalier ($$$) 30 Gloucester Street, Boston (tel: 617/262 3023). French and American cuisine; extensive wine list. In Back Bay.

Le Marquis de Lafayette ($$$) Lafayette Hotel, 1 Avenue de Lafayette, Boston (tel: 617/451 2600). Supreme French cuisine in Back Bay; formal dress.

Legal Sea Foods ($$) 64 Arlington Street, Park Square, in the Boston Park Plaza Hotel, Boston (tel: 617/426 4444). Also at 5 Cambridge Center, Cambridge (tel: 617/864 3400), Prudential Centre (tel: 617/266 4800) and Copley Plaza (tel: 617/266 7775). Chain offering top-quality seafood: simply

presented with very fresh ingredients.

Restaurant Jasper ($$$) 240 Commercial Street, Boston (tel: 617/523 1126). Highly esteemed new American cuisine in the North End.

Ristorante Lucia ($$–$$$) 415 Hanover Street, Boston (tel: 617/523 9148). Top-class North End Italian restaurant with specialities from the Abruzzi region.

Seasons ($$$) Bostonian Hotel, North and Blackstone streets, Boston (tel: 617/523 3600). International menu, American wines; expensive. Near Faneuil Hall.

Thai Cuisine ($–$$) 14a Westland Avenue, Boston (tel: 617/262 1485). Convenient for Symphony Hall.

Union Oyster House ($$–$$$) 41 Union Street, Boston (tel: 617/227 2750). Boston's oldest restaurant; an oyster house since 1826. On the Freedom Trail near Faneuil Hall. Seafood specialities, plus meat, poultry, salads and sandwiches.

CONNECTICUT
Connecticut River Valley

Chart House ($–$$$) West Main Street at Route 9, Chester (tel: 203/526 9898). Converted Victorian brush factory overlooking waterfall; well-prepared New England cuisine.

Copper Beech Inn ($$$) 46 Main Street, Ivoryton (tel: 203/767 0330). French cuisine; menu changes daily; reservations essential at weekends. (See also *Accommodation.*)

Fine Bouche ($$$) 78 Main Street, Centerbrook (tel: 203/767 1277). High standards of French cooking, and outstanding wine list to match. No lunches.

Griswold Inn ($$) 36 Main Street, Essex (tel: 203/767 1776). Old-fashioned character, with 1738 bar-room, cosy Gun Room, riverboat-style Steamboat Room, and a dining room constructed from a covered bridge. Traditional New England and classic American dishes. (See also *Accommodation*.)

Inn at Chester ($$$) Route 148, 318 West Main Street, Chester, (tel: 203/526 9541). The Post and Beam dining room at the inn serves renowned New England cuisine. (See also *Accommodation*.)

Pattaconk Inn ($) 33 Main Street, Chester (tel: 203/526 9285). Store-front eatery.

Greenwich

La Grange Restaurant, Homestead Inn ($$$) 420 Field Point Road, Greenwich (tel: 203/869 4459). Accomplished classic French cuisine; formal and elegant. Accommodation available.

Pasta Vera ($–$$) 88 East Putnam Avenue (tel: 203/661 9705). Somewhat cramped and with no frills but boasting exemplary Italian cuisine.

Hartford

Carbone's ($$$) 558 Franklin Avenue, Hartford (tel: 203/296 9646). Intimate and romantic; Italian-American food.

Frank's ($$$) 185 Asylum Street, Hartford (tel: 203/527 9291). By Civic Center; Italian and Continental cuisine.

Kashmir ($–$$) 481 Wethersfield Avenue, Hartford (tel: 203/296 9685). Northern Indian cuisine.

Margaritaville ($$) 1 Civic Center Plaza, Hartford (tel: 203/724 3331). Mexican and Southwestern cuisine.

Max on Main ($$–$$$) 205 Main Street, Hartford (tel: 203/522 2530). Excellent stone pies, with an imaginative blends of ingredients.

Municipal Restaurant ($) 485 Main Street, Hartford (tel: 203/278 4210). No-frills cafeteria; good value.

Litchfield Hills

Boulders Inn ($$$) Route 45, New Preston (tel: 203/868 0541). Looks on to Lake Waramaug; well presented fare such as filet mignon, duck with raspberry sauce or sea scallops provençal. (See also *Accommodation*.)

Chaiwalla ($) 16 Main Street, Salisbury (tel: 203/435 9758). Tea-shop with a tempting array of cakes and several varieties of leaf teas.

Fife 'n Drum ($$$) Route 7, Main Street, Kent (tel: 203/927 3509). Elegant dining draws aficionados. Wood-panelled walls and exposed brick interior; live piano music.

Freshfields ($$$) Route 128, West Cornwall (tel: 203/672 6601). Idyllically set by a covered bridge; outstanding New England cuisine.

Hopkins Inn ($$$) Route 45, New Preston (tel: 203/868 7295). Celebrated restaurant in a Victorian summer house.

Jessie's ($–$$) 142 Main Street, Winsted (tel: 203/379 0109). Bastion of Italian cooking, known for their own spicy clam soup.

Toll Gate Hill Inn ($$$) Route 202, Litchfield (tel: 203/567 4545). New England cuisine served in an 18th-century setting. (See also *Accommodation*.)

West Street Grill ($$) 43 West Street (Route 202), Litchfield (tel: 203/567 3885). Facing the village green; imaginative menu.

Mystic

Harbor View ($$–$$$) 60 Water Street, Stonington (tel: 203/535 2720). An intimate setting for French cuisine.

Randall's Ordinary ($$$) Route 2, North Stonington (tel: 203/599 4540). Everything is colonial: the menu, the building (which dates from 1685) and even the waiters' attire. (See also *Accommodation*.)

New Haven

Azteca's ($$–$$$) 14 Mechanic Street, New Haven (tel: 203/624 2454). Tex-Mex (Texas-Mexican) food served in stylish surroundings.

Bruxelles ($$–$$$) 220 College Street, New Haven (tel: 203/777 7752). Brasserie in the theatre district with a wide-ranging menu.

Frank Pepe's ($) 157 Wooster Street, New Haven (tel: 203/865 5762). Deservedly popular pizza-only establishment.

Norwalk

Silvermine Tavern ($$–$$$) 194 Perry Avenue, Norwalk (tel: 203/847 4558). From Merritt, Parkway exit 39. A romantic setting for traditional New England fare. (See also *Accommodation*.)

SoNo's Little Kitchen ($) 49 South Main Street, South Norwalk (tel: 203/855 8515). Jamaican specialities, including curried goat and coconut pastry.

MAINE
Acadia and Bar Harbor

124 Cottage Street ($$) 124 Cottage Street, Bar Harbor (tel: 207/288 4383). Dinner only: pasta, seafood and Oriental creations.

Asticou Inn ($$$) Northeast Harbor (tel: 207/276 3344). Formal fixed-price dinners in a stately setting; reservation essential.

George's ($$–$$$) 7 Stephen's Lane, Bar Harbor (tel: 207/288 4505). Romantic, candle-lit restaurant; dinner only, with a Mediterranean flavour.

Bath

Kristina's Restaurant and Bakery ($–$$) 160 Centre Street (tel: 207/442 8577). The bakery's pies and cakes are renowned; new American cuisine, seafood and grills.

Bethel

Four Seasons Inn ($$$) 63 Upper Main Street, Bethel (tel: 207/824 2755). One of the best eating-places in the region; classic French cuisine. Dinner only.
Mother's Restaurant ($$) Upper Main Street, Bethel (tel: 207/824 2589). Cosy Victorian-style house; eat on the porch in summer.
Sudbury Inn ($–$$) Lower Main Street, Bethel (tel: 207/824 2174, or toll-free 1-800/395 7837). Imaginative menu and excellent cooking; also inexpensive sandwiches and pizza. Accommodation available.
Sunday River Brewing Company ($) Sunday River Road, Bethel (tel: 207/824 3541). Popular hostelry near ski resort; own brewed beers, light meals.

Boothbay Harbor

Andrew's Harborside ($$) 8 Bridge Street, Boothbay Harbor (tel: 207/633 4074). Typical New England seafood restaurant with fine harbour view.
Black Orchid ($$–$$$) 5 By-Way, Boothbay Harbor (tel: 207/633 6659). Fine Italian cooking in a *trattoria*.

Eastport

Rolando's Harborview Restaurant ($) Eastport (tel: 207/853 2334). Italian pasta dishes, meat dishes and Maine seafood.

Freeport

Harraseeket Inn ($$$) 162 Main Street, Freeport (tel: 207/865 9377). Airy and spacious upstairs; hunting-lodge style downstairs.

Formal dinners and less formal lunches. (See also *Accommodation*.)
Harraseeket Lunch and Lobster Co. ($) Main Street, South Freeport (tel: 207/865 4888). Excellent value, no-frills eatery serving fried seafood and lobster dinners.

Penobscot Bay

Belmont ($$$) 6 Belmont Avenue, Camden (tel: 207/236 8053). Subdued atmosphere; changing menu features new American cuisine.
Blue Heron ($$) Dark Harbor, Islesboro (tel: 207/734 6611). Imaginative and sophisticated food and fine wines as well as delicious desserts; changing menu; dinners only.
Castine Inn ($$–$$$) Main Street, Castine (tel: 207/326 4365). New England cuisine. (See also *Accommodation*.)
East Wind Inn ($–$$) Tenants Harbor (tel: 207/372 6366). Rustic décor; menu features poultry and seafood. (See also *Accommodation*.)
Fisherman's Friend ($) School Street, Stonington (tel: 207/367 2442). Seafood, meat and poultry; fried fish on Fridays.
Gilley's Seafood ($) Water Street, Castine (tel: 207/326 4001). Good chowders, clams and the ubiquitous lobsters in this no-frills harbourside restaurant.
Pentagoet ($$$) Main Street, Castine (tel: 207/326 8616). Formal dinners available to the public; booking advised. (See also *Accommodation*.)
Village Restaurant ($–$$) 7 Main Street, Camden (tel: 207/236 3232). Overlooks the water; unpretentious fare and surroundings.
Waterfront Restaurant ($$) Bayview Street, Camden (tel: 207/236 3747). Great

for views, especially from the outdoor deck; seafood.

Portland

Back Bay Grill ($$$) 65 Portland Street, Portland (tel: 207/772 8833). Wide-ranging menu; jazz supplies the background mood; jacket advised.
Café Always ($–$$) 47 Middle Street, Portland (tel: 207/774 9399). Creative cuisine in art deco setting.
J's Oyster Bar ($) 5 Portland Pier, Portland (tel: 207/772 4828). No-frills shellfish and beer haunt, as popular with locals as with visitors.
Seamen's Club ($$–$$$) 375 Fore Street, Portland (tel: 207/772 7311). In a Gothic Revival building in the Port Exchange area, the restaurant serves excellent seafood dishes.
Street & Co ($–$$) 33 Wharf Street, Portland (tel: 207/775 0887). Among Maine's finest seafood establishments.

York and Kennebunkport

Arrows ($$$) Berwick Road, Ogunquit (tel: 207/361 1100). Subtly flavoured and well-presented offerings on a changing menu.
Cape Arundel Inn ($$$) Ocean Avenue, Kennebunkport (tel: 207/967 2125). Sophisticated dinner-only menu; overlooks the shore.
Dockside Dining Room ($$) York Harbor off Route 103 (tel: 207/363 4800). On its own island, unbeatable for views and seclusion; varied menu.
Hurricane ($$–$$$) Perkins Cove Ogunquit (tel: 207/646 6348). Good seafood entrées and desserts.
Mabel's Lobster Claw ($$) 425 Ocean Avenue, Kennebunkport (tel: 207/967 2562). A favourite haunt of George and Barbara Bush; family-style eatery.

One Fish, Two Fish ($$–$$$) Route 1 at York Corners, York (tel: 207/363 8196). Much-lauded seafood creations; dinner only.

Warren's Lobster House ($$) Route 1, Kittery (tel: 207/439 1630). On the waterfront; popular seafood venue with large salad bar.

York Harbor Inn ($$$) Route 1A, York Harbor (tel: 207/363 5199). Tempting lunch and dinner menus, and superb ocean views.

MASSACHUSETTS
The Berkshires

Church St Café ($$) 69 Church Street, Lenox (tel: 413/637 2745). Carefully considered style: classical music, art and greenery; varied fare.

Drummond's ($$) Jiminy Peak Ski Resort, Corey Road, Hancock (tel: 413/738 5500). In the ski-lodge mould, with cathedral ceilings, a wood-burning stove and views of the ski slopes; varied menu.

20 Railroad Street ($) 20 Railroad Street, Great Barrington (tel: 413/528 9345). Popular brisk-service bar-cum-restaurant.

Red Lion Inn ($$–$$$) Main Street, Stockbridge (tel: 413/298 5545). Oyster pie and scallops are among the New England specialities in this old-world dining room. (See also *Accommodation*.)

Sophia's Restaurant and Pizza ($) Routes 7/20, Lenox (tel: 413/499 1101). Nothing fancy about this eating-place; good, honest fare, including Greek salads, pasta, pizzas and grinders (filled rolls).

Williams Inn ($$$) On the Green, Williamstown, (tel: 413/458 9371). Stylish, formal dining-room in one of the area's finest hotels.

Cape Ann

Brackett's Ocean View ($$) Main Street, Rockport (tel: 508/546 2797). On the harbour.

Captain Courageous ($$) 25 Rogers Street, Gloucester (tel: 508/283 0007). Impressive as much for its seafood as its appropriately nautical atmosphere.

White Rainbow ($$$) 65 Main Street, Gloucester (tel: 508/281 0017). Fine candle-lit basement restaurant. Dinner only.

Cape Cod

The Bridge ($$) Route 6A, Sagamore (tel: 508/548 8510). Notable Yankee pot-roast; seafood and more.

Captain Linnell House ($$–$$$) 137 Skaket Beach Road, Orleans (tel: 508/255 3400). Classical Revival house with stylish interior; accomplished cooking.

Chillingsworth ($$$) 2449 Main Street, Route 6A, Brewster (tel: 508/896 3640). The finest French and nouvelle cuisine on the Cape, priced accordingly.

Ciro and Sal's ($$–$$$) 4 Kiley Court, Provincetown (tel: 508/487 0049). Authentic Italian restaurant. Highly recommended.

Coonamessett Inn ($$–$$$) Jones Road, Falmouth (tel: 508/548 2300). Old-world inn with regional fare. Accommodation available.

Dan'l Webster Inn ($–$$) 149 Main Street, Sandwich (tel: 508/888 3623). Lighter luncheons include inexpensive sandwiches, salads, soups; Sunday brunches; seafood and meats for more expensive dinners. (See also *Accommodation*.)

The Flume ($$) Lake Avenue, off Route 130, Mashpee (tel: 508/477 1456). Run by a Wampanoag chief; unpretentious seafood, including superb chowder.

High Brewster ($$$) 964 Satucket Road, Brewster (tel: 508/896 3636). Charming former farmhouse with exposed beams and panelling making a memorable setting for fixed four-course menus.

Land Ho! ($) Route 6A, Orleans (tel: 508/255 5165). Informal eating-place offering grilled fish, chowder, sandwiches and burgers.

The Paddock ($$–$$$) West Main Street Rotary (next to Melody Tent), Hyannis (tel: 508/775 7677). Formal sophistication; Continental-American cuisine.

Up the Creek ($$) 36 Old Colony Road, Hyannis (tel: 508/771 7866). Informal and lively.

Fall River

T.A. Restaurant ($$) 408 South Main Street, Fall River (tel: 508/673 5890). Portuguese-American fare.

Martha's Vineyard

Andrea's ($$$) Upper Main Street, Edgartown, Martha's Vineyard (tel: 508/627 5850). Continental and north Italian cuisine; a range of dining rooms, plus lighter meals in the bistro, which hosts live music.

Home Port ($$) North Road, Menemsha, Martha's Vineyard (tel: 508/645 2679). Unpretentious; wholesome fare with seafood and home-baked bread. Dinner only.

Lambert's Cove Country Inn ($$$) Off Lambert's Cove Road, West Tisbury, Martha's Vineyard (tel: 508/693 2298). Good for a romantic dinner. Accommodation available.

L'Etoile ($$$) 27 South Summer Street, Edgartown, Martha's Vineyard (tel: 508/627 5187)). French and New England specialities; elegant, antique-adorned setting.

Oyster Bar ($$$) 162 Circuit Avenue, Oak Bluffs, Martha's Vineyard (tel: 508/693 3300). American bistro in an art deco setting;

noted for fish, but pasta, pizza and specials are also featured. Dinners only.

Zapotec ($$) 10 Kennebec Avenue, Oak Bluffs, Martha's Vineyard (tel: 508/693 6800). Innovative Mexican cooking.

Nantucket

Brotherhood of Thieves ($) 23 Broad Street, Nantucket (no reservations). Like an old English pub with long tables, beamed ceiling and fireplace; entertainment. Sandwiches, chowder, fish, seafood and burgers.

Company of the Cauldron ($$$) 7 India Street, Nantucket (tel: 508/228 4016). Whitewashed interior, harp playing some days; fixed-price menu. Two seatings for dinner only.

Espresso Café ($) 40 Main Street, Nantucket (tel: 508/228 6930). Good value lunches and light snacks; small yard at back.

Jared Coffin House ($$$) Broad Street, Nantucket (tel: 508/228 2400). Formal dining: Federal-period furnishings; American cuisine. (See also *Accommodation*; and the *Tap Room* below.)

Tap Room ($–$$), Jared Coffin House, Broad Street, Nantucket (tel: 508/228-2400). Simple fish dishes; there is also a terrace.

Topper's ($$$) Wauwinet Road, Nantucket (tel: 508/228 8768). Elegant dining; new American cuisine.

New Bedford

Freestones ($$) 41 William Street, New Bedford (tel: 508/993 7477). Interesting place to eat in the historic area; a former bank, with mahogany panels and marble floors. Light meals and more ambitious entrées.

Newburyport

Firehouse Theater Restaurant (Ciro's) ($–$$) Mack Square (tel: 508/463

3335). Beside park and river. Excellent Italian food, and good value; generous salads, tempting desserts.

Scandia ($$$) 25 State Street, Newburyport (tel: 508/462 6271). Seafood and meats, well presented in candlelit dining room.

Pioneer Valley

Deerfield Inn ($$$) The Street, Deerfield (tel: 413/774 5587). The dining room is full of antiques and, suitably for this historic village, the menu often features recipes from the Historic Deerfield museum's cookery books. (See also *Accommodation*.)

Lord Jeffery Inn ($$$) 30 Boltwood Avenue, Amherst (tel: 413/253 2576). The menu features poultry, fish and game; the atmosphere is one of casual sophistication. (See also *Accommodation*.)

Whately Inn ($$) Chestnut Plain Road, Whately Center (tel: 413/665 3044, or toll-free 1-800/942 8359). Large dining room, but often booked up; dinners and Sunday lunches. (See also *Accommodation*.)

Plymouth

Inn for All Seasons ($$–$$$) 97 Warren Avenue, Plymouth (tel: 508/746 8823). Former summer mansion, now with three small dining rooms; seafood specialities. Closed Monday.

Lobster Hut ($) Town Wharf, Plymouth (tel: 508/746 2270). Excellent value seafood, best eaten outside on the deck overlooking the harbour.

Salem

Chase House ($$) Pickering Wharf, Salem (tel: 508/744 0000). Restaurant with lots of character; low ceilings and exposed brick walls. Mainly grills and seafood.

The Landing ($$$) Clark's Landing, off Front Street, Marblehead (tel: 617/631 6268). An apt waterside setting for seafood, including Ipswich clams and lobster.

Ravi's Fine Indian Cuisine ($) 6 Hawthorne Boulevard (Route 1A), Salem (tel: 508/744 6570). Meat, fish, and vegetarian food.

NEW HAMPSHIRE

Canterbury

Creamery Restaurant ($$–$$$) Canterbury Shaker Village (tel: 603/783 9511). Shaker-inspired cuisine with four-course dinners on Fridays and Saturdays, Sunday brunches and lunches.

281

Concord

Hermanos Cocina Mexicana ($–$$) 6 Pleasant Street, Concord (tel: 603/224 5669). Ably concocted Mexican dishes; leave room for the desserts.

Hanover

D'Artagnan ($$$) 13 Dartmouth College Highway (Route 10), Lyme (tel: 603/795 2137). An 18th-century building with exposed beams; dine outside on the terrace in summer. Country-French nouvelle cuisine; fixed-price meals.

Hanover Inn ($$$) Main and Wheelock streets, Hanover (tel: 603/643 4300, or toll-free 1-800/443 7024). The Daniel Webster Room is one of the state's top restaurants; lighter meals available in the Ivy Grill. (See also *Accommodation*.)

Lake Winnipesaukee

Corner House Inn $–$$) Route 113, Center Sandwich (tel: 603/284 6219). Cosy, old-fashioned inn; crab cakes and veal Oscar are among the highlights.

HOTELS AND RESTAURANTS

Hickory Stick Farm ($–$$) 60 Bean Hill Road, Belmont (tel: 603/524 3333). Dinner only; duck specialities; red meat, vegetarian cuisine and seafood too.

Le Chalet Rouge ($$–$$$) 321 West Main Street, Tilton (tel: 603/286 4035). Good French cooking.

Sweetwater Inn ($$) Route 25, Moultonborough (tel: 603/476 5079). Spanish fare and home-made pasta; salt-free cookery.

Tamworth Inn ($$–$$$) Main Street, Tamworth (tel: 603/323 7721, or toll-free 1-800/933 3902). New American cuisine. (See also *Accommodation*.)

Wolfeboro Inn: Tavern ($) 44 North Main Street, Wolfeboro (tel: 603/569 3016, or toll-free 1-800/451 2389). Old-world tavern room, no frills and often crowded; good-value food and worldwide beers.

Mount Monadnock Region

The Boilerhouse at Noone Falls ($$–$$$) Route 202, Peterborough (tel: 603/924 9486). By illuminated waterfalls; ambitious blow-outs and healthy spa meals. Well-chosen wine list.

Portsmouth

Café Mirabelle ($$) 64 Bridge Street, Portsmouth (tel: 603/430 9301). Cheerful informality; brunches, lunches and dinners.

Guido's Trattoria ($$–$$$) 67 Bow Street, Portsmouth (tel: 603/431 2989). Fine Tuscan dinners.

Molly Malone's ($) 177 State Street, Portsmouth (tel: 603/433 7233) Steaks, seafood and more; generous helpings.

White Mountains

The Balsams Grand Resort Hotel ($$$) Dixville Notch (tel: 603/255 3400, or toll-free 1-800/255 0600). One of

the finest restaurants in the state; jacket and tie. (See also *Accommodation*.)

Christmas Farm Inn ($$$) Route 16B, Jackson (tel: 603/383 4313). Mixed menus, including 'heart healthy' dishes. (See also *Accommodation*.)

The Darby Field Inn ($$$) Bald Hill, Conway (tel: 603/447 2181). Commendable specials as well as regular items; pine-panelled dining room. (See also *Accommodation*.)

Margaritaville ($) Route 302, Glen (tel: 603/383 6556). Family-run establishment which offers genuine Mexican food.

Polly's Pancake Parlour ($) Hildex Farm (I-93, exit 38), Route 117, Sugar Hill (tel: 603/823 5575). Home-made pancakes, waffles, French toast, quiches; uses home-ground flour.

Scottish Lion ($$) Route 16, North Conway (tel: 603/356 6381). Fine views of the mountains from the dining room; popular for Sunday brunch and American-Scottish evening fare. Fine selection of Scotch whiskies.

Snowvillage Inn ($$–$$$) Snowville (tel: 603/447 2818). A distinctive Austrian flavour to the cooking. Accommodation available.

Tavern at the Mill ($) Millfront Marketplace, Main Street, Lincoln (tel: 603/745 3603). On former sawmill property; Mexican, American and European cuisine; reasonably priced.

RHODE ISLAND
Block Island

Finn's Seafood Bar ($$) Water Street, Block Island (tel: 401/466 5391). Eat inside or outside.

Manisses ($$$) Spring Street, Block Island (tel: 401/466 2063). Elegant surroundings for dinner. (See also *Accommodation*.)

Bristol

Lobster Pot ($$) 119–121 Hope Street, Bristol (tel: 401/253 9100). Noted seafood haunt on waterfront.

Newport

Brick Alley Pub ($–$$) 140 Thames Street, Newport (tel: 401/849 6334). Cheerful, low-ceilinged restaurant; American cuisine and pasta; open late.

Christie's ($$) Off 351 Thames Street, Newport (tel: 401/847 5400). Prime position with a terrace right on the harbour; an apt setting for sampling seafood and Rhode Island wines.

Franklin Spa ($) 229 Spring Street, Newport (tel: 401/847 3540). Old-fashioned, with reasonably priced food.

Gary's Handy Lunch ($) 462 Thames Street, Newport (tel: 401/847 9480). Good stop-off for a sandwich and coffee (closed evenings).

Star Clipper Dinner Train ($$$) 102 Connell Highway, Newport (tel: 401/849 7550, or toll-free 1-800/462 7452). Three-hour rail trip along Narragansett Bay with four-course meals; murder mystery on Fridays.

Wave Café ($$) 580 Thames Street, Newport (tel: 401/846 6060). Not roomy, but good Italian food.

White Horse Tavern ($–$$) Marlborough Street, Newport (tel: 401/849 3600). America's oldest tavern (1673): beamed ceilings, whitewashed walls, small rooms. Champagne Sunday brunches, lunches, dinners.

Providence

Al Forno ($$$) 577 South Main Street, Providence (tel: 401/273 9760). Leading Continental/Italian restaurant. Rservations not taken.

Cecilia's West African Restaurant ($) 486 Friendship Street,

Providence (tel: 401/621 8031). Worth seeking out for Liberian food. Reggae at weekends.

Hemenway's ($$$) 1 Old Stone Square, Providence (tel: 401/351 8570). Top-notch seafood venue with a lively atmosphere.

Ocean Express ($–$$) 1-800/Allens Avenue, Providence (tel: 401/461 3434). Fresh seafood; ideal for family dining.

Thailand Restaurant ($$) 244 Atwells Avenue, Providence (tel: 401/331 0346). No frills, just appetising Thai fare.

Wes' Rib House ($$) 38 Dike Street, Providence (tel: 401/421 9090). American barbecue ribs and more; open until the early hours.

South County

Champlin's Seafood ($$) Port of Galilee, Narragansett (tel: 401/783 3152). Scallops are the speciality here; also oysters and lobsters. Sit outside on warm days.

Shelter Harbor Inn ($$–$$$) Route 1, Westerly (tel: 401/322 8883). Changing menu and a wine list as long as your arm. (See also *Accommodation*.)

South Shore Grille ($$$) 210 Salt Pond Road, Wakefield (tel: 401/782 4780). Fine waterfront restaurant with changing menu.

Tiverton

Evelyn's Nannaquaket Drive-In ($$) 2335 Main Road, Tiverton (tel: 401/624 3100). Just outside Fall River; diners can eat looking on to Nannaquaket Pond; generous portions of fried seafood.

VERMONT
Bennington

Alldays and Onions ($$) 519 Main Street, Bennington (tel: 802/447 0043). Deli

which opens as a restaurant in the evening; innovative menu.

Blue Benn Diner ($) Route 7, Bennington (tel: 802/442 8977). Typical diner with excellent breakfasts served all day, plus tortillas and burritos.

Bristol

Mary's ($$) 11 Main Street, Bristol (tel: 802/453 2432). Hung with Vermont paintings; unpretentious atmosphere. Beautifully cooked food such as lamb and egg-plant curry.

Burlington

Butler's ($$$) 70 Essex Way, Essex Junction (tel: 802/878 1100). Modern New England cuisine prepared by the New England Culinary Institute.

Grafton

The Old Tavern at Grafton ($$$) Route 35, Grafton (tel: 802/843 2231). Two dining rooms, one with Georgian furniture, the other with a low ceiling, panelling and exposed beams. New England specialities and local cheeses. (See also *Accommodation*.)

Manchester

Arlington Inn ($$$) Route 7A, Arlington, (tel: 802/375 6532, or toll-free 1-800/443 9442). The dining room draws admirers from afar for its American cuisine. Accommodation available.

Garlic John's ($–$$) Main Street, Manchester (tel: 802/362 9839). Italian *trattoria* opening for dinner only.

Quality Restaurant ($–$$) Main Street, Manchester (tel: 802/362 9839). Unpretentious, in heart of town.

Middlebury

Middlebury Inn ($$–$$$) Court House Square, Middlebury (tel: 802/388

4961). Village inn dating from 1827. (See also *Accommodation*.)

Woody's ($$–$$$) 5 Bakery Lane, Middlebury (tel: 802/388 4182), Modern art and jazz supply the background elements in this stylish restaurant overlooking Otter Creek.

Newfane

The Four Columns ($$$) West Street, Newfane (tel: 802/365 7713). An elegant setting for modern American cuisine.

Proctor

Vermont Marble Inn ($$–$$$) 12 West Park Place, Fair Haven (tel: 802/265 8383). An intimate dining room offering eclectic fare. Accommodation available.

Stowe

Villa Tragara ($$-$$$) Route 100 south of Stowe (tel: 802/244 5288). A former farmhouse graced with an intimate atmosphere; commendable fixed-price five-course dinners.

Woodstock And Quechee

Bentleys ($$) 3 Elm Street, Woodstock (tel: 802/457 3232). Graced with Victorian décor; the menu ranges from the standard to the ambitious; the desserts are recommended.

The Prince and the Pauper ($$$) 24 Elm Street, Woodstock (tel: 802/457 1818). Nouvelle French, served in colonial building.

Quechee Inn at Marshland Farm ($$–$$$) Clubhouse Road, Quechee (tel: 802/295 3133). Seasonal menu; the dining room has an elegant but rustic character. (See also *Accommodation*.)

Rosalita's ($–$$) Waterman Place, Route 4, Quechee (tel: 802/295 1600). Authentic Mexican cooking.

Index

INDEX

285

INDEX

INDEX/PICTURE CREDITS/CONTRIBUTORS

288

Picture credits

The Automobile Association would like to thank the following photographers, libraries and associations for their assistance in the preparation of this book.

ALLSPORT UK LTD 81a Boston Celtics Basketball, 81b Boston Celtics Robert Parish. BOSTON ATHENAEUM 32b *The Bloody Massacre perpetrated in King St*. BOSTONIAN SOCIETY 34a Shipbuilding, 35a 1392 Sailing Card, 35b Boston Wharf, 36a Macullar Parker Co, 38b John Fitzgerald, 38c Hugh O'Brien. BOSTON SYMPHONY ORCHESTRA 24b, 79a, 79b Boston Symphony Orchestra. BRISTOL COUNTY CONVENTION & VISITORS BUREAU 166 Fall River, 172 New Bedford. BROOKS DODGE 8b Dick Hamilton, 228 Skiing Black Mountains. TELFAIR H BROWN 106 CGC 'EAGLE'. DEPARTMENT OF ECONOMIC DEVELOPMENT CONNECTICUT 91b New England Carousel Mus, 93 Essex Train, 105 E Haven Shore Line Trolley Mus. JOHN EATON PHOTOGRAPHY 250 Horse & cart. MARY EVANS PICTURE LIBRARY 27 Landing of Pilgrim Fathers, 28/9 Indians attacking settlers, 28 John Cabot, 29 Pilgrim Fathers, 30/1 Pilgrim Fathers visited by Massacoit, 30 Metacomet, 31 John Winthrop, 32a Americans drilling soldiers, 33a Boston Tea Party, 42b John Quincy Adams, 42c Samuel Adams, 46/7 Tom Sawyer's band of robbers, 46 Topsy, 47b Louisa Mary Alcott, 55b Paul Revere, 148/9 Shaker women at work, 176 Emily Dickinson, 180/1 Miles Standish, 180 Mayflower, 181 Pilgrim Fathers, 183a Salem witches, 183b Salem witches Title page, 183c Salem witches arrest. FARNSWORTH ART MUSEUM 44 *Shipping in Down Fleet Waters* (F H Lane), 130 *Romance of Autumn* (George Bellows). B GRANT 204 Echo Lake. RONALD GRANT ARCHIVES 26a *The Whales of August*, 26b *The Bostonians*, 26c *On Golden Pond*. D HAMILTON 40a Menus Profile House, 40b Profile & Franconia Notch RR. HARVARD UNIVERSITY ART MUSEUMS 74 Matsumoto Koshiro. IMPERIAL WAR MUSEUM 150 *Freedom from Want* (Norman Rockwell). J LYNCH 9b Sweetgum leaf, 15a Waitsfield Farm, 135 Wiscasset Shipwrecks, 145a Sterling & Francine Clark Inst, 151a Cape Ann, 151b Gloucester Memorial, 167 Fruitlands, 168 Alcott sign, 169 Concord Bridge, 174 Amherst College Campus, 175 Deerfield Dwight House, 185b Masthead Salem Peabody Mus, 186 Marblehead, 187 Worcester Armoury, 199 Mt Monadnock. T LYNCH 16c Shelburne General store, 229 Dog sled racing, 232 Montpelier State House. MASSACHUSETTS OFFICE OF TRAVEL & TOURISM 194a Faneuil Hall. J McELHOLM 144 Oxford, 214 Newport Bridge, 218 Hammersmith. MUSEUM OF FINE ARTS BOSTON 45 *Boston Common at Twilight*. NATURE PHOTOGRAPHERS LTD 119 Baxter State Park (A J Cleeve), 164/5 Common Dolphin , 165a Great blue heron, 165b Cape Cod saltmarsh (P R Sterry).200a Labrador tea (R Burbidge). NORTHWEST AIRLINES 248 Plane. BART A PISCITELLO 38a Blessing the Fleet. PLYMOUTH PLANTATION 178 Plymouth. PORTLAND MUSEUM OF ART 44/5 *Boy in a Boatyard* (Winslow Homer). PRESERVATION SOCIETY OF NEWPORT COUNTY 216 The Breakers, 217 Rosecliff. MDC QUABBIN 182 Quabbin Dam. REX FEATURES LTD 43b George Bush. SCRIMSHAW WHALING MUSEUM 239a Bone pie crimper. STRAWBERY BANKE MUSEUM 13b Goodwin Mansion. THE MANSELL COLLECTION LTD 55a Paul Revere. GARY J THIBEAULT 124/5 Foxwoods Casino. TOPHAM PICTURE SOURCE 209b Robert Frost. VERMONT DEPARTMENT OF TRAVEL & TOURISM 237 Shelburne Boat, 253a Burlington Jazz Festival, 253b Maple Festival St Albans. WADSWORTH ATHENAEUM 33b *Battle of Bunker Hill* (Col John Trumbull), 42a, 43a Rauchenburg Robert Retroactive, 94/5 American XIXC Quilt. B YARVIN 99 Litchfield. ZEFA PICTURE (UK) LTD 70 Boston at night, 80 Café. S ZIGLAR 25 Tanglewood Lawn.

The remaining photographs are held in the Automobile Association's own photo library (AA PHOTO LIBRARY) and were taken by M Lynch with the exception of the spine, back flap and pages 3, 4, 5b, 6, 9a, 10a, 12b, 18, 22a, 23, 34c, 36b, 40/1, 50, 51b, 54, 55c, 59a, 60a, 63a, 63b, 65, 68, 69, 71, 75, 76a, 76b, 82b, 85, 86, 87, 89, 90, 92, 94, 95b, 101b, 103b, 108, 109, 110a, 110b, 111, 114a, 116a, 125, 133, 138, 140b, 141, 142, 143b, 145b, 146, 147, 148, 149, 158/9, 161, 162, 163a, 163b, 170, 184, 188, 189, 190a, 190b, 191, 196b, 203a, 205, 207a, 225, 236, 245, 255a, 256, 257b, 258a, 258b, 260, 261, 265b, 267 and were taken by R Holmes.

Acknowledgements

The authors would like to thank Sarah Mann at DIscover New England, and the staff of all the state and regional offices of travel and tourism, chambers of commerce and visitor bureaus who gave such valuable assistance in the planning, researching and checking of this book. Thanks also go to DestilNNations, Virgin Holidays, Virgin Atlantic Airlines and Northwest Airlines.

Contributors

Series adviser: Christopher Catling   **Joint series editor:** Susi Bailey
Copy editor: Eric Inglefield   **Designer:** Celsius
Verifier: Debbie Christensen   **Indexer:** Marie Lorimer